THE JEWISH PEOPLE
IN AMERICA

THE JEWISH PEOPLE IN AMERICA

A Series Sponsored by the American Jewish Historical Society

Henry L. Feingold, General Editor

Volume I
A Time for Planting
The First Migration, 1654–1820
Eli Faber

Volume II
A Time for Gathering
The Second Migration, 1820–1880
Hasia R. Diner

Volume III
A Time for Building
The Third Migration, 1880–1920
Gerald Sorin

Volume IV
A Time for Searching
Entering the Mainstream, 1920–1945
Henry L. Feingold

Volume V
A Time for Healing
American Jewry since World War II
Edward S. Shapiro

A Time for Searching
Entering the Mainstream

THE JEWISH PEOPLE IN AMERICA

A TIME FOR SEARCHING

Entering the Mainstream

1920–1945

Henry L. Feingold

The Johns Hopkins University Press

Baltimore and London

Second printing, 1992

The Johns Hopkins University Press
701 West 40th Street
Baltimore, Maryland 21211-2190
The Johns Hopkins Press Ltd., London

Library of Congress Cataloging-in-Publication Data

Feingold, Henry L., 1931-
A time for searching : entering the mainstream, 1920-1945 /
Henry L. Feingold.
p.   cm. — (The Jewish People in America ; v. 4)
Includes bibliographical references and index.
ISBN 0-8018-4346-4 (alk. paper)
1. Jews—United States—History—20th century.
2. Jews—United States—Politics and government.
3. Judaism—United States—History—20th century.
4. United States—Ethnic relations. I. Title. II. Series.
E184.J5F3765 1992   74307
973'.04924—dc20   91-45367

In Memory of Emily Paykin,
a Woman of Valor

CONTENTS

Series Editor's Foreword   *xi*

Preface and Acknowledgments   *xv*

Chapter One
Signals of Unwelcome   *1*

Chapter Two
Acculturation and Its Discontents   *35*

Chapter Three
The Contentment of Culture   *62*

Chapter Four
Crisis of Faith   *90*

Chapter Five
From Class Struggle to Struggle for Class   *125*

Contents

Chapter Six
Zionism and the Restructuring of
Jewish Political Life   *155*

Chapter Seven
American Jewish Political Behavior
during the Interwar Period   *189*

Chapter Eight
The American Jewish Response
to the Holocaust   *225*

Notes   *267*

Bibliographical Essay   *301*

Index   *315*

Illustrations follow page 140.

SERIES EDITOR'S FOREWORD

OVER the generations, there has been much change in the content of Jewish culture. Some writers argue that in the benevolent and absorbent atmosphere of America, Jewish culture has been thinned beyond recognition. But one ingredient of that culture—a deep appreciation of history—continues to receive the highest priority. The motto on the seal of the American Jewish Historical Society enjoins us, "Remember the Days of Old." It is taken from the Pentateuch, itself a historical chronicle.

Indeed, the Jewish community boasts almost one hundred local historical societies and two professional archives for preserving source material. The cherishing of its history goes beyond any biblical or cultural injunction. History is especially important for Diaspora communities because corporate memory rather than territorial space ultimately ensures their survival. That is what Bal Shem Tov, founder of the Hasidic movement, may have meant when centuries ago he counseled his followers that "memory is the key to redemption."

The American Jewish Historical Society offers this history of the Jews in America to both the Jewish community and the general reading public as a repository of memory. For Jewish readers this series provides an opportunity to enrich their self-understanding, quickening Jewry's energies and enhancing its potential for survival. We hope to remind the general reading public that, at a time when the American dream may be found wanting, the American Jewish experience is evidence that the promise of America can still be realized. Without the opportunities, freedom, and openness found in this land, American Jewry would not have been able to realize its energies and talents and become what it is today.

How that has happened over the generations is a story the American Jewish Historical Society is committed to tell. In fact, the society could think of no better way to honor its historical task and its rich hundred-year history than by recounting that story through this series. No single volume by a single historian can do justice to the multilevel historical experience of American Jewry. Drawing on the talents of five historians with a common vision and purpose, this series offers a historical synthesis at once comprehensible to the intelligent lay reader and useful to the professional historian. Each of these volumes integrates common themes: the origins of Jewish immigrants, their experience of settling in America, their economic and social life, their religious and educational efforts, their political involvement, and the change the American Jewish community experienced over time.

Predictably, the project encountered many conceptual problems. One of the most vexing stemmed from the difficulty of classifying American Jewry. To treat American Jews solely as members of a religious denomination, as was once the practice of the Reform branch, was a distortion, because most American Jews are not religious in the sectarian sense. And though some sociologists have classified Jews as a race, clearly that category does not adequately describe how they differ from other Americans. More than other ethnic communities, American Jewry is influenced by two separate historical streams: the American and the Jewish. To be sure, American Jewry is but one of the many ethnic groups woven into the American national fabric. Yet it is something beyond that as well. It is part of an evolving religious civilization that has persisted for millennia. This persistent tension between assimilation and group survival—the will to remain part of the universal community of Israel—is well evinced in the volumes of this series.

In this fourth volume, Henry L. Feingold notes that the decline of religiousness in the second and third generations of American Jews was balanced by the development of an activist political culture based on an elaborate organizational life, an effective fund-raising apparatus, and Zionism, with its notion of Jewish peoplehood. That reshaping of American Jewish individual and communal identity in some measure accounts for the insufficient response to the plight of European Jews during the Holocaust. American Jewry's remarkable achievement in the private sphere overshadowed its weakness in the public one.

On behalf of the society, I thank the many participants of this venture, which had its beginnings over fifteen years ago as a way of commemorating the society's 1992 centennial. Dr. Abraham Kanof, Rosemary Krensky, and the late David Lubart provided initial support for the project. Dr. Kanof has been repeatedly generous in his financial contributions over the years, while the Max and Dora L. Starr Foundation has provided additional welcome assistance. The authors, Eli Faber, Hasia R. Diner, Gerald Sorin, and Edward S. Shapiro, deserve special thanks. In addition, we are grateful to Ruth B. Fein and the late Phil Fine for their efforts on behalf of the project. For their technical and legal expertise in making publishing arrangements for the series, Robert L. Weinberg and Franklin Feldman need to be singled out. Words of thanks also go to Henry Y. K. Tom, executive editor of the Johns Hopkins University Press, and to his colleagues for their dedication and professionalism in bringing the society's dream to realization. Last, a special appreciation is in order for the society's untiring staff, particularly Bernard Wax and the late Nathan M. Kaganoff, for their administrative support.

Henry L. Feingold
General Editor

PREFACE AND ACKNOWLEDGMENTS

HISTORY does not flow evenly. Some epochs are crowded with stormy events; in others little of moment seems to happen. The years between 1920 and 1945 belong to the former group. American Jewish life and the American experience of which it was a part were so full that it seems the historical stream has overflowed its banks. The twenties not only witnessed the full emergence of a new urban-based culture but also saw the final elements of a modern market economy put in place. The prosperity of the decade was disrupted by the stock market crash, followed by the severest depression in American history. While reeling from the economic crisis, the nation was at the same time faced by a deterioration of international security that inevitably led to war.

A historical period bracketed by two cataclysmic wars is not the easiest material for testing the reconstructive and analytical talents of the historian. When such momentous events are viewed through the eyes of American Jewry—an important part of world Jewry that was pushed onto the cutting edge of history by an unprecedented threat to its physical security—the challenge becomes truly formidable.

By treating American Jews topically, I have tried to make sense of how they were affected by long-range shaping processes and by immediate events. There are chapters on economic, political, and cultural influences, on acculturation, and also on religious and organizational developments. Finally, I combine all these themes to examine how American Jewry responded to the Holocaust, the most significant event in recent Jewish history. The strategy that undergirds this approach considers that only a full knowledge of the American Jewish experience during the twenties and thirties will allow readers to make a balanced judgment regarding American Jewry's role as a witness during the Holocaust. It is the debate over that role that has become the focal point of American Jewish historiography during the interwar period.

This books tells the story of the children and grandchildren of the eastern European immigrants. Although I designate them "second generation," the term is used symbolically rather than chronologically, since those who arrived after World War I were actually first-generation Americans. Even more Jews were third- and fourth-generation Americans already acculturated, termed "alrightniks" in the patois of the immigrant. What bound them together was their common eastern European Jewish heritage and the trials of acculturation, made more difficult during the twenties by strong signals of unwelcome. Hostility was directed at all ethnics in the "new" immigration, but for second-generation Jews there was the additional burden of anti-Semitism, which intensified precisely when they seemed ready to discard much of their own culture, especially its demanding religion. No longer fitting easily into the transitional culture of their immigrant parents but not yet accepted by the host society, they were in some measure like the American writers of the twenties, a "lost generation." Yet that seemed hardly to interfere with their headlong drive to achieve middle-class status. They developed an ethnic economy of considerable depth. But that could not shield them from the ravages of the Great Depression, which temporarily halted their climb.

American Jews' mobility had virtually ceased and their remarkable fund-raising network had almost collapsed when the ominous events in Germany confronted them with yet another crisis, and they soon discovered they could not speak to the Roosevelt administration with one voice. Voluntarily associated through an elaborate network of organizations and congregations, American Jewry learned that it was no longer the cohesive community it had imagined itself to be: the freeness of America had altered its corporate character. Neither the regnant Zionist movement nor the myriad voluntary organizations had enough power to mount effective community action for the rescue of European Jews. As American Jewry assumed the mantle of world leadership, it was haunted by its helplessness in witnessing the destruction of its parent community. This searing sense of not having done enough during the years of the Holocaust helps explain its exertion in the establishment and nurture of Israel in the postwar years.

Many of the familiar characteristics of contemporary American Jewish life were set in place between the wars—not only its remarkable organizational and philanthropic network but also its abiding duality. The American

Jewish experience is, on the one hand, an episode in the millennial history of the Jews, another diaspora in a history full of diasporas. Some of the signals the community acts on and many of its shaping concerns stem from that linkage. Yet in these years Jews expended enormous energy in accommodating to America, in making themselves at home. They freely adopted values and behavior styles from the society with which they had cast their lot and reshaped their own distinctive culture to fit. The interplay between the two forces, America and Judaism, can be noted in much that American Jewry did and experienced between 1920 and 1945—in its distinctive political cutlure, its remarkable social mobility, the fragmentation of its "church" into three branches, and the advocacy role it assumed for world Jewry before the American government. This duality, which produced tensions and conflict as well as imaginative accommodations, is one of the binding themes of this book. It is a tension that can be found in the entire American Jewish experience, but it is particularly clear at the time when American Jewry was poised to enter the mainstream of American life.

A Time for Searching is the fourth volume in *The Jewish People in America* series, sponsored by the American Jewish Historical Society to celebrate its centennial. The series aims to present existing material in a form that will satisfy the standards of the professional historian while holding the interest of the intelligent lay reader. This historical synthesis reexamines existing monographs, memoirs and biographies, local histories, and newspapers as well as some original sources that were used primarily to add descriptive color. We are fortunate to have several repositories where such material is available. My task was made easier by the staff of the Jewish Division of the New York Public Library and the library of the American Jewish Committee, whose file catalog I found particularly useful. I am grateful to Daniel Epner for giving the manuscript a final reading. The dozens of others who patiently helped me to clarify my own thinking and to steer through the shoals of partisanship and sectarianism that abound in the American Jewish story are too numerous to mention. They know who they are, and I am grateful to them. I hope the fruits of their efforts show in an objective narrative composed by a researcher who, beneath it all, is concerned about the destiny of American Jewry. Ultimately the concepts that undergird this book were fashioned by years of reading and teaching American Jewish history. They are my own, as are the inevitable errors that have crept into the narrative.

A Time for Searching
Entering the Mainstream

CHAPTER ONE

SIGNALS OF UNWELCOME

THE JEWS of the generation that came of age in America in the 1920s were becoming an integral part of a new urban landscape. They danced the new dances, sang the new songs, drove Model T Fords, and cheered Lindbergh's safe landing near Paris. A growing number committed themselves to the pervasive business ethos and shared in the prosperity of the decade. But their dream of America was disrupted by the disturbing dissonance of anti-Semitism, which they perceived as threatening their security and their aspirations.

Undoubtedly some would gladly have ignored the growing signs of rejection, which were ambiguous enough to permit this. In the movement to restrict immigration, for example, anti-Semitism was not the exclusive motivation of Congress. Jews, after all, were not the only group in the "new immigration" that was targeted. The Congress that passed the restrictive immigration law of 1921 also passed the Lodge-Fish resolution confirming the promise of a Jewish national home in Palestine contained in the Balfour Declaration of 1917. Christian Seventh-Day Adventists joined Jews in their struggle against the Sunday laws. During the Harvard limitations case, President Lowell declared that he wanted to limit Jewish enrollment to 10 percent merely to prevent anti-Semitism. That percentage was considerably above the proportion of Jews in the general population and might have seemed sufficient to those who wondered why their sons would want to attend a school where they were not welcome. For the immigrants, who often viewed anti-Semitism as part of the burden of being Jewish, such signals were mild compared with what they had experienced in their former homelands. As long as discrimination did not interfere with earning a livelihood or living a Jewish life, it was best ignored.

The young Jews who came of age in the twenties had little in their background to help them muster such forbearance. Immigration restriction and limitations in Ivy League schools could be perceived as posing no insurmountable threat. But that was not the case with the anti-Semitic rantings of Henry Ford's *Dearborn Independent* or the blood libel incident at Messina or the dozens of slights they experienced in their daily lives. They were eager above all to enter the American mainstream, and any move to block their aspirations had to be fought in the name of what they understood to be the promise of America.

That generational difference in attitude itself reflected ongoing acculturation. The anti-Semitism of the twenties caught the second generation crossing between two worlds. Its members were not yet fully confident of their acceptance as Americans, but they had already surrendered some of their Jewish identity. Fearful and uncertain, they reacted to anti-Semitism with such sensitivity that one journalist spoke of the "pathological state of the American Jewish mind."[1]

By the eve of the Holocaust, American Jews had experienced two decades of rejection. During the thirties concern regarding domestic anti-Semitism was heightened by the virulent Judeophobia that swept Europe. Then their apprehension and insecurity become palpable. The emotional state of American Jewry is crucial in understanding Jews' response to the Holocaust, and the adequacy of that response is today a major issue in American Jewish historiography.

For ordinary Jews anti-Semitism was not an abstraction. Employment discrimination was common, especially in the white-collar fields where a growing number applied for work, but in entry-level employment as well. Western Union would not hire Jewish boys, and it was virtually impossible for Jews to become bank tellers or salesclerks in non-Jewish stores. The New York Telephone Company regretted that it could not employ Jewish women as operators: it found that their arms were too short to handle the switchboards. Want ads in the daily press found indirect ways of indicating a preference for non-Jews. In some cases the results were tragicomic, as in a *Variety* ad that sought young men as ushers. Applicants had to be blond and "have straight noses."[2] The growing number of educated Jews who qualified for professional positions as lawyers or teachers discovered that their opportunities for gainful employment were equally unpromising.

(handwritten margin notes: "Jobs, Education, Clubs, Employment, Housing)")

Even areas of business where Jews predominated were not exempt from the anti-Semitic animus, especially if they were imagined to have a mind-shaping propensity, as in the film industry. Discrimination also prevailed in the housing market. In cities where sizable Jewish population concentrations developed certain neighborhoods remained prohibited to Jewish home buyers and renters. In New York City during the twenties few Jews resided in the Park Slope and Brooklyn Heights sections of Brooklyn or the Fieldston and Riverdale sections of the Bronx. But in housing, the laws of the market were difficult to evade. A growing number of Jews had the money to purchase homes in such neighborhoods or to build their own, even if they lacked refinement. Money also helped circumvent the restrictionist policies of certain exclusive resorts and country clubs. By the end of the 1920s, American Jews had begun to establish their own.

In housing and social institutions, discrimination seemed to be maintained by an invisible hand. But in the case of the Ku Klux Klan, revived by a Dallas dentist in 1922 with a new hate list that included Jews, Catholics, and other foreigners, the source was visible. By 1924 the Klan's membership had grown to over four million, organized in forty-three states, mostly in the North and West. New chapters were established on some college campuses, and one was reported to be functioning in the United States Navy. The startling growth of the Klan became a source of alarm among Jews, who felt the truth of H. L. Mencken's observation that "the Klan was just what it pretended to be, an order devoted to the ideals most Americans held sacred."[3] Here circumvention was not possible, but Jews hoped that neglect might achieve the same goal. When the Klan issue came to the fore during the election campaign of 1924, the Jewish lawyer and civic leader Louis Marshall, who was president of the American Jewish Committee, opposed the inclusion of an anti-Klan plank in the Republican platform and repudiated the Hebrew American League of New Jersey, which proposed to campaign against Coolidge for his failure to condemn the Klan. At the Democratic convention Klan supporters were strong enough to prevent censure and helped withhold the nomination from Al Smith, who as governor of New York had signed an anti-Klan bill.[4] Not until the thirties did the Klan lose momentum.

For several reasons, the movement for rigorous enforcement of Sunday laws spurred by Protestant religious fundamentalists particularly vexed Jews. For the observant Jews who closed their businesses on their Sabbath (Saturday), the loss of Sunday's business could make the difference between

3

profit and loss. But it was the fundamentalist mind-set that caused the most concern. Fundamentalists inevitably spoke of the need to keep America a "Christian nation" and viewed the tribulation of the Jews as part of a divine scheme. Indeed, it was "God's rod of correction" for their rejection of Christ.[5]

During the nineteenth century, Jews usually chose not to challenge blue laws. The Tammany sachem Mordecai Noah argued that if Jews lived in their own sovereign nation they too would enforce their Sabbath laws. How could they in good conscience deny the Christian community the same prerogative?[6] Under pressure from congregants who wanted a common Sabbath with Christians, some Reform congregations in the South and West began to observe their Sabbath on Sunday. But the practice ran into opposition from Isaac M. Wise, founder of the Reform movement, who admonished that "you can desecrate the Sabbath, but you cannot consecrate the Sunday."[7] Although a growing number of Jews no longer observed the Sabbath, they were nevertheless prepared to join the Orthodox Jews in fighting for their right to have one, which meant the right to do business on Sunday. The stage was set for confrontation.

Throughout the twenties the conflict was fought in the courts of New York State. Fighting for the Sunday laws were the Lord's Day Alliance and the Sabbath Crusade Committee. Arrayed against them was a strange alliance of Orthodox Jews, Protestant Sabbatarians, especially the New York Conference of Seventh-Day Adventists, and the Jewish labor movement, which had embarked on a drive to make the five-day workweek a reality. Bills extending the closing law to Saturday were introduced into the legislatures of New York, New Jersey, and Oklahoma. "If this bill becomes law," observed a state senator from New York City, "it will give 1,000,000 Jews . . . no further justification for saying that legislation designed to compel them to observe Sunday laws involves discrimination . . . and a little more rest and leisure will do no harm."[8] The measures all went down to defeat. In 1927, however, some garment worker locals, followed by plumbers, carpenters, and printers, wrested the forty-hour week from their employers. By 1929, 240 manufacturers, employing 400,000 to 500,000 workers, had adopted the five-day workweek. The rest of working America would soon follow. A fortunate confluence of interest between Orthodox Jews, Jewish labor, civil libertarians, and Christian Sabbatarians carried the day.

If most American Jews treated Sunday laws and conversionary campaigns with equanimity, they were less calm about the blood libel incident that occurred in the small town of Messina, New York, on 23 September 1928, triggered by the disappearance of a four-year-old child, Barbara Griffith. Disregarding the Jewish High Holy Days of September, state troopers illegally entered the home of Rabbi Berel Brennglass, spiritual leader of Congregation Adath Israel, and removed him to the town hall for questioning by the mayor. There was no reason the rabbi should have been the focus of an investigation except that the police and the mayor had heard rumors that Jews required the blood of Christian children to perform some mysterious religious ritual. Although the child was found the next day in the woods near her house, the Jewish press let out an outcry. If this could happen in what was in many ways a typical small American town, then one had to assume that the religious hatred that had historically caused such suffering for Jews seethed just beneath the surface of American life. Since the Damascus case in 1840, such incidents had become relatively common in Jewish history but they were virtually unknown in the United States. But reinforced by the memory of the Mendel Beilis case in Russia (1911–13), Jewish leaders understood that the blood libel charge involved primal religious passions that, given the temper of the times, could become a physical threat to local Jews.

The case was quickly resolved when Louis Marshall, who placed inordinate stress on the public relations value of apologies, extracted one from the mayor of Messina. "This apology must be couched in such terms," he instructed the mayor, "as will meet with my approval, so that the world may know the remorse you express is genuine." If that was not done, he threatened to press the case before the appellate division of the supreme court of New York. The apology was quickly forthcoming, and Rabbi Brennglass accepted it without first showing it to Marshall. He was undoubtedly fearful that if the case was allowed to further excite the public imagination it would become impossible for the Jews of Messina to live among their Christian neighbors. Marshall then informed the rabbi that he considered him a "heroic and courageous Jew" worthy of the best traditions of the Jewish people,[9] and the incident came to an end. Though the case itself is of little significance, it is historically important for what it tells about Jews' state of mind at the end of a decade when they believed they were witnessing an explosion of anti-Semitism.

For more acculturated Jews, it was the Rosenbluth case that alerted them to the malignant spirit abroad in the land. Some saw it as an American Dreyfus case. A native-born Jew, Robert Rosenbluth had graduated from

5

Yale University School of Forestry and held several high positions in the federal civil service before he enlisted in the army. In October 1918 his commanding officer, Major Alexander Cronkite, was mysteriously shot to death. After four years of headlines, a grand jury indicted Rosenbluth on flimsy evidence. It took two years to vindicate him in the courts. Even then Henry Ford's *Dearborn Independent* cried for blood. The verdict, it claimed, had been wrung from the court by "shameful interference" and would compromise the confidence of the American people in their judicial system.[10] Jews, however, were convinced that Rosenbluth's indictment, especially after a four-year delay, reflected rampant anti-Semitism in the army and in the court system, and their suspicion was not fully laid to rest even after Rosenbluth was found not guilty. If a fully acculturated Jew, indistinguishable from other Americans, had been forced to undergo a six-year ordeal before he was vindicated, what hope was there for others intent on joining the American mainstream?

Few Jews doubted that they were witnessing an intensification of anti-Semitism. Some attributed it to the reversion to a vaguely pagan sensibility among Americans that had been triggered by World War I. Others spoke of the persistence of an "Anglo-Saxon tradition of exclusiveness." Many sought the cause in some flaw in the Jews themselves, such as their political radicalism, linked on the one hand to an imagined world conspiracy and on the other directly to the successful Bolshevik revolution.[11] This linkage of Judaism to political radicalism became the most persistent element in anti-Semitic propaganda, echoed in the highest echelons of government. As early as July 1917, Elihu Root attributed the failure of his mission to Russia to Jews who had returned there from New York's Lower East Side and were now, he insisted, in charge of managing the revolution. Similarly, Raymond Robins, the American representative for the Red Cross in Russia, decried the activities of these returned Jewish revolutionaries. The stories gained credibility because, of the approximately 2,500 immigrants who had returned to Russia in 1918, there were in fact about 864 "Hebrews." In 1919 this small group was supplemented by an unknown number of Jewish radicals deported after the Palmer raids aboard the S.S. *Buford,* dubbed the "Soviet Ark." Among these were the two well-known anarchists, Alexander Berkman and Emma Goldman. In both groups people who were Jews by circumstance of birth rather than conviction composed a tiny proportion of the total and were overshadowed by the far greater number of Jews who had left, or wanted to leave, the Soviet Union. Not all in the trickle of Jewish returnees were political. Jews had been returning to Russia since the beginning of the century because of homesickness. A Jewish writer, Maurice Hindus, saw them as "romantics" rather than as hardheaded revolutionaries. Only one prominent Bolshevik, Leon Trotsky, who returned to Russia from the Lower East Side in 1917 after less than a year's unhappy stay, fits the picture of Jews as leaders of the communist movement. Yet the story thrived in both Europe and the United States and became a mainstay of the anti-Semitic imagination.[12]

The charge of "Judeobolshevism" became the rallying cry of a group of loosely knit anti-Semitic publicists. In the United States its principal proponent was George A. Simons, a Methodist minister who as treasurer of the Methodist-Episcopalian Russian Mission had witnessed the Russian Revolution in Petrograd. After Simons returned in October 1918, he spared no effort to sound the alarm. Wearing his clerical collar, he testified before several congressional committees in 1919. His message was everywhere the same, that the men who made the revolution in Russia were overwhelmingly apostate Jews and that in the United States, too, nineteen out of twenty communists were Jewish. A news-hungry press only amplified his message.

Desperately, the American Jewish Committee (AJCOMM) published statistical data to disprove his case. One pamphlet featured a detailed ethnic breakdown of communist leaders in the Soviet Union that showed Jews to be but a small minority among the Bolshevik leadership. Another news release pointed out that Jews, as small merchants, were among the groups suffering most bitterly from Soviet expropriation and an antireligious public policy, including the closing of Jewish institutions of learning, academies, and synagogues. How could anyone imagine that Jews could support such a regime? Seeking to reeducate the public, the AJCOMM commissioned two books, Herman Bernstein's *The History of a Lie,* which exposed the spurious *Protocols of the Elders of Zion,* and another that called attention to the Jewish contribution to democracy—Joseph Jacobs's *Jewish Contributions to Civilization.*[13] But such counterpropaganda hardly neutralized the deluge of anti-Semitic publications warning of a worldwide Jewish conspiracy.

The pseudoscientific racist writings of men like John Jay Chapman, William Astor Chamber, David Starr Jordan, and Madison Grant had not drawn a large readership, but when simplified for the popular press and magazines, their impact was devastating. In 1922 Marshall demanded that the *Encyclopaedia Britannica,* a well-respected reference work, remove its article on Polish Jewry, which was full of anti-Semitic fabrications and slurs.

Of all anti-Semitic publications, the various versions of *The Protocols of the Elders of Zion,* which contained the idea of a world Jewish conspiracy in its purest form, raised the greatest alarm. Introduced in Europe by the czarist secret police, the *Protocols* had already been exposed as forgeries. Nevertheless, they were taken seriously by British and American intelligence services and received wide circulation during World War I. By 1919 the *Protocols* were being circulated at the highest levels of government in Washington. Only a timely warning regarding their authenticity prevented their publication as part of the committee hearings conducted by Senator Lee Overman during January and February 1919 to investigate the communist menace. Those hearings also featured the testimony of the Reverend George Simons.

In the United States, Boris Brasol, a czarist emigré who transferred his activities from Britain in 1918, promoted the *Protocols.* It was probably Brasol who convinced Ford to serialize them in the *Dearborn Independent.*[14] They appeared in print at roughly the same time, 1922–23, that Doubleday, Page and Company published a lurid series of articles in *World's Work* by Burton J. Hendrick, a muckraking Yale-educated journalist. Hendrick sought to halt what he believed was an impending invasion of America by Polish Jewish immigrants by exposing their dangerous character. They were "Typhoid Marys," he informed readers of his book *The Jews in America,* in which the inflammatory articles were collected.[15]

Shocked by what appeared to be a concerted anti-Semitic propaganda effort, Jewish leaders found themselves divided on how to respond. There were emotional outcries in the Yiddish press, but Jacob Schiff and Cyrus Adler advised "controlled silence" lest Jews advertise themselves. The Anti-Defamation League (ADL) issued guidelines to publishers for the use of "Jewish" and "Jew." It counseled against using these labels either for criminals or for notables such as physicians, because "in neither case has the man's Jewishness any connection with his disgrace or honor."[16] But Marshall's warning to Doubleday that they were "stumbling" perilously close to criminal libel did not prevent Henry Ford's seven-year campaign to force American Jews out of public life.[17]

The capriciousness of Henry Ford's character makes it difficult to find motivation for his anti-Semitic campaign. Some, like Rabbi Leo Franklin of Detroit, who knew him personally, were convinced that the gullible industrialist was being manipulated by others, including C. C. Daniels, brother of the former secretary of the navy, the czarist Boris Brasol, David Starr Jordan, president of Stanford University, and E. B. Cameron, who eventually assumed much of the responsibility for the campaign. In some measure this view was shared by Louis Marshall, who considered Ford "an illiterate and mentally unbalanced fanatic."[18] Others observe that Ford's rural background made him an ideal candidate for the populist brand of anti-Semitism. In assigning a conspiratorial role to Jewish bankers, Ford reflected the mentality of thousands of Michigan farmers who also clung to that myth. His trouble with Wall Street reinforced his conviction. In 1919 he had borrowed $75 million in a desperate effort to retain family control of the company. A decline in sales during the 1920 economic downturn made it impossible to redeem the loan, compelling the Ford Company to go public to raise necessary capital. Ford was dismayed. He understood little of the intricate finances involved in such a procedure and never forgave Wall Street for what he believed was an intrusion into his personal fiefdom.[19]

In 1919 Ford had purchased a nearly defunct newspaper with a circulation of only 72,000, then invested $5 million in it. By 1925 its circulation had risen to 700,000. When Ford's anti-Semitic campaign started, thousands of copies of the *Dearborn Independent* were delivered free to the local clergy and other community agencies. So intent were the publishers on making their views known that Ford auto dealers were compelled to distribute a monthly quota of the newspaper and readers were requested to share the cost of the campaign. The purchase of the newspaper and the mobilization of the dealership network may have been part of a strategy to groom Ford for political office. Whatever the case, the actions that followed went beyond the caprice of a wealthy and powerful man.

E. G. Pipp, editor of Ford's magazine, was replaced by W. J. Cameron, who became editor of the *Dearborn Independent.* The change signaled an anti-Semitic campaign that ran for ninety-one issues and reached its zenith with the serialization of the *Protocols,* later distributed in book form as *The International Jew.* Supported by limitless funding from the Ford industrial empire, the message reached millions of Americans. Coming with the publication of other anti-Semitic propaganda and with evidence of exclusion, it shocked and frightened American Jews.

How to respond to the onslaught left Jewish leaders in a quandary. There was no way to silence Ford, and counterpropaganda was expensive and ineffective. Half-convinced that a personal appeal to Ford would have little effect, Louis Marshall nevertheless sent a long cable to Detroit detailing the poisonous effect the attack was having not only on Jews, but on the morale of the nation. The cable ended with a plea to halt the campaign: "Three million of deeply wounded Americans are awaiting your answer." Two days later Marshall received an insulting response accusing him of using the language of a "Bolshevik orator" and informing him that the discussion he requested would take place "when [he had] attained a more tolerable state of mind."[20]

Fearing a wrenching battle of words in the public arena, Marshall was inclined to agree with Cyrus Adler that silence was the best way to protect the dignity of the Jewish community. But that would also leave the field to the *Dearborn Independent,* which, with Ford's resources, could go on with its campaign indefinitely. A suggestion from the militant Yiddish press to boycott Ford products was also thought unsuitable by Marshall and Adler. (Eventually local Jewish communities in the Midwest organized such a boycott without Marshall's approval, and it contributed to bringing Ford down.) Instead, in July 1921 Marshall communicated directly with Warren G. Harding, who was on good terms with Ford's social circle, asking the president to intercede in the name of justice. "If you fail," he noted, "at least you will be on record as having supported the American spirit."[21] The muting of the *Dearborn Independent*'s anti-Semitic rhetoric after July 1921 may be attributable partly to Harding's compliance with Marshall's request, but it would take more than presidential intercession to silence Ford. By 1924 his anti-Semitic diatribes had again reached fever pitch.

Surprisingly, though Marshall had threatened to use the courts in several other cases of anti-Semitism, he hesitated to do so in the Ford case. He believed the libel laws were not strong enough to win such a case, and in 1922 he urged the governor of New York to sign an amendment strengthening the state's libel law. Only when he had sufficient evidence to ensure victory did Marshall venture forth, and then not to the courts, but into the public arena. One such foray occurred in March 1925, when he had evidence that Ford was misusing the United States mail. He wrote to Calvin Coolidge offering photostatic evidence that the Ford Motor Company was illegally coercing its dealers to order and distribute the *Dearborn Independent* through the mail.

Marshall understood better than most that the Jewish community was involved in a public relations battle that was best fought with images rather than lawsuits. Ford's folk-hero image had to be deflated by making him look the fool. To accomplish that Marshall needed the help of America's media and opinion-making elites. Throughout fall 1920 he consulted with prominent Catholic laymen to establish contact with church officials like Cardinal James Gibbon of Baltimore, Cardinal William O'Connell of Boston, and Archbishop Patrick Haynes of New York. With the additional help of the Federal Council of Churches of Christ, he launched a tolerance campaign, financed largely by the AJCOMM. After the *Dearborn Independent* stated that Benedict Arnold had "served as a Jewish front," the stage was set for a proclamation, published in leading newspapers on 15 January 1921, in which 121 prominent Americans, including all living former presidents, denounced Ford's divisive and un-American campaign. Making certain to couch all his activities in terms of the American interest, Marshall rarely mentioned Jews directly. Rather, Ford was pictured as posing a threat to American values that Jews cherished. When the carefully planned public relations strategy conceived by Arthur Brisbane, the syndicated Hearst Press columnist retained by the AJCOMM, was disrupted by a public message rebutting Ford issued by several national Jewish organizations, Marshall was dismayed.[22] Answering Ford's charges directly focused public attention on a negative image of Jews rather than on Ford's hate peddling.

It was another "loose cannon" that gave Marshall the opportunity for a public relations coup, though even there he disapproved of using the courts. Beginning in April 1924, the *Dearborn Independent* featured a series of articles dealing with Jewish exploitation of farmers' organizations. A particularly bitter personal attack was launched against Aaron Sapiro, general counsel for the National Council of the Farmers' Cooperative Marketing Association. Sapiro was committed to the idea of farm cooperatives as a solution to farmers' problems and had played an important role in establishing a division of cooperative marketing in the Department of Agriculture. The articles accused him of being part of "a conspiracy of Jewish bankers who seek to control the food market of the world." Over a dozen separate libels were listed in Sapiro's answering $1 million suit. The case was so complicated that several judges disqualified themselves. By the time it came to trial, in March 1927, much of Ford's passion for "exposing" Sapiro had waned.

The strategy for the defense was to place Sapiro himself on trial by linking him to a cabal of Jewish bankers including Bernard Baruch, Julius and Lessing Rosenwald, Otto Kahn, and Albert Lasker, who were supposedly involved in a conspiracy to control farmers. But from the outset the court chose to focus on the intricacies of cooperative marketing, and Sapiro was getting a fair hearing. To protect Ford, his lawyers used E. B. Cameron, who had written the libelous material, as a foil. Although there was evidence that Ford had personally ordered the vendetta against Sapiro, Cameron testified that the tycoon never discussed the content of the paper with him. But when the court issued a subpoena for Ford to testify, the defense case fell apart. Afraid he would look foolish in public, Ford's attorneys tried desperately to prevent his appearance. A declaration of a mistrial in June offered Ford respite until September. Finally, rather than take the witness stand, he decided to settle out of court.

Working through two prominent intermediaries, E. J. Davies, former assistant attorney general, and Joseph Palma, a United States Secret Service official, secret negotiations were begun. As a basis of settlement Ford offered to "repair" the damage. There now began delicate negotiations between Marshall and Sapiro on what repair meant. Marshall was interested in the "moral effect upon the public mind" that could be achieved through a formal public apology by Ford. There had, after all, been damage to the entire Jewish community.[23] Sapiro, a highly secularized Jew uninvolved in Jewish affairs, merely wanted to recover costs for personal damages and compensation for the expense he had undergone for the trial. He also hoped for a special scholarship fund to be established for needy students in agricultural colleges and a subsidy for a farm journal. Marshall's fear was that Sapiro's request for a monetary settlement would compromise the effect on public opinion that he wanted to achieve.

Sapiro ultimately received $140,000, and with Brisbane acting as intermediary, Marshall helped formulate a public apology for Ford to make. Released on 8 July and given nationwide publicity, the apology was skillfully designed to avoid humiliating the tycoon. But Ford's professing ignorance of seven years of vilification that was being done in his name made him look ridiculous. For Marshall that appearance was imperative if anti-Semitism itself was to be denigrated. Ford asked for forgiveness, and Marshall was able to respond that "the spirit of forgiveness is a Jewish trait," striking a note that would be understood by all believing Christians. He cautioned that the effect of the apology would be negated by derision.[24]

Although skeptical about its sincerity, Jews everywhere greeted the apology with joy. A man of great wealth and power who had done "grievous wrong" to the Jewish people had been brought low. There was surprisingly little rancor. Marshall spoke of receiving great *nachas ruach* (spiritual satisfaction) from the disposition of the case. But noting that the *Protocols* were still being widely distributed, Stephen S. Wise spoke for many who felt that the damage done was irremediable.[25] Ford did not comply with alacrity with the part of the agreement that ordered the destruction of the remaining copies of *The International Jew* and the withdrawal of the reprint rights given to Theodor Fritch, a Leipzig publisher. Another suit filed by Herman Bernstein, a concerned Jew, was settled quietly, much to Marshall's satisfaction. There had been enough publicity.

The significance of the Ford case goes beyond the damaging impact of the publication of anti-Semitic material. Few American Jews were denied access to the promise of America because of such publications. We shall note presently how many second-generation Jews made the rapid leap to the middle class during the 1920s. But ultimately the ideas formulated with such charged words do affect attitudes that influence public policy. Ford's campaign reviling Jews undoubtedly contributed to a latent attitude of anti-Semitism that is difficult to measure because it remains concealed. American Jews reacted with great concern because they were aware of the long-range significance of access to the instruments shaping public opinion. They would not have responded so strongly had Ford's racial fixation remained private, but he had the wealth and power to amplify a private sentiment and project it into the public arena. Even then, Ford's machinations might have come to nothing had anti-Semitism not been "in the air" in the early years of the twenties. Jews were facing not only Ford, but a host of other hostile incidents and processes. The *American Hebrew* referred to them collectively as "sinister tendencies," that needed to be resisted.[26] In the Ford case, they were. In that outcome may lie its historical significance. After Jewish leaders groped for a suitable strategy without finding one, a fortuitous libel suit and perhaps a change in the economic fortunes of the Ford Company presented an opportunity to hit back in an acceptable manner. Jews discovered that it was possible to fight anti-Semitism and win.[27] The lesson was not forgotten.

For the second generation, Ford's anti-Semitic fulminations disrupted a dream of America. The Harvard limitations case and the immigration restriction laws, because they dealt with access, suggest denial of the dream. In both cases quotas were the mechanism used. Small wonder the idea of quotas retains its negative connotation among American Jews to this day.

The Harvard limitations case agitated American Jewry between 1922 and 1925. Though it is another example of anti-Semitism in the private sector, this time we see a private institution limiting Jewish enrollment and, at least in theory, curtailing the possibility of education and certification. Although the limitations policy directly affected only a comparatively small group of Jewish students, because it dealt with formal education, to which Jews attached inordinate value, the movement to rescind such limits became a community crusade. In a sense such agitation was a perverse tribute to Harvard, for it was the university's reputation for excellence that led Jews to single it out rather than the dozens of other universities that had embarked on a limitations policy earlier and more blatantly.

The Harvard case is best viewed in the context of eastern Jewry in the second half of the nineteenth century. For a stratum of eastern European "enlightened" Jews, the conviction grew that a university education was, in the words of Abraham Cahan, "a symbol of spiritual promotion," and that educated people were the "real nobility" of the world.[28] The esteem given to education was reinforced by a more practical consideration: before World War I, evidence had already accumulated that formal education was transforming American Jewry from a proletarian immigrant group to a middle-class one. By the 1930s, the over 4,400,000 Jews who composed 3.5 percent of the population were supplying 10 percent of the student population. The percentage was considerably higher in areas of Jewish population concentration.[29]

That fervor for education drove the sons and daughters of the immigrants, and frequently the immigrants themselves, to enroll in schools at all levels. The movement was not limited to the United States. After *numerus clausus,* a law to limit the number of Jewish students enrolled, was imposed in Russia in 1887, Jewish young people migrated to Germany, Switzerland, France, and even Turkey to enroll in universities. Between 1912 and 1913, 2,500 attended German universities alone. One of the first tasks the world Zionist movement set for itself, after the Balfour Declaration of 1917 promised a Jewish homeland in Palestine, was to establish a world-class university. Everywhere Jewish students exhibited the same characteristics: extraordinary drive, coupled with "high visibility, [and] strong institutional and disciplinary concentration."[30] Predictably, almost everywhere they appeared in numbers, quotas followed. In the United States the rush of young Jews to enroll in the universities was more pronounced, because they could do so without leaving home. If he lived in a large city like New York or Boston, the budding doctor or lawyer could become a "subway" or "tram" student. The proximity of the university put the dream of a college education within reach of thousands of Jewish families who might otherwise have applied their limited resources to more immediate goals. In the case of Columbia University, physical access was fortuitous. A relocation of the campus to Morningside Heights had just been completed in 1910: the trustees assumed that its distant location and the Protestant character of the campus would deter Jewish enrollment. But one trustee, William Parsons, helped design and then invested in the Broadway subway line that traverses Manhattan's West Side. No one could have been more surprised to discover that direct access had been furnished to secularized Jewish students, concentrated in lower Manhattan and in Harlem. With public transportation available, Columbia's Jewish enrollment soared. University officials called it an invasion.

Between 1890 and 1910 Jewish enrollment was limited mostly in professional schools and hardly at all at the undergraduate level. But after World War I the policy shifted toward outright limitation. It became most manifest in elite private colleges, especially those near Jewish population centers, and in schools of medicine, law, and engineering. That Jewish enrollment remained above the Jewish proportion of the population was sometimes cited by university officials to justify quotas, but that rationale did not take into account that the Jewish population produced a higher percentage of potential college students. In the secondary schools, from which a growing number of Jews graduated, they were likely to enroll in the college preparatory track. Immigrant parents understood that formal education and certification would yield dividends and were willing to invest their hard-earned dollars.

By 1920 the recently expanded Washington Square campus of New York University was 93 percent Jewish, a higher proportion than in the tuition-free institutes of City College of New York or Hunter, whose estimated Jewish enrollment varied from 80 to 90 percent. That same year Columbia's Jewish enrollment reached 40 percent, which it whittled down to 22 percent in two years. Schools some distance from Jewish population centers, such as Yale, Syracuse, Dartmouth, and Princeton, predictably had lower Jewish enrollment. In fifty-one non-elite universities, situated away from urban areas or in the Midwest, surveyed by the *Jewish Daily Bulletin,* exclusion of Jews was virtually nonexistent. The *State,* a newspaper in Columbia, South Carolina, advertised for Jewish students. An accompanying editorial observed that if Jews would only seek out smaller state institutions like the University of South Carolina, both the Jews and the universities would benefit. But often compelled to work part time and unable to afford board, most Jewish students considered these schools out of reach.[31] Sending a Jewish son to college was in most cases fraught with uncertainty, and education was frequently disrupted by a change in family fortunes.

Situated in Cambridge, within easy reach of Boston, which in 1920 had almost 80,000 Jews, Harvard saw its Jewish enrollment rise by 10 percent between 1918 and 1920. Jews became 20 percent of the student body, but considerably fewer took an active part in campus activities. Tensions had developed on campus. A sizable portion—perhaps a majority—of students and faculty supported a policy to limit Jewish enrollment. Like Columbia, Harvard had experienced no difficulty in absorbing the sons of German Jews. "But at the turn of the century," observed the university's eminent historian Samuel E. Morison, "the bright Russian Jewish lads from the Boston public schools began to arrive. There were enough of them in 1906 to form the Menorah Society and in another fifteen years Harvard had her 'Jewish Problem.'"[32]

Harvard's organizational culture was more liberal and merit-oriented than that of any other Ivy League school, but as in all such universities, segregation of Jewish students from the social life of the campus was the rule rather than the exception. The 40 percent of Jewish students who lived on campus were housed in two dormitories, one of which was dubbed "little Jerusalem." As at Columbia, the feeling against commuting "tram" students, who did not fully join in campus life, was strong.[33] On 5 June 1922, in response to a recommendation by President Abbott L. Lowell, the Harvard Board of Overseers created a committee to examine the "principles and methods for more effectively sifting candidates for admission." Jewish alumni, suspecting a strategy for the imminent limitation of Jewish enrollment, reacted quickly. A prominent Cleveland lawyer and officer of B'nai B'rith communicated directly with Lowell to protest the specific mention of Jews. His letter echoed a note sounded by many Jewish Harvard alumni: rather than accommodating to anti-Semitism, the Harvard tradition would be better served by combating it. In the exchange of letters with Jewish alumni, Lowell pointed out he had not used a method of indirection commonly employed at other universities, because he thought everyone agreed that reducing the number of Jewish students would lessen anti-Semitism: "If their number should become 40 percent of the student body, the race feeling would become intense."[34]

Lowell, who was known among Jews as a staunch restrictionist and as opposing the appointment of Louis Brandeis to the Supreme Court, had in fact been remarkably candid. The composition of the committee, three of whose thirteen members were Jewish, suggested that support for limitations was not a foregone conclusion. Moreover, the committee took seriously its charge to consult fully with the administration as well as with "thoughtful" Jews. A student committee composed of five Jewish and five non-Jewish students served primarily as a safety valve to release campus tensions. It was the discussions within this committee that revealed to Harry Starr, president of Harvard's Menorah Society, what was really at stake. He began by believing that the tension stemmed only from the dislike of certain Jewish "tram" students, but eventually he became convinced that "bad or good, . . . rich or poor, brilliant or dull, polished or crude, *too many Jews,* were not liked."[35]

An untoward incident on Christmas Eve 1922 revealed more than Lowell intended. During a six-hour delay on the New York Central between Boston and New York, he discussed the case with Victor Kramer, a Jewish alumnus. Kramer turned what Lowell undoubtedly believed was a private conversation into a media event. It was, as Starr had suspected, not a matter of quality but of quantity. "You are Menorah boys, we are Crimson boys, and the two just don't mix," Kramer reported Lowell as saying. As the evening wore on Lowell revealed that he believed the real answer was for Jews to abandon their religion, which had been superseded by Christianity. "To be an American is to be nothing else." Lowell's response to Harvard's Jewish problem was to absorb such Jews, but that could be done only if they remained below 15 percent.[36] Kramer's revelations focused Jewish attention on Harvard and changed a local problem into one that concerned the entire community.

When the committee finally delivered its report on 9 April 1923, public criticism of the university was intense and much goodwill had been lost, especially among an influential and generous group of Jewish alumni. Predictably, the committee's report was designed as much to reduce such hostility as it was to propose a suitable admissions policy. The quota system was repudiated as running counter to Harvard's tradition of "equal opportunity to all regardless of religion." The report recommended that henceforth no preference be given to sons of alumni, thus upholding the merit principle. Proportional representation for each group and any "novel process of screening" or "covert devices" were rejected. Academic admissions requirements would be raised by employing the "highest seventh system" for preparatory schools west of the Mississippi. On the surface it looked like a clear-cut victory for the merit principles of admission, which most Jews supported. But two key recommendations—to raise the proportion of students from the interior and to limit the size of the entering class to one thousand—would have much the same effect as quotas: they would lower the proportion of Jewish "tram" students.[37] The admissions screen was simply altered so that Jewish applicants had less access, as did other urban minorities. Within less than a decade Harvard's Jewish enrollment declined again to 10 percent, without the use of formal quotas. Privately a form of limitation prevailed, but publicly it was rejected. For the moment, that served the interests of both sides.

Behind the Harvard case there lies a web of culture conflict between Jews and the guardians of establishment institutions. We observe a highly motivated group of second-generation Jews seeking an accelerated rise in station through formal education and certification. A few sought such education at universities that were historically the leadership-training ground of the native elites. Rather than receiving approval for the merit and academic effort that were esteemed by their eastern European Jewish cultural heritage, Jewish students were made to feel like intruders and rejected for not understanding and fitting into the culture of the institutions.

Conflict between arriviste and established Jews also occurred within the community. The limitations policy focused on the "new" Jewish immigrants and their children and barely touched the acculturated and established Jews who had descended from the nineteenth-century German-Jewish immigration. Some of these Jews undoubtedly resented being tarred with the same brush. Others had imbibed enough of American values to understand and even sympathize with its hostile attitude toward the descendants of the "pushy" eastern European Jews. "One of the saddest features of the whole matter," observed Louis Marshall, "lies in the fact that some of our Jewish snobs are openly favoring a limitation which would exclude a large percentage of the Russian Jews."[38] One such was Julian Morgenstern, president of Hebrew Union College, the rabbinical academy of the Reform branch. The problem was with the "day students," he asserted, who had arrived at the university a full generation too early. It was essentially a problem of the "not yet American Jew."[39] A Jewish alumnus writing to the *Philadelphia Jewish Exponent* saw the roots of the problem in the strident secularism of the new breed of Jewish students. "It is not the Jew who practices his Judaism," he wrote, "but the Jew who neglects it, besmirches it and disgraces it" who finds himself held in contempt.[40] The *American Hebrew,* which served as the voice of the more acculturated segment of American Jewry, became exasperated with the constant cry of anti-Semitism. To be sure, there were difficulties for Jewish youth on campus, but "the right kind of Jewish youth" could overcome them without crying wolf.[41] The right kind of students were those who went out for the athletic teams and otherwise accepted American values.

At the root of the conflict was a cultural dissonance that centered on the different value each group assigned to education. Harvard's aims were totalistic. It not only sought to produce trained minds, it wanted to shape the entire student so he could take his rightful place among the governing elite of the nation. The university served as a socializing agency, as did other Ivy League schools. That was a far cry from the Judaic value system, which assigned character training to the home and viewed secular education as merely an instrument for building a better life. Jewish values permitted far less intrusion into the private area that Harvard officials called "character."

Had Jewish applicants been attuned to the university culture and its indifference to the values they cherished, they might have thought twice about seeking admission. They came with an instrumentalist view of education that was part of their immigrant culture but anathema to the universities they sought to enter. That partly explains why Yale's dean of freshmen saw Jewish students as a "foreign body in the class organism" and why Lowell felt there was "no use talking of a spirit of common brotherhood between the graduates of St. Marks and the Menorah Society."[42] Harvard students who favored limits spoke of the Jews' poor hygiene, competitiveness, and disdain for athletics. They complained that Jewish students were dishonest and violated the honor system. "When a Gentile is a crook, he is a crook," one Jewish student observed, "but when a Jew is a crook, he is a Jew."[43] Yet these were surface manifestations of a deeper fear that Jews were an alien force seeking to take over a native institution.

The cultural conflict centered ultimately on two related issues—the status of the "day" or "tram" students, and team sports. Repeatedly the complaints of Christian students focused on tram students, whose general and financial circumstances ruled out their participating in the social life of the university. Yet Jewish students who lived on campus were no more welcome in the social life of the college, and ultimately they founded their own fraternities, as their parents founded Jewish country clubs. By 1922 the best known of these Jewish fraternities, Zeta Beta Tau, boasted thirty-two chapters.[44]

It was primarily college sports that became the symbol of the conflict of cultures. As one Harvard professor put it: "If the Jews have a complex on athletics, our boys have one on the Phi Beta Kappa society." There was no mistaking who "our boys" were. A Yale official spoke of students' being disinclined to compete with Jews for scholastic honors. The Yale Y was considered preferable to the Phi Beta Kappa key, just as football scrimmage was preferable to debating. The primacy of athletics was less pronounced at Columbia University, where the "handsome, well-mannered youth of caste" did not completely rule the campus because of the comparatively high proportion of Jewish students, which persisted even after quotas were imposed, and because of the more cosmopolitan ambiance of New York City. Columbia's organizational culture was also less prescriptive, and academic excellence was held in higher esteem.[45] At the heavily Jewish City College of New York (CCNY), where the physical education department was dominated by West Point military procedures, a coach is reported to have exhorted his class: "If you want to be a he-man go in for football; if you want to be a nut like Einstein, stick to the books." The preference of the nearly all Jewish student body of CCNY became clear in 1925 when students struck against ROTC-required military drills.[46]

Concerned about what it considered a misperception of Jewish cultural values, the *American Hebrew* devoted an entire issue, bearing the long title "Who's Who in the Colleges? A Bird's-Eye View of the Jewish Undergrads Who Give the Lie to the Prejudicial Assertion That Jews Do Not Participate in College Activities," to proving the opposite. The number of Jewish students who had earned letters in sports was impressive, according to a study conducted by Zeta Beta Tau. In ten major universities, excluding the three that followed a limitations policy, Jewish students earned 7 percent of the varsity letters awarded for sports. But they earned 16.7 percent of the honors awarded for excellence in publications.[47]

Clearly, the perception that Jewish students were "Egyptian mummies in tortoise shell spectacles" was as overdrawn as the image of all Christian students as "jocks." Athletics had in fact become a major acculturation instrument within the Jewish community. The public enthusiasm of the young fans who greeted the all-Jewish Hakoah soccer team from Vienna in 1927 was equal to that of the crowds who welcomed Albert Einstein when he visited New York in 1921. When the predominantly Jewish Seward Park

High School, which serviced the Lower East Side, won the city's baseball championship, even though the team had no field to practice on, the Yiddish dailies played the story to the hilt.[48]

The supposed reluctance of Jewish students to go out for sports, so frequently complained about, may have reflected a general unhappiness with their entire set of unacceptable cultural values. There was something different about the student culture produced by the sons of the eastern European immigrants, who were very unlike the German-Jewish students the universities had grown accustomed to. According to the drama critic Walter Eaton, they were more "ambitious" and "aggressive," generating an "atmosphere disturbingly at variance with the spirit of the place [they] enter."[49] Jewish students were more likely to apply their energies to their studies. "They memorize their books!" complained one student who was nettled by the lack of appreciation of common sense. "History is full of examples where one race has displaced another by underliving and overworking," complained another. A Columbia medical student thought it was in the psyche: "Somehow or other they have an emotional intensity that drives them longer and harder than the average." But the noted scholar Horace Kallen, himself a Harvard graduate, was convinced the problem lay not in their differentness, but in the speed and completeness with which they adopted the universities' values and style.[50]

Kallen's observation notwithstanding, Jewish students were seen as different by both Christian and Jewish observers. It was not so much that they behaved badly as that they had little understanding of the concept of behavior. Morris Cohen, celebrated mentor of many Jewish students at CCNY, described his colleagues' disappointment at the "bad manners" of Jewish students. But Cohen saw much to praise, too. They were crude, to be sure, but that was because their idealism had not been tempered by "hard cold realities." There was "an extraordinary attachment to the values of the spirit" that made them worthy successors to their parents.[51] They looked different, too. Ludwig Lewisohn, who received a graduate degree from Columbia in 1922 but was rejected for a teaching position, looked in the mirror and noted with "dull objectivity" his dark hair, his "melancholy eyes," and his "unmistakingly Semitic nose" and knew he did not belong.[52] Like many others, Lewisohn probably would have liked nothing better than to be accepted, but he could not change his appearance or the poverty that compelled him to take the subway home rather than participating in campus activities. The sons of the eastern European immigrants who attended college were usually the first in the family to do so, and they were sent at considerable financial sacrifice. It was an investment made by the entire family, and the young man was expected to focus on immediately attainable goals—to get on with the job of making something of himself.

In colleges where the sons of eastern European Jews composed a sizable portion, like CCNY and New York University (NYU), there prevailed a rough give-and-take intellectual atmosphere. Ideas and ideology were taken seriously, and often the students were highly politicized. An observer noted quickness of speech, informal dress, and an almost total absence of what was called "school spirit" at NYU's Washington Square campus. Jewish students were enthusiastic sports fans but had little time to take part in organized college athletics or any other extracurricular activity. Most had some kind of part-time employment. Campus fraternities, when they existed at all, were weak.[53] Yet there were those who took pride in what they believed was a superior student culture. Addressing the perennial complaints regarding the poor personal hygiene of Jewish students, one journalist argued that a lack of bathing ought not to conceal the "beauty of the spirit." "The garb of the dirty immigrant may clothe the grandson of Isaiah." As for fraternities, what were they, argued the Jewish principal of a New York public high school, but snobbish institutions that interfered with proper socialization? Better to create for students "a society in which membership is open to all who measure up to a high standard of character and scholarship. . . . the one is open while the other is dark."[54] There was communal pride in the academic achievement of Jewish students. Their superior performance on the newly conceived intelligence tests developed by Lewis M. Terman was used to flay the "Nordics." The Regent scholarship winners list in New York State "reads like a confirmation roster at a temple," boasted the *American Hebrew*.[55] At Columbia 22 percent of the student body was Jewish, but Jews made up nearly half the members of Phi Beta Kappa. By 1930, six of the nine editors of the *Columbia Law Review* were Jewish. Professor Charles H. Grandgent, chairman of the committee Lowell appointed to examine the Harvard admissions policy, reported his astonishment at the number of Jews from poor districts "who became remarkable students."[56] Everywhere Jewish students generated a vital campus intellectual life in which sports became an informal activity while student drama and publications were upgraded.

Yet despite their superior academic performance, or perhaps because of it, Jewish students at Harvard, Yale, and Princeton remained outsiders.

Some undoubtedly paid a price, especially in the Ivy League colleges. Many were in the process of distancing themselves from the immigrant culture of their parents when they were brought up short by the hostility of the university. No longer buttressed by their own faith and culture and not yet welcomed by the new, they could suffer a devastating blow to their mental health.57

The Harvard quota case was merely one aspect of a struggle for status that was also occurring in the professional and business world. But within the university the confrontation between conflicting cultural values seemed to become enlarged. Both cultures were clearly elitist but differed on what standards to impose. The Jewish view that such an elite ought to be based on academic ability departed sharply from Harvard's, which acknowledged brainpower but in practice preferred to select the core of its student body based on class background. Publicly it was the Jewish view that prevailed: Harvard renounced quotas. But several other standards in the new admissions policy effectively reduced the Jewish presence to 10 percent by 1930. In effect Harvard had won a private victory that entailed no public humiliation for Jews. Yet even that victory was temporary. By 1940, under the pressure of impending war, Jewish enrollment rose to 25 percent.

For American Jewry the struggle against Harvard's limitation policy had primarily a symbolic significance. It occurred along with other events that signaled to upwardly mobile Jews that the promise of America might be curtailed. That perception prevailed even though public universities and private ones away from areas of Jewish concentration continued to accept Jewish applicants and though there was the alternative of establishing a Jewish university, much as the Catholics had done. By 1922 there were 20,000 Jewish students at the expanded city colleges, and six years later Yeshiva College was founded. But for acculturated Jews these alternatives were unacceptable. They understood that a quota system at Harvard would influence the conventions of the American university for generations and serve Jews poorly. Jewish universities, they felt, would resegregate Jews and slow acculturation.58 For various historical reasons, Jews had selected formal education as a preferred instrument of mobility, and so they had to fight to retain access to higher education. The struggle was couched in the language of the American ideal of democracy and merit. "What is at stake . . . is something far greater than the privilege of education in a few endowed universities. . . . *It is the American Ideal,*" declared the *American Hebrew.* When Harvard recognized merit as the major criterion for admission, Jews naturally saw it as a great victory. "The alignment of Harvard with liberal American universities will carry its influence far beyond Cambridge," commented one editorial writer, "like the shot first heard at Concord Bridge, it will be heard 'round the world."[59] Of course, it helped Harvard too. The contributions of the Warburg, Lehman, Sachs, and Straus families to Harvard's $10,000,000 fund-raising drive in 1924 were more generous than ever. But for the Jewish man on the street, who would never aspire to attend Harvard, the limitations case was simply one more signal of unwelcome.

The impact of the immigration laws of the 1920s on the demography and culture of American Jewry was clearly far greater than that of the Harvard limitations case. I shall note in the final chapter that during the 1930s these laws meant life or death for thousands of European Jews. But the historian must tread carefully before classifying restrictionism as an example of anti-Semitism in public policy. Instances of such official anti-Semitism are comparatively rare in American history, and the nativist animus that drove the new laws was not directed only against Jews.[60]

Immigration restriction sentiment was triggered originally by suspicion aroused by German-Americans who had become disaffected during the war. Three decades of a massive influx of immigrants had engendered a feeling among the elite as well as among ordinary Americans that the nation needed to be restored to its "rightful" inhabitants. Although Woodrow Wilson probably would not have gone as far as his former ambassador to London, Walter Hines Page, who is purported to have suggested that "Americans have got to . . . hang our Irish agitators and shoot our hyphenates," he too came to be wary of the immigrants' power after Irish-Americans had swallowed their pride and largely supported Henry Cabot Lodge's campaign against treaty ratification.[61] In the post–World War I period opposition to immigration had become widespread.

Jews seemed merely to be another unwanted eastern European group to which the laws incidentally applied. When Gedaliah Bublick, editor of the Orthodox *Tagblatt*, gave voice at the congressional hearings to what most Jews suspected, that the proposed immigration law was aimed at barring Jews, he was reminded by a committee member that had Jews lived in Scotland they would have fallen under the more generous English quota.[62] Cairoli Giglotti and Salvatore Cotillo, two leaders in the Italian-American community, were equally convinced that the laws were aimed at barring their kinsmen. Senator "Cotton Ed" Smith, a major supporter of the legislation, wanted to exempt Jews from the quota system. Their "thrift, their economy, their love of learning" appealed to him, as they did to Congressman John L. Burnett, who helped steer the measure through the House. But both retained their contempt and fear of Italian immigrants. The brunt of nativist hostility was borne by the vastly more numerous Catholic immigrant laborers. When in 1919 the Catholic bishops' circular letter, "Social Reconstruction: A General Review of the Problems and Survey of Remedies," called attention to the plight of immigrant labor, it only supplied grist for the restrictionist mill.[63]

Yet sensitized by the Ford case, most Jews remained convinced that restrictionism was more than incidentally anti-Semitic. Most ominous were the "scientific" grounds for the concept of Nordic supremacy. If the problem was in the germ plasm, there could be no hope that the "new" immigrant would eventually become a good American. But biological determinism was precisely what academic experts like Henry Fairchild Osborn of Columbia and Professor Edwin G. Conklin of Princeton were proposing.

At the hearings for the emergency immigration law of 1921, there was only one clear-cut indication that it was Jews who were the target of the restrictionists. The incident concerned a report prepared by the director of the Consular Service, Wilbur Carr, and approved by Secretary of State Charles E. Hughes before it was released to the Associated Press. Compiled from the reports of the consuls in Poland, the report spoke of the Jews as "filthy . . . often dangerous in their habits . . . lacking any conception of patriotism or national spirit." It also warned that 350,000 to 5,000,000 of these "low physical and mental types" were poised to flood the United States. Before Senator Albert Johnson, chairman of the Immigration and Naturalization Committee, could deliver his report to Congress, including the derogatory reference to Polish Jews, Marshall protested. The report was inflammatory and erroneous: "That Jewish economic life has been destroyed by the great war is a misfortune, not a crime." The consuls, Marshall insisted, had far exceeded their authority when they expressed personal views about any group of potential immigrants. Polish Jews, protected by the minority rights clauses of the Treaty of Versailles, were not poised to flood the United States, and there were only 3,000,000 not 5,000,000. An embarrassed Hughes instructed his consuls to henceforth confine their reports to statistics and hard data, but the damage had already been done.[64]

The movement to restrict immigration, reinforced by new support from the South and Midwest, gained momentum in 1917, when for the first time Congress overrode a presidential veto of a literacy test bill. But the law would have had little effect on Jewish immigration because most Jewish immigrants qualified for exemption based on reunification of families. Between 1919 and 1920, of the 119,000 Jews who entered the country, only 689 did not come to join their families.[65] Moreover, there had been great strides in abolishing illiteracy among the prewar Jewish population of eastern Europe.

At the end of the war pressure increased for restricting immigration. Restrictionism had broad nationwide support and sometimes took an ugly nativist turn. A flood of restrictionist legislation was introduced into the Sixty-fifth Congress in December 1918. Among the proposals was the Barnett bill (H.R. 14163), which sought to restrict immigration from the former Central Powers for fifty years and all other immigration for twenty years. There were seven other legislative proposals to suspend immigration of radicals and other undesirables. At the hearings for these bills in February 1919 the first specific anti-Semitic rhetoric aimed at Polish Jewry was articulated by Rev. George Simons. The need for "emergency" immigration legislation was being established.

The House Committee on Immigration and Naturalization, which met in 1921 to consider such emergency legislation, had been exposed to the idea that the nation was facing not only a biological crisis, but also a demographic one. The members believed that millions of potential immigrants, including Jews, were ready to overrun the nation. A logjam at Ellis Island that caused ships loaded with immigrants to be diverted to Boston fueled the rumor that the nation was about to be flooded with immigrants.[66] Robert Ward, a Harvard professor who founded the Immigration Restriction League, had earlier apprised Congress that a well-organized Jewish mass immigration was imminent. On 5 January 1919, Frederick Wallis, commissioner of immigration at Ellis Island, testified that unlimited numbers were "clamoring to come to this country," including a million Italians. Though only 311,000 passport applications were on file in Poland, there was a rumor that 8,000,000 Jews were ready to come to the United States. He ended his testimony by informing the committee that he was convinced "that all of Europe is bending this way, not that they are all coming . . . but all who can make it."[67] Convinced of the flood story, Senator Albert Johnson, the cosponsor of the legislation, became concerned that Jewish agencies like the Hebrew Immigrant Aid Society (HIAS) were abetting the influx. At the 1921 hearings the testimony of John L. Bernstein, director of HIAS, was twisted out of context to support the flood rumor. "If there were in existence a ship that would hold 3,000,000 human beings," Bernstein had written in a memorandum, "the 3,000,000 Jews of Poland would board it to escape to America." Vainly Bernstein tried to inform the committee that his statement was merely a metaphor expressing the dire condition of Polish Jewry. The testimony by a special agent for the Federal Immigration Commission that the proportion of Jews in the Polish immigration stream had actually declined to about 40 percent had little impact.[68]

That millions of Polish Jews were about to land on American shores was an exaggeration. But that Polish Jewry was in a desperate situation was not. The war, which in the East had been waged in areas of Jewish population concentration, had ruined the economic base that supported Jewish life. The ten-month Russian occupation of Galicia alone drove 600,000 Jews from their homes. Relief workers estimated in 1916 that half of the Jews of Russia were without means of support. The situation was aggravated by anti-Jewish depredations during the Russian civil war. In Russia hundreds of towns had been devastated and thousands of Jews had become nomads. In the port cities of western Europe there were 200,000 Jewish refugees from eastern Europe, dependent on local Jewish communities for succor. These communities were clamoring for help from Jewish welfare agencies. Prostitution and procuring, which by 1914 had been all but eliminated in most Jewish communities, showed a resurgence.[69] This desperate situation in the Jewish communities of eastern Europe could easily be imagined as a spur to mass emigration.

Against such a backdrop, Marshall stood little chance of convincing the Committee on Immigration and Naturalization that the minority rights treaty clauses he had fought for finally made a good life possible for Polish Jewry, so that after the emergency was over few Jews would need to emigrate. Congressman Emanuel Celler, then a freshman House member from an almost all-Jewish district in Brooklyn, recalled the mood in Congress: "When I finally rose to talk I knew it was in vain. I used every device at my command. I pleaded and I reassured and realized finally they simply didn't want any more 'wops, dagoes, Hebrews, hunkies, bulls.'"[70] After some conflict over the precise formula to be used, the emergency immigration law of 1921 was signed by President Harding.

Marshall's warning that the law had been too hastily thrown together was quickly confirmed. Quotas were staggered to allow a fifth of the yearly total to be filled every month. The result was that ships arrived with immigrants when the monthly quota had already been used up. In November 1923, for example, 4,800 immigrants arrived to discover that only 3,800 quota places were available. No one had bothered to explain the system to the shipping companies or to the consuls issuing visas. The administration of the law was so rigid that no exemptions were allowed. When such immigrants were returned to their ports of embarkation, often penniless, the result could be cruel. Dozens of cases of "stranded" immigrants and other "humanitarian" stories of immigrants who had fallen afoul of the law were reported in the Yiddish press. The 1921 law succeeded in reducing immigration but it had not yet solved the problem.

Such a solution was hoped for from a permanent immigration law, to be in place by 1924. A more restrictive bill was introduced by Senator Johnson in December 1923 that proposed to shift the census used for determining quotas back twenty years to 1890. The intent of the restrictionist was unmistakable. "Why not 1880? Why not 1860 or 1850?" Marshall cried in anger. "There is a reason . . . those who have agitated for this kind of legislation wish to keep out of the country certain races."[71]

There was little hope of stopping the restrictionist tide, which had grown stronger since 1921. Not only was Jewish opposition subdued, but German- and Scandinavian-Americans, who had once favored an open door for immigrants, had changed their position. The National Liberal Immigration League and the Interracial Council, once in the vanguard of the liberal opposition, had slipped quietly out of existence. A minority report by two Jewish congressmen, Adolph Sabath and Samuel Dickstein, challenged the validity of the Nordic supremacy idea and proposed that the president determine the annual immigration figure based on the nation's needs. But even though 1924 was an election year, which gave those favoring a liberal immigration policy some additional leverage in states with large immigrant populations, few who favored such a policy had any hope of achieving it. Support in Congress for the measure was so overwhelming that a presidential veto would have been easily overridden.

Marshall, who was not opposed to restrictionism, but merely to the kind the new law proposed, offered only token opposition to its passage. The fear was that open agitation would stimulate anti-Semitism while failing to appreciably alter the law. Better to accept the inevitable and then humanize the administration of the law. Let leaders of other hyphenated groups take the lead; Jews were already too much in the limelight. When the Yiddish press continued its emotional response, Marshall argued that it was better to reestablish an economic base for Jews where they were. They could not all come to America. The Joint Distribution Committee, whose board Marshall served on, was already planning to spend millions on just such a policy.

The law, which President Coolidge signed on 26 May 1924, was the harshest version of the several under consideration. It was, as Marshall foresaw, passed by an overwhelming vote, 326 in favor and 71 opposed in the House, and 62 for and only 6 opposed in the Senate. Coolidge, though apprehensive about the provision to exclude the Japanese, "heartily approved of its main features." Few noticed that, at the behest of the California fruit-growers' lobby, Mexico was exempt from the law. That feature would loom large during the refugee crisis of the thirties. But in the interim Marshall's fear that quotas would be difficult to determine and would cause great hardship was confirmed by events. It took almost three years to determine accurately what each national quota should be. During that period the British quota rose from 34,000 annually to 73,000, while the German quota declined from 51,000 to 23,000.

Most persistent was the problem of 15,000 "stranded" refugees, those who had been caught in countries of transit by the change in the law or had otherwise fallen afoul of it. Heart-rending cases of family separation were highlighted in the Jewish press. Seven months after the new immigration act became law, Marshall, Stephen S. Wise, and Nathan J. Miller formed a committee to raise $500,000 for victims of immigration restriction. Thirty-three Jewish organizations met in August 1924 to form the Emergency Committee on Jewish Refugees; by November they had aided 4,000 stranded Jewish immigrants. Not wanting to call attention to the Jewish aspect of the problem, Marshall opposed an amendment to give 35,000 stranded family members preference on the quota lists.

The immigration laws of 1921 and 1924 were effective in their primary purpose, cutting back the immigration flow from eastern and southern Europe. The combined quota of Poland, Russia, Romania, and the Baltic countries, which before World War I furnished about 100,000 Jewish immigrants annually, now was fixed at 9,443. The effect on Jewish immigration was drastic. Only 73,000 Jewish immigrants settled in the United States between 1924 and 1931, a small fraction of the 656,000 who had come between 1907 and 1914.[72]

Ironically, by the end of the twenties the influence of Nordicism, one element in the restrictionist bloc, began to wane, weakening the solid support for the movement. Aware of the economic implications of restrictionism, Herbert Hoover, Secretary of Commerce, and Andrew Mellon, Secretary of the Treasury in the Harding administration, had earlier called for a modification of the quota system to achieve a labor surplus. The provision excluding the Japanese became worrisome for Coolidge and for Secretary of State Hughes, who had seen evidence of Japanese sensitivity on the immigration issue at the Washington Arms Limitation Conference. Senator Albert Johnson, the restrictionist chairman of the Immigration and Naturalization Committee, introduced a bill in 1927 that proposed to abandon the national origins idea altogether. Fearing there would be a political and economic price, congressmen from urban districts also had second thoughts. Subsumed by the related religious issue, immigration policy was no longer a major concern in the "Brown Derby" campaign of 1928. A conference of restrictionist organizations, which included the Sons of the American Revolution and the Junior Order of American Mechanics, was barely able to grind out proposed amendments to the 1924 law to be considered by the Seventieth Congress in 1929. Meeting in January, the first session of that Congress postponed considering the amendments, although new quotas had to be in place by April 1929 to ensure proper implementation at the beginning of the new fiscal year. Hoover called a special session of Congress to consider a new immigration bill, but the proposal was tabled by the Senate.

For the proponents of Nordic supremacy, too, the laws proved a disappointment. Together with the Volstead Act, the immigration laws of the twenties showed how difficult it was to legislate social change. The ethnic composition of the nation in 1890 could not be restored by government fiat, because "Nordic pioneering stock," so idealized by some restrictionists, proved reluctant to pioneer in America. Between 1922 and 1924, Denmark and the United Kingdom used little more than half their quotas, and Norway and Sweden used considerably less. At the same time, the quotas for eastern and southern Europe were oversubscribed. Those who were wanted would not come, and those who would come were not wanted.

Given the role of the American dream in shaping their lives, the rejection embodied in the quotas set by the immigration laws and to a lesser extent by Harvard stung the self-image of American Jews. "*America* is a *Religion* for the Jews of Eastern Europe," observed John Bernstein, director of the Hebrew Immigrant Aid Society, "and they come here as to the Holy Land, and if one is not admitted he feels as though he were ejected from a Holy Temple."[73] It was not that Jews took seriously the slanders regarding Polish Jewry; the perception of self, especially among committed Jews, usually remained high. At the congressional hearings Louis Marshall spoke of Jewish immigrants as dynamos: "Would we reject a gift of 100,000 dynamos a year?" Marshall pleaded. "Yet we are now talking about the rejection of these human dynamos. . . . Have they not brought gifts to us? Have they not brought moral convictions?"[74] More than esteem, they required asylum. "The question of emigration is to most of our brethren one of life and death, not merely of economic betterment," explained a columnist for the *Jewish Morning Journal.*[75]

The sense that the struggle against restrictionism was hopeless, which prevailed among some "uptown" leaders, may have been reinforced by their ambivalent attitude toward the "new" Jewish immigrants and their offspring. Marshall, who often expressed admiration for Yiddish-speaking Jews, nevertheless became convinced that the heavily accented and overemotional testimony of the president of the Federation of Polish Jews and the editor of the religiously oriented *Jewish Morning Journal* had made an "unfortunate impression" by resorting to "the usual method of ward politics."[76] Like many uptowners, he was easily exasperated by their political radicalism, the constant agitation of their unions, and the stridency of their political Zionism. Together with other AJCOMM members, he hoped that over the years this human clay could be reshaped into something more acceptable. Yet at times the noise from the "congested quarter" must have seemed unbearable and Americanization painfully slow. But Marshall would not go as far as Simon Wolf, Washington agent of B'nai B'rith, who suggested that the process could be accelerated if synagogues withheld membership from those who had not demonstrated an intent to become citizens. What Marshall found offensive was the basis on which restrictionism was legislated, not that it was done.[77] The racial slander contained in the Nordic supremacy concept would not go unanswered. The Jewish press used the term "Nordomania" and poked endless fun at those who claimed superiority merely because they were of certain racial stock. Fiorello La Guardia, the new Yiddish-speaking congressman from the heavily Jewish Harlem district in New York City, informed the committee that in his district drunkenness was more prevalent among the native-born than among the immigrants, and that illiteracy was far more prevalent in Georgia and

Tennessee. The AJCOMM made a similar point when it circulated a bulletin of the United States Public Health Service indicating that during the past two decades, judging from a survey of inmates in public asylums, immigrants from western Europe had a higher incidence of mental illness than the new immigrants.[78]

Jews had received many negative signals since the end of World War I. "The country seems to have reached a period of bitterness, disillusion and active hatred," observed one editorial writer.[79] But it was the long-range impact of restrictionism that ultimately made it the crucial factor affecting the well-being of all Jews between 1920 and 1945. American Jewry has always depended on biological and cultural supplementation from abroad. The Sephardic Jews of the eighteenth and nineteenth centuries would have vanished had it not been for the timely arrival of the Jews from central Europe, especially those who came from the German principalities after 1820. Similarly, that succeeding German Jewish community could not have supported a distinctive Jewish culture without the arrival of the "Jewish Jews" of eastern Europe. The restrictionist laws blocked the arrival of that biological and cultural supplement from eastern Europe. As the number of Jews entering the immigration stream waned, the impact on American Jewish demography could be seen in the decline of readership of the Yiddish press and attendance at the Yiddish theater and in a further decline in religious observance. There were ominous predictions that American Jewry would not survive such a blow.[80] Cyrus Adler's response to these fears was wrathful: "If three and a half million Jews in America cannot maintain Judaism without a constant stream of immigrants," he maintained, "then they are unworthy of Judaism." Others, like the newly elected president of Central Synagogue, Dr. Elias Solomon, were more sanguine, believing that with "proper care and cultivation" American Judaism could be made secure without a constant supplement from abroad.[81]

For eastern European Jews the denial of the "resettlement of choice" in America was catastrophic. By the end of the twenties both the Bundist solution, which sought Jewish survival in a "just" socialist order, and the solution of the American Jewish establishment, which sought legal protection of Jewish minority rights through treaty clauses guaranteed by the League of Nations and financial support for relief, retraining, and resettlement, were clearly not working. Jewish cultural institutions were being decimated in the Soviet Union, while Poland and Romania were reluctant to implement the minority rights clauses. At the same time the Zionist solution, to resettle eastern European Jews in Palestine, seemed premature, since the country's economy was not yet able to absorb them. That push-pull calculus left only the United States as a potential haven should flight become necessary. Now America, the traditional haven of choice, was no longer available. Marshall's rejection of an "asylum exemption," advocated by both Orthodox Jews and the Jewish labor movement, stands out in retrospect. Such exemptions, based on religious persecution or family reunification, might have furnished rescue advocates during the Holocaust with a legal instrument based on a distinction between normal immigrants and refugees in dire need, which the immigration law did not contain.

In 1924 Jewish leaders could not know how desperate the Jewish condition would become in just a few years. Steadily improving conditions in the East and the absence of emigration from the Soviet Union concealed the problem. After 1919 the main reservoir of potential Jewish immigration no longer was Russia but became Poland, Romania, Hungary, and the Baltic countries. The flow would be supplemented in the thirties by German Jews. The stage for the catastrophe of the thirties and forties was thus set—there was no place for Jewish refugees to go.

The immigration laws of the 1920s, which at the time did not seem to be aimed exclusively at Jewish immigrants, would prove crucial for Jewish survival in the thirties. Their significance could not be fully perceived at the time because Jews grouped the legislation naturally with other hostile events—the Harvard limitations case, Ford's anti-Semitic fulminations in his *Dearborn Independent,* the strident anti-Semitic propaganda in popular journals and books, and the daily humiliations Jews experienced in a troubled period of xenophobia and nativism. At the time, Jewish leaders might have taken some comfort from seeing that Jews were not the only targets of the restrictionists. But during the refugee crisis of the thirties it became clear that the laws posed a separate and distinct threat to Jewish survival.

As the twenties drew to a close, there were signs that the nativism and xenophobia that gave rise to virulent anti-Semitism had run their course. As the war receded into memory, hostility toward immigrant ethnics declined, assisted off the historical stage by the prosperity of the twenties. Organizations like the National Civic Federation and the Daughters of the American Revolution, which had taken the lead in the campaign to restrict immigration, were having difficulty filling their coffers and had to cut back on their activities. The Ku Klux Klan, which in its heyday claimed a membership of 4,500,000, declined to 30,000 during the Great Depression. Jewish public life concerned itself with mundane things—the Palestinian riots of 1929 and the adverse effects of the depression on the community's ability to maintain its elaborate social service network and meet the mortgage payments on the structures built to house its new congregations and agencies. One observer hopefully saw "the candle of intolerence . . . spluttering in its socket, about to breathe its last gasp."[82] That, we shall see, was hardly the case, but for the moment it was comforting to believe it might be.

CHAPTER TWO

ACCULTURATION AND
ITS DISCONTENTS

FOR JEWS, who are a wandering people, acculturation—the reshaping immigrants undergo—is a familiar experience. Over the centuries Jews earned a reputation for adaptability, and that is really what acculturation is about. It is a process of change in which behavioral norms and values in all areas of life—courtship, family life, religion, even culinary tastes—are refashioned. It begins the moment immigrants set foot in their new homes and continues for generations, and it is rarely painless. Host cultures are less than eager to receive them as they are, but immigrants naturally resist the discomfort of change and cultural denuding. For the Kobatchniks of Philadelphia, name changing, which for some became part of the acculturation process, was not trouble free. Their decision to change their family name to Cabot aroused the ire of the illustrious Boston Cabots and sparked protest from the Pennsylvania Society of the Order of Founders and Patriots. The family nevertheless persevered, and the *American Hebrew* mournfully observed that "Kobatchnik with its rich, sneezing tonal effects, is no more."[1] Giving up the old family name was only an outward manifestation of change—the least that was lost.

After the restrictive immigration laws went into effect, the influence of the immigrant generation diminished. Their children, the second generation—used here more in the cultural than the chronological sense—now set the pace and determined the direction of change. The web of kinship and communal associations, part of immigrant life, fell into disuse even while interdependence of the generations remained. What had been a comforting family incubator often became the setting for generational conflict. Not only were children unable to talk to parents about what had come to matter, but parents saw children rejecting their cherished values and ways. Nor could parents serve as models. "I can't be friends with Gentiles at school and at work and stick up for European ways too," complained a Jewish son from an observant home; "that's why I don't like to stay at home. I don't want to hurt my parents and I can't follow their advice."[2] Among those who took seriously the commandment to pass on the tenets of the faith, the disruption of the cherished chain of generations was especially painful. The second generation was transitional, belonging fully to neither culture. Its members were bound to experience a sense of marginality. Speaking of the new type of Jews resettling in the Bronx, a writer observed that they were "quite distinct from the east-side Jews":

> It's the second-generation Jew with all the outward characteristics
> minus beard and mustache, playing baseball, great fight fans, com-
> mercial travelers, clean-shirted, white-collared, derby-hatted, creased-
> trousered. The women are stylish and stout, social workers, actresses,
> stump-speakers, jazz dancers with none of the color and virtues of the
> erstwhile bearded bewigged parents, and a few vices of their own
> acquisition. But they bathe frequently.[3]

And at Bay Parkway Temple, in one of the new neighborhoods in Brooklyn where modernizing Jews were settling, the sermon topics on one September weekend hint at a decline in traditional moral standards. On Friday night a Reform rabbi sermonized on "Jazzing through Life," and on the Sabbath his topic was "Home Wreckers." The sense of no longer fully belonging to the immigrant culture, yet somehow bearing its stamp, was felt by Alfred Kazin, who notes that he learned to accept his parents' and consequently his own Jewishness, but "without being part of any meaningful Jewish life or culture."[4] Second-generation Jews were strongly drawn to American ideals and values. Theirs was a headlong rush to Americanize, observed Charles Bernheimer, one of the founders of Jewish social work.[5] It took different forms, including the commitment to universalist political ideologies and devotion to new religions like Christian Science and Ethical Culture. Louis Marshall, who was dismayed at the wholesale abandonment of religion, noted with regret that any "ism" seemed preferable to Judaism.[6]

The tension of having to live in two worlds took its toll. The outward trappings of acculturation, such as dress, could be learned much faster than changes that required basic alterations in character and values. Moreover, the process of change occurred during a decade of "heightened anxiety" caused by rapid changes in American culture.[7] The Jews of the twenties were changing their cultural garments while riding an escalator. There are indications, in the rudimentary statistics available, of the enormous stress the second generation was experiencing. Yet they did comparatively well in maintaining their mental health. Between 1918 and 1920, when 20 percent of the population of New York City was Jewish, they furnished only 14.5 percent of the inmates of state mental hospitals. Jews produced fewer psychotics but more neurotics and people who suffered from what was then called "nervousness." Neurosis traceable to family conflict seemed to be more prevalent among Jews than non-Jews.[8]

One of the symptoms of stress was a wave of suicides among Jewish youth in the spring of 1927. All kinds of reasons were given, from "too much freedom" to the loss of religion and direction. Speaking before the United Parents Association, Rabbi Stephen Wise pointed to the consequences of the new "modern" materialistic standards:

> There is this acquisitive passion—the dominance of things and things and things. Children are given thrills instead of responsibilities. There is too much education and too much psychology, fostering the idea that life is self-expression, self-fulfillment and self-realization until it reaches the newest most tragical and final manifestation—the extinction of life itself.[9]

But few others were so certain about the cause of the malaise. Did change first require the weakening of family bonds, as a potter softens the clay, or did family bonds naturally weaken? Whatever the case, the twenties saw a loosening of the ties of kinship, and ultimately the large extended family was replaced by a small nuclear one. Family clans that had settled in the same neighborhoods dispersed. The nuclear family was then compelled to bear alone the stress of rapid change or decline in fortune. Occasionally families cracked under the strain, but most often the changed Jewish family survived and continued to live as before—or as much so as was possible. Jewish social workers were convinced that the rise in crime and other forms of social pathology was also related to the weakening of family life. Undoubtedly tongues clucked when a marriage broke up or a neighbor's child "went bad," but few suspected that they were themselves undergoing a sea change that was radically altering their lives. The startling rise in the number of deserted children that the press publicized was happening on someone else's turf. People no longer thought in terms of community.

Strictly speaking, the loosening of family ties was not exclusive to the second generation. The National Desertion Bureau was established in 1911 in response to the alarming increase in desertion, and in August 1912 the Kehillah established a Bureau of Social Morals to counter the burgeoning crime and vice in the ghetto.[10] Before World War I, Jews had the highest divorce rate in the city of New York, and that probably held true in all urban areas where Jews concentrated. The immigration process itself sometimes weakened family bonds. Husbands often preceded their families to prepare the way and earn enough to pay their passage. Sometimes such separations lasted for years, and in the meantime a man started another family. The war aggravated the situation by lengthening the period of separation. We have noted how the hard-nosed implementation of the immigration laws of 1921 and 1924 stranded thousands more and left families separated. Sometimes such husbands, having already undergone some acculturation, no longer found their bewigged, starkly plain wives pleasing when they finally did arrive. Or a wife, quick to grasp the new opportunities for women, would find her slower, traditional-minded husband no longer suitable. Often there was a family boarder who might become a constant temptation or might meddle in family affairs. An alienated father, steeped in Old World ways and unable to speak the language, lost parental authority in the eyes of his children, who took their behavioral cues from friends on the block. "Green" parents turned to their Americanized children for succor. Parents became children, and children were unwillingly pressed into the role of parents.

The rudimentary statistical portrait we possess of the maladies that attend such family stress suits the twenties better than the pre–World War I period. In 1919, under the auspices of the AJCOMM, the three major statistical collection agencies combined to form the Bureau of Jewish Social Research. Desertion and divorce rates, incidence of juvenile delinquency, and other manifestations of disruption of family life were recorded by communal social workers, who complained of chronic shortages of qualified workers and inadequate budgets. The figures were then channeled to the bureau. Surveying the problem of child dependency in New York City for that year, the bureau found that there were approximately 50,000 dependent Jewish children in New York City alone and that those in foster care fared better than those who were institutionalized. Between 1902 and 1922, social-work agencies had recorded 12,413 such cases. In 1922 the National Desertion Bureau tried to cope with the rising rate by mobilizing an international network of Jewish agencies and the courts to bring wayward husbands home or, failing that, to make them pay child support. One of the most nettlesome problems was to find means of compelling husbands who had started second families to support the families they had abandoned in Europe.[11]

The hedonistic character of the Roaring Twenties also contributed to breaking down the standards of morality that Jewish family life was based on. Buttressed by laws of family purity that were more demanding than the Victorian standards the bourgeois family of the non-Jewish world adhered to, family life for the observant seemed a bastion of security. But it was rooted in norms that were everywhere being challenged, especially regarding the position of women. In the Old World the sexes remained largely separate for work and play. It was as if an imaginary *mekhitzah,* the curtain separating men and women during prayer, also ran through their family lives, defining specific roles for husbands and wives. During the 1920s that separation began to break down. Small apartments, women in the workplace, social dancing in dance halls, and more freedom for children created unprecedented contact between the sexes. In the America of the twenties, Jewish men and women were finally coming to live in the same world. That change was accompanied by a general elevation in the status of women, officially marked by the granting of the ballot in 1920. Focused on mimicking men, especially in clothing and hairstyles, the first thrust of women's emancipation may have appeared superficial. But the stage was being set for more profound changes.

Fear of pregnancy had become minimal as a result of the safer birth control devices. They were widely used among Jews, who eventually became the nation's most efficient contraceptors.[12] It is unlikely that young Jews read Freud, but they did read popular magazines like *True Story,* whose circulation rose from 300,000 in 1919 to 2,000,000 six years later, and they did see the new advertisements that presented a less wicked-seeming version of the unleashed libido by coupling it with the allure of romantic love. The highly literate children of immigrants could see at a glance that the aspiration of the age was for "increasing carnality." There remained little in their cultural baggage that might help them resist the seduction. They were becoming part of an age in which the consumption of material things for pleasure and self-gratification had high priority. Sexual gratification, now viewed as a right, was merely further along the entitlement continuum.[13]

Judaism recognizes that both sexes are entitled to sexual gratification but insists that it be sought within marriage. It is what the marriage partners owe to each other. Adultery was one of the few crimes in ancient Jewish law punishable by death through stoning. But the injunction to chastity was increasingly difficult to heed given the permissive ethos of the twenties. Old World courting patterns became defunct in the new social environment, which gave the highest priority to self-gratification. In the shtetl of eastern Europe, marriage prospects grew naturally out of the network of kinship and community, helped along by the matchmaker (*shadkhan*). It was assumed that physical attraction and romantic love, if they had to play a role, would develop after marriage. Arranged marriages did not disappear at once, but the second generation found such matches increasingly unacceptable.[14] They lacked two requisites for young moderns—free choice and romantic love. Anxious to see his widowed sister remarried, a brother was surprised when she rejected his suggestion of using a matchmaker to find a new mate. "Marriage to her," he wrote to the editor of the *Forward,* "means the union of two people bound by friendship and love," while going to a matchmaker seemed "like going on the slave market . . . to be weighed and measured like a cow at a fair."[15] The sister, who was earning her own livelihood, no longer required the protection and the support of a male breadwinner. She was less apprehensive about the prospect of a life lived alone. "Don't take pity on my years," wrote the author Anzia Yezierska to a friend; "I'm living in America, not in Russia. I am not hanging on anybody's neck to support me. In America, if a girl earns her living, she can be fifty years old without a man and nobody pities her."[16] Spinsterhood remained undesirable, but it was no longer shameful, and frequently it was unavoidable, especially for girls who had educated themselves out of their class only to find a diminished number of acceptable suitors. Such potential suitors, especially if they had attained professional status, became "overly conscious" of their worth and desired to marry women of still higher station. Their elusiveness was a source of bitter complaint in the press.[17] The social spaces where boy usually met girl in the Old World—family gatherings, clubs, and youth movements—had diminished in importance in the new. They were partly replaced by new locales where relationships might blossom, such as the school, union hall, shop, and above all the block. But the new network did not offer respite from the frenetic pace of city life or privacy from the prying eyes of neighbors. The tenement roof was hardly conducive to the romantic image of love and marriage that was replacing the practical, hard-headed approach of former generations. Nevertheless much meeting, matching, and courtship took place in this neighborhood setting. Most urbanized,

American-born Jews found their mates within a twenty-block radius of their homes and therefore within acceptable social proximity as well. But the rules of the courting game had undergone radical change.

To bring marriageable men and women together, there developed summer resorts providing an environment conducive to courtship. These hotels and hostelries became especially popular among young women, who hoped to achieve middle-class status by a "good" marriage. For working-class girls, Jewish unions and fraternal orders also arranged for members to cavort in the country at reasonable rates, as did settlement houses. In June 1924 the Jewish Working Girls Vacation Society began its annual registration of single women at the Educational Alliance. For eight dollars a week, an affordable price for working women, there was a choice of two resorts— Bay House in Bellport, Long Island, for beach enthusiasts, or Lehman House in Big Indian, New York, for those who preferred the seclusion of the mountains.

Most of the summer resorts were run for profit and cost the guests considerably more, but it was considered a worthwhile expenditure for those seeking a better class of mate. Some women spent a good portion of their savings to conceal any telltale signs of lowly origins. An expensive wardrobe could make the humblest salesclerk look like a teacher or a private secretary or—best—the daughter of a doctor. Such simulation was possible because the "guests" did not know each other. Anonymity permitted them to assume a role they believed would attract the desired mate, but it also introduced an element of misrepresentation that could have tragic consequences.

The vacation week itself was carefully organized, with social games, amateur theater, and other group activities to throw the guests together as much as possible. There was, however, a chronic shortage of male suitors. To fill the gap, the male staff, composed of college men chosen for their good looks and charm, was pressed into service to "romance the dogs." The basic tension of the resort was embodied in the way the men sought sex without commitment to marriage while the women wanted at least a promise of marriage before granting sexual favors. "The wonder is not that there's so much sex at South Wind, but that there's so little of it," observed Herman Wouk. "Most of the people get nothing and the handful who do go farther with it, skulk and crawl in the dark as though they were committing a crime."[18] Relatively few matches were consummated considering the expense involved. The key to the success of the resort lay not in the number of couples it brought together, however, but in its ethnically and religiously controlled social environment. The dreaded specter of intermarriage, especially between poor Jewish girls and the sons of Italian immigrants, had arisen. There were about one hundred such marriages a year on the Lower East Side in 1923.[19] Parents, who often subsidized such "vacations," may have noted that their daughter returned with a "bum," but at least he was a Jewish bum.

The need to accommodate to the new freedom of women placed considerable strain on the Jewish family, especially if it had remained observant. Judaism assigned women the sacred task of maintaining the purity of the family, whose holiness was based on its mission as the principal transmitter of the faith. Despite the religious tradition that gave priority to modesty, immigrant Jewish women generally were not slow to learn and use the prerogatives of the new ethos. Their response was conditioned by class and cultural background. The middle-class daughters of the prior German-Jewish immigration had in some ways already achieved a status to which the working daughters of immigrants still aspired. But their independence seemed tame compared with the actions of the small group of radicalized women associated with the Jewish labor unions' struggle to organize. These women far outpaced their upper-class sisters in their liberated behavior and their assumptions about the role modern women should play in society.

Jewish women of all stripes were in the forefront of the campaign to ratify the Eighteenth Amendment. The impetus came not only from "uptown," represented by the Reform movement and the social workers of Jewish settlement houses, but also from the newly organized American Jewish Congress, which insisted that Jewish women be allowed to vote in its nationwide communal election in 1918. Further leftward along the political spectrum, the Jewish labor movement, the socialists, and even the anarchists were active in the struggle for women's rights. Once the ballot was granted, it was taken more seriously among the politically conscious "downtown" second-generation working-class women than among their German Jewish uptown sisters: "Our women are quick to adopt the latest fashions in dress," complained a spokesman for the National Council of Jewish Women, whose members were drawn largely from the old German-Jewish middle class, "but our minds . . . are centuries behind the fashion."[20] There was also support, which went considerably beyond that of other immigrant groups, for the panoply of related legislation. The movement for fairer divorce laws and laws to protect working women and children that accompanied the women's movement also had its strongest support among second-generation Jews.

That support was rooted in the enthusiasm with which Jews accepted the precepts of modernity generally. Predictably, the "liberation" of women was high on the agenda of the Reform movement and the Jewish labor movement, and with the exception of the ultra-Orthodox, there was little organized opposition to it among the clergy. Admired figures such as Rose Schneiderman and Rabbi Stephen Wise were passionate in their advocacy of women's rights. The cause was buttressed by the ample evidence of women's contribution to Jewish social and economic life. They were already indispensable as volunteers in the organizational network, which in the twenties was staffed by middle-class women. The franchise was naturally viewed as a logical culmination of women's growing role in public life. In immigrant families, too, it was often women who first attained language fluency and social competence.

In a sense, politics followed economics in the second generation, whose women increasingly worked outside the home. In the immigrant generation, as the day of the wedding approached the prospective bride trundled her *katerinka* (sewing machine) to the middle of the shop floor as a sign that her shop days were over and the family phase of her life was about to begin. In 1905 only 1 percent of Jewish wives worked outside the home.[21] By the twenties the situation had changed. A small percentage of Jewish women would remain in the work force, since for every four women there were only three potential breadwinners. Among these women was a stratum who had attained an educational level that permitted them to aspire to "finer" things like becoming teachers. But primarily it was the need to supplement the family income that compelled women to work after marriage. The young immigrants were in the most fecund age bracket. Although family size had begun to diminish from the high point it had reached in Europe, in 1918 25 percent of the Jewish population was still under age fourteen. Then, too, immigrant Jews and their offspring aspired to a higher living standard, which may have included buying a house or sending a son to college. Such aspirations would have come to naught had there not developed opportunity for women's employment, especially in the women's apparel industry. World War I also created a temporary shortage of labor, which during the twenties was accompanied by a rise in real wages and a reduction of working hours. There was at once a need, an opportunity, and a new ethos that encouraged women to work after their families had been properly cared for.

There had always been some Jewish women, who voluntarily or involuntarily, remained in the work force. The poorest immigrant women often found employment as domestics in the homes of wealthy uptowners. Among the observant there persisted the notion that the *talmud chacham*, the talented scholar, who in the Old World may have been supported by his in-laws (*eidem oif kest*), should continue to be supported by his wife. When we add to this small group the Jewish women who became entrepreneurs, a fuller picture emerges of the growing importance of women in the economy. It is likely that a good percentage of the subcontracting in the garment industry, which earlier had produced the infamous sweatshop, was done by women or by couples working together. It is difficult to find hard evidence for this, since most such businesswomen registered the business under the husbands' names. Of the five thousand entries in the 1926 issue of *Who's Who in American Jewry,* 10 percent belonged to women, but only three Jewish businesswomen warranted an entry.[22] We will never know how many Jewish women entrepreneurs there were, since they were never registered, but by the twenties the role concept that preferred to keep women in the home had undergone considerable change and had brought with it a change in the relations between the sexes. A growing number of second-generation women had some work experience outside the home, and its broadening effect can hardly be overestimated. It helped empower women in the family, where much of Jewish life was lived.

But on the level of family life, working could prove a mixed blessing, since working women usually carried a double load. Few husbands stepped in to help with domestic work, which still had to be done. Most second-generation men still viewed doing housework as an intolerable feminization. Wives who earned extra income frequently discovered that they had added that burden to their responsibility for the care of the home and family. Some men could not reconcile themselves to their wives' new higher status, which undoubtedly was behind much of the increase in family conflict. Few women were strong enough to manage both job and home without an enormous increase in stress. Middle-class women might counsel that "a business woman should have a maid even if it means that she can't afford to eat anything more than bean soup," but that was not an option for most second-generation working-class women.[23] Women feared that the double burden would age them before their time, while men were concerned with the enticements their wives and daughters faced in the workplace. Working mothers also meant less supervision for children, a problem discussed endlessly in the press and inevitably linked to the increase in juvenile crime.[24]

Had there been sufficient income, it is still doubtful that the old domestic arrangement, which sought to keep women at home, could have been maintained. Many middle- and upper-class women of German-Jewish background had already abandoned an exclusive homemaker role in favor of outside activity. But they faced a "peculiar restriction." The athletic clubs (*turnvereins*) and glee clubs that existed in the German-American communities were usually limited to men. Instead, their energy was channeled into organizational work, which kept them away from home for long hours but brought no income. The path for Russian-Jewish women was entirely different, since they left the home to become members of an industrial proletariat and often participated in labor unions.[25] Theirs was not merely a cosmetic change, and their leap from the domestic role to factory work was far more wrenching.

Aside from its impact on their individual development, the involvement of middle-class Jewish women in organizational work played a significant role in the growth of Jewish organizational life. The "professional board lady" who emerged in the twenties may not have had her worth validated by a paycheck, but the tasks she performed and the responsibilities she bore were far more broadening than housekeeping. Often such volunteers supervised sizable professional staffs and handled budgets as big as that of any middle-sized corporation. The long hours they worked and the often bitter power struggles they waged showed that the world of Jewish organizations was not one of make-believe. Many of these volunteers were in fact full-time professionals in all but name and salary. For many, experience in the organizational world was their first opportunity for self-actualization outside the home. The increased participation of Jewish women as volunteers thus both reflected the new emancipatory spirit and helped generate it.[26]

Women became crucial in the operation of organizations like the National Council of Jewish Women (founded in 1893), Hadassah (1912), and the Union of American Hebrew Congregations' National Federation of Temple Sisterhoods (1913). Before their role was circumscribed by the advent of paid professionals, volunteers not only performed most program and fund-raising functions but filled the entire gamut of social service and Jewish education positions, which were the mainstay of these organizations.[27] Their influence was also felt in national and Jewish politics. By 1923 the National Council of Jewish Women not only was advocating strong positions on matters of war and peace, but was also lobbying for better housing, improved working conditions, and antilynching laws. By 1923, through the efforts of Rebecca Kohut, the International Jewish Women's Organization was established, and it played an important role in ameliorating the vexing Jewish relief problem in eastern Europe.

By the late twenties an increasing number of wealthy Jewish women were joining the women's division of their local Jewish federations, which through their control of fund-raising and allocation would come to occupy a central role in Jewish organizational life. Like most Jewish women's organizations, their programs emphasized reform and amelioration. The National Federation of Temple Sisterhoods, for example, sought to strengthen religious adherence by building a dormitory at Hebrew Union College in Cincinnati. It then began to subsidize new congregations, and finally in 1931 it became the principal sponsor of the Jewish Braille Society.[28] The Zionist organizations that focused their good works on Palestine were even more skillful in mobilizing women volunteers. Hadassah devoted itself to building a public health infrastructure in what it believed would one day become the Jewish national homeland. Among the most noteworthy of these organizations was American Mizrachi Women, which came into being as a separate organization for religious Zionists in 1925. By 1927 national Jewish women's organizations boasted 115 chapters and branches in the New York metropolitan area alone.

There were few formal organizations among the wives and daughters of the wealthiest stratum. Many of these women belonged to nonsectarian clubs such as the Town Club of New York, the Philomath Club of San Francisco, or the North Carolina Club of Jewish Women, and their officers were customarily drawn from the most established Jewish families, who made their homes available for rounds of social teas and fund-raising dinners.[29]

It was not long before the larger women's organizations developed separate priorities and programs. In 1920 Rebecca Kohut of the National Council of Jewish Women requested that the Joint Distribution Committee grant them a $100,000 subsidy and full participation in the crucial fund-raising campaigns. Similarly Hadassah, which had become the largest single constituent organization in the Zionist Organizations of America, took a firm stand in support of the Brandeis/Mack faction during the 1921 Cleveland convention debacle. Two years later it withdrew from the ZOA and affiliated separately with the World Zionist Organization.

For the small group of radical Jewish women of the twenties, separate women's organizations to demand women's rights were hardly necessary. Their militancy, which stemed from socialist and anarchist ideology, outdid anything their genteel middle-class sisters could advocate in the Jewish organizational world. They spoke of "free love" and used the pejoratives of Marx and Engels to express disdain for the institution of the bourgeois family. Needless to say, they made little headway in the Jewish community, which revered the family. They usually were associated with the Socialist party and the labor movement, especially the Women's Trade Union League. Most were involved in the bitter struggle to organize the Jewish labor movement before World War I. Prominent among them were such women as Theresa Malkiel, Clara Lemlich, Pauline Newman, Rose Schneiderman, and Rose Pastor Stokes. Although not cut from the same cloth, they represented a special kind of pace-setting feminism in their ideology and lifestyle. Behind them was a larger group of unsung first- and second-generation radical immigrant women, part of a loosely organized, intensely secular Jewish subculture. Except for a strong commitment to Yiddish, their link to the Jewish world of synagogues and organizations was tenuous. In a sense they represented that segment of the community that was least Americanized and least willing to be so. Their emancipation ideology stemmed as much from socialism as from the conditions of their lives. Paradoxically, the Socialist party was strongly male oriented and separated women in auxiliary groups.[30]

Most Jewish women remained firmly ensconced in family life and possessed little sense of separate gender interest. When they achieved such awareness, it was individually. More likely the growth in consciousness should be attributed to the second generation's increase in formal education. But that drive for education, in evidence among Jewish women as well as men, was directed as much toward attaining middle-class status as toward "liberation." With their broadened horizons, such women became active in a series of causes later encompassed in the liberal agenda: welfare-state legislation, the peace movement, racial tolerance, and improved public health. "Emancipation of women" was merely one such cause. It was their general concern with "progressive" goals that helped fuel the remarkable activism of Jewish political culture in the thirties and forties.

For most second-generation couples the liberation offered by the new contraceptive devices was revolution enough. It profoundly affected the relations between the sexes by making it possible for women, at least theoretically, to express their sexuality almost on an equal footing with men.

But for those still ensconced in the traditional family mode, the price for such experimentation by women remained awesome. The double standard, which closed its eyes to pre- and extramarital relations by males but virtually ostracized women for "loose" behavior, still held. Birth control remained a taboo in most secular Jewish homes and posed a special problem for observant women, whose family lives were subject to the biblical injunction *peryah v'redyah* (be fruitful and multiply). With the consequent large families, Orthodox women were inevitably more dependent and beleaguered. Even after the socialist press took up the cry for more information on birth control, Orthodox women were unlikely to heed the example of the "moderns." Birth control remained largely a matter of class and means and was more likely to be practiced by native-born aspirants to the middle-class, which included a growing number of Jewish men and women. The widespread use of birth control was reflected in the declining size of the Jewish family. During the twenties a favorite Jewish joke concerned unemployed *mohalim*—the men who performed the rite of circumcision. By 1938, 50 percent of Jewish families produced two or fewer children. The new Jewish professional group had the fewest.[31] Jews were on their way to becoming America's most efficient contraceptors.

Though most Jewish families adjusted well to the stresses of acculturation and modernization, there was a disturbing rise of criminality in the immigrant generation. Crime was nothing new to the eastern European Jews. There were the *betteljudn* (beggar Jews) and *voiljudn* (lazy Jews), the procurers and smugglers, who composed a network of criminality in most sizable Old World Jewish communities.[32] Among the first-generation immigrants certain kinds of "white-collar" crime such as embezzlement and failure to pay wages as well as gambling, petty larceny, procuring, and prostitution were more prevalent than crimes of violence. Crime may not have been as rampant as suggested by Police Commissioner Theodore Bingham, but it was certainly prevalent enough to cause concern among Jewish leaders, who in 1908 established the Kehillah in New York City, with its Bureau on Social Morals (1912), to eliminate what was considered a shameful aspect of Jewish life.[33] With the exception of Pittsburgh and Baltimore, every sizable Jewish urban community had its Jewish criminals. But so small was the number of individuals involved and so atypical the idea of living outside the law that one must take care not to assign Jewish crime a greater weight than the facts warrant.

Many contemporary observers believed first-generation criminality was a passing condition associated with the difficulties of immigrant adjustment. But though Jewish criminality generally declined by the mid-twenties, it did not entirely disappear, and its character changed.[34] To assume that Jewish crime was caused by the deterioration of a supportive family life, as some did, does not fully explain its persistence. Prohibition and conflict within the ethnic economy and in the Jewish labor movement furnished new opportunities for a more organized criminality. Jews' inordinate drive to enter the middle class sometimes led them to use illegal means. But by the end of the thirties Jewish criminality was largely confined to a comparatively small group. Its commercial character gave way to a preference for violence, including murder, but the new criminals were only incidentally and usually marginally Jewish.

Before World War I prostitution and procurement had been all but suppressed by community self-policing: the number of Jewish women arraigned for sex offenses fell from 18 percent before the war to 11 percent in 1924. But the impoverishment of Jewish communities in eastern Europe following the war gave the trade a new lease on life that was also reflected in the United States. One study of three hundred pimps in Chicago in the early 1920s identified forty-seven as Jewish. The monitoring activities of the Kehillah probably gave New York City a lower number. As in other parts of the world, Jewish procurers were organized into a syndicate confined to a few families. Yet considering that the American Jewish population had increased, the decline in this form of vice was noteworthy.[35]

Some of the slack was taken up by the conditions created by the Volstead Act. By all rights the "noble experiment" of Prohibition should not have interested Jews much, since they were indifferent drinkers. But as it affected the organized criminal community, the Volstead Act, particularly article 7, which exempted the production and sale of wine for sacramental purposes, also acted like a growth hormone for the Jewish underworld. Article 7 furnished an opening for a flock of false rabbis to serve as outlets for the sale of "sacramental wine." Many of these rabbis organized their fictional congregations in the wine districts of California, where they had also established the Association of Hebrew Orthodox Rabbis of America.[36] In New York City alone almost three million gallons of sacramental wine—more than a gallon for each Jewish man, woman, and child—were supposedly drunk during the fiscal year ending in June 1924. Overshadowing the activities of the "wine rabbis" were the Jewish entrepreneurial criminals who were attracted to bootlegging by the easy profit to be made. Between

1924 and 1932, when Jews composed slightly over 3 percent of the population, close to 12 percent of those indicted for bootlegging were Jewish. The "Big Seven" consortium of rum runners also had a strong Jewish representation.[37]

The effect of the wine rabbis and bootleggers on the Jewish community was twofold. It stimulated Jewish criminality and, in the words of Cyrus Adler, it brought "the rabbinate and the Jewish people into disrepute [by] . . . creating a public scandal."[38] There was fear that such conspicuous lawbreaking by Jews would serve as an excuse for anti-Semitism. The public already recognized the names of the most notorious bootleggers, such as "Waxey" Gordon, Irvin Wexler, "Longy" Zwillman, and "Dutch" Schultz. The foremost anti-Semitic propagandist of the early 1920s, Burton J. Hendrick, repeatedly informed his readers that Jews were producing a disproportionate share of bootleggers.[39] For some acculturated Jews the abuse of the sacramental wine clause and the high number of Jewish bootleggers posed a danger to the entire community. Insecure and anxious to present a good image, they demanded that something be done to control lawless Jews.

The "scandal" widened the gulf between Reform and Orthodox Jews. In 1922 the executive committee of the Central Conference of American Rabbis (CCAR), the rabbinic organization of the Reform branch, petitioned the commissioner of the Internal Revenue Service to revoke article 7 of the Volstead Act, the exemption clause. Jewish leaders in California petitioned the state assembly to crack down on the fake rabbis. Rabbi Louis Ginzberg, a highly respected scholar at the Jewish Theological Seminary, was asked to determine whether Jewish religious law mandated fermented wine rather than mere grape juice for the kiddush and other sacraments. Ginzberg responded that unfermented wines were permissible. But Orthodox rabbis did not accept Ginzberg's decision, nor could they forgive those Jews who had turned to secular authority to adjudicate what was clearly a matter of religious law.

Another condition that abetted organized Jewish criminality during the twenties was the persistent conflict in the garment industry and in the kosher poultry and meat slaughter business. Not only did labor and management resort to using underworld "muscle" to resolve labor disputes, but so did communists vying for control of the union locals. The practice in the garment industry goes back to the turn of the century and became even more commonplace after the signing of the "Protocol of Peace" in 1911.

During the early period the criminals were merely hirelings, receiving a salary of twenty-five to fifty dollars a week to back up the "bosses" as well as the union leaders. Their task was primarily intimidation and protection during periods of strife, but it did not take long for gangsters to realize they could control, and even own a share of, the business they were hired to protect. By the 1920s the opportunistic use of criminals developed into full-fledged racketeering. Once criminals were invited into the industry, it proved impossible to remove them. Even so, it remained an intracommunity affair, as Jewish unions and businessmen retained Jewish gangsters to do their bidding. The community itself was still insulated enough to permit such a paradoxical development.

Protection became a profitable business for "die Shtarke," the name given to the first criminal gang to penetrate the garment industry, but it was the strike of 1926 that led to its entrenchment. That strike occurred after communist-controlled locals, 2, 9, and 22 of the International Ladies Garment Workers Union (ILGWU) disregarded warnings and led the union into it. Beginning during the slack season and lasting twenty-six weeks, the poorly planned strike was a disaster for the fifty thousand workers involved. But for the thugs, working for both sides, it was a boon. The communist-controlled locals retained the strongarm services of "Little Augie," while the manufacturers hired a former bootlegger, Jack "Legs" Diamond. The union leaders soon discovered they could sustain the strike only by illegally using the membership's compensation fund to buttress a lost cause. Finally both sides turned to Arnold Rothstein, the racket-involved son of a pious garment manufacturer, for an arbitrated settlement. The lost strike left in its wake bankrupt locals and entrenched racketeers who were removed only with the help of government authority.

If the Jewish community could view criminals in the garment industry with equanimity, the same was not true of their penetration of the kosher poultry industry. Its annual sales of $50 million between 1925 and 1935 made it one of the most profitable businesses in the ethnic economy. That its very reason for being was based on Jewish law made it inseparable from Jewish concerns. Yet the kosher poultry business, like other businesses that dealt with *shechita* (ritual slaughter), seemed rarely to be free of troubles, and at the turn of the century there were bitter "kosher meat wars." The myriad aspects of Jewish law required a recognized rabbinic authority for adjudication, but no such unified authority existed in the American Jewish community—nor could it. The result was that any rabbi, or group of rabbis, could claim power and enter the lucrative business of certifying kosher foods. In 1901, for example, a group of Orthodox rabbis attempted to subsidize the post of chief rabbi for Rabbi Jacob Joseph, whom they had brought from Europe, by imposing a tax on kosher meat. They ran into the opposition of a group of kosher slaughterers and consumers who would not consent to such a tax.

In the twenties, following the pattern of the garment industry, the contending parties resorted to settling disputes by strongarm methods. Desperate, some turned to secular authority for help. But laws passed in New York State in 1917 and 1922, which established working conditions and criminalized misrepresentation of meat not slaughtered according to religious law, proved of little avail. Instead, the chaotic conditions hastened the entrée of Jewish criminals hired to impose order on the industry. Competition among Orthodox factions became so keen that in 1926 officials in New York's Department of Health, which had the authority to grant licenses to operate slaughterhouses, succumbed to bribery and extortion. Forty-nine employees were forced to resign. Three years later officers of the "Official Orthodox Poultry Slaughterers of America," which acted as the chamber of commerce of the industry, were indicted for violating the Sherman Anti-Trust Act.

The trial lasted seven weeks, and special bleachers were constructed in the courtroom for the 125 witnesses. The court proceedings drew the intense attention of the socialist-oriented Yiddish press, which was gratified by the public display of the "dirty linen" of the Orthodox community. On 22 November 1929, sixty-six of the eighty-five defendants were found guilty. But the trial did not halt the assaults, beatings, destruction of vehicles, and extortion that characterized the kosher poultry business. The rank and file was reluctant to purge the criminal elements, since under their auspices working hours declined from as many as twelve hours a day to as few as fifteen hours a week and weekly salaries rose to $65 in the wholesale trade and $45 for retail slaughtering.[40] Small wonder there was keen competition for such employment.

The inability of Orthodox Jews to bring order into the world of *kashrut* (kosher certification) was no less apparent in the burgeoning processed-food industry that developed during the twenties. Like the kosher poultry business, which was organized by voluntary trade associations, the processed-food business was supervised by the Union of Orthodox Jewish Congregations, which used a special symbol, Ⓤ, to indicate its approval.

But again there were ever more "religious" groups who denied the validity of the certification and insisted on imposing their own.

A modicum of order was finally achieved in the kosher poultry business by levying a tax of seven cents a pound to pay the "boys" who had worked their way in. The lucrative poultry business had fallen under the control of Arthur "Tootsie" Herbert, the shady business agent of local 167 of the International Brotherhood of Chauffers and Teamsters. His brother controlled local 440, to which many of the ritual slaughterers continued to belong even after it was expelled from the United Hebrew Trades.

The problem of kosher meat and poultry was not finally solved until government imposed its authority. We have already noted that the back of the kosher poultry trust was broken in 1929, after a seven-week trial. In 1930 the Kashruth Association enlisted the help of Mayor James "Jimmy" Walker and then his successor, Fiorello La Guardia, to bring order to the industry. But the process was painfully slow and the situation continued to embarrass the community. After a strike in 1934 by ritual slaughterers, it was apparent that secular authorities could do little to legally prevent dissident Orthodox groups from entering the lucrative kashrut business. "Tootsie" Herbert remained a power in the business until he too was indicted.

Arnold Rothstein, who was assassinated in 1928, was involved in every shady business imaginable, as an underworld business manager rather than a thug. As a type, he is comparable to Meyer Lansky, the business "brains" of the mob in the 1930s. But increasingly the Jewish criminal of the thirties was not a businessman who preferred to work outside the law but a thug addicted to violence, especially contract murder. The members of violent gangs like Murder, Inc., in Brooklyn or the Purple gang in Detroit represented an urban rather than an ethnic phenomenon. They flourished first in the outlying satellite ghettos of New York City, like Brownsville and Williamsburg, which in the late twenties retained a kind of lawless frontier atmosphere.[41] Such gangs had two outstanding characteristics—their proneness to violence and their ethnic ecumenism. "Bugsie" Siegel and Abe "Kid Twist" Reles seemed simply to enjoy inflicting pain and taking life. And the interaction between Italian, Irish, German, and Jewish criminals, though subject to sporadic violence, was often superior to that of their counterparts in "respectable" society.

Whether they were involved in gambling, narcotics, policy games, prostitution, or numerous legal businesses, the rackets were controlled by a few insiders who were in crime to make money. There was a division of labor among the gangs. To Murder, Inc.—a journalistic term originated by Harry Feener of the *New York Telegram*—was assigned the role of "extermination squad." The gang members killed on contract, and their victims were usually criminals who were earmarked for death because of some trespass of the criminal code. Contrary to popular belief, their violence was rarely random but was confined to their criminal brethren. In a peculiar way Murder, Inc., earned a grudging respect from certain Jews, who welcomed the notion of Jewish power represented by willingness to shed blood. What is certain is that by the thirties Jews no longer viewed Jewish criminals with anxiety or as reflecting badly on the Jewish community. They were not considered part of it.[42]

That view marked a change from the pre–World War I attitude, when crime and vice among Jews were considered a cause of shame and anger. There were endless arguments about causes. For the religious, crime was the price of resettling in a godless *medine* (society) that encouraged breaking the Jewish moral code. More worrisome in the twenties was the fear that Jewish conspicuousness in the criminal underworld would fuel anti-Semitism. For Henry Ford and the anti-Semitic publicists, the notion of a "Jewish crime wave" became standard fare, as did the cry from within the community that something must be done.

The task was now more difficult because Jewish community leaders no longer had the influence they had in 1908, the year the Kehillah was founded in New York. Paradoxically, Jewish crime became more organized just when the community had become less cohesive. We have noted how crime in the garment industry and kosher poultry industry fed on that disorganization. Moreover, the business-mindedness of Jewish criminals was not that different from the ambitions of ordinary businessmen, who also occasionally broke the law to turn a bigger profit. It was an extralegal way to achieve middle-class status. A generation or two later, no one would ask the descendants of criminals where their money had come from. The headlong drive for place, which we will observe in the economic climb of Jews during the twenties, may furnish historians the best clue to the persistence of Jewish criminality.[43]

In exploring the background of the Harvard case we noted that the craze for education lay behind Jews' reaction to quotas. The culture of the university proved especially seductive for Jewish students. Had men like Lowell and Butler been aware of how the college environment accelerated acculturation, they might have encouraged rather than limited Jewish enrollment. But the number of Jewish students affected by enrollment limitation at the college level was insignificant compared with the rising proportion enrolled in secondary schools. In New York City in 1918, 53 percent of high-school students were Jewish—a considerable increase from 1908, when Jews made up only one-third of a smaller high-school population.[44] A building program that started in 1924 produced 130 new schools, partly because of Jewish agitation. Many were in new Jewish neighborhoods in Brooklyn and the Bronx, including Thomas Jefferson High School in the Brownsville section of Brooklyn, which in 1922 was the largest school building of its kind, housing an overwhelmingly Jewish student population of over four thousand.[45] The large number of children in Jewish neighborhoods, who increasingly attended until graduation, brought congestion leading to morning and afternoon sessions. By 1923 on the Lower East Side most of the seven thousand Jewish graduates of elementary schools were enrolled in secondary schools, and though not all would graduate, the proportion who did outpaced that in other ethnic groups. In addition, thousands more continued to attend evening school. Second-generation Jews, like their parents, viewed formal education as a worthwhile investment. By the mid-1930s, graduation from high school was well on the way to becoming the norm among Jews.

That second-generation Jews should become the staunchest defenders of public education is not surprising. In 1922, using the slogan "Keep the home folks learning," Jewish organizations complained that not enough funds had been appropriated for citizenship education and that underpaid and poorly trained teachers were incompetent to teach English to foreigners. The least the city could do, they argued, was to raise the salaries of teachers of Americanism.[46] It did not escape the notice of survivalists that the public schools might also strengthen Jewish identity if Jewish content could be grafted onto the curriculum. In 1928 the Jewish school system reached only 23.2 percent of Jewish children of school age. The public school was therefore viewed as the primary avenue of acculturation and mobility, since it reached all Jewish children. The instrument at hand was the Hebrew language, which had been revived in modern form by the Zionist movement.

The rationale for such ethnic identity reinforcement could be found in Horace Kallen's notion of cultural pluralism, first developed in a noted article in the *Nation* (1915) and then more fully in his book *Culture and*

Democracy (1924). The idea that democratic societies should encourage and sustain diversity was not new. Kallen had learned it from William James and from Harvard's noted literary authority Barrett Wendell. But neither figure would have supported, as Kallen did, a strategy to strengthen Jewish culture through the public school curriculum. They held immigrant culture in low esteem. Undoubtedly some agreed with Lothrop Stoddard's view that Kallen, as an archchampion of the hyphenates, was himself proof that assimilation could never work. But Barrett Wendell did recognize the special role the tenets of Judaism had played in shaping the founding principles of the republic. In their love of Hebrew and their use of the Zion metaphor, the Puritans especially used an Old Testament model. At the laying of the cornerstone of a Jewish community center in the capital, President Coolidge repeated the historian William Lecky's observation that "a Hebrew mortar cemented the foundation of American Democracy."[47] Hebraism was not alien to the prevailing Protestant culture.

It may have been that awareness that encouraged a small group of Zionist educators—Isaac Berkson, Alexander Dushkin, Mordecai Soltes, Mordecai Kaplan, Stephen Wise, and Samson Benderly—to extend the cultural pluralism idea one step further. Combining it with John Dewey's view that education was itself a social process, they argued that teaching the Bible as literature and Hebrew as a classical language not only was academically justifiable but would help socialize the children of Jewish immigrants while enriching American culture.

Educators like Isaac Berkson, a leader in the movement to bring Hebrew to the schools, sought to enhance the socialization aspect of education, reinforcing Jewish culture by infusing into the curriculum a secularized neutral element like Hebrew.[48] That was the thrust of his 1920 doctoral dissertation, "Theories of Americanization: A Critical Study with Special Reference to the Jewish Group." In 1929 the New York City Board of Education had rejected the teaching of Yiddish, the language actually spoken by the immigrant generation, on the grounds that it would reinforce immigrant ethnicity. That left an opening for the teaching of Hebrew, favored by the Zionist movement but vigorously opposed by the socialist-oriented Yiddishists. If Yiddish culture was declining, they argued, Hebrew had never gotten started in America, since none of the requisites for its use were in place. It was a purely aesthetic endeavor.[49]

The prospects for teaching Hebrew in the high schools were not promising. In 1921 the Menorah Society had petitioned the administration of CCNY to accept the New York Board of Regents' Hebrew qualification test toward admission to the school. The petition was rejected, and the test itself was discontinued in 1923 over the protest of the Hebraists. In 1929, spear-headed by Avukah, the intercollegiate Zionist organization, a group of prominent Jewish leaders drawn from the Jewish Congress and the Conservative movement again presented a proposal for teaching Hebrew in the high schools. Echoing the educational philosophy of John Dewey and the cultural pluralism approach of Horace Kallen, they argued that Hebrew was a living language and, in "progressive" terms, could serve as a vehicle for developing social awareness and an appreciation of foreign cultures. In a word, it could produce better citizens while at the same time helping Jewish children overcome psychological maladjustment. These arguments and others were included in the eloquent memorandum presented to the board by Israel Chipkin, president of the Jewish Educational Association. But the board would not be persuaded. It pointed out that the proposal was impractical, since colleges did not accept Hebrew, and that there were neither sufficient texts nor enough trained teachers nor any real demand.

Undaunted, the Hebraist group pushed ahead, helped by the fact that Italian had been introduced into the curriculum during World War I and was enrolling ten thousand students yearly. Moreover, the Hebraists pointed out that the board, which had rejected the teaching of Yiddish, ought to make some concession to its growing Jewish constituency. Hebrew, unlike Yiddish, was sectarian and cultural and would promote rather than hinder acculturation. The board reconsidered, and in 1930 Hebrew was introduced experimentally into two predominantly Jewish Brooklyn high schools, Abraham Lincoln and Thomas Jefferson.

The following year the experiment was proclaimed a success, and a two- and three-year language sequence was established. Even though Hebrew remained unacceptable for most college admissions requirements, the program grew. By 1938 there were two thousand students registered in sixty-five Hebrew classes in forty schools, and positions for fifty Hebrew teachers had developed. The program also took hold in Boston, Chicago, Saint Louis, and Schenectady. It was supported by, and it in turn buttressed, a small, dedicated Hebrew cultural nexus that included the weekly *Hadoar,* whose circulation reached fifteen thousand in 1940. The newspaper was published by an agency for the dissemination of Hebrew culture and language, Histadruth Ivrith. By 1936 there were a special Hebrew Week and a Hebrew Flower Day. The growing Zionist youth movement also furnished programs to popularize Hebrew.

But the hope of using the public school system for ethnic reinforcement was never realized. It became clear that public secular institutions could not fill the breach left by the failure of communal institutions. After World War II, enrollment in Hebrew classes began to decline. A practical rather than an ideological motivation actually fueled the early success of the program: one of its principal attractions for Jewish students, who had learned a smattering of Hebrew in the Jewish afternoon school system, was that they could receive credit for these studies in the secular high school. The primary significance of Hebrew in the high schools remained symbolic but, as Kaplan had foreseen, it helped legitimize a secular version of Jewish culture based on Hebrew.[50]

Rooted in a linkage of faith and familiar cultural patterns, the influence of the immigrant generation would persist for years, but gradually it was emptied of its content to become a source of nostalgia and humor rather than identity. The decline was most apparent among the young, especially college students, who replaced the particularistic values of Jewish immigrant culture with universalistic ones that often stemmed from the academic subculture they had joined. Younger Jews pursued careers with a fervor their ancestors had reserved for religion. Predictably, the high status of the rabbi declined, to be replaced by a new esteem assigned to professionals—especially doctors and lawyers. The synagogue, once a principal cultural conduit, now competed for attention with a host of secular organizations.

In the large cities the bonds of neighborhood continued to support familiar ethnic and religious modes.[51] The pull of at least nominal religious observance could be seen on religious holidays, when attendance at the neighborhood public school was down and Jews could be seen in their "Sunday best." The Jewish delicatessen, bakery, or kosher butcher, the periodic "drives" for charity, and the occasional Yiddish "benefit" theater performance identified the neighborhood as Jewish without making specific demands for adherence. But as the years passed there was little to distinguish Jewish neighborhoods on the Sabbath, when it was business as usual. If parents lived in neighborhoods, their children lived on the sidewalks of those neighborhoods, and a seasonal cycle of street games and sports formed a subculture of youth, tenuously linked to a Jewish presence only when the games were interrupted by the chore of attending the afternoon Talmud Torahs.[52]

Aside from proximity, what bound Jews together was not only the nationwide secular organizations that proliferated in the twenties, but the grass-roots mutual benefit societies, sometimes called anshes or chevras or, most frequently, landsmanshaften. Although their preoccupation with parochial interests conferred little weight at the national level, after 1920 they formed the most extensive organizational network in the Jewish community. In 1938, when the landsmanshaften were already past their peak, there still were over three thousand such societies, with a total membership of about 500,000.[53] Although they eased the painful acculturation process by furnishing opportunities for socialization, their primary purpose was to provide mutual aid through loans, insurance, employment and business opportunities, even cheap burial plots and summer vacations. Initially their binding thread was the venting of nostalgia for the Old World towns they stemmed from, but as hometown ties became tenuous their membership was randomly drawn from immigrants from different locales. At the outset their charitable activity consisted of sending financial relief to their old communities, many of which had been devastated during World War I. By the 1920s, some larger landsmanshaften threw themselves into the struggle against immigration restriction, but most remained purely local and fraternal in interest. Minutes were written in Yiddish, and only gradually did English become more prevalent. Their membership was composed primarily of immigrants and their children, but occasionally one could find a member of the third or fourth generation on their rosters who joined for the benefits rather than out of nostalgia for the old home. Many groups eventually affiliated with larger fraternal orders like B'rith Abraham and Workmen's Circle, which promised a fuller and cheaper choice of benefits.[54] The landsmanshaften were a part of the transitional immigrant culture that filled an important social welfare and fraternal function, but continuing acculturation and the welfare state eventually caused their demise.

For those descendants of eastern European Jews who had gone beyond the "alrightnik" stage to become affluent and Americanized, there was membership in the Jewish country clubs that proliferated during the twenties. By 1924 there were sixty-nine such clubs, originally organized by German Jews and devoted to golf and social activities. Eventually some also became centers for Jewish philanthropic pursuits and organization hubs of the federations, many of whose donors belonged to them. Periodically the *American Hebrew* exhorted the clubs to assume more responsibility for Jewish philanthropy, but basically they remained what they had always been—an alternative to the country clubs that did not welcome Jewish members.[55]

For the less acculturated and affluent, the adult summer camps, which also proliferated during the twenties, served as the equivalent of the summer homes owned by affluent Jews. Virtually every movement, whether its organizational impulse stemmed from the Yiddishists, Hebraists, Labor Zionists, Socialists, or the various communist factions, offered the use of its camp as part of its benefits. The camps were distinguished by their rich cultural fare—a marathon of lectures, symposia, music and poetry recitals, drama and dance performances, and of course an endless round of formal and informal discussions on politics. Such cultural and intellectual stimulation more than compensated for the lack of privacy and the primitive facilities. In their impulse for collective endeavor and their fondness for ideology, the camps were recognizably an eastern European habitat. Their life span was thus also limited.

Paradoxically, it was American popular culture that increasingly acted as the cultural cement for all segments of American Jewry. The crossword-puzzle craze of the twenties swept the more acculturated. Prominent Jews like Walter Lippmann and Eddie Cantor were known to be enthusiasts, and in 1924 a young Jew won the national crossword-puzzle tournament. Simon and Schuster, a Jewish-owned publishing house, published the first crossword-puzzle book, which became a best-seller. Other Jews participated in popular pastimes such as ballroom dancing and singing, and Jews increasingly wrote the popular Tin Pan Alley music, as well as jazz and blues. Jewish composers like George Gershwin and Irving Berlin became the toast of popular culture. Also noteworthy was the growing enthusiasm for sports that swept the younger generation. The exploits of Benny Leonard, a Jewish boxer, were celebrated. According to the press, which faithfully tracked such stars, he was "a decent Jewish boy, unspoiled by success, who accorded proper respect to his mother." In 1923 a European strongman who advertised himself as "the modern Bar Kochba" attracted long lines of Jewish youngsters to watch his performance. The popularity extended to Jewish baseball players like Mose Solomon and to the three Hungarian-Jewish medalists in marksmanship, fencing, and swimming at the 1924 Olympic Games in Paris. When the Hakoah all-Jewish Viennese soccer team played at the Polo Grounds in New York in 1927, wearing its blue-and-white uniforms, it took the Jewish community by storm, particularly the younger generation. When the motorcade of Chaim Weizmann and Albert Einstein passed through Jewish neighborhoods in November 1921, they were enthusiastically welcomed and many Jews uttered the prayer customarily saved for princes and sages: "Blessed art thou O Lord, king of the universe, who bestoweth of his wisdom and dignity upon those of flesh and blood."[56] Wisdom and learning rather than athletic prowess were valued by the immigrant generation. Happily, things were changing, observed one Jewish weekly: "The average American is slowly rectifying the false impression that Jewish college students are intellectual grinds."[57] It had long advocated sports as a powerful acculturation instrument. When Jewish baseball stars like Hank Greenberg made their debut in the thirties, no one would tout their athletic prowess more proudly than second- and third-generation American Jews.

CHAPTER THREE

THE CONTENTMENT OF CULTURE

A CULTURE of acculturation develops out of mediation between the values of the host society and of those trying to find a place in it. The immigrants and their children naturally created such a culture. But another kind of culture, that contrived by writers, poets, playwrights, journalists, and filmmakers, also reached its zenith in the 1920s. Elliot Cohen, editor of the *Menorah Journal,* spoke of it as composite and heterogeneous,[1] ranging from the "high" culture of the Yiddish Art Theatre to the "low" culture of borscht-belt resorts. That heterogeneity makes finding its core a challenging task for the contemporary observer.

Other immigrant groups developed distinct cultures, but few did so as extensively as the Jews. Jewish writers and artists seemed obsessed with the need to probe the condition of the larger society and their uneasy relationship with it. What was remarkable about American Jewry was that its culture was produced, and prodigiously consumed, by an impecunious audience, burdened with enormous problems and responsibilities. One imagines that Jews ought to have found more practical things to do than write and read books and attend theater performances in which their condition and that of the world were explained and generally fretted over. Where did that energy come from?

The comparative freeness of American society was certainly a condition for the energy's release. It furnished the openness for Jews who desired to make their mark as writers and artists. But that hardly explains the abundance of creative types that flourished in the Jewish community. An astute observer of the foibles of American Jewry thought that this exuberance reflected a "Leonardo Da Vinci complex" frequently found among Jews.[2] A less mocking explanation may suffice. Historical circumstance had made Jewish culture portable. Unlike other immigrant groups, Jews were able to bring their full culture to America, including writers, poets, and sundry culture producers. It possessed a separate language, Yiddish, that permitted them to think and encode separate thoughts. In a word, the requisites for the flowering of a distinct Jewish culture in America—the artists and writers, the language, and above all the mass audience eager to hear and see—were present.

Ironically, no sooner did an American Yiddish-speaking culture flower than the number of people speaking the language declined, and cultural energy followed suit. Dearly held regional loyalties that were once a source of acrimony became merely a matter for humor and were ultimately replaced by conflict based on class and ideology. But this brief historical flowering established the transition to a truly cosmopolitan Jewish culture. America served as its incubator.

From the outset this new culture was beset with special problems. Its creators were secular Jews who were often alienated from the organized Jewish community and from the religious wellsprings that shaped its social values. Everywhere that modernity touched the community, Jewish identity was weakened, and nowhere was that more apparent than among the writers and artists who were inevitably in the vanguard of secularization. The emerging culture tended to detach itself from the communal roots of Jewish life even while it exploited its customs. Jewish cultural institutions lacked financial security, leading to periodic desperate calls for more support. For one writer responding to such an appeal, the very notion of a culture produced from the "top down" and supported by an institutional network seemed unnatural. "The truth is that a healthy culture is least likely to be found among those who pant for it," he insisted. Certainly building a specifically Jewish culture could not be assigned to those who were themselves uncertain about its content. For Maurice Samuel, an ardent Zionist, the real problem was to isolate a core Jewish identity that could define such a secular culture.[3] That quest preoccupied some Jewish writers throughout the interwar period.

One thing was certain: the diminution of the religious element in Jewish culture could not be reversed. Some turned to the notion of Jewish "peoplehood," a vague amalgamation of ethnicity and universalism promoted by Labor Zionists and socialists. But that too posed problems of content and language. Urban cosmopolites who wrote the new plays and books were inevitably more concerned about the cosmos than about a particular tribe within it. These writers and artists spoke of the masses but jealously maintained their apartness.

A generation of immigrant writers would continue to use Yiddish and confine themselves mostly to Jewish concerns, and there was also a small group of writers who wrote in Hebrew as well as Yiddish. But these were eventually overshadowed by a new group, primarily the sons and daughters of immigrants, who wrote in English and sought their audience in the majority culture. They had become American writers who happened incidentally, and in some cases unhappily, to be Jewish. Some worried about whether there was enough energy to feed both cultures.[4]

The Yiddish theater, which continued to flourish for most of the twenties and was an important component of the Yiddish tier of that culture, poses a mystery for the historian. Except for the *Purimshpil* (Purim plays), little in traditional Jewish culture predicted a flowering of the theater arts.[5] Yet not only did American Jewry far outpace other ethnic communities in this area, it more than matched the legitimate American stage.

In part that efflorescence may be attributed to the continuous flow of plays and theater companies from the centers of Jewish culture in eastern Europe. Aware that a large Yiddish-speaking audience had developed in America, the Vilna Troupe, which had a long record of success in Poland, sought a new home here in 1924, and the Habimah Troupe arrived from Moscow two years later. Many actors also sought to make their mark individually. The Yiddish theater thus became a bridge between avant-garde Continental drama and American drama, bringing the latest plays and acting methods demanded by the more sophisticated Jewish theater audience. The major source of these innovations was the Moscow Art Theater.[6]

The cry to purge theater of *shunde* (trash) could already be heard at the turn of the century, when it was voiced by Jacob Gordin. Ironically, such elevation would probably have shortened the life of the Yiddish theater, which began as a popular art form and was after all a commercial venture that depended on its audience and communal institutions for support. Its fare in the first decades of the century catered to the lowest common denominator of the mass audience, and the cathartic release of emotion was its primary function. Within the improvised formula plays, associated first with playwrights like Morris Horowitz and Joseph Lateiner, almost any device, from chanting the prayer for the dead to a patriotic peroration, was employed to arouse the audience. The working-class audience was not seeking an experience in "high culture"—it was aroused by raw emotion and a virtuoso performance, much like the Elizabethans. It was an actor's rather than a writer's theater, and its analogue was Italian opera, not a play by Henrik Ibsen.[7]

But with the growing dominance of a more sophisticated second-generation audience, the Yiddish theater was compelled to upgrade its fare. It now required plays that could bring in an audience that was distancing itself from its working-class neighborhoods and roots. Jews had always been urban, but now they were becoming urbane. The traditional *shunde* improvisational techniques, which the actors used mercilessly to arouse the immigrant audience who still fondly recalled the traditional religious homes, now worked less well. The second-generation audience had little authentic religious experience to draw on, and a higher education level made it less manipulable.[8]

An elevation featuring ensembles and repertory theater and substituting good plays for formula plays was introduced through the Art Theater movement that began in Moscow in the 1880s. In 1918 it made its debut in New York with Ben Ami's production of *A Secluded Nook*. (*Farworfn Vinkl*). But it was Maurice Schwartz who combined the requisite vision, acting skill, and entrepreneurial energy to make repertory theater work in America. Not an aesthete or a purist, he "yoked together all the conflicting impulses of the Yiddish theatre and made of them an exuberant tension," observed Irving Howe.[9] In 1918 he organized the first ensemble company at the Irving Place Theater in New York. A year later Ben Ami, unable to work with the star-oriented, domineering Schwartz, organized the Jewish Art Theater, soon called Naye Theater. Its leading spirit, Peretz Hirschbein, had trained with the Moscow Art Theater and then founded the prototype of the noncommercial Yiddish Art Theatre in Odessa in 1908. Abandoning the old *shunde* productions, Hirschbein favored realistic plays and translations of the most noted European playwrights—Shaw, Ibsen, Schiller, Tolstoy, Andreyev, Strindberg, and others. New, talented young actors like Rudolf Schildkraut and Muni Weisenfreund (Paul Muni) made their debut. In the meantime the Schwartz troupe, spurred by his remarkable acting talent, had its most successful season in 1923, with the production of Leonid Adreyev's *Anathema*. The visit of the Moscow Art Theater in 1922 further stimulated the new movement. The Stanislavski method, a kind of exaggerated realism, became popular, and on the stage itself the mechanics of production and movement of scenery were now sufficiently developed to allow "spectacle and pageantry." Rather than a one-play run, the repertory system was adopted, and many troupes provided themselves with studios where they rehearsed plays and where apprentice actors could learn their craft.

Most important, the ensemble system replaced the star system, adding more breadth to the productions. Ensemble theaters proliferated. Most popular were the Folksbiene, the Vilna Troupe, the Bronx Art Theater, the Yiddish Ensemble Theater, and the New York Dramatic Troupe. Yiddish theater went from folk entertainment to a sophisticated art form that matched anything offered on the revitalized American stage. Plays like *Farworfn Vinkl, Green Fields, The Dybbuk,* and *Yoshe Kalb,* retained their Yiddish flavor and yet were modern, a combination that made them immensely popular with Jewish audiences during the twenties. To some it seemed Yiddish theater was entering its golden age.[10]

But beneath the surface, trouble was brewing. Even the best theater could not reverse demographic trends, and the Yiddish-speaking audience was decreasing yearly. By 1927 a malaise was evident among Yiddish theater aficionados, which deepened after the stock market crash of October 1929. The depression decade of the thirties radicalized many of the playwrights and a portion of the Jewish audience. Some of the drama became unabashedly ideological and didactic, a theater of preaching and advocacy. One could imagine that the socially conscious proletarian fare that swept Jewish culture during the depression was ideally suited for the working people it extolled, but these remnants of the Yiddish-speaking immigrant generation were not drawn to the "new" theater. The Art Theater movement had infused a new spirit, but it was based on an anomaly. Many Jews had achieved middle-class affluence well before they achieved full fluency in English, and they continued to prefer Yiddish. But the shrinking middle-class audience no longer generated the spirit that had permeated Yiddish theater before World War I.

For a time the decline of Yiddish theater was concealed by an infusion of money and talent from the government-sponsored Yiddish Division of the Federal Theater Project and the patronage of certain Jewish unions like the ILGWU, whose prize-winning *Pins and Needles* attracted audiences until World War II. Amateur groups like the Folksbiene were able to survive through a subsidy from Workmen's Circle, and Artef (workers' theater groups) received a subsidy from the Communist daily *Freiheit.* Creative energy, and in some cases acting talent, continued to come from a far-flung amateur theater network in the Jewish communities of Poland and America. It also emanated from organizations of the extreme left wing of the

Jewish political spectrum, who saw in theater yet another agitprop instrument to reach audiences they desired to "educate." At the same time a much diminished commercial theater, featuring such stars as Menashe Skulnik and Molly Picon, continued to attract the surviving remnants of the old Second Avenue audience. The subsidies of these political groups gave the Jewish theater a flush of health but could not in the long run substitute for commercial viability.

The surest symptom of loss of vitality was the growing number of Jewish theater people who transferred their talents to the American stage. The resulting Jewish presence in American theater was conspicuous enough to generate a concern about an "ethnic invasion" among some critics. The proponents of neither Yiddish nor American theater were happy with the situation. The former because they were witnessing a hemorrhaging of the resources of their enterprise, the latter because, in the words of *New York Times* critic John Corbin, the transfer of talent was bringing a presence "animated by the spirit of a separate minority" and "collective grievance" about America that produced a "drama of acid intelligence" rather than good dramaturgy.[11]

Stella and Luther Adler's Group Theater, many of whose actors and directors came out of the Yiddish Art Theatre, was a major instrument of this radicalized Jewish infusion. During the thirties the Group Theater favored plays of social significance, many written and produced by Jews and acted in English by Jewish actors. It would serve as the nesting ground for Lee Strasberg's Method School of acting, a variation of the Stanislavski approach. That theater would reflect the spirit of the times and become more socially conscious could have been predicted. But that Jews should be so conspicuously represented in that change was for some a disturbing development. Much of the ferment originated with the Jewish Left, which had been energized by the collapse of the economic system it foresaw— indeed, hoped for. Featured were not only plays that addressed social problems but also realistic acting by amateurs who were often ordinary workers. That strategy employed by Artef, an ensemble group founded by the Communist party in 1928, lent new authenticity to the stage performance. Under the direction of Benno Schneider, it became the avant-garde of the Yiddish theater, especially when it eschewed political ideology and focused on dramaturgy. The practice of recruiting raw talent from the shops was also followed by Arbeiter Theater Farband (1925), one of fifty-three ethnic workers' theaters in America organized by the Left.[12]

From the Jewish historical perspective the influence of these theater groups outweighs the contributions of individual Jewish playwrights like Samuel N. Behrman, Moss Hart, Lillian Hellman, and the most popular, Clifford Odets. For these playwrights and writers, Jewishness had become only an incidental part of their identity—it was not a part of their art. They were Jewishly connected in the sense that they sometimes wrote about the problems of people whose reaching for middle-class status had been interrupted by the depression or had led to catastrophe. Sometimes there was a Jewish sensibility in the humor they brought to bear or in the distinctive speech rhythms they employed. Yet they were no longer merely children of immigrants but were highly secularized and acculturated types.

Despite the occasional organization of new companies like the Yiddish Ensemble Theater (1931), the New York Dramatic Troupe (1934), and the Yiddish Dramatic Players (1938), by 1940 the decline of the Yiddish theater was apparent. From its high of 538,000 theatergoers in 1916 and twenty Yiddish theaters in New York City alone, by 1940 the potential Yiddish theater audience had declined to 246,000.[13] More important, the supportive culture on which Yiddish theater depended had lost much of its drawing power. For the theater, that meant fewer "benefit" performances and loss of promotion by the Yiddish press, which, we shall note, had also experienced a steep decline in readership. The flight of its best talent was accompanied by a loss of organizational energy. Like other Americans, second- and third-generation Jews were drawn to the new media—film and radio. Residual hunger for Yiddish was partly satisfied by the establishment of WEVD in 1926, a radio station sponsored by the *Forward* and named after Eugene V. Debs. For a time Yiddish films were widely popular, but they too lost their audience to Hollywood. The theater of social protest may have echoed a deeply held sentiment among many American Jews, but it did not nurture a specifically Jewish culture. It addressed American problems in the English language. Only Maurice Schwartz, who skillfully mixed his dramaturgy with the business aspects of commercial theater, was able to maintain the Yiddish Art Theatre until 1950. Most others had lost their audience by the advent of World War II.

At the peak of its influence, Jewish theater contributed much to creating an American Jewish cultural presence. But its language, Yiddish, confined it to a specific time and place. By the twenties its continued influence depended on how well it reshaped itself from the folk theater it once was to a sophisticated art theater that addressed its audience in Yiddish. In that, it was never fully successful. Second-generation Jews spoke English as a matter of course and preferred to satisfy their cultural appetites in that language.

Normally journalism would not fit into our working concept of culture, but an exception must be made for the Yiddish press. Jewish immigrant culture could not have been sustained without it, and it was itself a cultural instrument, approached in influence only by the Yiddish theater. When its readership declined in the twenties, it was a sign that the entire cultural apparatus was losing vitality.[14] Like the American penny press, the Yiddish newspapers did not confine themselves to news. Their columns were devoted to advice on health and interpersonal relations, reviews of the latest Yiddish plays, serial installments of the works of Jewish writers, and always a superabundance of political commentary. They served as the equivalent of a university extension course, especially in the area of culture and citizenship education.

The Yiddish press reached its zenith between 1914 and 1916, when hunger for news from the eastern war zone led to the printing of extras, sold by vendors in Jewish neighborhoods. The press's success was also based on a highly literate readership that had developed a keen interest in politics. An informal survey in 1924 showed that its most intense readers were ordinary workers. In 1922 there were still over twenty Yiddish newspapers with a total readership of over 400,000, far outpacing other ethnic groups, which published about 1,500 newspapers in thirty-three languages.[15] But even the intense loyalty of such readers could not halt the decline in circulation.

It was primarily an organ press; the newspapers and magazines either were directly sponsored by a political, religious, or cultural organization or had otherwise come to be identified with a specific constituency. By 1920 the socialist-oriented *Jewish Daily Forward,* edited by Abraham Cahan, with a circulation of 147,000, was the most influential and profitable of the Yiddish dailies. It published twelve editions in major Jewish communities and showed a profit of $1.5 million, some of which went to support socialist organizational efforts.[16] Following the *Forward* in importance was the *Day/ Warheit,* which addressed a more centrist, nonsocialist readership and also favored a purer Yiddish than that of the *Forward.* Its daily circulation in 1922 was 64,000. The *Tageblatt,* which was still further right on the political spectrum, printed about 60,000 copies daily, and the *Jewish Morning Journal,* which represented a traditionalist conservative position, had a daily circulation of about 77,000. There were in addition several smaller transitional newspapers, which appeared and disappeared with amazing frequency.

The major dailies also served as an outlet for Yiddish writers. "Die Yunge," a group of poets, were featured in the *Day,* while writers like David Pinski, Jonah Rosenfeld, Isaac L. Peretz, Abraham Reisen, Sholem Asch, Israel J. Singer, and later his brother Isaac found their readers in the press. But the result was a factionalization of literary fare based on the political proclivities of the publishers and editors. There was irony in the reinforcing role the press played in Yiddish culture, since it also promoted the Americanization that eventually brought the demise of Yiddish culture. Many of its features were aimed at interpreting America for its readers and teaching citizenship and American values. By 1927 Jewish readers had begun to buy English-language newspapers and looked to the Yiddish press only for Jewish news. When circulation continued to decline, the major dailies began to publish English supplements in a desperate effort to win back readers. But as with the Yiddish theater, a change of fare could not alter demography.

As the Yiddish press lost influence, the vacuum was partly filled by the developing Anglo-American press, mostly in the form of weeklies and monthlies published by the growing number of national Jewish organizations or as private or communal publishing ventures. Between 1920 and 1940, 132 such journals appeared, serving about 250,000 readers in 61 communities. There were 44 newspapers and magazines published in English, and an additional 58 journals were either organizational or trade organs. Ten of these journals had been established in the previous decade, but three, the *American Israelite,* the *Jewish Times* (San Francisco), and the *American Hebrew,* were survivors from the earlier German-Jewish migration. Akin to small-town booster papers, they focused on news of the Jewish community or their sponsoring organizations.[17] It was a far tamer press, but that was not unwelcome to Cyrus Adler, who had little love for the provocative reporting of the Yiddish press and had been arguing for years that it was necessary to transform its ideologically "hot," advocative character. Now he counseled Jacob Landau, founder of the Jewish Telegraph Agency, to place his news service on a sound business footing so that he might better withstand political pressure and focus on news of the Jewish community in America and abroad.[18] Yet such a focus, using a daily news bulletin, hardly allowed for the transmission of cultural fare. It became, in the words of one observer, a "bleak expanse"—hardly a fit successor to the vibrant Yiddish press. But though the Anglo-Jewish press did not play a cultural role, its growth did portend a transition to a new kind of community in which secular organizations programmed cultural activities.

As in the case of the Yiddish theater, a growing number of young Jews embarking on careers in journalism chose the national press to develop their talent. Before 1920 some major newspapers such as the *Washington Post* and the *New York Times* were owned by Jews, and there was also Jewish representation among reporters, editors, columnists, and feature writers. That representation had a precedent, during the German-Jewish period, in the careers of Mordecai Noah, the renowned editor of the *National Advocate;* Joseph Pulitzer, who as publisher of the New York *World* introduced many of the techniques of modern journalism; Adolph S. Ochs, who became principal owner of the *New York Times* in 1896; and the several other Jews who had made names for themselves in journalism.[19] But there were no Jewish names to be found among the owners of the powerful newspaper chains that had developed during the twenties, and Jewish journalists wrote for the American reader. Nevertheless, the prominence of Jews in journalism and the media generally became a source of apprehension, since it was possible to imagine a Jewish conspiracy to shape public perception by controlling the flow of information. That notion became a mainstay of the anti-Semitic imagination in the early twenties.[20]

The success of Jewish journalists depended on their ability to find what would arouse the interest—prurient and otherwise—of the American newspaper-reading public. Like any other product, news was subject to the rules of the market. Journalists like Simeon Strinsky of the *New York Times;* S. J. Kaufman, who wrote the popular feature "Round the Park" for the *Evening Telegram;* Heywood Broun, whose "Conning Tower" appeared in the *World;* and the cartoonist Rube Goldberg were popular because they pleased the appetite of the public. Jewish journalists would probably have lost their readers had they attempted to advocate a sectarian point of view. Moreover, Jewish publishers and journalists were aware of their delicate position, and some, like Arthur Hays Sulzberger, took great pains to avoid even the appearance of being tainted by Jewishness. The *New York Times* underplayed all news of Jewish interest, including the Russian pogroms of the twenties.[21] The most influential of the Jewish journalists, Walter Lippmann, harbored an intense distaste for his nouveaux riches Jewish brethren, and he had almost nothing to say about the slaughter during the

Holocaust.[22] What is puzzling is not the sensitivity of Jewish newspaper publishers and journalists to their exposed position, but that so many displayed an unerring instinct for the popular mind-set.

We have noted that the Yiddish press served as a major outlet for Jewish writers and poets. Its decline naturally had a negative effect on them, for many of the autodidacts who created that culture were part-timers, dependent on the press for their livelihood. Like the Yiddish theater, and for much the same reasons, Yiddish literature entered a new phase in the twenties. The poetry and literature of social protest, which the "sweatshop poets" and writers of an earlier period were so taken with, fell into disuse after World War I. Their strident advocacy and limited sense of style and form were considered naive by the more formally educated succeeding generation of poets.

More conscious of language and more formal in style, the new generation of writers and poets divided into two schools: those who took their cues from the poetry emerging in eastern Europe, and those who were influenced by the West. "Die Yunge," as the first group were pejoratively dubbed, took their cultural cues from Russian and German poetry, drawn to the aesthetics of poetry and the purity of the language. They aspired to be something more than "the rhyme department of the Jewish labor movement."[23] Two of the group's best-known poets, Halper Leivick, who had experienced exile in Siberia, and Moshe Leib Halpern, favored a strong lyrical quality and rejected the advocacy of the earlier poets. Like their predecessors, they were unable to earn a livelihood by writing alone; both Leivick and Halpern were paperhangers and wrote for the *Day* and *Freiheit*. But for the most part Die Yunge kept themselves apart from the immigrant world, preferring to write for small journals like *Literatur, Shriftn,* and *Inzel.* They aspired to modernism even while rooted in the workaday immigrant world, and their reward was isolation and contempt from those who lived in that world. The movement toward a modern form of writing and poetry, begun by Die Yunge, was completed during the twenties by a successor group of writers and poets dubbed "In Sikh" (Introspectivists). In the sense that they received some of their signals from the ultramodern poets of the Anglo-American world—T. S. Eliot, Ezra Pound, and Robinson Jeffers—these writers were also reacting against the formalist tendency of Die Yunge. Their stress was on creating poetic imagery, but it was rendered in an intuitive, lyrical manner and made imaginative but more informal use of the Yiddish language. Since they were further along in their acculturation, their work was less ethereal and more inclined to break rules. More acculturated and boasting some formal education, "In Sikh" writers like Jacob Glatstein were more receptive to the American experience and its literature.[24]

Writers, poets, and sundry culture carriers require an ambiance in which to socialize and exchange ideas. For the Yiddish artists this environment was furnished by the cafés and cafeterias of the Lower East Side of New York City. The best known was the Café Royal, on the corner of Second Avenue and Twelfth Street opposite the Yiddish Art Theatre. By the twenties there were other meeting places in mid-Manhattan and Brooklyn that attracted their own clienteles. There the "artists" and hangers-on nursed their glasses of tea as they discussed, argued, socialized, and shaped a world governed by their rules. Despite the small number and social marginality of the artists and writers, the cafeterias furnished the setting for conflicts among the groupings of that world. To maintain a modicum of tranquillity, they would be seated in different sections of the café. Actors from the Yiddish stage and writers who held journalists in contempt were seated separately in order to avoid altercations. Only poets were permitted to cross the geographic line between the two camps, and that was because they were held in even lower esteem. They were called *zaydene yungermanchikes* (silken youth) or simply "whores." At the same time the literati who depended on various Yiddish dailies for publication also received the contempt reserved for their benefactors. Those who wrote for the *Forward* were called "concubines," doubtless to mock the control sometimes exercised by Abe Cahan. There were more earthy pejoratives for those who wrote for the communist *Freiheit*. As in the immigrant theater and like the style of the New York Intellectuals of the thirties, there was little civility in discourse when it came to serious things like culture and politics.

Those who wrote in Hebrew formed a small, self-contained group that eventually became influential enough to challenge Yiddishist hegemony, at least concerning the school curriculum. The conflict between the two groups during the twenties was a minor echo of the language war then occurring in Palestine. The assumption that Yiddish would be the preferred language for the transmission of culture was natural. It was, after all, the language most people spoke. Yet in terms of fervor for their cause—revival of the Hebrew language—the Hebraists would prove formidable contenders. The producers and consumers of Hebrew literature came primarily from a small Hebrew-speaking group of teachers, bibliophiles, and Zionists. Among them were the educators who gathered around the noted educator Samson Benderly. Others were religious Jews who had become "enlightened" and no longer thought of Hebrew as a holy tongue to be spoken only in prayer. Like the Yiddishists, the Hebraists faced the challenge posed by a second and third generation that overwhelmingly preferred to speak and write in English and no longer experienced even the limited contact with Hebrew that stemmed from religious training. At the turn of the century approximately twenty Hebrew journals, most of them monthlies and quarterlies, appeared and disappeared with some frequency. But by 1920, when the major journal *Hatorem* was forced to cease publication, most were no longer in existence.

But the times seemed to favor the Hebraists. World War I led to the demise of the Ottoman Empire, and the Balfour Declaration, which promised a Jewish national home in Palestine, expanded the prospects of the Zionist enterprise and the revival of Hebrew it fervently advocated. The establishment of the Hebrew University in 1921 gave Hebraists a powerful instrument to propagate their culture in the Diaspora. In 1916 a central agency for the dissemination of Hebrew culture, Histadruth Ivrith, was established. By 1927 the circulation of its weekly *Hadoar* was almost 20,000. An additional source of hope came with the visit in 1925 of the poet laureate of Hebrew literature, Hayyim Nahman Bialik, which did much to hearten the Hebraists in spite of the poor response to their national conference to foster Hebrew culture.[25]

The Hebrew enterprise gained its strongest support from the burgeoning Conservative movement and from such rabbinic leaders as Mordecai Kaplan, whose Society for the Advancement of Judaism (1922) placed Hebrew at the center of its ideology and program. Despite its small constituency, a thriving alternative Hebrew culture developed, so that by the end of World War II American Jewry furnished an important outpost for Hebrew literature. One of its major redactors was Simon Halkin, who wrote in Hebrew about the American physical and social landscape.[26] That Hebrew ultimately prevailed over Yiddish is attributable to the Holocaust, which decimated the Yiddish-speaking population centers in eastern Europe. Then came the establishment of Israel, with Hebrew as its official language, and today it is Hebrew rather than Yiddish literature that flourishes. The cultural soul of American Jewry could not be won by either Hebraists or Yiddishists, and the demise of both was inevitable after the biological replenishment that the Yiddish-speaking immigrant culture depended on was all but cut off by the immigration laws of 1921 and 1924.

By 1927 more of the twenty-nine Yiddish dailies, weeklies, bimonthlies, and quarterlies had ceased publication, and the rest were in financial difficulties. The rejection by the Orthodox of Hebrew as a possible vernacular partly accounts for the decline in journals written in Hebrew. The circulation of the Yiddish press declined from 717,146 in 1916, its peak year, to 536,346 in 1927, a fall of 25.3 percent. The circulation of Yiddish books in the New York Public Library dropped by 71.8 percent during the same period. In 1923, 25 percent of the 286 recognized Jewish writers were over age fifty-five. By the census of 1930 only 1,750,000 listed Yiddish as their mother tongue, and ten years later the figure was down by another 500,000. In 1940 *Hadoar,* the major Hebrew newspaper, had only 14,000 readers.[27] Another symptom of decline was the waning vitality of the Yiddish schools and teachers' institutes. Small and often more ideological than cultural, these institutions nevertheless provided crucial support for the Yiddish-speaking enterprise. Like the Yiddish theater, that nexus was adversely affected by the overall decline in the number of Yiddish speakers. "Between the Scylla of Zionism, which looked to Hebrew as the recognized tongue, and the Charybdis of fervent nationalism which seeks to assimilate the Jew . . . Yiddish has no chance," observed the *American Hebrew.*[28]

Despite the clear portents, the atrophy of the transitional immigrant culture and the languages that transmitted it shocked its members. In the European world they came from, Polish and Russian had not, after all, posed a serious challenge to the thriving of a separate Jewish culture. What was wrong in America? They could not understand that here a centripetal force gathered Jews in. Though America's pluralism promised space for ethnic cultures to develop, its seductive solvent ultimately threatened to melt down all ethnic cultures.

The English-speaking Jewish culture that gradually replaced the Yiddish-speaking one between the wars was multifaceted and amorphous. Its practitioners were formally educated and, like its consumers, increasingly middle class. It was a culture that was moving, like the second generation itself, from "downtown" to "uptown." Because its members were highly individualistic rather than folk oriented, they sustained varying intensities of interaction with Judaism. Some novelists wrote lovingly of the Jewish scene, others produced kitsch for the popular audience with little trace of their Jewish origins. One self-consciously Jewish group of writers, eager for a more positive definition of Jewry in America, gathered around the *Menorah Journal.* But more often the cultural sensibility of such writers was cosmopolitan universalist rather than particularist. Such a cosmopolitan culture had already developed in the great urban centers of Europe, where it produced a culture in which Jews were heavily represented. This cultural milieu also produced the operational elite—the technocrats, scientists, doctors, lawyers, and managers required to administer modern societies. These cosmopolitan elites operated within the national culture but also remained apart from it. The president of the American Philosophical Society, Professor Hartley B. Alexander, wrote perceptively of the apartness of the Jewish cosmopolite: "He lives in Rome, and is not as the Romans, he is in Asia, in Europe, in Africa and is not Asian, nor European, nor African, but is everywhere a kindred apart, related to all men but confused with none."[29] If Jewish cosmopolites looked to the cosmos rather than the tribe for enlightenment, that did not mean they rejected the Jewishness they had once adhered to: viewed through the new cosmopolitan prism, Jewish values and thought compared well with those of other cultures. They did not reject Jewish culture so much as they removed themselves from it and viewed it objectively. They might admire its precepts, but they did not live by them.

Three distinct groups made up this emerging cultural community. The first were the direct inheritors of the Yiddish intellectual mantle and resembled the eastern European intelligentsia: they were the most Jewish of the cosmopolites. Writers like Chaim Zhitlovsky, who advocated cultural nationalism, the noted writer and lecturer Nahman Syrkin, who was a major spokesman for labor Zionism, the literary critic Shmuel Niger, and perhaps the most cosmopolitan of all, the essayist and editor of the *Yiddisher Kemfer,* Hayim Greenberg. All had been uprooted by emigration and wrote for a culture that was slowly fading. Although the New York Intellectuals of the 1930s bear a strong resemblance to them in fervor and interest, this small cadre of Yiddish intellectuals was really the last of a type. Most boasted a European university education for which they were unable to find a specific use or institutional anchor in America. Like the New York Intellectuals of the thirties, they remained independent and marginal, earning their living by lecturing and occasionally writing for small Yiddish journals. They were scholar-intellectuals rather than academics. The absence of a university or other institutional connection is noteworthy. American Jews were the only ethnic group to support such an independent intelligentsia. Its impact on Jewish, and ultimately American, political culture was profound. They differed from other Jewish cosmopolites in their strong interest in Jewish national resurgence, which most expected to come through some synthesis with socialism.

Although different in approach and more varied in membership, the

English-speaking successor group that comes closest to the Yiddish-speaking secularists were the essayists who wrote for the *Menorah Journal*. Founded by Henry Hurwitz in 1915, the *Journal* was an offshoot of the Menorah Society founded at Harvard in 1906. By 1920 the society boasted eighty chapters on American campuses. Self-consciously Jewish in content, its leading light after it became a bimonthly in 1926 was Elliot E. Cohen, its managing editor. Although unable to sustain his own writing, he soon gained a reputation as an imaginative editor and attracted a coterie of gifted writers to the *Journal*. With the exception of Felix Morrow, who stemmed from an observant family, writers like Lionel Trilling, Herbert Solow, Clifton Fadiman, Henry Rosenthal, Tess Slesinger, Louis Berg, Albert Halper, and Sidney Hook were raised in secular homes and possessed little knowledge of Jewish culture, but they could be engaged by topics of contemporary Jewish interest such as the virulent anti-Semitism in America and the condition of Jews in Europe.

By the 1930s the *Menorah Journal* was attracting the best of the new Jewish writers, including Waldo Frank, Lewis Mumford, and Ludwig Lewisohn, and such scholar-intellectuals as Harry Wolfson (Harvard), Adolph Oko (Hebrew Union College), Horace Kallen (Oxford), and Irwin Edman (Columbia). Under Elliot Cohen's editorship the *Journal* gained influence among educated American-born, second-generation Jews. Predictably, its tone and style were far from those of the Yiddishist intellectuals headed by Zhitlovsky. Unlike their predecessors, members of this group were familiar with American literary conventions and were inclined to support a vaguely humanistic social order rather than formal socialism. They present us with the first glimpse of what the American-Jewish amalgamation would be like—less ideological, and motivated by a cerebral interest in things Jewish rather than an emotional one. That some of these writers supported the Arab cause in the 1929 riots indicates that defense of the Jewish interest could no longer be assumed.[30] As the depression deepened, many in the *Menorah Journal* circle were drawn into the maelstrom of radical politics, but their strong inclination to "oppositional thinking" made them poor disciples of any political or cultural line,[31] and they disdained political as much as religious orthodoxy. After the Moscow purge trials began, these writers were among the first to note that the Soviet experiment, which had seemed so hopeful to many Jewish intellectuals, was a failure. In that sense they might be considered precursors of the modern grouping known as neoconservatives.

Related to both the Yiddish secularists and the writers who gathered around the *Menorah Journal,* and sometimes overlapping them, was the group that coalesced during the thirties, later dubbed the "New York Intellectuals." In their socialist proclivities and their fondness for polemic they resembled the former; in their use of English and their avoidance of a direct link to the Jewish interest, the latter. The New York Intellectuals stemmed mostly from lower-middle-class or working-class immigrant families. Lacking urbanity, their dialogue had a rough give-and-take quality not far removed from the street debates so popular in Jewish neighborhoods. Yet they also had a serious interest in political economy that defines the boundaries of the group. They differed from the writers in the Algonquin Circle—George S. Kaufman, Moss Hart, and Dorothy Parker—who displayed a similar need to be brilliant but whose interests ran to theater rather than political theorizing. At the same time, though the New York Intellectuals considered themselves students of Marxism—unlike writers like Joseph Freeman, Michael Gold, Bertram Wolfe, and Will Herberg—they never came under the discipline of the Communist party.

More than anything else, these intellectuals were fashioned by the depression. They had attended college, where their radicalization often began, only to discover upon graduation that there was no niche for them. "The Depression," according to one observer, "added a new barrier beyond that of discrimination to the educational difficulties and obstacles of Jewish students." Yet the powerful ambition and drive so characteristic of such students could not simply be set aside. The depression had forced them to become *luftmenschn,* and now they made that unemployed condition the basis of a new profession—"intellectual." Assisted by a dose of barely digested Marxism, they simply transmuted the problem of their own future into a critique of society.[32] The nation had never seen anything like it. In search of a rationale for their argument, they jumped easily from one discipline to another. To the dismay of more orderly minds, there seemed to be no ground rules for the discipline they practiced. Any cudgel was used to beat down the opponent in intellectual discourse. It was winning the argument, rather than the search for truth, that was of primary importance. They were not preoccupied with the academics' need to publish or to document their arguments. Morris Cohen, whose classes some attended at City College and who served as a model, was not a prolific writer. His reputation rested on his probing questioning and his acerbic teaching style. Like him, they brought ineluctable—one is tempted to say Talmudic—argumentation to their intellectual discourse.

Writers like Philip Rahv, William Phillips, Lionel and Diana Trilling, Meyer Shapiro, Clement Greenberg, Elliot Cohen, Paul Goodman, Harold Rosenberg, Sidney Hook, and Lionel Abel were part of a cohort that had fallen between two chairs, neither belonging to the Jewish culture of their parents nor feeling fully part of American culture. Perhaps that deracination encouraged their seeking roots in the socialist community: they needed to invent themselves from scratch. But if they were on the way to losing their last traces of Jewish identity, there was something familiarly Jewish about their penchant for polemic and their assumption that the intellectual avocation was worthwhile in its own right. Such passionately engaged types were not uncommon in the Jewish community. Their values were secular and universalist, and the only thing they had in common was their utter rejection of the Soviet experiment under Stalin, usually after an initial flirtation with it. One can detect no common philosophy in the *Partisan Review,* which served as their publication outlet. They produced no identifiable stream of thought like the Frankfurt school's amalgamation of Marxism and Freudianism.[33] Some undoubtedly used their socialism to rationalize the sharp break with religion generally and their immigrant Jewish families specifically. Serving as a substitute for family and community, the social network of New York radical politics offered an entrée to wealthy homes and a continuous round of parties that permitted contacts with publishers and easy sexual liaisons.[34]

Even so, the intellectuals found themselves ideologically stranded by the perceived failure of the socialist experiment in the Soviet Union, on the one hand, and the strident anti-Semitism of the Right on the other. They understood instinctively that they stemmed from the very alien, rootless world that formed the core grievance of writers like T. S. Eliot and Ezra Pound, yet they were discerning enough to realize that these were the great poets of the age. Small wonder they became "an intellectual order from the lower ranks . . . created by those who were rejected by other classes." Less exalted was the observation by art critic Harold Rosenberg, who saw his fellow intellectuals gathered around *Partisan Review* as "a herd of independent minds."[35]

The New York Intellectuals were of a certain time and place. World War II dispersed them from their beloved New York. The second generation—Irving Howe, Irving Kristol, Daniel Bell, Delmore Schwartz, Leslie Fiedler, Seymour Martin Lipset, Nathan Glazer, Alfred Kazin, and others—discovered a more open post-Holocaust world, willing to absorb a formerly disaffected sect of free-lance intellectuals. And the intellectuals proved more than willing to make a career of what they had inadvertently become. Once absorbed by the accepting world of the university and publishing, their brilliant commentary, now mellowed by war and prosperity and their own approaching middle years, lost some of its edge. A critical examination of public policy replaced their penchant for advocating social engineering. One wing, having seen the alternative, became eloquent defenders of Western culture against the Marxist critique.

In their wake the New York Intellectuals left an awareness of the crucial role independent thinkers could play in American cultural life and a free society. From the Jewish perspective, America saw a self-conscious intellectual cadre, mostly Jewish, assume the role of "identifiable players on the stage of American intellectual life." They had gotten there through a circuitous route, but they eventually gained acceptance and an opportunity to leave their mark.[36]

More remote from the Jewish ken were the novelists and sundry writers who wrote for a general American audience. We need say little about those such as George S. Kaufman, Lillian Hellman, and Simeon Strinsky who, like George Gershwin and Irving Berlin in music, betrayed little in their work that was identifiably Jewish. Most were eminently successful and fully accepted as interlocutors of American culture and politics because they spoke in a language the general public understood. Why American Jewry produced a disproportionate number of such interlocutors, especially in the film and entertainment industries, remains a mystery. Although a direct bridge is difficult to find, the skill may have been honed in the world of Yiddish theater and entertainment. To be commercially successful, after all, *shunde* plays required an understanding of what fare the "popular mind" found most suitable. But surely that is not the entire explanation.

Those who retained some measure of Jewishness in their art can tell us much more. Best known among these are three women writers—Anzia Yezierska, Fannie Hurst, and Edna Ferber. The last became enormously popular and deserves special attention because she was the first to break away from the caricatured presentation of Jewish life and write simply as an American. In 1924 when she was awarded the Pulitzer Prize for her novel *So Big,* the citation read that her work "best reflects the wholesome atmosphere of American life and the highest standards of American manners and manhood."[37] For Ferber, born into a Wisconsin Jewish family and a keen observer, a loving rendition of life in middle America was not difficult to conceive. Clearly she was able to speak to America not solely out of a fictive imagination, but from firsthand knowledge of her neighbors. Only with her autobiography *A Peculiar Treasure* (1939), were her readers presented with a portrait of second-generation Jewish life in middle America. A similar pattern is discernible in Myron Brinig's novel *Singermann*. Brinig stemmed from a Romanian Jewish family that had settled in Montana. In the same vein, Sidney Miller wrote of the acculturation of his Russian Jewish family in California (*Roots in the Sky*). For Jewish readers in urban areas, the adjustment of a Jewish family in Chicago pictured by Meyer Levin (*The Old Bunch*), may have been more familiar. Easily the most insightful novel of the ordeal of acculturation, one that peeled aside the idealization of ghetto life on the Lower East Side and realistically detailed the price exacted by the transplantation process, was Henry Roth's *Call It Sleep* (1934). It is this novel by a Jewish author that has best endured the test of time: some place it among the five greatest American novels written in the twentieth century.

There would be much hand-wringing when the Jewish writers of the thirties produced a scathing portrait of American Jewish life. The *American Hebrew* echoed the apprehension of many Jews about the effect of the candid depiction on non-Jewish readers: "On the whole we are proud of the Jewish men and women who are making a place for themselves in contemporary American literature"; but the great novel about Jewish life in America, stated the editorial, had yet to be written.[38]

That portrait emerged partly as a result of the Depression, which radicalized many Jewish writers. With the exception of Meyer Levin and Nathaniel West, a host of Jewish writers of the thirties—Benjamin Appel, Nathan Asch, Edward Dahlberg, Daniel Fuchs, Samuel Ornitz, and Isidor Schneider—fell under the spell of the socialist realism school. If earlier writers like Anzia Yezierska and Mary Antin composed paeans to America and sentimentalized ghetto life, writers like Albert Halper and Michael Gold (*Jews without Money*), found little in the American Jewish experience to be thankful for. "America is so rich and fat," observed Gold, "because it has eaten the tragedy of millions of immigrants." Ignorant of Jewish culture, they were harshly judgmental about the entrepreneurial impulse of their parents, which they viewed as exploitative and lacking class consciousness. That impulse was depicted in Jerome Weidman's *I Can Get It for You Wholesale* and *What's in It for Me?* Sometimes it became flagellation, as in Ben Hecht's *A Jew in Love* and Budd Schulberg's widely read *What Makes Sammy Run?* Paradoxically, Jews were being condemned for what they had become at the juncture when the Depression was sweeping away many of the small businesses through which they hoped to enter the middle class. The candid exposure by Jewish writers of the naked ambition and crass materialism they imagined to be at the center of Jewish life has been attributed to self-hatred, a common "mark of oppression." But it is just as likely that the public washing of dirty linen, which so distressed the insecure Jewry of the thirties, was part of the new literary mode introduced by Sinclair Lewis, who was equally frank about general American life in his popular novels *Main Street* and *Babbitt*.[39]

For committed Jews the literary odyssey of Ludwig Lewisohn was more satisfactory. He began as a critic of American society but became a defender of the New Deal. His anticommunism and Jewish self-consciousness, which included a staunch advocacy of Zionism, went against the leftist Jewish literary trend. Lewisohn, who was dismissed from a college teaching position for his pro-German sympathy during World War I, went on to become the drama critic of the *Nation* until 1924, when he settled abroad for ten years. It was that experience and his alarm about the rise of Nazism in Germany, sounded in a seminal article in the *Nation* in May 1933, that led him to advocate a return to the religious tradition and some form of Hebraic culture represented by Zionism. In *Upstream* and *The Island Within* he had already linked the virulent anti-Semitism of the thirties with the futility of the strategy of assimilation. There would be no acceptance of the Jews even if they turned themselves inside out. He was particularly distressed at the way some highly assimilated German Jews responded to the ordeal they faced. "So long as there is discrimination," he cautioned American Jews, "there is exile."[40]

It was in drama rather than literature that Jews achieved the greatest distinction. Of the twenty-one Pulitzer Prizes awarded between 1917 and 1938, four were won by Jewish playwrights. The theatergoing public came to know the names of Elmer Rice, George S. Kaufman, Sidney Kingsley, Clifford Odets, Irwin Shaw, Lillian Hellman, and Samuel N. Behrman. Some became better known for their wit than their profundity, and in most cases their Jewish identity played little part in what they wrote. If Jewish writers sought to explain politics and life, Jewish playwrights seemed content to find the popular vein and exploit it. They were often critized for their banality, especially in the depiction of Gentile-Jewish relations in the popular *Abie's Irish Rose* by Anne Nichols. The negative portrait of the ethical conduct of Jewish businessmen by the popular Jewish comedy team of Potash and Pearlmutter, who in skits like *Partners Again* were forever outwitting their rivals in the cloak and suit business by fair means or foul, suggests that acculturation itself entailed swallowing unfavorable caricatures.[41] Nevertheless, the prominent Jewish presence on the stage gave the second generation a sense of belonging. At the same time, complaints regarding trivialization and caricature of Jews were rooted in their growing insecurity. We have seen that in the twenties and thirties there was much evidence that the nation did not welcome Jews. Like many arrivistes, they were preoccupied with decorum. One should not reveal family secrets, especially if the host was less than friendly. Jews had a vision of middle-class respectability that they sought to preserve at all costs.

American readers and theatergoers, eager to be entertained, probably cared little about the ethnic or religious origins of their favorite writers. The test was whether the songs were singable, the novels readable, and the plays edifying. Using that measure, Jewish artists did disproportionately well. The sheer wit and comical vision of Rube Goldberg, Montague Glass, Bruno Lessing, Fannie Hurst, and Edna Ferber made audiences laugh and let them see themselves as they never had before. Even from an aesthetic viewpoint there was something to be said for the passion and engagement Jews brought to the cultural arena, which sharpened the use of language, as one observer put it, beyond the "frugal 800 words of the peasant's vocabulary." Their contribution enriched American culture just when it was ready to accept it. More important, the Jewish contribution provided a useful corrective to that "lethal smugness" that frequently blights the culture of insular, self-contained nations like England or Sweden.[42]

There is some risk in identifying a specific Jewish thrust in American literary life. The seven small but prestigious publishing houses founded by German Jews, which included Knopf, Simon and Schuster, and Viking, served the American book-buying public and did not favor Jewish authors. Publishing Judaica and promoting Jewish scholarship fell to the Jewish Publication Society of America (JPS), founded in 1888. But JPS showed little interest in publishing Jewish novelists, many of whom did not write on Jewish themes and were themselves only incidentally Jewish. If there was something distinctive about Jewish-owned publishing houses, it was the frequency with which they introduced innovative marketing techniques like the Little Leather Library, the Modern Library, the Book-of-the-Month Club, the Literary Guild, and the Book Find Club. These techniques helped Jewish writers indirectly by vastly expanding the market for their books.

What may have encouraged Jewish writers—or writers who happened to be Jewish—most of all is the development of a specialized Jewish reading public that maintained some nostalgic interest in things Jewish. After 1920 American Jews became the largest identifiable segment of the book buyers' market, a fact commercial publishers would have to take into account.[43]

As radio and film developed during the twenties, a continuous flow of new material was needed to retain audience interest. Like their non-Jewish counterparts, aspiring Jewish writers and theater people viewed writing and producing screen and radio plays as a promising new field. As an increasing number of Jews found their way to these careers, the conviction grew in anti-Semitic circles that they were dominated by Jews, especially the radio industry, which developed rapidly after the federal government lifted the ban on privately owned radio sets in 1919. By 1922 mass production of radio sets began, and by 1929, 40 percent of American families owned radios. The first nationwide network, the National Broadcasting Company, was organized by the Radio Corporation of America in 1924, and the Columbia Broadcasting System followed in 1927. In both cases Jewish entrepreneurs played the leading role. But as the source of capital to build these networks and in the ownership of local stations, of which there were 562 by 1924, there were few Jews to be found.[44]

The story of the film industry is somewhat different. After the development of the "talkies" in 1927, films had become so popular that they alone among the entertainment businesses staved off the negative impact of the depression of the thirties. "Going to the movies" had become the most popular form of American mass entertainment.[45] But its rapid development compelled the movie "moguls" to turn to Wall Street for capital. By 1936 ownership had become diversified, and only three of the "big eight" studios were still owned by Jews. Jewish representation in film distribution had also declined.[46]

If the building of the "dream factory" were merely another example of the penchant of Jewish entrepreneurs to develop a new, nonpreempted area of the economy, our story would end here. But the film industry also exemplifies the marketing of a new type of product and the developing of a new industrial organization to go with it. It was Adolph Zukor who transformed the industry into a modern, integrated business enterprise. He combined stars and good stories with production facilities and distribution capacity, building movie palaces in the downtown areas of the nation's cities, and by controlling these three elements he enhanced the potential for films to earn back at least their production costs. Nevertheless, it took some doing to convince conservative investors that there was money to be made in the projection of celluloid images. When that finally occurred, the film industry developed into the peculiar amalgam we witness today—at once an art form and a lucrative private business.

Unlike the theater, film was a mass-consumption industry with a unique propensity to influence public perception and behavior. It was the fear of having such a powerful instrument wielded by "foreign" entrepreneurs of an alien faith that aroused the custodians of morality. That fear grew even though Jewish moviemakers concentrated on pure entertainment and paid little attention to the medium's supposed power to shape the mind-set of the viewing public. The founders of the three major networks (William Paley, David Sarnoff, and Leonard Goldenson), and the men who founded the major film studios were only marginally identified as Jews. When the noted producer Harry Cohn was solicited for refugee relief during the virulently anti-Semitic forties, he replied: "Relief for the Jews? What we need is relief from the Jews."[47] For the Jewish moguls, entertainment was a business like any other. It had no special message but to anticipate the public mood and capitalize on it. "We have got to adjust our entertainment to this mood," observed Leonard Goldenson, who reorganized Paramount Pictures after 1933.[48]

A downturn in business in 1921 triggered an attack on the "morality" of Hollywood. During March 1921, Rev. Harry Bowlby of the Lord's Day Alliance blamed the Jewish-controlled film industry for encroaching on the sacredness of Sunday worship.[49] The "unchristian" values projected by the films and the immoral behavior of its stars became fodder for local scandal sheets, especially in the Bible Belt. Concerned about the growing number of Jews involved in the legitimate theater, one critic complained that Jews had "secured to a remarkable extent, control of the physical theatre," where their "rudeness of manners, lack of courtesy . . . and general vulgarity" were offensive and posed a threat to American values.[50] It was the first in a series of thinly disguised attacks on "Jewish" Hollywood, which became foreboding in the thirties. Jewish spokesmen tried to counteract the campaign. Jews were being pilloried as "commercial, sordid, devoid of morals and ethical responsibility," complained the *American Hebrew,* when the truth lay elsewhere. "We favor reform and progress, but we are utterly opposed to the sort of puritan hysteria that wallows in slander and vilification."[51] In 1922 the industry consented to an office of voluntary censorship, headed by Will Harrison Hays, to monitor the moral content of films based on a code all the studios would adhere to. But even the censorship of the Hays office did not eliminate the fears of the custodians of morality.

Though the moguls were little interested in the mind-shaping potential of their business, the creative types who proliferated in the Jewish community welcomed a new outlet for their talents. When Samuel Goldwyn asked Anzia Yezierska to join his staff she accepted with alacrity, not only because she believed that filmmaking was "destined to be the greatest of the arts," but also because it was "the newest language of democracy." Similarly Clara Beranger, who became a highly successful screen writer and adapter of the pathbreaking *Dr. Jekyll and Mr. Hyde,* saw the future of "creative" Jews not only in the business end of the industry but in the artistic side.[52] The significance of the Jewish influence in radio and film was as much in the outlet it provided for Jewish talent in writing, directing, and acting as in the pioneering of a new industry. Many young Jewish writers followed a well-trodden path to Hollywood.

Jews were also avid consumers of the products of the "dream factory" and naturally were influenced by the way they were depicted in films. Strangely enough, despite Jewish prominence in the industry, the screen image of Jews projected before 1920 was based largely on the negative caricature prevalent in popular cartoons. They were shown as alien con men, scheming merchants, swindlers, especially in fire insurance fraud, and only occasionally as innocent victims or heroes.

A new generation of Jewish film producers, Harry Cohn, Louis B. Mayer, the Warner brothers, Irving Thalberg, Budd Schulberg, the Schenck brothers, and Marcus Loew, finally produced a positive image of Jews during the twenties by skillfully exploiting the immigrant acculturation saga. For the first time the American filmgoer was given a glimpse of life in the congested urban ghetto that seemed so little part of America, with the projection of a "Jews are like everyone else" image. Two aspects of the acculturation experience were usually at the heart of the story plots: one was the "making it" theme and the price it entailed—a thinly disguised immigrant version of the American success story. The second was the "melting pot" theme, which dealt with ethnic interaction, especially between Jews and Irish-Americans. In three dozen films, of which *Humoresque* (1920) was the successful prototype, the movie audience was given a positive view of American Jewish life. The new sentimental image of the Jews, which stressed warm family ties, aspiring, talented young men—usually startlingly handsome—doting mothers, and kind, long-suffering fathers was hardly more accurate than the negative one that had preceded it, but it was far more acceptable to the Jewish filmgoing audience. *The Jazz Singer* (1927) sums up the saga of the upwardly mobile Jewish son who breaks away from religion and family. But instead of feeling bitter at the "loss" of their son, his parents recognize its inevitability. The father's last line as he watches the career success of his son, trained to be a cantor, is: "He's not my son any longer—now he belongs to the world."[53] It was an acceptable solution for Jews, and it assured Gentiles that Jews would, after all, assimilate. More gratifying for Jewish audiences, too, was the final scene, in which Jacob Rabinowitz chooses to chant the prayers in his father's synagogue on the Lower East Side. It meant that the call of blood will always bring assimilating Jews back to the fold. *The Jazz Singer,* which starred Al Jolson, earned $3,000,000 and established sound film as commercially viable while demonstrating that the immigrant saga could play in the heartland. That ability to show a profit was scarcely perceptible in prior ghetto films such as *The Good Provider* (1922), *Hungry Hearts* (1922), *Salome of the Tenement* (1925), *Little Miss Smiles* (1922), *Cheated Love* (1921), *The Barricade* (1921), and *Solomon in Society* (1921).

But projecting a more acceptable image of Jews seemed to be possible only by dejudaizing them. The films usually portrayed them as Americans with a slight ethnic wrinkle. Increasingly non-Jews were cast as Jews, and ethnic conflict, formerly projected by stock characters like the Irish policeman and the grasping, cringing Jewish merchant, also underwent changes. Cultural conflict would be resolved by intermarriage, which was in fact well under way among the Jewish producers, directors, and writers, whose second wives invariably were not Jewish. The daughter of the Irish policeman, beautiful and full of spirit, would, after much hand-wringing, marry the kindly, talented son of the Jewish merchant. In the prototype of this theme, *Abie's Irish Rose* (1928), which had been produced as a stage play four years earlier, the children have none of the undesirable ethnic traits of their parents. They are able to fall in love because they have their Americanness in common. For Jewish filmgoers Hollywood's message was unmistakable: success could be found by giving up the separating Jewish culture in favor of the bounty America offered. Included in that bounty was acceptability as a mate, which proved irresistible in the postwar era.[54]

During the interwar years, strong pressure to break down the immigrant Jewish culture emanated not only from the host society but also from within the Jewish community. The earliest signs of a weakening were seen in the gradual abandonment of the Yiddish language and the culture it produced. The more Americanized Jews, associated with the Reform movement and the American Jewish Committee, viewed Yiddish as inhibiting Americanization. Such Jews tended to view their Jewishness in denominational rather than cultural terms. For some the complete demise of Yiddish and the "foreign" culture it generated could not come soon enough. "The traits which distinguish Jews from non-Jews will disappear," wrote the editor of the *American Hebrew,* and "the Jews will differ from the non-Jews only in religion."[55] Not all "uptowners," however, were indifferent to the beauties of the mother tongue. Men like Louis Marshall and his brother-in-law Judah Magnes grew to appreciate the Yiddish language, if not those who wielded it with such vituperation against the "court Jews." They believed that the passionate Jewishness of Yiddish culture and even the nationalistic spirit engendered by Zionism would become important assets in the struggle for Jewish survival in America. When Louis Marshall received a worried letter about the need to curb the influence of the Yiddishists, he pointed out to his correspondent that Yiddish seemed to be dying a natural death, which would prove a loss for the Jewish community. Yiddish homes, he observed, were producing masterly writers in English.[56]

Marshall's observation was accurate. A survey in 1940 showed that, with the exception of a few stock phrases, knowledge of Yiddish had almost totally disappeared among native-born Jews. Second- and third-generation Jews were convinced that Jewishness was a "matter of the heart" and not of being shaped by a particular culture or religion.[57] With the decline of Yiddish as a working language, the elaborate cultural institutions that had served the immigrant generation so well would also be transformed. Unlike the Jews of eastern Europe, American Jewry would not sustain a separate secular culture with its own language that could break the fall of those abandoning Judaism.

Yet despite the decline of Yiddish and Hebrew, a Jewish cultural presence persisted in the twenties and thirties. Jews continued to feel Jewish and to identify themselves as such. How would such inchoate sentiment find cultural expression? American Jewry would produce writers, thinkers, filmmakers, and sundry culturists who found an outlet for their creative energies through the institutions of American culture. They wrote, produced, and acted in films and plays for the general American audience using the American idiom. There may have persisted telltale signs of a Jewish sensibility—a certain humor, an outsider's penchant for questioning established conventions—but primarily they were becoming Americans who happened to be Jewish. Sometimes it seemed the only thing that kept them in the Jewish fold was others' insistence that they belonged there. Exclusion from a country club or law firm could bring them up short. But few could muster the certainty of their parents and grandparents about the content of Jewish culture. Except for the organizations and congregations that proliferated in the twenties, there was no central cultural core or agency to define what being Jewish meant. The cultural pluralism Horace Kallen advocated had created space for a particular Jewish culture, but Jews no longer were certain what should be planted in that space. Instead, American Jewry was becoming a voluntary association. At its core was the religious congregation, but a growing percentage of Jews were choosing not to be affiliated with it. Examining the growing separation of the religious dimension from the remainder of Jewish life is our next concern.

CHAPTER FOUR

CRISIS OF FAITH

A SECULAR Jew believes one can be Jewish without being Judaic. We have noted how the separation of Jewishness from Judaism posed problems of self-definition for the custodians of modern Jewish secular culture. In this chapter we learn that Judaism—the religious component, without ethnicity—was equally vulnerable when confronting the powerful drive toward secularization. Its three branches, Reform, Conservative, and Orthodox, tried, each in its own way, to rejoin Jewishness and Judaism, but to little avail. Faith had become a separate component of American Jewish identity, and for a growing number it played little role in their lives.

In the libertarian atmosphere of America, Judaism—buttressed by myriad laws (*Halakah*) that dictated the behavior of the observant virtually every moment of the waking day—was difficult to maintain. Rabbis had no power to order Jews to sustain their Judaism, and the number who chose to break all ties or to maintain only tenuous ones grew yearly during the twenties and thirties. Second-generation Jews coming of age during the twenties, immersed in their private lives, remained oblivious to the crisis of faith the rabbis often spoke about. The organization of new congregations and the building of new synagogues to house them concealed the waning of piety and learning, the traditional sources of vitality. Even committed Jews could not agree on the state of the faith. The debate between the transformationists, who insisted that Judaism could accommodate to the American environment, and those who saw tampering with religious tenets as evidence of assimilation and decline continues to this day.

The development of what might be called the Jewish church was especially apparent during the twenties. By 1929 there were over three thousand registered Jewish religious congregations in America. (The figure would be considerably higher if we included the less formal minyans and chevras usually found in the Orthodox branch.) The growth was most apparent in the Reform and Conservative branches, where the number of congregations more than quintupled between 1912 and 1922. Aided by the growth of the Jewish Center movement, which by 1929 claimed 100,000 members, the Conservative branch had begun to move ahead of the Reform in the number of families affiliated, if not in the actual number of congregations and the size of their budgets. The Conservative movement was particularly success-ful in organizing congregations in new areas of settlement.[1] There was also a synagogue building boom, based partly on the need to house new congre-gations. In 1927 alone sixty-seven synagogues were completed and an addi-tional thirty-four were under construction. The stock-market crash brought the building boom to a precipitous halt, but not before saddling con-gregations with serious budgetary problems. Those seeking to join congre-gations during the Depression were undoubtedly discouraged by the high cost caused by their indebtedness. In New York City the per capita mort-gage debt was $13.10, and in smaller communities it was almost $15.00.[2]

Yet during the twenties the Jewish religious establishment appeared to be vital. The Jewish Theological Seminary (JTS, Conservative), Hebrew Union College (HUC, Reform), and the Rabbi Isaac Elchanan Yeshiva (Orthodox) had been established to meet the demand for an indigenous rabbinate. By 1924, 231 candidates for ordination were enrolled, the major-ity, 107, at HUC.[3] Through the efforts of Rabbi Stephen Wise, who had earned his own ordination by studying privately with the noted Viennese Rabbi Adolf Jellinek, the Jewish Institute of Religion (JIR) was established in New York in 1922. The Orthodox branch furnished additional institu-tions and individual rabbis with authority to grant ordination. The Hebrew Theological College was established in Skokie, Illinois, in 1922, and rab-binic training could also be obtained from such institutions as Yeshiva Torah Vodaath, Rabbi Chaim Berlin, Tifereth Jerusalem, and Ner Israel in New York City. By the twenties the perennial problem of producing an indigenous English-speaking rabbinate was finally on the road to solution.

But there was little agreement among the three branches on what constituted a rabbi or how best to train for the pulpit. An effort to unite JTS and the Rabbi Isaac Elchanan Theological Seminary (RIETS) in 1927 failed partly because no agreement could be reached on the role of Jewish law and on the activities of Mordecai Kaplan, whose proposed changes in ritual and theology were anathema to Orthodox Jews. The Reform branch sought to attract second-generation candidates, who tended to view the rabbinate as a profession. Orthodox rabbinic training paid little heed to the "modern" pastoral function that so concerned the Reform and Conservative rabbinic institutes. For Orthodox candidates to the rabbinate, study of sacred texts remained an act of devotion. The emphasis was on *lernen,* which consisted primarily of Talmudic study. The notion of the rabbi as a professional was unacceptable, and though the overflow of rabbis stemming from the Orthodox yeshivas often filled vacancies in Conservative and Reform congregations, many preferred to become religious functionaries such as kosher food and slaughter inspectors. Somewhere between the Reform and Orthodox stood the Conservatives, who tried to emulate the tradition of scholarship and religious devotion of the Orthodox but also to employ the modern *Wissenschaft* approach to the study of religious texts. At the same time some attention was given to training for pastoral duties such as family counseling and administration of a religious congregation. Graduates from these institutions were all designated rabbis, but there was a world of difference in their background and training.

The Reform rabbi could hope to earn a respectable livelihood from his pulpit position. In 1925 the rabbi of Temple Emanu-El in New York City, the congregational flagship for the Reform branch, earned $20,000 annually, and there were a half-dozen Reform rabbis who earned $15,000 a year. But in smaller congregations the yearly salary was only $1,800 to $2,000, making such pulpits far less desirable. That problem led Cyrus Adler, Chancellor of JTS, to propose a central fund to supplement the income of small-town rabbis.[4] Linked to differing views on the permissibility of ritual and theological changes required to accommodate to the American environment, wide differences also developed between the three branches regarding the communal role of the rabbi. At the heart of the conflict were conflicting views about the function and orderly development of rabbinic law called Halakah. In the modern period Judaism had no priesthood, but learned rabbis were authorized to interpret Jewish law. As long as a self-contained Jewish community existed, the law had broad sanction, but in a free society the rabbi's authority to intrude into the lives of the faithful was based on voluntary compliance.

Deep in the throes of secularization, American Jews sought a new role for the rabbi. For the second generation, eager above all to gain acceptance, the image the rabbi presented to the non-Jewish world outweighed in importance his knowledge of religious texts. The model of respectability was the priest or minister. Some had in any case come to believe that conceptually Judaism and Christianity were cut from the same cloth. By the twenties the Conservative synagogue and the Reform temple had gradually taken on recreational, social, and educational functions that often overshadowed the religious one. The rabbi was expected to be an efficient administrator, to officiate at life-cycle activities, to represent the Jewish community to the Gentile world, and to maintain the religious standards that the laity no longer was inclined to meet. The rabbinate was becoming a profession, one of many a Jewish son could train for. Rabbis might bemoan their loss of authority and status, but in the established temples of the Reform branch and in a growing number of Conservative synagogues there was adequate monetary compensation. Each branch's rabbinic association functioned like a professional society. Increasingly, too, rabbis were sought to lead and add legitimacy to the growing number of secular organizations.5 The synagogue would remain the basic building block of Jewish communal life, found wherever there were aggregations of Jews, but it was developing into an adjunct of the Americanization process. The growth of the Jewish church thus seemed inversely related to the decline of traditional faithfulness. The *American Hebrew* viewed the increase in synagogue building as "striking testimony to the vitality of Judaism in America," but it frequently suggested, tongue in cheek, that the most practical architecture for such synagogues would be an "accordian shape," enabling them to accommodate both the small number of worshipers who attended services weekly and the crowds who packed the synagogues during the High Holy Days. For many, services had in fact become a once-a-year affair.6

The decline of attendance at religious services was merely the most visible part of the general decline in religious observance. Between 1914 and 1924, consumption of kosher meat, usually the last thing to be abandoned by secularizing Jews, had declined by 30 percent. The picture for religious education, also central for the faithful, was even gloomier. Such education was poor in quality and usually stopped after confirmation for the boys, and for girls religious education was neglected altogether. Religious observance became increasingly symbolic. Thus confirmation ceremonies (bar mitzvahs), which had never loomed large in religious observance, became the occasion for expensive celebrations. Hanukkah and Passover, which fell near Christmas and Easter, assumed greater importance. Few would have gone as far as James Wise, son of Rabbi Stephen Wise, who on withdrawing from JIR stated categorically that "Judaism as a religion has ceased to play a vital part in Jewish life." For most second-generation Jews, however, primordial religious practices like the memorialization of the dead through prayer retained a strong hold. Even the most secularized Jew attended services for a few hours on holy days to chant the *yiskor* (memorialization) prayer for the dead, and burial in a Jewish cemetery continued to be the rule. But Jewish law no longer determined the basic contours of life. "We have to see to it that our children grow up as Jews and this has nothing to do with religious ceremonies," a respondent informed a survey researcher. "One must be a Jew in his heart."[7]

Discomfort with formal religion was particularly prevalent among Jewish college students, for whom the liberal secular environment was most seductive. As early as 1923 the convention of the Conservative United Synagogue established a fund to bring rabbis to the campuses for weekly religious services. A year later, aware that Jewish fraternities did not fill the religious vacuum, B'nai B'rith, the largest and oldest fraternal order, founded Hillel, which supplanted a poorly financed university welfare program sponsored by the Union of American Hebrew Congregations (UAHC). But its efforts to Judaize the student population met with some resistance on the campuses of several midwestern universities. Jewish students rejected a discussion of the normal Hillel fare, which focused on their role in the Jewish community. It was too boring.[8]

The decline in observance did not escape the notice of Christian missionaries, who wanted to believe that the long-awaited conversion of the Jews was at hand. The Presbyterians' Department of Jewish Evangelization saw "a menace and an opportunity" in the Jewish condition. A menace because the failure of Judaism would inevitably lead to an increase in criminality, an opportunity because these unevangelized Jews would welcome a crusading church whose founder was a Jew. In the same vein, the World Conference of Protestant Christianity, meeting in Budapest in 1927, counseled greater tolerance toward Jews because race prejudice is "a great stumbling block to the acceptance of the Christian message." But the book issued by the conference, *The Christian Approach to the Jew,* culminated with a plea to meet the "urgent and growing need" for evangelism among the Jews. Strangely, with the perceptible weakening of observance among Jews, their fear of missionary activity and Christian hegemony grew. That accounts for the outcry in the Jewish press when in 1922 the War Department proposed placing marble crosses on the graves of all American war dead, regardless of religion.[9]

Yet on religious matters Jews could no longer speak with coherence: each branch was convinced it was the wave of the future. But behind that confidence they were aware that when the congregations of the greater New York area attracted only 20 percent of Jews, something was amiss. "We have withstood oppression and persecution but our prosperity has been our undoing," complained one journalist. None of the branches seemed able to cope with the erosion. Mordecai Kaplan, the most perceptive observer of the crisis of faith, became convinced that "the salvation of Judaism cannot come either from Orthodoxy or from Reform." But he was virtually alone in calling the situation a crisis.[10]

Others preferred to view it as a transformation. A Jewish student at the University of Wisconsin felt that only Jewish religious particularity was giving way—that Jewish students still believed in God "as a superior controlling force." Others described a privatization of religious belief. "A religion that insists on our making a show of our religious feelings . . . is not and cannot be sincere and heartfelt," answered one respondent to a "state of the faith" survey. Some insisted that "real" religion is a "matter of the spirit" and therefore can never be lost. Still others expressed doubt that a "priest class holds the keys of heaven." David Sarnoff, founder of the National Broadcasting Company, was certain that what was occurring was merely "a change in religious conceptions" that would ultimately prove to be a gain rather than a loss to religion. Felix M. Warburg, a leading Jewish philanthropist, thought Judaism remained essentially vital even if there was some waning of observance. That notion was probably closest to the ideas of most Jews. Forms and dogma were no longer crucial, and undoubtedly some shared the view of Edna Ferber, the much admired writer, that the transformation would produce something "less personal and much lovelier."[11]

Predictably, rabbis were less sanguine about the decline in religiousness. The weekly press listing of sermon themes repeatedly bemoaned the impact of newly adopted values. Topics included intermarriage, the decline of observance, the headlong race to accumulate wealth, the loss of spirituality, and especially the indifference of Jewish youth to the tenets of their ancient faith.[12] There was something in the air of a free society that eroded tradition, just as secular rationalism and science undermined the ability to believe. "We are not satisfied to rest content with the tales which history and science have proven untrue," a writer complained. The "modern Jew" wants a religion "less of preaching, . . . more of happiness, less of sorrow."[13]

Behind the malaise lay a profound change in perception that affected all religions. Church attendance was also declining. The *Harvard Alumni Bulletin* published statistics, collected by Professor Julian L. Coolidge, that showed a "marked religious slump." After its stridency at the beginning of the decade, Christian fundamentalism, spurred by the Scopes "monkey trial," had begun to lose moral authority. The foreign missions in which so much had been invested showed little return. Jews and Catholics were actually doing better than the Protestant denominations. But the category on Coolidge's survey that showed a startling 50 percent increase was the one labeled "not interested." "A religious depression," according to one historian, "preceded the economic depression in the United States."[14]

There was little agreement among Jewish thinkers regarding the source of the malaise. Cautioning against underestimating the seriousness of the crisis, Mordecai Kaplan saw the "appalling poverty of spirit" linked to the uncritical absorption of the faith-eroding practices of modernity. Even more pessimistic was Horace Kallen, who blamed much on the American rabbi, whom he saw as a surrogate retained to talk about faith and to observe religious laws that few Jews still cared enough to follow. In such a situation "[Judaism] can survive, but it cannot live," he concluded.[15] In January 1927 the convention of the Intercollegiate Menorah Association condemned the new professional rabbinate for its general lack of Jewish learning. But in turn the *American Hebrew* condemned the Menorah group for being "spiritually and religiously at sea" and failing to realize that what American Jewry now needed was that "the Rabbi be human, yes human, rather than merely academic."[16]

In the interwar period the communal and religious tensions within American Jewry were exacerbated by the extreme individualism inherent in American culture. Jews performed most religious duties, including prayer, in groups. The covenant was made with the Jews as a people, as well as with each individual Jew. Religion could not be neatly tucked away for practice on the Sabbath, nor could Jewish ethnicity and religiousness be separated as had happened in Protestantism. Holidays like Hanukkah and Purim were national more than religious festivals. The advocacy of Jewish peoplehood employed by the Conservatives, the Reconstructionists, and the American Jewish Congress movement was successful precisely because it capitalized on the persistence of a sense of nationhood or tribe. It was that sense of belonging, rather than religion per se, that kept many secularizing Jews in the Jewish fold. They somehow continued to feel ethnically Jewish.[17] But without a separate language, there was little assurance that the drawing power of ethnic Jewishness could continue indefinitely.

To accommodate to American society, where the individual made the decisions formerly made by the community, required an alteration of Judaism's legalistic and corporate character. It was difficult for "modern" Jews of the second generation to define their Jewishness purely in terms of creed, as had the German Jews before them. Sometimes nationalism like that embodied in Zionist ideology or ethnicity like that inherent in various stripes of socialist *yiddishkayt* was substituted. Secularizing Jews could thereby still consider themselves Jews and avoid the self-abnegating effects of assimilation. Sometimes an amorphous universalism or "moralism" rooted in the Prophets was the preferred form of ideological accommodation. It was most prevalent in the Reform branch but was also favored by Conservatives and Reconstructionists. Responding to the question, "What makes a good Jew?" the men's club of New York's Temple Beth El opted for both nationalism and universalism. First the members chose the prophetic ideals of justice, mercy, and humility, second "a conscious continuity of the history and traditions of our people," and third, "service to and unity among the Jews of the world."[18] Observance of religious law, traditionally the anchor of Jewish religious identity, was not mentioned. Yet the respondents did not view such changes as a back door out of Judaism. These values were merely the modern way of being Jewish. By stressing such things as the Golden Rule and the human family rather than the need to keep the 613 rules associated with being observant, Judaism could fit neatly into the developing civil religion. The hallmark of that public faith was religiousness rather than a particular religion. How successful Jews were in making that transition became evident during the thirties and forties, when it was no longer uncommon to see rabbis delivering invocations on public occasions.[19]

For the acculturating American Jew, the increasing cost of synagogue membership may also have played a role in the growing reluctance to join a congregation. Membership dues in the new congregations could be nine times those in the old, and that did not include admission tickets for the holidays, the occasional sponsoring of the sacramental kiddush, charity drives, and other incidental expenses. The sale of tickets for the High Holy Days caused an annual outcry in the Jewish press as nonmembers complained that religion was being reduced to a commercial transaction and, infinitely worse, that there was discrimination against the poor. But for the hard-pressed synagogues there was no other way to meet rising expenses.

For the wealthier Reform congregations the funding problem was less dire. Many congregations associated with the UAHC had begun to set up pension annuities to enable their rabbis to retire at age sixty-eight. With the help of a $100,000 bequest made by Jacob Schiff, a group insurance fund for rabbis was established. In 1924 at its Chicago convention the UAHC planned to spend almost $500,000, to be contributed by member congregations, to bring the HUC out of the "mendicant class." The Conservative movement, on the other hand, had trouble raising funds to keep itself in operation. Its 1923 $1,000,000 endowment drive for the seminary failed to reach its goal partly because pledges were not redeemed, even though Louis Marshall, Jacob Schiff, and Felix Warburg, associated with the Reform movement, made sizable contributions.[20] When the Depression struck, some Conservative congregations had insufficient reserves to weather the storm.

Influenced strongly by the Protestant model of religious pluralism and by sharp economic as well as social divisions within the Jewish community, the differentiation of the Jewish "church" into three branches became irreversible by the end of the twenties. In 1927 the Conservative and Orthodox branches, not yet considered separate, failed to find common ground for unifying their rabbinical academies. There was competition for limited financial resources. The leaders of JTS counseled Julius Rosenwald not to contribute to building a library for the newly established Yeshiva College because it was "not modern" and would cut into its own library development. Five years after founding JIR, Rabbi Stephen Wise, stung by the difficulty and the recriminations involved in fund-raising, regretted he had embarked on the venture.[21] The tripartite division of the faith tended to dissipate resources and energies.

Insecurity in its faith also caused confusion in the laity, which was now free to choose as if shopping in a department store. A severely monotheistic Judaism seemed uncertain how to worship its one God. The divisions reflected class and social groupings, which in turn rested on the differing rates and terms of acculturation. The poorest, least acculturated Jews were usually Orthodox, while Jews who had achieved middle-class status were attracted to the Reform branch. The Conservatives fell somewhere in the middle. In a peculiar way, which branch would ultimately dominate would be related to economic developments. The Reform movement hoped that, as they gained middle-class status, the second- and third-generation children of the eastern European immigrants would find a comfortable niche in their

congregations, as had the German Jews before them. To some extent that
was happening, perhaps more in the proportion of second-generation sons
drawn to the Reform rabbinate than in terms of members of Reform
congregations. The converse, however, would not hold true. The loss of
prosperity during the Depression did not strengthen the ranks of Orthodoxy. Not until after World War II did a middle-class Orthodoxy develop,
able to compartmentalize the sacred and the secular. Unforeseen was that
an all-encompassing political ideology like Marxism or some form of socialism would prove especially attractive to children from Orthodox families. A leap from Orthodox Judaism to Orthodox communism was not
uncommon during the Depression years. Moreover, once the branches became associated with economic and social class, much of the antagonism
and hostility between the classes devolved upon the synagogue. If there
always seemed to be a synagogue that an American Jew "would not be
caught dead in," it had as much to do with class and culture as it did with
theology.[22]

On the surface its superior organization, relative affluence, and what its
spokesmen believed was a confluence with "the spirit of the age" gave the
Reform branch a good chance to attract the second generation. A survey
done by the UAHC in large cities showed a membership firmly in the
middle class: 20 percent belonged to city or country clubs; 57 percent were
independent entrepreneurs; 23 percent were professionals; and 20 percent
were high-salaried employees.[23] The movement's domestic growth was supplemented by new branches of liberal Judaism in England and France. A
fourth-day school for five hundred pupils was established by the UAHC in
the New York area in 1922. Its social action programs lent the Reform
branch an air of being morally engaged; it was in the process of revising its
Union Prayer Book. Reform seemed infinitely flexible. In the early years of
the century its wealthy supporters even mustered the confidence to contribute to the Conservative seminary in order to check the hemorrhaging of
Orthodox youth. Believing that Orthodox Jews were not yet ready to
worship in Reform congregations, they hoped they would be attracted by
the Conservatives, a movement they viewed as a "vestibule to Reform."[24]
The president of Hebrew Union College, Dr. Julian Morgenstern, foresaw
"gradual convergence" between the Reform and Orthodox branches. As
early as 1921 Julius Rosenwald expressed his readiness to make a large

contribution to consolidate HUC and JTS and abandoned the idea only on the advice of Jacob Schiff.[25]

By the thirties, however, the growth of the movement had come to a virtual halt as a result of historical and sociological forces only vaguely understood by its leaders. By 1940 the 61,609 families that belonged to the Union of American Hebrew Congregations had declined in number. At the congregational level services had become formal and lifeless, and activity was listless. The three traditional functions of the synagogue—as a house of prayer (bet tfiloh), a house of study (bet midrash), and a meeting house (bet knesset)—had been abandoned by Reform, so that there was neither a community of memory nor faith to buttress it.[26] A new lease on life would require a radical departure from the classical principles of Reform first set down in the movement's Pittsburgh platform.

Even the assumptions regarding the children of eastern European immigrants proved difficult to realize: they were not malleable human clay to be shaped by the movement. By the twenties 50 percent of Reform rabbis, many of eastern European background, tended toward Zionism, at least in the cultural sense. The growing Zionist presence in the movement suggests that the relation between Reform and its new adherents was in fact transactional. Their influence was also apparent in the movement to restore more Hebrew to the service and in such practices as Friday night candle-lighting service, the blowing of the shofar on holidays, and the restoration of such "nationalist" holidays as Purim and Hanukkah.[27] Rather than joining the Reform movement as some had envisaged, a greater proportion of the second generation sought membership in Jewish secular organizations like the American Jewish Congress, B'nai B'rith, and Hadassah, which better reflected their secular self-image. Many no longer affiliated at all.

The Zionization of the Reform movement is in some measure attributable to the second generation. A group of Reform rabbis led by Stephen Wise, Gustav Gottheil, and Judah Magnes and joined in the twenties by Philip Bernstein, Barnett Brickner, Bernard Heller, and Abba Hillel Silver, gradually succeeded in altering the antinationalist stance of classical Reform. As early as 1920 the convention of the Central Conference of American Rabbis (CCAR) passed resolutions condemning the imprisoning of Vladimir Jabotinsky and another on the death of Joseph Trumpeldor at Tel Hai. After some debate the same convention acknowledged the San Remo protocol, which implemented the Balfour Declaration. In 1923 a resolution supporting the Jewish settlement in Palestine was approved. Some leaders of the Reform movement came to consider themselves "cultural" Zionists, and by 1927 at least 10 percent of the members of the CCAR accepted the position that a Jewish homeland should be reconstituted in Palestine. Leading supporters of the Reform branch invested in the Palestine Development Fund established by Louis Brandeis. When the co-opting of non-Zionists for the expansion of the Jewish Agency for Palestine finally became a reality in 1929, some prominent members of the Reform movement were involved. Finally in 1935 an outspoken Zionist, Rabbi Felix Levy, was elected president of the CCAR.[28]

Reform's conversion to Zionism was embodied in the Columbus platform, which has been identified as the "most radical transformation of any in Jewish history."[29] In forty-eight years Reform became the opposite of what it had been, a reflection of its inherent flexibility. There was sufficient ambiguity within its ideology to permit accommodators to harmonize the old with the new. Those interested in change argued that the Pittsburgh platform stated only that the Jews were "no longer" a nation, not that they had never been one or could not be one again. There could therefore be a belief in the reestablishment of a Jewish homeland in Palestine, not as the only hope of Jews, as many Zionists maintained, but as a unique hope. Anti-Zionism, they maintained, was not essential to Reform, as atheism was to socialism. It was possible to conceive of Palestine as an experiment where Progressive ideas could be carried forward. That was the approach of Louis Brandeis. Why could not a model just society, a basic tenet of Reform Judaism, be established in Palestine?[30] Such thinking gained additional favor during the thirties, which saw the development of a nonideological rationale for supporting the *yishuv,* the popular name of the Jewish settlement in Palestine. The refugee crisis had made finding a haven for hapless Jewish refugees imperative. America, together with most other receiving nations, proved extremely reluctant to accept Jews. With a little diplomatic adroitness "refugeeism," which contained no nationalist implications to nettle "classic" Reformers, could be made acceptable, since it promised a "renewed lease on life" for Jewish refugees. That was the argument presented by Rabbi Abba Hillel Silver in 1943 when American Zionists finally approved the idea of a Jewish commonwealth in Palestine.

These factors also brought in their wake the reversal of classic Reform ideology on the significance of the exile in Jewish history. The exile, which Reformists viewed as permanent and not a form of divine punishment, underpinned Reform ideology. The committee to draft a new set of guiding principles, established in 1935, included only one staunch anti-Zionist, David Philipson. Ratified two years later, the "Guiding Principles of Reform Judaism," soon known as simply the Columbus platform, while continuing to reject the notion of the election of Israel and extreme forms of nationalism, now spoke of "Judaism [as] the soul of which Israel is the body." That was a bold attempt to rejoin ethnic Jewishness and Judaism, which earlier Reform thinkers had done much to separate. Taking a page from Mordecai Kaplan, Judaism was now defined as "the historical religious experience of Jewish people." But basic religious principles, like the primacy of prophetic Judaism and the idea of mission, were retained. Jews would still be bound up with the "destiny of faith, brotherhood, freedom, justice, love, truth and peace," stated a declaration presented to the CCAR in 1936. But the new emphasis on Jewish peoplehood, coupled with the practical rationale of refugeeism, enabled the Reform movement to legitimize the idea of a Jewish homeland: "We affirm the obligation of all Jewry to aid in its upbuilding . . . by endeavoring to make it not only a haven for refuge for the oppressed but also a center of Jewish culture and spiritual life." By placing on a back burner a problem that had been plaguing the movement since the Balfour Declaration, the Reform movement positioned itself closer to what had become the consensus in American Jewry.

Although the cadre of Zionist Reform rabbis ultimately carried the day, victory came at a price. The classical Reform position of the Pittsburgh platform, which stated that Reform Jews considered themselves "no longer a nation but a religious community," was not easily abandoned, even after an address by Rabbi Silver challenging the existence of the mission idea central to the ideological superstructure of Reform. A number of leading laymen continued to be unalterably opposed to Zionism and fought a stubborn rear-guard action over every concession. That included the granting of an honorary Doctor of Hebrew Letters degree to Chaim Weizmann in 1928 and the inclusion of the Zionist anthem, "Hatikvah," in the proposed new Reform hymnal in 1930. It was from these holdouts that the militantly anti-Zionist American Council for Judaism founded in 1943 was drawn.

The Columbus platform had little to say regarding the crucial issue of Jewish law in the practice of Judaism. Without Halakah, Reform became a faith that intruded little into the lives of the laity. But rather than winning greater commitment from its adherents, the laxness simply produced a low level of religious observance. Reform continued to face the problem of differentiating itself from a liberal Protestant sect or the liberal political culture of the Left. The growing number of young Jews drawn to the peace movements and other forms of radical activism during the thirties rarely chose the Reform movement's social action program to express their desire for peace and social justice. Yet such young Jews advocated these causes with a religious fervor. A well-known Zionist spokesman thought Reform lacked drawing power because it reduced Judaism to "lecture values" and "ethical principles" and so had become hopelessly "dull with little distinctively Jewish in its content."[31] Its universalism went well with the times, but viewed through a Judaic prism it seemed in danger of becoming a kind of "Christless Christianity," according to Emil G. Hirsch, speaking at the CCAR convention in 1925. "If we come to consult really who are our co-religionists," he stated, "we shall discover that we have more in common with the Unitarians and Ethical Culture people than with Orthodox Jews."[32] If it was possible to be ethical without law, or God, or Torah, then why be Jewish at all?

Events in the Jewish world were moving quickly during the late thirties. It would be only a matter of time before the cataclysmic events of the Holocaust would require a response. With the radicalization of the Zionist movement, the issue of political Zionism became white-hot. The debate crystallized around the idea of a Jewish army. When the CCAR endorsed the idea in February 1942, the lines were again drawn. Arguing that the CCAR could not speak for the Reform rabbinate, the UAHC objected to the resolution. A group of sixty-three Reform rabbis, meeting in Philadelphia in March 1942, again proclaimed that the CCAR's support of a Jewish army did not represent the will of the Reform rabbinate. A special conference called at Atlantic City in June to heal the breach led instead to the establishment of the American Council for Judaism, which would not disband when called on to do so by the CCAR convention in June 1943. Like so many institutions of American Jewry, the Reform movement remained divided during the crucial years of the Holocaust.

If the Reform movement needed to reformulate its basic principles, the Conservative branch suffered from the absence of any founding principles. Aspiring to unite American Judaism and never intending to be merely another branch of it, Conservatism became instead a protest against the extremes of classical Reform and a critique of an overly rigid Orthodoxy. Its position was not enviable, since Conservatism depended on Reformers for much of its funding and on Orthodox candidates to fill its rabbinical academy.

Despite the movement's growth during the twenties, that decade did not begin auspiciously. Only eight rabbis were ordained in 1921, while twenty-five received diplomas from its Teachers Institute. Its financial situation was precarious, and for a time the chairman of its executive committee, Louis Marshall, was supporting the Jewish Theological Seminary out of his own pocket. Paradoxically, a Conservative organizational structure had been established and a leadership developed, but despite the rising number of congregations affiliated with United Synagogue, no clearly differentiated laity devoted to supporting the movement had fully emerged. Few moneyed supporters identified themselves as Conservative: Conservatism in the twenties was really the neoorthodoxy of its day, and that is the image its leaders wanted to project. They imagined that such a policy would help in recruiting students for the seminary. Indeed, by 1923, JTS's enrollment had increased to 226. The most successful branch, enrolling 81 of these students, was the Teachers Institute headed by the dissident Mordecai Kaplan. The enrollment in all divisions would grow until the end of the decade, but the identity problem that stemmed from being a halfway house between Orthodoxy and Reform was not resolved.

It took special dedication to devote one's life to the Conservative rabbinate, and relatively few sons of observant families heard the call. The candidate trained for four to six years, only to find himself, after ordination, officiating in a small congregation with few amenities and low status and pay. Some of the students at the Seminary College were enrolled as extension students while registered full time at nearby Columbia University. Norman Podhoretz, one such part-timer, noted that most students at the seminary had backgrounds similar to his own—a moderately observant eastern European family usually more ethnically than religiously Jewish. "The point was to be a Jew," noted Podhoretz, "and the way to be a Jew was to get a Jewish education."[33] JTS did not always serve the function its founders envisaged—a safety net for those rejecting Orthodoxy. What was developing instead was a "pick and choose" Judaism. The laity understood little of such ringing phrases as "catholic Israel" or "positive historic Judaism" that fell from the lips of its leaders. The certainty they sought in faith was difficult to find in a movement that could boast neither the crusading iconoclasm of the early Reform movement nor the single-mindedness of Orthodoxy. Instead it adopted a position between moderate Reform, concerning ritual and custom, and a flexible Orthodoxy as it related to Jewish law. Like all halfway houses, it tended to be merely a stop on the way to somewhere else.

But in the twenties Conservative leaders were only dimly aware of these weaknesses. There was a sense of triumph based on the growth of United Synagogue and the growing reputation of its seminary as the place for a rigorous regimen of Jewish learning. At the 1927 convention of the Rabbinic Assembly its president, Rabbi Max Drob, informed his colleagues that Conservatism was the sole hope for American Jewry. But he overlooked signs that the movement's unresolved ideological problem would make the thirties a period of uncertainty. Despite its desire to be the "folk" religion of American Jewry and its rhetoric concerning Jewish peoplehood, the movement was in fact a "vertical democracy." It possessed the clearest divison between the elite church, embodied in the faculty of the seminary, and the folk religion. The congregations were dominated by the seminary and its Rabbinic Assembly, established in 1919. The rationale for such hierarchical control was contained in the principle of "positive historical Judaism," which maintained that not only the present generation but the chain of preceding Jewish generations had a claim. The elite centered on the seminary represented eternal Israel as well as catholic Israel. In fact, Conservatism was catholic, more in the Roman sense than in that of K'lal Yisrael (the universal community of Israel). Given such preeminence, the Conservative rabbinate tended to become a surrogate ministry, doing the things required of an observant Jew that the laity was no longer willing to do. Predictably, the laity became increasingly less observant.[34] As happened with the Reform movement, making things easier did not necessarily make Conservatism more popular. Nor did the presence of distinguished rabbis at the seminary produce a distinctive Conservative ideology. But Conservatism was far ahead of the Reform branch in recognizing that Zionism, which contained the peoplehood element in its most pristine form, offered an opportunity to bridge the gulf between the ethnic and religious components of Judaism. Its leaders became the staunchest proponents of cultural Zionism and among the earliest to advocate political Zionism. What was a problem for the Reform movement, which viewed the faith in purely denominational terms, became an opportunity for the Conservatives. The movement also avoided the cold rationalism of Reform ideology in favor of something more emotional and historical.

But in trying to balance the claims of the religious tradition and modernity, the Conservative movement fell between two stools. It preserved most traditional rituals and revitalized others that had fallen into disuse. Several holidays were restored to their original grandeur and celebrated for their full length. Hebrew continued to occupy a central place in prayer. Prayer shawls and skullcaps were worn during services. Dietary laws were observed, at least at public functions, and a *get* (religious divorce) was required for remarriage. At the same time some of the changes in ritual the Reform movement introduced to enhance decorum were also adopted. In most Conservative synagogues the *mekhitzah,* the curtain that separated the sexes, was abandoned in favor of family pews. The new United Synagogue prayer book eliminated the petition for the renewal of the sacrificial system. Reference to the resurrection of the dead was changed to suggest God's creative power. In 1935 the Rabbinic Assembly approved a resolution permitting those who lived great distances from the synagogue to drive to services on the Sabbath. Most important, the scientific study of Scripture, the *Wissenschaft* approach to study of Jewish texts, was finally adapted with certain modifications to fit it into the "positive historical" approach that Conservatives held up as the ideal. The study of Talmud continued. An attitude of reverence toward the historical process to which Judaism was subject was encouraged. Conservative leaders spoke of a living tradition but also insisted on ancient prerogatives such as the notion of chosenness.

In no branch of American Judaism was the tension between tradition and modernity more keenly felt; Conservatives tried to meet both claims without losing credibility. But the successive adjustments required by modernity brought with them a constant confrontation with Jewish law. That law, Conservative rabbis argued, had to remain alive through constant reinterpretation, lest Judaism become a fossil. As a Conservative spokesman put it in an address before the Rabbinic Assembly: "We have felt that Reform Judaism abandoned Halahah [*sic*] while Orthodoxy permitted Halahah to abandon us."35 But the middle ground was proving untenable. The claims of secularization were unending, and if Conservatism was to avoid a collapse from within, it would be compelled to firmly anchor its ideology or go the way of the Reform movement or Orthodoxy.

In the interwar period the Orthodox branch had the least hopeful prognosis for survival. Its all-encompassing demands, embodied in a strict interpretation of Jewish law, meant that its adherents had to make an agonizing choice between being observant and earning an adequate live-lihood. A garment worker who observed the Sabbath, for example, could not work overtime during "the season" and frequently missed work because of holidays. The demands of earning a living often won out, giving Ortho-doxy the highest attrition rate during the twenties. By preselection, its adherents were less affluent and less acculturated. With few exceptions Orthodox congregations tended to be small, but these chevras and minyans in which the Orthodox Jews prayed and studied might have been the envy of the other branches, since these small groups really formed "communities of faithful," so conversant with the ritual and rhythm of religious Jewish life that they required no central authority. Many functioned without a rabbi and were none the worse for it. But organizationally such autonomy at the grass roots could be a liability, too. Weak authority at the top meant a proliferation of schisms, so that by the outbreak of World War II few could say with certainty who spoke for Orthodoxy. The cement binding Ortho-doxy together was the observance of Jewish law and a keen suspicion of the Christian religion and the modern secular world. Some ultra-Orthodox Jews preferred to insulate themselves from American culture lest they be contaminated. But that also meant that they could not directly confront or even acknowledge the problems modernity posed for the average worshiper.

Paradoxically, the Orthodox believers, whose religious ideology most required centralized authority, developed none that might help the branch hold its own in the free atmosphere of America. Orthodox rabbis of various stripes rarely could be convinced to accept the fiat of another, especially when it came to matters of kashrut. More than the other branches, author-ity came to rest in the individual congregation or charismatic rabbi. The malaise stemmed partly from the position assigned to the rabbis. They were not primarily religious leaders or congregational administrators but were men of learning, which gave them the enormous prestige requisite for lead-ership. For the Orthodox, a rabbi was one who, because of his knowledge of Jewish texts and law, had the authority to rule on questions of religious law. All who had earned *s'micha* (rabbinic ordination), usually by study at a yeshiva or with an individual rabbi, technically had authority to make such judgments.

In 1898, in response to the establishment of the Reform branch's Union of American Hebrew Congregations (1873), the Orthodox movement estab-lished its congregational arm, the Union of Orthodox Jewish Congrega-tions (UOJC). But the UOJC experienced inordinate problems in winning compliance from the various groups that composed the Orthodox world. By 1941 it had drawn less than 10 percent of the three thousand Orthodox congregations into its membership.[36] Its most authoritative rabbinic body, founded in 1902, Agudath HaRabbanim, supported the Rabbi Isaac Elchanan Theological Seminary (RIETS), which after 1897 became the major Orthodox rabbinic seminary in America. But as early as 1908, when students of RIETS went on strike over the issue of instruction in English, the relationship between the two bodies was a stormy one, especially when the question of rabbinic ordination was involved. During World War I, under the administration of Bernard Revel, RIETS began to diversify its program, which for the ultra-Orthodox conjured up fears of secularization. A Talmudic academy and high school was established in 1916, and in 1921 the Hebrew Teachers Institute sponsored by Mizrachi (the religious Zionists) was absorbed. Finally, a year after the collapse of the unification negotiations with JTS in 1928, Yeshiva College was established. Again there was opposition from Agudath HaRabbanim which feared the introduction of secular subjects into the curriculum. The leadership of the highly regarded Rabbi Joseph B. Soloveitchik in 1932 did not still the voices of opposition. Viewing the Ph.D. degree that Soloveitchik had earned at the University of Berlin as evidence of dreaded secularism and seeing Yeshiva College itself as a "nest of atheism," the ultra-Orthodox refused to enroll their children. That same year an alternative rabbinical seminary was established by Rabbi Judah Levenberg, which made no concession to secular studies. But faced with financial problems in Cleveland, where it had finally relocated, it became a casualty of the Depression.

Its demise did not end the conflict between Europeanists, who insisted that no concessions to modernity could be allowed, and Americanists, who realized that in the dynamic environment of America some accommodation was required. The Europeanists were usually recent arrivals, who after leaving the great yeshivas of eastern Europe, clung tenaciously to tradition. The Americanists were younger, usually American-born and English-speaking, and saw the possibility of living in the modern world while adhering to the Halakah. It was this group that eventually produced modern or neo-orthodoxy.

In day-to-day practice the questions of Jewish law the rabbis faced may have seemed banal to Americanized Jews. Could electric appliances, which became popular during the twenties, be used on the Sabbath? Could one ride in an elevator or drive one's car on that day? Was it permissible to use the new Schick electric razor rather than a depilatory for shaving? Could one use a *gompo,* a mechanical clamp, for circumcision? There were also the perennial questions concerning kashrut and *shekhita* (ritual slaughter), which did not diminish until the 1940s, when packaged foods became popular. In 1941 the UOJC was finally barred from making kashrut decisions. Most divisive of all were the questions concerning relations between the sexes. Most agreed that coed dancing, which had reached new popularity during the twenties, was not permissible; but what about family seating in the synagogue? In Orthodox congregations in the South and West, women congregants, who played an important role in congregational life, were insistent on this concession to modernity, and a number of congregations had joined the modern Orthodox or Conservative United Synagogue over this issue. Inevitably Orthodoxy became entangled in the web of law, and the divisions within its fold were based on its broad or narrow interpretation.[37]

After the death of Bernard Revel, the guiding spirit of RIETS, the Agudath HaRabbanim, which viewed itself as the legitimate organization of Orthodox rabbis, renewed its challenge. It had opposed the founding of Yeshiva College in 1928. Now it created a "Committee of Seven" to oversee the activities of RIETS and the new college. The move was rejected by Samuel Levy, chairman of the board, who preferred to assign such a role to the Rabbinic Council of America (RCA), whose members were primarily RIETS graduates. It had been founded in 1926 by Rabbi Leo Jung, who was trained in Europe and had earned a doctorate at the University of London. The RCA was strengthened in 1942, when it was joined by the Hebrew Theological College of Chicago, but it never mustered sufficient strength to speak for the entire Orthodox rabbinate in America.

The Europeanists eventually organized their own yeshivas in the New York metropolitan area and other areas of Orthodox settlement. The first of these religious day schools was Rabbi Jacob Joseph Yeshiva. The model for the more advanced religious academies was Mesifta Torah Vodaas, which expanded its activities after 1921 under the energetic administration of Rabbi Shraga Mendlowitz. A renewed spurt of energy occurred in 1935 when Rabbi Shlomo Heiman became *rosh yeshiva* (chancellor). Orthodoxy was also reenergized by the transplant of European academies like the Telshe and Mirrer Yeshiva, which in the face of the Nazi threat reestablished themselves in the United States.

In 1941 the high point of this reenergizing was the establishment of an advanced seminary (*kollel*), Beth Medrash Govoha, in Lakewood, New Jersey, by Rabbi Aaron Kotler, perhaps the most remarkable of the group of Orthodox immigrant rabbis who arrived during the late thirties. Sometimes called the "Harvard of yeshivas," the seminary did not offer ordination but encouraged study for its own sake. Another such transplant was the Breuer community (K'hal Adath Jeshurun), which moved from Frankfurt to Washington Heights in New York City in 1940. Made up of followers of Rabbi Samson Raphael Hirsch, among the earliest religious leaders to attempt a synthesis between Orthodoxy and modernity, the Breuer community permitted its followers to attend secular schools but linked itself to Agudath rather than its next-door neighbor, Yeshiva College. In addition the Hasidic courts also successfully transplanted themselves to American soil, and with the decline of the traditional hostility between them and the Mitnagdim (rationalists), the strength of Orthodoxy increased. Between 1938 and 1946 the number of yeshivas grew from fourteen to eighty-four and the number of students from 4,000 to 17,500. By 1944 the National Society of Hebrew Day Schools (Torah Umesorah), founded under the auspices of Agudath Israel of America, boasted five hundred such schools.

While the Holocaust was destroying the base of Orthodoxy in eastern Europe, a seed was being planted in America that would finally give the Orthodox enterprise a firm American base. The initial attempt to establish order in the Orthodox world by founding a branch of Agudath Israel in 1922 did not succeed, but the second attempt in 1939 flourished. The infusion of Orthodox leaders, institutions, and thousands of committed believers from Europe was important in fueling the resurgence of Orthodoxy after the war. But the chaotic lack of organization that characterized the world of Orthodoxy persisted. By 1945 four distinct types of Orthodoxy could be discerned, sometimes more hostile to each other than to the "outside world." The right wing was composed of ultra-traditionalists, consisting of Agudath Israel and most of the Hasidic communities. In the center were the traditionalists, whose adherence to religious law was somewhat more flexible. Next came the modern Orthodox gathered around RIETS, now called Yeshiva University, whose attitude toward modernity was that one could thrive in both worlds if they were compartmentalized. Many in this group were college graduates and had professional training. On the periphery of Orthodoxy were the nonobservant Orthodox, Jews who were in fact secular but recognized Orthodoxy as the only authentic Judaism even though they no longer adhered to its tenets.[38] Given the persistence of these splits and the freeness of the American secular environment, Orthodoxy would become far more dominant in Israel, where it faced no competition from other branches. That dominance, coupled with other factors, gives contemporary American Orthodoxy the sense of triumph that in earlier decades characterized the Reform and Conservative branches.

We come finally to Reconstructionism, which did not become a fourth branch of American Judaism in the interwar period but whose influence on Conservatism and Reform and on Jewish secularists was pervasive. So attuned was the Reconstructionist approach to the needs of secularizing Jews that one can say most American Jews were Reconstructionists without knowing it. The movement's brilliantly edited biweekly journal, the *Reconstructionist,* helped create that impression.[39]

Mordecai Kaplan, founder of the movement, perceived early how deeply the assumptions of American secularism, especially its notion of individual fufillment, had taken hold among Jews. He became convinced that American Judaism was in a crisis that neither the Orthodox nor the Reform branch—the former excessively rigid and the latter "a negation of Judaism"—was able to address. He proposed Reconstructionism as a philosophy and as a strategy to confront the problems of American Jewry as an "organic whole."[40] So powerful were Kaplan's intellectual constructs and his charismatic appeal to students and intellectuals that it was difficult, while he was alive, to implement his ideas by creating institutions to house them.

Born in June 1881 into a Lithuanian Orthodox Jewish family that nine years later resettled in New York, Kaplan followed a typical second-generation pattern. His early education was almost completely Orthodox. He received a B.A. from City College in 1905 simultaneously with ordination from the Jewish Theological Seminary. He then accepted a post as rabbi at New York's Kehillath Jeshurun, an Orthodox congregation. But when Solomon Schechter in 1909 offered him a seminary position as a teacher of homiletics, he abandoned the pulpit. It is to Kaplan's interest in sociology and anthropology—his majors at Columbia University, where he studied for a master's degree—that many of his formulations can be traced. Reconstructionism, in effect, replaces theology with cultural anthropology and sociology as a guide to Jewish survival. Much of his thinking on religion was influenced by the French Jewish sociologist Emile Durkheim, while the notion of organic community can be traced to the writing of Ahad Ha'am. The new social scientists becoming entrenched in American universities were particularly influential.

As director of the newly founded Teachers Institute of JTS, he soon attracted a coterie of loyal students. Included in this group were two who would become important thinkers in their own right, Rabbis Milton Steinberg and Max Kadushin. The support of these students, who went on to fill key Conservative pulpits, later enabled Kaplan to withstand the opposition of Rabbi Louis Ginzberg, the seminary's most noted scholar, and Cyrus Adler, who became its president in 1925. Ginzberg opposed Kaplan for his radical departures from tradition. Adler, on the other hand, found Kaplan's Zionism and his heterodoxy unacceptable but appreciated the fact that Kaplan remained an observant Jew.

Kaplan's first love was teaching at the seminary, which he never left, despite two tempting offers by Rabbi Stephen Wise, founder of the Jewish Institute of Religion. But his "poisonous doctrines" were considered heretical by the Orthodox, who tried as early as 1921 to convince Cyrus Adler to dismiss him. He experienced considerable discomfort at the seminary, and in 1927 he withdrew his resignation only after Adler convinced him that despite the effect of his activities on fund-raising and the unification talks with RIETS, the seminary would not engage in "heresy hunting."[41]

Kaplan's problems at the seminary stemmed from several articles published in the *Menorah Journal,* which later were incorporated in his book *Judaism as a Civilization* (1934). The founding in 1921 of the Society for the Advancement of Judaism (SAJ), which Kaplan first called the Society for Jewish Renascence, was not an attempt to establish yet another branch of Judaism. Reconstructionism posed more of an ideational than an organizational challenge. Its principles and practices, insisted Kaplan, were designed to restore vitality to what he perceived as an American Judaism on the brink of disaster.

Kaplan's alarm about the condition of American Judaism was first aroused by the behavior of his students at the seminary. Orthodox Judaism, he noted, seemed ill suited to the modern rational temper that shaped their perceptions. The students seemed no longer able to draw spiritual succor from the faith of their ancestors. Many despaired at the disabilities they faced for a religion they neither understood nor believed in. He was dismayed at the self-hatred he observed, which he saw as a formula for disaster. Judaism was not in consonance with the times and had therefore to be "revised from a social viewpoint." If it were to survive, its center of spiritual interest had to shift from abstract dogmas and codes of law to the "pulsating life of Israel." He came to the paradoxical conclusion that the spiritual restructuring of American Jewry required that religion no longer be its exclusive preoccupation. In its place there would be Jewish peoplehood, expressed through Jewish organic communalism—what Durkheim called the "conscience collective."[42] He conceived of Judaism as an evolving civilization with its own culture and ethos, which needed to be fit into American society. It was only later that the word "religious" was added to "evolving civilization." He assumed that the two cultures were in consonance, since both were basically democratic and Hebraic. But American Jewry would have to live in two worlds and balance the claims of both.

To achieve that goal Kaplan proposed refashioning Judaism along communal lines. Judaism he defined as the "*tout ensemble* of all the elements that enter in what is usually termed the cultural life of a people, such as language, folkways, patterns of social organization, social habits and standards, spiritual ideals, which give individuality to a people and differentiate it from other people." In a word, Kaplan proposed to rebuild a Jewish community rooted in a knowledge and celebration of its own millennial culture. Only such a community could withstand the atomizing impact of modernity. Religion would become merely one of several forces binding Jews into a community.[43]

To fit the modern secular mind-set, supernatural and otherwise unacceptable notions like covenantial chosenness and revelation would have to be abandoned. Religious law, which Kaplan noted was more honored in the breach than in the observance, would have to be modified. Since modern people found moral preaching that did not bear on behavior inauthentic, the commandments for doing ethical deeds—the individualized, inner-directed mitzvot—would now also be realized by collective deeds to achieve social justice. During the depression the Reconstructionists, by advocating public ownership of all natural resources and basic industry, came close to the socialist approach to organizing society.

But what seemed so right in theory proved difficult to put into practice. Few lay people understood Kaplan's notion of God as process and his stress on "this worldly salvation." Except for those modern Jews who needed a rationale for their commitment, Reconstructionism seemed too cerebral. It made few concessions to the extrarational, on which faith was often based. But the substitution of *sancta,* the sacralization of the customs and traditions of the Jewish people, for the restrictive Jewish law made sense to many. Reconstructionist *havurot,* the small social communities of worshipers Kaplan favored, became known for their exciting services and rich intellectual and cultural fare. By the late twenties, Reconstructionism was making inroads among select educated, professionalized Jews, who supported the Society for the Advancement of Judaism and several small congregations. Few noted the anomaly of an elite group's attempting to restore a Jewish folk religion.[44] To critics it seemed that the Reconstructionists, by substituting ideas about religion for the piety that had formerly bound the Jewish people together, were inadvertently becoming students of religion rather than believers. Reconstructionism was not "an organic growth from within," observed one critic, but rather a contrived, man-made attempt to reshape an ancient faith to meet the needs of the moment.[45]

Most troublesome of Kaplan's proposed changes was the concept of chosenness, which, because of its inherent special claims for election, was incompatible with upholding a religion that fit into the general American civil religion, especially the idea of pluralism and egalitarianism. Kaplan proposed to replace it with the notion of vocation or calling, which also had roots in American Puritanism. By avoiding the implication of Jewish superiority, the notion of vocation—that is, devotion to one's professional field, to be considered equivalent to the study of Torah—would circumvent the invidious distinctions inherent in the doctrine of chosenness. It was the unacceptability of the idea of election that first led Reform and Conservative thinkers to attempt to refashion it. But where Kaufmann Kohler, the ideologue of classical Reform, converted chosenness into mission and denied peoplehood, Reconstructionism proposed to celebrate peoplehood and deny chosenness. For Orthodox and traditional Jews generally, however, the election of the Jews remained at the very heart of their religious sensibility, and they made their opposition to Kaplan's tampering clear.

Still another problem concerned the supernaturalism embodied in the idea of the existence of a personal God and revelation. For these, we have noted, Kaplan emphasized the idea of Jewish peoplehood. Reconstructionists went beyond Conservatives in their advocacy of Palestine as a new center of Jewish culture. "Take Palestine out of the Jew's life," Kaplan stated, "and the only sphere of influence that remains to him as a Jew are the synagogue and the cemetery."[46] But at the same time Kaplan was primarily concerned with integrating Jews into American life and, like the Conservatives, did not advocate emigration to Palestine or the "negation of the Diaspora," which was then an integral part of Zionist ideology. Palestine was considered a haven for all Jews should it be required, which fit neatly into the "refugeeism" that was behind the emerging Zionist consensus during the thirties.

But changes in *minhag,* the order of worship, and alteration of the content of prayers created endless problems for Kaplan's followers. Such popular Reconstructionist practices as a "cultural" evening at the home of a congregant, or teaching sessions on Jewish ceremonies and history, or the working out of a "code of ethical practices" so that Judaism could become a seven-day-a-week affair remained internal affairs and aroused little ire. But when the SAJ synagogue followed the Reform precedent and eliminated the popular Kol Nidre prayer, chanted on the eve of Yom Kippur, because it did not meet the test of sincerity and truth, protests were loud and clear. Substituting Psalm 130, which Kaplan proposed in its stead, was unacceptable; the familiar chanting of the Kol Nidre was too close to the hearts of the observant and formerly observant.[47] Many Jews, after all, attended services only on that one evening, and they expected to hear what they had always associated with the faith they were in the process of abandoning.

Reconstructionists also followed the Reform lead and deleted from the prayer service references to revelation, the resurrection of the dead, and the restoration of sacrifical cults. It was part of an effort to modernize the service and make it more aesthetic by avoiding monotonous repetition. In 1941 two of Kaplan's disciples, Eugene Kohn and Ira Eisenstein, published a new Passover Haggadah that not only contained contemporary material but omitted mention of the ten plagues. That earned a rebuke from the authorities at the seminary. In 1921 Judah Magnes, former chairman of the Kehillah and soon to be chancellor of the Hebrew University, submitted a thirteen-point criticism of Kaplan's program. He found it too cerebral and lacking transcendence. Kaplan, he felt, was "tinkering" and replacing traditional customs with "inconsequential minutiae" without regard to "traditional sanctions" and "Jewish religious psychology."[48]

But the traditionalists would hardly agree that the changes Kaplan proposed were "inconsequential." In 1941 the Reconstructionists published *A Guide to Jewish Ritual,* which summed up all the proposed alterations. Aside from denying the binding character of Jewish law, it proposed a change in how the sacredness of the Sabbath should be observed. The day would be used for recreation, because the "will to live most happily and effectively must supersede the observance of the Sabbath."[49] When the

Reconstructionist Sabbath Prayer Book with the proposed alterations was published in 1945, it aroused a storm of protest. A group of heads of yeshivas belonging to the extreme Orthodox Agudath HaRabbanim met in a ballroom of a midtown hotel on 12 June 1945 and unanimously judged the siddur "blasphemous." A rabbinic convocation was convened to excommunicate Kaplan and a group of his closest associates. Again there was apprehension at JTS that Kaplan's presence was causing incalculable damage. Although the *cherem* (writ of excommunication) actually demonstrated the lack of authority of the Orthodox rabbis, it saddened Kaplan for the remainder of his long life.

In that Reconstructionism remained a movement without structure and its innovations affected relatively few Jews, it might be considered inconsequential. Yet in one area, the notion of rebuilding an organic community, its influence was important. "Whatever helps to produce creative social interaction among Jews belongs to the category of religion because it contributes to the salvation of the Jews," wrote Kaplan.[50] Therefore Jews ought not only to pray as Jews, but also to play and work and socialize and fulfill their social needs together. The idea was taken up by American Jewry in the Jewish center movement.

Kaplan had played a leading role in the New York Kehillah, which lost momentum by 1918 and expired by 1922. It seemed impossible to reestablish the European experience of the *kahal*—a formally organized community with governing power—in America, where the central authority was absent and the centrifugal forces within the community could not be contained. Kaplan therefore proposed restructuring community on a smaller scale by replacing the synagogue, which served as the matrix of the community, with small kehillot (formal community structures) that would include social and cultural activities as well as religious worship.

Eventually the idea emerged in the form of Jewish centers, soon dubbed "a shul with a school and a pool." It was not a new idea, having been tried in different form by a Cleveland Reform congregation, "the Temple," in 1901 and by Temple Sinai in Chicago a few years later. But Kaplan's idea for Jewish centers was part of a larger strategy to bring Jews together not only for worship but for all social and cultural activities outside the home. That would include sports, Jewish education, in which "cultural Zionism" would be a major part of the curriculum, and other forms of cultural activity. Unlike the country club, which had become a favorite haunt of affluent Jews, the center's identity would be clearly Jewish, though not exclusively religious. That was, after all, what the second generation was already doing, Kaplan argued. With SAJ's Jewish center on West Eighty-sixth Street in New York as a model, the center idea was soon picked up by the Reform and Conservative branches. The construction of Jewish centers was an important part of the synagogue building boom of the twenties and attracted thousands of members. The center became the temple of the second generation.

But it soon became clear that as an organizational device the center could not gather all Jewish communal activities under one roof. Jewish secular organizations would not easily surrender their sovereignty to become part of someone else's strategy to restore Jewish communalism. More important, organizing the manifold activities of the center required an expensive administrative staff and larger buildings. The budgets of the centers would hypothetically be divided into thirds: one for the synagogue, one for Jewish education, and the last for secular cultural activities. In practice this meant that the centers increasingly were limited to middle-class members who could afford the high cost of membership. Moreover, their budgets soon reflectd the fact that secular activities overshadowed religious ones in popularity. The Jewish center became a community center with a synagogue rather than the reverse. In most cases, one researcher observes, the center became "a powerful metaphor for community," but rather than acting as a rejudaizing agent, it reflected the powerful thrust of secularization.[51] It would take more than buildings and programs to recommunalize American Jewry.

Kaplan understood that survival required an ethos that did not conflict with the second generation's dearest objective, integration into American society. He saw that most Jews were using their newfound freedom to remove the yoke of a confining religion. What American Jewry was experiencing went beyond a crisis of faith. It was also a crisis of community that threatened to leave Jews, no longer supported by the immigrant ethnic culture, part of the atomized, lonely American crowd. Kaplan hoped to revitalize it by stressing Zionism and other community-building devices such as the Jewish center. But Reconstructionists would learn that organic community could not be contrived. It required first a people who felt they belonged to a special group. The problem was how to instill such a belief in an intensely secularizing society that tended to detribalize its citizens.

Most Jewish leaders did not share Kaplan's gloomy prognosis, but they were aware of the growing trend toward disaffiliation.[52] Their response was to teach the worthwhileness of the culture, which could no longer be learned at home with one's mother's milk. Marshall spoke of duplicating in religious education the Jewish experience with public education. He was convinced it would "save Judaism from dissolution."[53] Formal education was, after all, achieving a great deal for American Jewry in the economic sphere. Why not in the religious?

But such confidence regarding the ability to deliver ethnic or religious identity was hardly warranted by the ramshackle Jewish education system in areas of Jewish population concentration. As early as 1910 the New York Kehillah had established a Jewish Board of Education directed by David de Sola Pool and assisted by Alexander Dushkin. A grant of $50,000 was duly made by Jacob Schiff. A "state of the field" survey revealed dismal conditions. A small cadre of inadequately trained, usually foreign-born teachers was, in effect, teaching a decreasing proportion of Jewish children. The religious elementary schools were graduating only 3 to 5 percent of their pupils. But except for the development of a cadre of professional educators, the picture was dismal.

Leading this cadre of professional educators was the Palestinian-born Samson Benderly, who had abandoned a career in medicine to establish a Jewish education system in Baltimore. Also in the group was Mordecai Kaplan, who headed JTS's Teachers Institute, where he experimented with various curricula and teaching approaches, and Israel Friedlander, who was killed in the Ukraine in 1921. Their efforts were eventually reinforced by a younger group that included Alexander Dushkin, I. B. Berkson, Israel Chipkin, and Emanuel Gamoran. The group had many differences but generally agreed that Jewish education should be communally sponsored. Aware that the number of Jewish students completing high school was increasing, they decided to focus their efforts on the secondary level of Jewish education. A Hebrew high school had been established in New York City in 1918, using the Dalton plan for individualized instruction. Four years later a small centralized system was put in place in New York City. Students met every Sunday at the Barney building on Ninth Street in Manhattan. The organizers hoped to convince Jewish students attending secular high schools to devote one day a week to their Jewish education. In 1928 Benderly, who had assumed leadership of the board, turned his attention to the majority of Jewish adolescents who were receiving no Jewish education at all. He commissioned a simple primer, an *Outline of Jewish Knowledge,* so that students might educate themselves. But left unanswered were the questions of motivation and of how to get the new material into their hands. By the end of the decade a fairly comprehensive system was in place. Of the 871 American Jewish communities, 98 percent had some form of Jewish school organization, with an enrollment of 249,109 students.[54]

According to one observer, a major problem was "how to integrate the training of the Jew and the training of the American citizen."[55] Clearly, a community interested in accommodation would be unwilling to support the heder system, the religious schooling associated with the Old World. Aside from the financial problem, the greatest obstacle to establishing a rational education system was that the communal structure it had to be based on was torn between secularists, who favored the teaching of "Jewish culture," and religionists, who did not acknowledge the deep division that had developed between Jewish culture and religion. Futhermore, within the secular and religious camps there was little agreement on what to teach. In fact, a variety of educational systems were developing; religionist schools ranged from the ultra-Orthodox to the Conservatives, and secular schools were split between those who focused on Hebrew and on Yiddish. In the first category there existed about 717 privately supported congregational schools and 97 community schools called Talmud Torahs, attended primarily by preconfirmation boys. The Hebrew schools like the Herzliah Institutes in Boston, Philadelphia, Baltimore, and Chicago were supplemented by Hebrew high schools like Marshalliah in New York. Supported partly by the Zionist movement and partly by tuition, their thrust was cultural Zionism and the teaching of Hebrew. More complex was the organization of the Yiddish secular schools, which religious Jews did not consider a legitimate part of the educational system. Following the Jewish political spectrum, there were three primary types and some random institutions that fell in between: the Farband National Workers' Alliance schools (Poale Zion), the Sholem Aleichem *folkshuln,* which were ostensibly Yiddishist and nonpolitical, and the Arbeiter Ring (Workmen's Circle) schools, which were secular, socialist-oriented institutions reminiscent of the Bundist academies of Poland but now affiliated with the American Jewish labor movement. On the fringe stood the communist Internationalist Workers Order schools, which, though they were fiercely Yiddishist and enrolled 10,000 to 12,000 students by the mid-twenties, were not accepted as a legitimate part of the Jewish community.[56]

During the 1930s the most common type of school, the congregationally linked religious school, moved into the new neighborhoods where

Jews were settling. In 1929 the Hebraists won a victory that accelerated the decline of Yiddish: helped by the political influence of Rabbi Stephen Wise and Judge Otto Rosolosky, Hebrew was finally accepted as part of the official high-school academic course in New York City.

Such triumphs tended to conceal the drastic impact of the Depression on the endeavor to maintain Jewish culture through education. In 1935 Isaac Berkson, one of "Benderly's boys," was commissioned to survey the state of Jewish education in New York City. Presumably his findings would apply to other Jewish communities as well. His report was not hopeful. The percentage of Jewish children receiving some form of Jewish education had risen since the twenties: about 35,000 were attending such schools, mostly boys preparing for confirmation. The percentage attending nationwide was in fact higher than in New York City, and Berkson failed to include the 15,000 children still attending hederim (elementary schools). To bring central organization to these far-flung schools, Berkson recommended that Benderly's Bureau of Education and Chipkin's Jewish Education Association, both empires for dominating personalities, be merged. The centralization took four years to carry out and required setting up yet another agency, the Jewish Education Committee, to be headed by Dushkin, to which the original Bureau of Jewish Education, a leftover of the defunct Kehillah, surrendered its activities.[57] The aspiration to make Jewish education an instrument for Jewish religious and ethnic survival was not fulfilled. By the mid-forties more Jewish children were receiving some sort of Jewish education, but for the most part its impact remained minimal.

Using the public schools to achieve that end offered a better hope. Almost all Jewish children could be reached through the public schools, whereas the weak eclectic Jewish school system reached only 27 percent. But some way had to be found to circumvent the constitutional mandate separating church and state. We have already noted, however, that the teaching of Hebrew in the public high schools was barely able to sustain itself. Moreover, its rationale was secular, which left unaddressed the problem of strengthening religion.

The movement to do so began not with a direct assault on the line separating church and state, which Jews overwhelmingly supported, but simply with an attempt to adjust the school calendar to Jewish religious needs. In 1922 the Federation of Jewish Women's Organizations petitioned New York's Board of Education not to schedule such activities as graduation ceremonies and teacher examinations on Friday night or Saturday.

Anxious to avoid tension, the board shifted the decision to the district superintendents and ignored the matter of examinations. Soon there were requests to recognize Passover as well as Easter as a religious holiday. Finally in 1930 several Jewish organizations petitioned the board to permit excused absences for Jewish students who observed Rosh Hashanah and Yom Kippur, which fell at the outset of the fall term. Finally the Jews joined the Protestant-sponsored campaign to conduct "religious training" outside the school during "release time."

As early as 1913 a plan for a weekday church school, begun in Gary, Indiana, by its school superintendent, Dr. William Wirt, had spread through the Middle West. By 1933 the release-time system involved 383 communities in forty states and serviced 227,210 students of all faiths. But there was opposition in the Jewish community as well as among non-Jews. In 1926 the superintendents' chapter of the National Education Association split on the release-time issue. In the Jewish community, secularists found the system pernicious.[58] Nevertheless, pressure from mainline Protestant churches helped expand the program. In 1940, over the strong opposition of Parent-Teacher Associations, school administrators, and "progressive" educators, New York State passed the Coudert-McClaughlin bill, which allowed each district to find its own way through the maze. The Board of Regents guidelines required that the system be noncompulsory and that participating students have written permission from parents. The churches and synagogues where instruction was to take place were required to file a weekly card of attendance. But no sooner had Governor Herbert Lehman signed the bill (9 April 1940) than a bitter controversy resurfaced in the New York City system. Jewish local organizations did not actively oppose a trial run scheduled for the Bay Ridge district of Brooklyn, but there was concern that the program would draw invidious distinctions between "observers" and "nonobservers." The Jewish Education Association and the United Synagogue proposed an alternative dismissed-time plan that would close down the schools completely one hour a week for religious instruction and avoid drawing such distinctions among the students. But the dismissed-time plan was opposed by Protestant churches.

By 1943 the release-time program had lost momentum. The number of teachers disapproving rose from 16 percent in 1942 to 31 percent the following year. Older students were unenthusiastic, there was much truancy, since the program was difficult to administer, and the participating students seemed to gain little from the experience. By 1947 the program was almost completely phased out. Jewish survivalists who had initially viewed the program favorably did not attempt to sustain it. They had discovered that the various religious congregations and centers to which the students were sent did not, in any case, have a program to teach Judaism. The released students made the same discovery and increasingly voted with their feet for more entertaining activities.[59]

Systematizing Jewish education, finding a place for Hebrew in the high school and the liberal arts curriculum, and programs like release time were supported by those who feared imminent dissolution of the religious and ethnic culture. These survivalists sought to halt the dissolution by actively teaching the culture. Any means to reach the Jewish masses was considered acceptable, even the use of the new, popular radio. In September 1923 the United Synagogue arranged to have services broadcast over WEAF in New York City and WMAS in Massachusetts. Such survivalist strategies sometimes posed problems for acculturating Jews, who wanted above all else to become American. They therefore looked askance at the sectarianism inherent in the attempt to teach Jewish culture and religion.

Such secular Jews were less concerned with preserving the traditional culture than with creating space for an acceptable modified Jewishness that would fit easily into the majority culture. They eventually sought their answer in a nonsectarian religiousness. As early as February 1915, Horace Kallen had advocated pluralism in an article in the *Nation* using the analogy of the symphony orchestra. All the instruments, each playing a different tune, produced a harmonious melody. According to Kallen, each group's right to develop its separate culture and religion should itself become a basic principle in democratic societies. If that happened, Judaism would become part of a kind of secularized public faith centered on the democratic ideal of tolerance.[60] Ultimately the citizenry would, at least for public purposes, be converted to a "shared culture" in which religiousness, if not a particular faith, would play a major role. In the late twenties that idea was manifested in the growth of interdenominationalism.

The movement for Christian-Jewish amity began in earnest before World War I with the founding of the Committee on Goodwill between Christians and Jews of the Federal Council of Churches of Christ, which was part of the "goodwill" enthusiasm of the Social Gospel movement. Liberal Protestantism was more concerned to address the strident fundamentalism of the early twenties than to counteract the anti-Semitism such fundamentalist groups generated. There was detectable in the goodwill movement an element of Protestant triumph. In its early form it barely distinguished between Americanizing the immigrants and Christianizing them. That missionary impetus caused some concern among Jewish advocates of religious tolerance, who predictably were mostly associated with the Reform branch. The problems involved in Jewish-Christian relations were again taken up at the annual meeting of the Central Conference of American Rabbis held in Cincinnati in 1925. Two years later the Permanent Commission of Better Understanding between Christian and Jews was organzied by Rabbi Isaac Landman. That same year thirty-nine Christian and Jewish organizations banded together to found the National Conference of Christians and Jews, which became the major national agency advocating Christian-Jewish goodwill.[61]

Interdenominationalism required ideological as well as organizational support. Christians and Jews would necessarily have to tone down their particularism and stress those spiritual factors they held in common. The Judaic notion of election, for example, did not fit easily into a society that aspired to democratic egalitarianism, nor could it be reconciled with pluralism, which was at the heart of the idea of religious tolerance. It was partly for that reason that the Reform branch and the Reconstructionists abandoned the notion of chosenness.[62]

How difficult it was to probe the division that separated Christians and Jews was illustrated by the bitter recriminations that followed Rabbi Stephen Wise's speech on the subject of Jesus. Speaking on 20 December to a full house at Carnegie Hall, Wise expatiated on Joseph Klausner's recently published book *Portrait of the Historic Jesus*. Using Midrashic and Mishnaic sources, Klausner had concluded that the teachings of Jesus did not depart appreciably from Jewish beliefs at the time and that Jesus had no intention of starting a new religion. Wise, a good ecumenicist, took Klausner's findings one step further by adding that Jews ought to recognize Jesus' teachings as falling into the prophetic sphere.

Wise was taken aback by the reaction to his sermon in the Jewish community. Many Reform rabbis believed that Wise's interpretation was basically correct but felt he had not been circumspect in saying so during the Christmas season. So emotional was the reaction from the Orthodox branch that an attempt to explain that Wise had been misquoted in the press proved of little avail. Rabbi Meier Berlin, who represented the religious Zionists (Mizrachi) on the board of the United Palestine Appeal (UPA), insisted that Wise resign as chairman of that major fund-raising agency. Wise and others learned that interfaith ideas could be pushed only so far among observant Jews.[63]

Despite numerous setbacks, the movement for interdenominationalism reached its zenith as World War II approached. Conservative and Orthodox leaders now joined the Reform vanguard in speaking of religious pluralism as an integral part of American democracy. Paradoxically, although a new, virulent strain of anti-Semitism had made its debut, the idea that there existed a Judeo-Christian continuum was gaining acceptance among Jewish and Christian opinion leaders. Later a prominent Jewish sociologist of religion would note the existence of a religious triad in which Judaism was granted full partnership with Protestanism and Catholicism.[64]

But all was not suddenly sweetness and light. Will Herberg, who first noted the acceptance of Judaism as one of the three founding religions, later came to doubt the confluence of Christianity and Judaism. He wondered whether in the formation of the American civil religion in which Protestantism, Catholicism, and Judaism became variants of the national faith, each was losing its reason for separate existence. The forces of darkness at work in Nazi-occupied Europe overshadowed interdenominationalism and the rhetoric of goodwill.

In the end, few of the programs to halt the erosion of faith proved effective. The cooling of religious passion was part of modernity, which nothing seemed able to slow. For the faithful there was little satisfaction in knowing that the cooler temper promised to enhance Jewish security. The price—emptying Judaism of its particularist content—seemed too high.

CHAPTER FIVE

FROM CLASS STRUGGLE
TO STRUGGLE FOR CLASS

Historians agree that the interwar years served as a lever that pried the children of Jewish immigrants out of the working class. By 1945, when our examination ends, American Jewry was primed to produce its third commercial elite, the "egghead millionaires."[1] But there is little agreement on how Jews achieved middle-class status fully a generation before other groups of the "new" immigration.

The launching platform for Jewish economic ascendancy was the general prosperity of the twenties. The years before the crash of 1929 saw an 11 percent rise in real income and a shortening of the workday. The resulting rise in the general standard of living was based partly on a 40 percent increase in productivity stemming from the development of cheap new sources of power and the further mechanization of production. It also freed Americans, encouraged by the new advertising and the installment plan, to pursue consumerism. A persistent depression in agriculture and 5,174 bank failures between 1921 and 1929 suggested that the prosperity of the twenties was fragile, but for the children of immigrants such forebodings hardly mattered. Their enterprising spirit and their intense striving for place were in consonance with the business ethos of the decade.[2] The parent generation had been proletarian, but in the twenties there occurred a drive for white-collar employment and ultimately for the professions. That development warrants special attention, since it would be in the professions as much as in business that Jews would make their mark.

The paucity of reliable statistics on Jews' economic condition at the outset of the twenties compels us to turn to other sources for clues to their economic mobility. The most noteworthy of these emanates from the far-flung Jewish social service network, which issued periodic reports on family dependency. Between 1915 and 1924 such dependency fell off sharply. The enrollment in orphanages, the number of paupers interred by free burial societies, even the number of juvenile delinquents institutionally maintained declined 50 to 75 percent. In Brooklyn, which by 1920 housed one of the largest Jewish communities in the nation, dependency declined 64 percent.[3] In part the decline reflects the effects of the new workers' compensation law, which compelled the state to assume some responsibility for dependent families. But the prosperity of the twenties, especially the high level of employment, also contributed.

On the higher economic rungs the picture was still more hopeful. Although Jews held almost no ownership or management positions in basic industry, they were well represented among the nation's wealthiest families. Of the 449 people listed in Henry Klein's *Dynamic America and Those Who Own It*, 33 were Jewish. The Guggenheim family, which had made its fortune in copper mining, was one of four richest families in the nation, and Jewish family names, mostly from the prior German Jewish migration, dotted the list of second-rank fortunes in the $20 million range. We shall see later how being closed out of some important areas of the economy compelled Jewish entrepreneurs to pioneer in high-risk areas. Willy-nilly, Jews again assumed their familiar role of "courageous enterprisers" and accrued the special rewards America holds out for pioneers.[4]

It was on the middle rungs of business that Jews found their niche. By 1929, 45 to 50 percent were involved in trade, more frequently as employees than as proprietors. An estimated 15 to 20 percent were involved in small-scale manufacturing and sales, especially clothing, millinary, and furs, printing and stationery, and the manufacture and assembly of simple finished goods like gloves, costume jewelry, cigars, and increasingly, footwear. By 1937 two-thirds of the 34,000 factories and 104,000 wholesale and retail establishments in New York City were owned by Jews, but only a third of their work force was Jewish. A steady stream of Jewish workers became proprietors, usually of small stores or factories. There was also a growing representation in service industries, especially small restaurants, hotels, and laundries.[5] The marked proletarianism of the pre-World War I decades was gradually giving way to occupations able to support a middle-class life. The normal generational sequence was from shop work to owning of a small business and finally to the professions, but that pattern was not always predictable. In the 1920s there was already a hint that the Jews' sojourn in small business would be no more permanent than their stay in the working class. The heartbreak of parents whose sons rejected the family business was a familiar theme in Jewish literature and theater. Increasingly the children aimed for careers in the professions or the arts rather than in business. They became doctors, lawyers, accountants, and dentists. A 1934 survey of 46,600 Jews in thirty-six middle-sized and small cities shows that professionals composed between 7.8 and 12 percent of the Jewish work force. They were especially well represented in medicine.

Professionalization reflected a general upgrading of the Jewish work force. Unlike their mothers, during the twenties and thirties Jewish working women were more likely to be white-collar workers, and this shift applied to men as well. Second-generation Jewish men were more likely to choose sales over tailoring or house painting as a lifetime occupation. A survey of 408 Jewish youths taken in Baltimore in 1940 showed that though only 4.7 percent of the fathers who reached maturity during the twenties could be classified as professional or technical, 13.4 percent of their sons were aspiring for such careers. By the mid-thirties a new Jewish occupational profile had emerged. About 35 to 40 percent of the Jewish work force was in commercial occupations, compared with 13.8 percent of the general population. Commerce overshadowed manufacturing, which drew only 15 to 20 percent, compared with 26.3 percent for the general population.[6]

Most surprising was the speed with which the second generation entered the middle class. Social mobility comparisons are easiest with Italian-Americans, with whom Jews often arrived in the country. The two groups together composed 43 percent of the population of the New York metropolitan area. Jews consistently outpaced Italian-Americans in attaining middle-class rank. In 1925, 13.2 percent of the Jewish work force (down from 15.1 percent in 1905) was classified as white collar, compared with 2.4 percent of Italians. The figures are reversed for unskilled workers. Here 26.8 percent of Italian workers are so designated, compared with 3.6 percent of Jews. By the time Italian-Americans became skilled and semiskilled workers in the thirties and forties, Jews were moving on to managerial and professional positions.

To some extent the same comparison holds with other ethnic groups of the "new" immigration. A survey of Jewish students entering college during the 1960s shows that their parents, who reached adulthood in the thirties and forties, were almost twice as likely to run independent businesses as were non-Jews.[7] Despite considerable job and professional training discrimination, Jews had taken a conspicuous lead. We shall note presently that some were convinced such rapid mobility had a price. They see the virulent anti-Semitism of the Depression partly rooted in conspicuous Jewish success.

The upward surge did not ensure that Jews would continue to dominate in areas of business developed by the preceding generation of German Jewish entrepreneurs. Despite their role in the growth of commercial banking in the early decades of the century, Jewish banks played almost no part in the rapid development of finance during the twenties. When Max Warburg, whose family had helped establish Jewish banking in America, visited the United States in 1920 to renew connections after the disruption of war, he found little of the German Jewish banking nexus left. His cousin Paul Warburg extended credit to the bankrupt Hamburg-American line, but in 1924 Kuhn, Loeb, the Warburg house, turned to the non-Jewish Dillon, Reed and Company to form the American Continental Corporation to extend credit for rebuilding German industry. After the death of Jacob Schiff in 1921, Jewish investors no longer sought to fulfill their capital needs through the Jewish banking "crowd," whose banking houses had in any case lost much of their Jewish character. As early as 1911 Kuhn, Loeb took on a non-Jewish partner, and Goldman, Sachs followed suit in 1915. Lehman Brothers had lost its Jewish family stamp by 1924. Clearly, banking enterprises based on a sectarian organizational principle could no longer keep pace with the complexities of a developing world economy. With the exception of Goldman, Sachs, these Jewish banking houses had made a successful transition to the post–1933 government-regulated banking environment, but they had also become dejudaized in order to gain complete access to the economy. August Belmont and Company was dissolved in 1930, Speyer and Company broke up in 1939, and the Seligman Company also curtailed direct investment activity that year. Unstable conditions triggered by the worldwide depression and government regulation of the banking industry made private commercial banking difficult. With the exception of an investment house established by Carl M. Loeb in 1931, which merged with Rhoades and Company in 1938, only one small Jewish bank was established—the Manufacturers Trust Company of New York, organized in 1925 by Nathan S. Jonas. The breakup of the Jewish banking nexus also indicated that the barriers to Jewish investment capital had come down. But that change was not true of Jews' employment in banking. In 1936 a *Fortune* study revealed that "there are practically no Jewish employees of any kind in the largest commercial banks."[8]

There was a similar decline in an area where one would least expect it—large-scale merchandising, in which Jewish department-store founders had made a name for themselves. In the early years of the century the Jewish merchants' influence in town-site development could scarcely be overestimated. "There is scarcely a village in any state of the union that does not have a 'Jew storekeeper' and his family," noted one observer.[9] But though small-scale merchandising kept pace, especially in specialty products like furniture, jewelry, tobacco, and clothing, Jewish merchant kings rarely participated in the next stage of the development of merchandising—the chain store. Sears, Roebuck, the largest Jewish-owned merchandising enterprise in the nation, fell on bad times during the recession of 1921. Only the timely investment of a portion of Julius Rosenwald's personal fortune kept the business afloat.[10] Established early in the century, Jewish department stores did business primarily in the cities of the East. Filene's, founded in Boston in 1881, was as well known as Macy's, Gimbel's and other Jewish department stores, but it limited its stock to clothing and accessories.

If Jewish entrepreneurs and managers were rarely to be found in basic industry, they did gain important footholds in secondary industries, including the burgeoning automobile spare parts, used car, and private transportation businesses, which came into their own after 1925. John D. Hertz, a Czech Jewish immigrant, founded the Yellow Cab Company and went on to become America's leading car renter. Similarly, though few Jews could be found in the steel industry, the scrap-metal business, capitalized at over $300 million in 1924, was 90 percent Jewish-owned.[11] Jews were also represented in real estate development, construction, printing, shoe and textile manufacturing, hotel keeping, and the entertainment business. Paradoxically, while the percentage of Jews observing dietary laws declined steadily, the advent of the processed food industry triggered an expansion in the kosher food business. By 1934 it boasted a sales volume of $200 million in New York City alone, not including the sale of kosher poultry.[12] If one disregards concerted efforts to restrict Jewish business in certain areas, the best clue to a Jewish presence in a particular aspect of the economy relates to three factors: riskiness, since Jews were pushed or drawn to the more marginal areas; ready access to capital; or conversely, the need to raise little start-up capital.

All three factors played a role in the development of the film industry, which attracted a disproportionate number of Jewish entrepreneurs. The growth of entertainment industries based on images and information began in earnest during the twenties. Commercial radio expanded rapidly after the government ban on private commercial broadcasting was raised in 1919, and Jewish entrepreneurs and capital played a prominent role. But local stations were usually owned by non-Jews.[13]

A similar pattern prevailed in three other areas of the information industry—newspaper and book publishing and advertising. Although some well-known newspapers like the *New York Times* and the *Washington Post* were owned by Jews, the powerful newspaper chains that developed during the twenties and the wire services had little Jewish representation.[14] Jews were also conspicuously absent from the mushrooming advertising business; only six of the two hundred full-service agencies were owned by Jews. Few Jews were employed in non-Jewish agencies, and none at all worked in the most desirable position of accounts manager, where "looking" American was considered crucial. Inevitably some Jews did "pass," which triggered a popular joke: "He used to be Jewish, but he's all right now."[15] In publishing too there were few Jewish firms to be found before 1915. By 1925 there were seven small Jewish-owned quality houses, which included Knopf, Viking, and Simon and Schuster, founded by scions of the German Jewish immigration. Many of the new mass-marketing strategies, including the Little Library and the Book-of-the-Month Club, were initiated by Jewish entrepreneurs.

Of all the industries Jews were drawn to, their presence in the new film business became most conspicuous and ultimately most troublesome. Strangely, the founding Jewish filmmakers were not people interested in the creative arts but the typical small businessmen who proliferated in the Jewish community. Harry Cohn had variously been a cobbler, a trolley-car conductor, and a vaudevillian; Jesse Lasky had once been in the shoe business; Carl Laemmle was a former clothing salesman; Louis Mayer got his start in the junk business; the Warner brothers were once cobblers and bicycle repairmen. Marcus Loew, theater-chain owner, began as a factory worker, while William Fox was a garment cutter and Samuel Goldwyn began as a glovemaker. Most went on to become proprietors of storefront nickelodeons, a street business that attracted hundreds of aspiring Jewish entrepreneurs in the first decade of the century.[16]

By 1907 there were five thousand such nickelodeons nationwide. From the beginning, the moving images on the screen captivated the public.

When after 1927 the development of audio permitted these images to talk and a further improvement in technology, called movietone, eliminated jerky, unsynchronized movements, the American love affair began in earnest. A new, lucrative—but also, because of the peculiar nature of its product, extremely risky business—was born. By the mid-thirties the film industry was capitalized at $2 billion, employed 325,000 people, and could distribute its product to 23,000 movie theaters with a seating capacity of 11,300,000. It was estimated that an average of 115,000,000 Americans attended a movie at least once a week.[17]

In a little over two decades a small group of Jewish entrepreneurs developed a marginal street business into a major new industry based primarily in southern California. "Hollywood" became a code word for glamour. But the rapidity of its development compelled the Jewish moguls to turn to outside sources for capitalization, bringing on the decline of Jewish dominance in the industry. By 1936 only three of the "big eight" studios were still owned by Jews, and Jewish representation in the crucial film distribution end of the business also declined. Jews remained prominent in all phases of the film industry, but actual ownership and control had become diverse.[18]

The film industry was unique because of its imagined power to influence ethical values and life-styles. Such a powerful instrument in the hands of alien Jews sparked fear among the custodians of morals, ensconced primarily in the churches, and led to a move to control it through censorship. Yet the moguls were primarily interested in profits and paid little attention to film's power to shape the mind-set of the public. The best way to make a profit was to offer pure entertainment and to follow public taste rather than trying to fashion it. According to Leonard Goldenson, the goal of the moviemakers was "to anticipate the public mood as best you can."[19] Jewish Hollywood preferred to follow rather than to fashion public taste.

Despite the commercial orientation, after the downturn in business volume in 1921, the fear of untoward Jewish influence in the film industry became a lodestar for anti-Semitism. "Jewish Hollywood" was attacked for the sleazy values it projected. Jews had physical control of the theater, one critic complained, although "they are rather ludicrously unfitted to control the destinies of fine art."[20] The moguls at first tried to counteract the movement for censorship, but they soon concluded that a seal of approval might attract the middle-class audience they sought. In June 1923 Adolph Zukor urged producers to recognize their "peculiar powerful responsibility" to set higher standards for the screen and offered a $10,000 annual prize for the best story produced as a motion picture.²¹ It availed little. By the thirties the attacks on "Jewish Hollywood" had resumed. Joseph Kennedy, Roosevelt's ambassador in London, and Charles Lindbergh, America's most popular folk hero, warned Hollywood to mute its voice on foreign policy issues lest it confirm its advocacy of a Jewish view on intervention.

Many young Jews, seeking an outlet for their creative energies, went to Hollywood, where many were destined to be disappointed by its prevailing commercialism. Nevertheless, the significance of the Jewish impact in the mind-shaping industries was not confined to the business pioneers who played an important role in developing them. It also belongs to the screenwriters and directors who helped develop the "product" that had such an enormous impact on audiences the world over.

Lest I create the impression that all Jews were on their way to middle-class status or even aspired to it, we need to recall that most remained in the work force as wage earners. Many of these workers were employed in "Jewish" industries related to the needle trades, which were part of an ethnic economy comprising a concentration of businesses owned by Jews and employing Jews. We therefore consider next the singular development of the Jewish labor movement, which tried to upgrade living standards by collective action. This was an area where Jews had power, if only over other Jews, and therefore gives the historian an opportunity to determine whether they exercised power responsibly.

In eastern Europe Jews had entered the working class in mass only during the last third of the nineteenth century. Once settled in America, Jews rarely worked in basic industries like steel and automobiles and therefore did not become members of the large industrial unions. They were not the sons of workers, nor would they produce sons who were workers—they were workers more by circumstance than by birth. Their intense working-class consciousness, so much in evidence in the first generation, was as much a product of intellectual rationale, which may have included a cursory knowledge of socialist theory, as of objective circumstances. Jewish workers idealized the working class, but they aspired to rise above it rather than with it. Ironically, while other ethnic workers had largely severed themselves from radical parties and programs and accepted the idea of "bread and butter," nonideological unionism advocated by Samuel Gompers, president of the American Federation of Labor, Jewish workers were more disaffected and radical. Yet they also possessed a strong impetus for self-improvement that suggested they believed their situation was not as hopeless as proclaimed by the radical intellectual labor leaders who tried to convince them to define their lives through class struggle. When in 1921 the New York State supreme court handed down a favorable decision regarding the right of the International Ladies Garment Workers Union to organize and bargain collectively, confidence grew that unionism might after all offer a way to improve their lives. But Jewish workers, especially in the needle trades, looked to their unions for more than merely security: they hoped they would bring a "new day."[22]

Accurate figures on the number of Jewish workers belonging to "Jewish" unions are difficult to come by. The rank and file of the Jewish unions was not necessarily Jewish, and not all Jewish workers were unionized. By the mid-thirties Jewish workers in the garment industry were outnumbered by Italians. In 1933 there may have been as many as 210,000 workers in the unions belonging to the United Hebrew Trades; the bulk were members of the Amalgamated Clothing Workers of America (ACWA) and the ILGWU. An additional 5 percent of the Jewish labor force belonged to unions associated with other trades, construction, printing, or entertainment. During the twenties, resistance by management and the bitter political strife within the unions had brought membership down to a lower number. The figure of slightly less than half a million unionized workers was reached only during the New Deal period.

The Jewish labor unions had from their inception been volatile: members were individualistic and difficult to control. Jewish workers were quick to strike but had little tenacity or discipline. Communal support during strikes was difficult to mobilize because Jewish unions had distanced themselves from central institutions like the synagogue and the Jewish defense organizations and were only weakly linked to the national organized labor movement. Yet they did wring improvements for their members from resistant employers who were also Jewish and whose profit margins were usually low. A series of successful strikes in the needle trades between 1918 and 1921 shortened the workweek to forty-four hours and brought improvements in working conditions. In some cases the perennial problem of an uneven flow of work, causing a slack season, was mitigated by guaranteeing workers at least forty-one weeks of work a year. After the first round of strikes in 1920, Secretary of Commerce Herbert Hoover was called on to try to bring peace to the industry. But the temptation to use the unions to realize ideological goals tended to overshadow "bread and butter" issues and resulted in perpetual agitation.

After World War I the strategy of the world communist movement called for using the Jewish unions and related fraternal orders, like the Workmen's Circle, as instruments to penetrate the American labor movement and bring it into the communist fold. Capitalizing on the generally favorable view Jewish workers still had of the Russian Revolution, the communist organizers employed all kinds of tactics. "Fainting brigades" were used to disrupt "right wing" speeches, and "spit brigades" unnerved rank-and-file members who had not yet joined the communist side.[23] The struggle for control of the unions kept them in constant turmoil.

By 1924 a militant communist group, probably numbering no more than 1,500 but strengthened by a greater number of sympathizers, had gained control of three ILGWU locals, 1, 9, and 22, and were also strong in the waistmakers' union, local 25, which boasted a long tradition of radicalism. In July 1926, already affected by the impending Lovestonite-Fosterite split, the communist group, against the advice of more experienced leaders, called its 50,000 members out of the shops. Before the strike was settled the ILGWU, a kingpin of the Jewish labor movement, was in shambles. Both sides resorted to the use of thugs, which during an earlier troubled period had gained a foothold in the garment industry. In dire fear of being ideologically outflanked on the left and subject to the devastating charge of "right-wing opportunism," the communist leaders rejected a settlement proposal made by the Governor's Advisory Commission in the eighth week of the strike. Both sides dug in. Pressure on the owners to settle was minimal, since the season had passed. In December, after the unions were exhausted, David Dubinsky, manager of the staunchly anticommunist cutters' local 10, finally dissolved the communist-dominated Joint Board that had so mismanaged the strike. It was later revealed that the communist faction had misused $800,000 of the security fund. After twenty-six weeks and a cost of $3.5 million, the unions were compelled to settle virtually on the terms offered at the outset. It was a bitter lesson for the Jewish workers.

The communist faction was broken, but so too was the ILGWU. The union's members were demoralized, its treasury was depleted, its leverage in the industry was gone. The gangsterism and racketeering the "civil war" had left in its wake were widespread and would not be brought under control until the thirties, when government prosecutors lent a hand. Slowly the locals were reorganized and the mass of workers returned to a free union. Many of the most skillful strategists associated with the communists rejoined the ILGWU; Charles S. Zimmerman ultimately accepted the post of vice president under David Dubinsky. Victory eluded the communists by a hair's breadth. They might easily have carried the day had they not been compelled to comply with the strategy of a distant Moscow leadership unfamiliar with American conditions. But the Communist party line changed again in 1928, and after the threat subsided the needle trade unions could get on with the business of ameliorating conditions for their members rather than fighting for the more remote realization of a classless society. The internal threat weakened in the nick of time, since the effects of the depression were already creating a dire situation in the industry.[24]

During the thirties the unions drew closer to the Jewish community, which they had formerly ignored. In 1934 they helped establish the Jewish Labor Committee to counteract the strident anti-Semitism of the thirties and the Nazi threat, and many European labor leaders owe their lives to its rescue efforts.[25] Its anti-Zionist stance, an inheritance of its socialist-Bundist roots, was also abandoned, and close links were established to the Labor Zionist Mapai party in Palestine and to its labor federation, the Histadrut. But that concern for the welfare of the Jewish community became manifest only when the Jewish membership of the garment unions had fallen below 50 percent and the industry itelf was being dispersed from its New York locale.

For our purposes it is important to understand the impact these unions had on the Jewish ethnic economy. As early as the first decade of the century, some labor leaders realized that much of the "sweatshop" situation was caused by the fragmented character of the garment industry, which pitted contractor against worker and allowed for such a narrow margin of profit that neither could hope to thrive. The key to improved working conditions lay in restructuring the garment industry so that the numerous small subcontractors did not have to assume all the responsibility for higher wages and better working conditions. To realize that goal, the more profitable jobbers and wholesale segments of the needle trades, whose labor costs were low, had to be convinced to share the cost of better wages and working conditions. The unions fought for a guaranteed period of work, a cut in the workweek to forty hours, an increase in the minimum wage, and industry-financed unemployment insurance. A few years later the ILGWU's program for improving the conditions of labor found its way into the New Deal labor program. It became substantially the substance of the Wagner Act—the so-called Magna Carta for labor—passed in 1935.

During the twenties the unions helped modernize the clothing industry. A plan to streamline production was first inititated by the ILGWU in Cleveland in 1919. In 1941, encouraged by the need to increase production, the union submitted a program for industrywide planning and modernization that included minimum standards of managerial efficiency. The union leaders came to realize that workers ultimately bore the cost of the widespread inefficiency in the industry. The obligation to run the shops efficiently was incorporated into the union contracts, and the ILGWU established a management-engineering department that the manufacturers could consult. For the first time, the union would provide industrial engineers to help solve technological and managerial problems. It established reasonable prices and even conducted the despised time-motion studies to improve labor efficiency. The ACWA established a similar "stabilization" program. The unions became deeply involved in production, and in many cases their cooperation was indispensable for solving production problems. In certain cases the union, rather than standing by while a shop went bankrupt and its members became unemployed, extended credit to save the business and union funds were also used to help employers promote the market. Stimulated by military contracts, wages and work conditions in the industry improved steadily during World War II.

Finally, as conditions in the garment industry became more stable and costly strikes became a thing of the past, the union coffers filled. The ILGWU became one of the wealthiest unions in the nation and searched for ways to use its money to realize its traditional humanitarian goals. One of its major aspirations was to meet the housing needs of its members and of friends of labor by subsidizing cooperative housing. In 1927 the ACWA underwrote the building of the first housing cooperative, in the Van Cortland section of the Bronx. Soon the typographical and kosher butcher unions followed suit. Ultimately Jewish fraternal orders of all political stripes became organizers and sponsors of housing cooperatives. The Jewish unions extended credit for these projects, and the ILGWU entered the cooperative housing field directly and built thousands of affordable apartments for the working people of the city. These investments in the "not for profit" sector not only stimulated the construction industry but did much to support the economy of the city.

The Jewish labor movement marked a transitional phase of the inter-war Jewish experience. By the end of the war the leadership of the unions was still Jewish, but the Jewish rank and file had either retired or moved on to other endeavors. But in their time the impact of the Jewish unions on the ethnic economy was matched only by their role in shaping a unique American Jewish political culture. In retrospect the major problem was to find a way to reconcile their idealism, rooted in socialist ideology, with the practical needs of an industry compelled to operate in a capitalist economy. The unions raised the standard of living of Jewish wage earners, keeping wages on a par with those in heavy industry. But Jewish unionists seemed to have to fight harder merely to keep up. That condition was inherent in the nature of the garment industry, which was composed largely of marginal, under-capitalized units. There seems little doubt that working conditions would have been much worse without the unions. Yet with all the ameliorative programs, better pay, shorter hours, pensions, unemployment insurance, and paid vacations, Jewish workers seemed little better off than those belonging to less militant unions or to no unions at all. They had to run merely to keep up.

Then what was the attraction of the union movement? It may have been the psychic income it offered. It uplifted workers who resisted becoming mere cogs in the production process. Why strike when victory was hopeless? Because at that brave moment "seventy thousand zeros became 70,000 fighters," full of courage and purpose.[26] Like so much in American Jewish history that seems otherwise inexplicable, the struggle of Jewish unionists may have had as much to do with a search for transcendence as with improving their working lives.

Most distinctive about the Jewish economic profile of the twenties was its "curious . . . distribution in particular squares of the checkerboard,"[27] reflected in the peculiar path Jews followed to the middle class. Another puzzle is why Jews were able to arrive so much faster than other immigrants.

There was a historical precedent for the intense and ultimately successful Jewish commercial activity of the twenties. During the colonial and early national periods, a Jewry dominated by a Sephardic elite had prospered through ocean commerce, developing new areas of the economy such as the fur trade, capitalizing on traditional Jewish crafts such as soap manufacture, and selling new products such as spermaceti oil, which replaced the more expensive tallow for making candles. In their turn the German Jews who were part of the great nineteenth-century migration developed a commercial elite that evolved primarily from merchandising and pioneering in new areas such as the Great Lakes fishing industry, shoe manufacturing, and the export of wheat and beef and culminated in the Jewish commercial banking nexus popularly known as "Our Crowd."[28]

It has been suggested that the third commercial surge by the descendants of eastern European Jews was based partly on a "demonstration effect." The children of the eastern European immigrants, the argument runs, had before them the model of success and sometimes an entrée to the actual businesses of the German and Sephardic Jews who came before them. In the garment industry and many merchandising areas, second-generation Jews simply crossed an ethnic bridge to establish themselves.[29] But it is difficult to determine whether business decisions were affected by such an ethnic consciousness. Not only were the two groups removed from each other and often antagonistic, but the national economy in which the second generation would play its role had undergone radical changes. "Shoestring capitalism," the ability to establish a small business with almost no capital—a familiar feat for Jewish entrepreneurs—had become more difficult in the incorporated economy of the twenties. On the other hand, the new economy required a better-educated work force and people with professional skills to replace the "jack of all trades." Specialization would be the sine qua non of the emerging economy. Strategies for mobility employed by the second generation, to the extent that they existed at all, were shaped by these new needs. The route to success could sometimes be shortened by a direct ethnic connection, but more important, ethnicity had a long-range impact, especially when it involved the transfer of capital.

The drive for achievement and success, the "dirty little secret" of American culture, became a reality for the ambitious Jews of the second generation.[30] Speculation concerning the rapid mobility of Jews in modernizing societies is not confined to American Jewry. Werner Sombart's thesis, which together with the work of Karl Marx, laid the foundation for virulent anti-Semitism based on antagonism to the capitalist system, attributed the very origins of capitalism to the Jews, especially in North America,[31] theorizing that it was based on an inherent "Levantine" instinct. Indeed, Jewish economic life within the Russian Pale was predisposed toward small business dealings among artisans. A disproportionate Jewish representation in trade also holds for the economies of western Europe during the nineteenth century: 90 percent of the Jews of rural Bavaria, for example, were involved in small trade before World War I, and many more examples of Jewish middleman roles could be cited.[32] But for the second generation in America the case is not so clear-cut. Researchers cannot agree on whether Jewish mobility was realized through small business or formal education or a combination of both.

Some social scientists also attribute the Jewish penchant for business enterprise to a series of historical constraints rather than to inherent cultural characteristics. These range from the prohibition against owning land to a "heritage equipment restraint" that traces the enterprising spirit to the socializing and education within the Jewish family. There was also a "latecomer constraint" that compelled Jews to pioneer in undeveloped areas of the economy, since they often were allowed to become active in business only after many of the most desirable areas had already been developed.[33] The Jewish inclination for risk taking in new areas has also been attributed to a religious culture that sets high value on individuals' taking full responsibility for their lives. Operating in the least developed and structured areas allows greater opportunities for control: there are few rules on the frontier.[34] Such a taste for risk taking might also be ascribed to prohibitions against Jews, who have often been restricted in the management of more established industries. In the interwar years Jews rarely could be found in the management tier of heavy industry, the railroads, the automobile, or the new petrochemicals industry. Jewish entrepreneurs usually began as shoestring capitalists practicing free enterprise in the riskiest areas of the economy. That was certainly the case in the film industry. The willingness to take risks is central to the entrepreneurial spirit, but we cannot automatically assume that Jews welcomed risk. They had little choice. Did Jews make occupational choices, such as small business and the independent professions, to better control their working lives? Or did the control stem from the choices they were compelled to make? In either case, the challenge produced an autonomous economic agent better able to manage adversity.

I have saved for last a frequently cited reason for Jewish achievement in business: the priority Jewish culture gives to education and study. Briefly stated, that rationale sees in the culture of *lernen*—close study of texts—a high level of abstraction and decoding, honing skills that can be applied in modern industrial societies. The Jewish preference for a career in the law, according to the theory, is rooted in the study of Talmud, which is essentially a law text. But aside from its self-serving cast, even if one could show that such values were embedded in the traditional culture, there would remain the problem of showing how secularizing Jews retained sufficient knowledge of that culture for it to shape their economic activity. Surely the static education of the heder of eastern Europe, where learning was based on rote memorization, was no more suitable for conversion to modernity than learning the Catholic catechism. If the religious culture had an effect at all, it would be in the development of specialized businesses, such as kosher foods or the manufacture and sale of religious items. Undoubtedly a portion of the Jewish ethnic economy was based on filling this special need.

If cultural factors cannot by themselves explain the successful Jewish drive to attain middle-class status, then perhaps the answer can be found in the objective conditions in which the second generation lived their economic lives. Provided poverty and exclusion are not so extreme as to erode the will to achieve, "have-not" groups in America usually harbor the desire to raise themselves. Jews were precisely such a group, poor and having experienced a wave of exclusionary anti-Semitism, but hardly defeated. "I had no very acute sense of being deprived, or any notion that I was the victim of social injustice," writes Irving Howe of his youth in the thirties.[35] The same seeming immunity from the hard external conditions of life was true for most young Jews growing up during this period. A protective family mantle seemed able to shield them from the worst effects of poverty and exclusion even while knowledge of such obstacles sharpened the appetite for achievement. We have already noted the militant Jewish reaction to the attempt by elite educational institutions to limit Jewish enrollment. Jewish students simply worked harder to attain their goals. In business, too, discrimination could release enormous new energies to overcome the hurdles it imposed. An extra measure of effort was most manifest among those preparing for the professions, where competition for place was keen. Between 1925 and 1930, when only one out of every thirteeen Jewish applicants to medical school was accepted, a struggle for place developed among Jewish students. Jewish aspirants to a career in medicine understood that they had to be better. For those preparing for careers in law, competition was less keen; the comparative cheapness and ease of entering law school attracted a larger, less affluent pool of Jewish applicants. "Jewish boys [go] into law," according to testimony presented before the New York State court of appeals hearings, "because it is the easiest and cheapest profession they can enter."[36] The resulting overcrowding led the legal establishment to search for a way

Louis Marshall (1856–1929), president of the American Jewish Committee, who dominated Jewish organizational life during the first third of the twentieth century.

Cyrus Adler (1863–1940), president of the American Jewish Commmittee and the Jewish Theological Seminary, was the most prominent Jewish leader after Louis Marshall.

Rabbi Stephen S. Wise
(1874–1949), principal
American spokesman for
Zionism during the
interwar period, founded
the American and World
Jewish Congresses.

The faction of Justice Louis
D. Brandeis (1856–1941)
lost its leadership of the
Zionist movement in 1921,
but he continued to exercise
behind-the-scenes influence
in Zionist and general
Jewish affairs.

As a brilliant mathematician, humanist, and victim of Nazism, Albert Einstein (1880–1955) had enormous stature among American Jews.

Professor Morris R. Cohen (1887-1947) was a cultural hero to the second-generation Jewish students attending his philosophy classes at City College of New York.

An evening class for immigrants, the Irene Kauffman settlement house, September 1921.

Baltimore Hebrew Congregation, Madison Avenue, c. 1930.

"Tom Thumb wedding" at Baltimore Hebrew Congregation, 1923.

Yiddish theater poster for David Pinsky's *The Dumb Messiah*, Jewish Art Theater, 1918.

Al Jolson as a cantor chanting the Kol Nidre prayer in *The Jazz Singer*, 1927.

Director Anatole Citvar discussing a scene with Edward G. Robinson at Warner Brothers studio in 1938.

This New York City building at Twenty-first Street and Fifth Avenue was filled with Jewish-owned clothing companies.

Abe Sherman's newsstand, Battle Monument Square, Baltimore, 1924.

Dan's Confectionery, Light Street, Baltimore, c. 1939.

Sunshine Cleaners, Charles Street, Baltimore, 1926.

This Store is
AUTHORIZED
....to Accept
RELIEF
TICKETS

מיר נעהמען
רעליף טיקעטס

Sign in a Depression-era Jewish neighborhood grocery store.

Sussman and Lev Deli, Baltimore, 1940

A favorite theme of anti-Semitic propaganda during the interwar years — that Roosevelt was controlled by his Jewish advisers determined to bring the nation into war.

An indication of continuing anti-Semitism in the interwar period: uniformed members of the German-American Bund march at a Madison Square Garden "Americanization" rally in celebration of Washington's birthday, 21 February 1939.

Herbert Lehman on 31 December 1938 taking the oath of office for a third term as governor of New York administered by his brother, Judge Irving Lehman.

Mrs. Julius Ochs Adler, chair of the Defense Recreation Committee, selling a ticket to composer Irving Berlin for the 1942 Army-Giants football game.

A 1947 U.S. postage stamp of the four chaplains who went down with the *Dorchester* in February 1943—their story served to counteract wartime anti-Semitic propaganda.

HELP RESCUE THROUGH EMIGRATION **HELP**

שיפֿן מיט גערעטעװעטע דורך האַאָס

קומען צו אונזערע ברעגנן!

העלפֿט זײ קומען

װײזט אײער דערבאַרמונג הײנט

העלפֿט האַאָס העלפֿט

אין דער הײליגער רעטונגס אַרבעט

שנדר'ט פֿאָר האַאָס

CONTRIBUTE TO HIAS

HEBREW SHELTERING and IMMIGRANT AID SOCIETY

10 TREMONT STREET, BOSTON, MASS.

During the Holocaust years, HIAS, the oldest of the immigration agencies, appealed for money to sustain its rescue of Jewish refugees.

Courtesy of the American Jewish Historical Society

An early anti-Nazi protest rally held at Madison Square Garden (27 March 1933).

Courtesy of the American Jewish Historical Society

Protests against the British White Paper of 1939, which closed the doors of Palestine to Jewish immigration at the height of the refugee crisis.

Jewish war hero Sgt. Meyer Levin in his B-17 bombadier's seat.

General Eisenhower viewing the carnage in a concentration camp in 1945.

to restrict Jews. The strategy it hit upon was to raise educational requirements to prevent law school mills from churning out "unqualified" lawyers.
But behind this change was the familiar distaste for "pushy" Jews who, it
was claimed, lacked honor and displayed a tendency for unethical legal
practices. In Philadelphia and other cities, the Protestant-dominated legal
establishment used various devices—including preceptorships and grand-
father clauses that required every applicant for the bar to be descended from
a native-born American—to dam the flood of Jewish lawyers. Blocked from
joining large, established law firms, these law school graduates became
"solo practitioners," barely able to earn a living. By 1934 the law had
become for Jews "a dignified road to starvation." But a small group did
adjust their careers to perceived opportunity and lowered their sights. They
persisted in private practice, sought government employment, or became
teachers.[37]

Sometimes anti-Semitism could bring an unforeseen boon. To ensure
security, Jewish merchants frequently bought the downtown buildings in
which their stores were located. It often developed into the best investment
they made, since downtown real estate rose in value after World War II. But
more often it put a damper on Jewish commercial activity. Jews may have
moved out of the lower ranks earlier than other ethnics, but their climb to
the next rung of the ladder was blocked. Few Jews could be found on the
boards of large corporations, banks, or insurance companies even when
organizations, such as Sears, Roebuck, the National Broadcasting Company and Columbia Broadcasting System, American Smelting and Refining, and Kennicott Copper had been founded by Jews. At the same time, a
special price was exacted for being too successful in business. Some of the
hostility between Jews and Italian-Americans in the thirties stemmed from
friction in the garment industry, where Italians remained workers while
Jews climbed to management or ownership.[38]

Much has also been claimed for Jewishness itself as offering certain
advantages, especially in the ethnic economy. There was sometimes an
ethnic connection that enhanced entrance into a particular business. In the
nineteenth century the German Jewish banking nexus depended for investment capital and banking intelligence on Jewish banking houses in Germany, France, and England. I have noted that an ethnic bridge gave eastern
European Jews access to the garment trade, which in the nineteenth century was dominated by German Jews. Jewish capital from the East Coast
helped Jewish merchants establish themselves in San Francisco and other

western cities. The same ethnic bridge could lead to ownership of small businesses founded by German Jews or earlier-arrived eastern European Jews, which were sold or otherwise transferred to newcomers. The Jewish press was filled with advertisements placed by people wanting to sell or buy businesses.

But the most important Jewish asset was the credit lines that permitted capital to be transferred from one generation to another and from one group to another within the community. Such internal credit lines, developed partly in response to R. G. Dun's effort to deny established sources of credit to Jewish entrepreneurs, helped circumvent the need to raise capital from scratch. Before 1925 only one bank in all of New England and one in the Middle Atlantic extended credit to Jews, and 85 percent of the Jewish population was in any case too poor in collateral to qualify for bank loans.[39]

By 1927 there were in existence 509 loan societies, 83 percent of them affiliated with religious congregations. In addition, 2,367 mutual benefit societies also extended small no-interest loans. The Hebrew Free Loan Society was the most active. Out of a fund totaling a quarter of a million dollars, it lent over a million dollars in interest-free loans for the fiscal year 1922–23, and a total of about $15 million to 400,000 borrowers over a thirty-year period. The loans were small and of very short duration, and losses were minimal. The fund's purpose was to tide clients over temporary emergencies and help them get established in self-supporting employment, either in small businesses or through training or education.

Jews also used the existing credit unions, which, though nonsectarian, were often managed by Jewish directors. In 1927 Boston had 139 credit unions, 75 percent of them managed by Jews. Strangely enough, the societies made loans to all who applied. In 1942, 22 percent of the loans were made to non-Jews.[40] Supplementing the credit unions were the *aktsiyes,* a term derived from the German *Aktiengesellschaft* (joint-stock company). These were private credit agencies not subject to government regulation. It was estimated that by 1930 the *aktsiyes* had disbursed $50 million in loans. Credit unions could spring up anywhere, from synagogues to landsmanshaftn. Frequently wealthier German Jews would serve on the boards of directors while credit-needy descendants of eastern Jews were the applicants. The free-loan societies thus served as a bridge to transfer capital from one community subgroup to another. Undoubtedly these formal credit agencies were overshadowed by credit given within the extended Jewish family, but the crucial role of family circles and cousins' clubs in making capital available to family members cannot be documented.

By 1941 the credit unions alone had assets of $322 million, but though most survived the Depression, their days were numbered. Sensing that there was business to be done among ethnics, the savings banks, now separated from commercial banks, established personal loan departments that the free loan societies could not compete with. Banks were preferable because they could make larger loans over longer periods, but in their day the loan societies, *aktsiyes*, and credit unions were important in helping Jews establish themselves in business and improve their skills. They were part of a cohesive "ethnic economy" that filled a credit vacuum created by the established banks' reluctance to extend credit to Jews.[41]

New research indicates that before World War I formal education was not greatly relevant to occupational succcess. The German Jewish immigrants did not give academic training particularly high priority. Contrary to what is popularly assumed, first-generation eastern European immigrant Jews tended to have as high a school dropout rate as other immigrants, since the educational system was not geared to transmit needed skills.[42] But in the consolidated economy of the post–World War I years, when the opportunity to pioneer in new areas diminished, education and all forms of skill enhancement joined the tradition of small business as a path to the middle class. Whereas the over 70,000 Jewish immigrants who arrived between 1921 and 1927 were as often as not compelled to start at the bottom of the economic ladder, the children of earlier arrivals often could aspire to the professions through education.

Formal education and certification, as a mobility instrument, developed fully during the twenties. We have seen how the hunger for formal education accounted for the "invasion" of universities in the vicinity of Jewish population centers. In 1917 Jews' college enrollment in the New York metropolitan area was already far above their proportion of the population. It reached 73 percent at CCNY.[43] Jewish students were attending high school longer and were more likely to graduate. The higher the educational level, the more disproportionate the Jewish presence. The value of formal education became a Jewish immigrant folk ethic touted by parents and promoted by the Jewish press and by word of mouth. When a Jewish student at DeWitt Clinton High School attained the highest score on the state scholarship examination, the *American Hebrew* proudly editorialized that "it is from the ranks of these conspicuously bright students that our future

Einsteins, Bergsons, Michelsons, Loebs and Plotzes . . . will come."[44] That was more an aspiration than a prediction, yet when 80 percent of New York's 310 Regents scholarship winners in 1921 were Jewish, one can assume that achievement measured by academic performance reflected a cherished Jewish cultural value, supported not only by the tradition of "learning" but also by the prospect of reward. That reward was especially attainable for those who could convert their facility for formal academic study into a professional career. But there were also income and status rewards for less conspicuous forms of self-enhancement. Entering the professions was one part of a process that upgraded the entire Jewish work force. The lowliest finisher in the garment industry aspired to become a cutter; the salesman, a sales manager; and the clerk, a bookkeeper. The eastern European Jews' ascendency was more difficult to negotiate than that of their German Jewish predecessors, since they were compelled to start lower on the economic ladder, often in low-paid manual work, and the basic requisites for social mobility had first to be established.

Gender differences in occupational patterns in the second generation were marked. Investment in education or specialized vocational training was far more common for a son than for a daughter. The customary pattern was for boys from poor families to leave school at the age of fourteen and then complete high school at night. Formerly that would have been the end of their education, but even for them the pressure for schooling had risen by the twenties. For women the preferred pattern was to enroll in a six-month business course after graduating from public school in order to learn stenography and typing. Attaining a position as a bookkeeper directly upon graduating from high school was even better if a family could manage it. Both were considered good jobs for women, which improved their prospects for marriage. That goal continued to receive the highest priority. Predictably, the earliest thrust toward the professions was limited largely to men.

A trickle of Jews had entered the professions during the first generation; they became neighborhood doctors, dentists, and pharmacists, and in a few cases they rose to more exalted stations. But the category "professional" did not fully come into its own until after World War I, when certification procedures and educational requirements were formalized. In the legal profession bar associations raised requirements as part of a restrictive strategy to limit the number of Jews.[45] Quotas for Jewish candidates for medical school had the same objective.

But restriction did little to dampen the drive to enter the professions, and Jews continued to do so in disproportionate numbers. By the mid-thirties 50 percent of the applicants to medical schools were Jewish. One survey based on thirty-six middle-sized and small cities in 1934 shows that the number of Jews in the professional category varied from 7.4 to 12 percent, with considerable variation from city to city. In Cleveland, where 8 percent of the population was Jewish in 1938, 21 percent of the physicians, 18 percent of the dentists, and 23 percent of the lawyers were Jews. In smaller cities like Buffalo, Stamford, and Trenton, the percentages were even greater.[46] A study of 106 educational institutions near Jewish population centers, undertaken by the Bureau of Jewish Social Research during the 1918–19 academic year, showed that Jews were far outpacing other groups in preparing for the professions. Though they were only 3.22 percent of the general population, they composed 10.7 percent of all students taking professional and vocational courses, and 85 percent of them were preparing for careers in medicine, engineering, law, or dentistry. The preference, though not necessarily the enrollment figures, was in that order. Dentistry and pharmacy served as substitutes for applicants who were denied acceptance to medical school. In the Jewish commmunity D.D.S. was jokingly spelled out as "disappointed doctor or surgeon."[47]

A massive alteration of the American Jewish occupational profile began in the twenties. When it was completed three decades later, American Jewry would be the most firmly middle-class ethnic group in the nation. By 1930 the majority of the Jewish work force had become white collar. In 1950, 15 percent of the Jewish work force fell under the heading of professional and technical, and by 1970 that figure stood at 30 percent. The rapid changes took a little getting used to. A Jew was supposed to do well in trade, observed the writer John Erskine, "but in America he is distinguishing himself more and more in the professions." He predicted that the "Nordics" would go into public affairs while the Jews would "pursue the things of the mind."[48]

The change in American Jewry's class structure is crucial to understanding its reaction to the Holocaust. Professionalization and general skill enhancement entailed more than a change in job description and economic status. They meant a profound shift in mind-set in which self-actualization tended to be valued above group identity or religious belief. Loyalty and commitment to profession received the highest priority. Indeed, professionalization seemed to require such a priority to be realized. Social mobility was thus accompanied by a dilution of ethnic identity as part of the trade-off for gaining access and acceptance. It was an outlook that emphasized individual rather than communal realization of goals and therefore weakened the cohesiveness of American Jewry, lessening its ability to respond collectively to the crisis of the thirties.

Our examination would be incomplete without considering the event that had the most profound impact during these decades—the Great Depression. It acted like a storm, bending a trend here, delaying mobility there, and generally upsetting the mental state of Jews as it did that of all Americans. Had it not occurred, American Jewry would have undoubtedly established itself in the middle class earlier. But it would also have missed a testing process that deepened its commitment to social welfare.

Although they were fully reported in the English and Yiddish press, few Jews linked the happenings on Wall Street in October 1929 to their own working lives. But more affluent German Jews and earlier-arrived eastern European Jews who had become involved in stock market speculation were not immune from the effects of the crash. Writing to his daughter, Cyrus Adler related that a friend had told him that "at Lehman's everybody was saying oi, oi, oi, so he got tired of it and went over to Morgan's where young Morgan and young Lamont were saying the same thing with an American accent."[49] For most Jews the full impact of the economic collapse did not become apparent until 1930. After that year unemployment doubled virtually every year. By 1932 it stood at over 12,000,000—25 percent of the work force. Many more were underemployed. Adler now spoke of the effect the sudden reversal of fortune had on once wealthy men: "Men seem to think that the ground is crumbling under their feet," he observed; "it is as though the nerves of our people here have failed them."[50] For 400,000 Jewish bank depositors in New York, the full meaning of the crisis may have been fathomed only after the failure of the Bank of the United States, established with such pride in 1913. Despite its official-sounding name, it was a Jewish-owned enterprise with headquarters on Delancey Street in New York. Its failure and the indictment of its officers shook the confidence of Lower East Side Jewish wage earners.

The Depression brought with it cases of desperate poverty among Jews, duly recorded by the welfare agencies. A Jewish divorcée in Los Angeles, with two children, was discoverd on the edge of starvation. She would not swallow her pride and ask a welfare agency for help. A destitute Jewish family in Omaha was discovered suffering from malnutrition, too weak to move. These were usually families separated or deserted, in desperate straits, and too proud to turn to the Jewish community for help. The worst cases occurred where no support structure or extended family existed to offer relief. Such cases were probably less common among Jews, where family closeness remained a cherished value.

For Jews the psychological effects of loss of the American dream may have been more painful than for less driven groups. The Depression distorted the academic atmosphere of New York's city colleges, whose student bodies had become overwhelmingly Jewish. Students still able to attend faced uncertainty concerning their futures. Many were compelled to abandon their education to help support their families. The character of student protests, which had been primarily pacifist in the twenties, changed as more students became convinced that capitalism had reached its final crisis. Unable to pay their bills or to compete with chain stores for the dwindling number of customers, the merchant fathers of these students joined the growing pool of the unemployed, as did salesmen and other white-collar employees. Since Jews were concentrated in the sale of luxury goods— jewelry, furs, amusement, tobacco, and furniture—they were the first to feel the economic contraction. Between 1929 and 1933, the 2,855 largely Jewish-owned fur-goods firms were reduced to 1,463, and jewelry stores dropped to half their number.[51]

More accustomed to the vagaries of the business cycle, which brought slack seasons and periodic unemployment, Jewish garment workers may at first have seen the Depression as more of the same. They did not conceive of their worsened condition as a personal failure. But to those who had begun to climb the ladder of success and now found themselves destitute after years of hard work, the readjustment of life goals could be painful and sometimes led to emotional breakdown. For those resilient enough, part-time employment—formerly frowned on—was eagerly sought. Unable to practice their professions, doctors and lawyers drove taxicabs. If they were lucky they could retrain themselves as teachers or land jobs in the municipal, state, or federal civil service. Earning certification as a teacher was not easy, since examinations were used to weed out candidates with real or imagined imperfections. In some cases that included minor accents, which many Jewish candidates were convinced were used as an excuse to deny them positions. But once they earned a license teachers were in an enviable position. They had steady work at good pay, something few possessed. "We were considered rich because the high school teachers were making seven fifty a day," one successful candidate observed, and therefore "the brightest people became teachers."[52]

Other newly minted independent professionals were not so fortunate. For doctors, lawyers, dentists, and accountants, earning a livelihood often became a problem. Medical and dental care were not considered necessities and were the first thing to be cut out of the family budget. Having mastered all the hurdles and received his license, a starting Jewish doctor still had to set himself up in practice, an expense that required going deeper into debt for an uncertain income. That uncertainty also stemmed from the reluctance of Jewish doctors to practice in small towns, where income was lower and the possibility of anti-Semitism had to be taken into account. They congregated in big and middle-sized cities, where they competed fiercely with each other for the limited number of patients still able to afford their services. Jewish students continued to flood into law, which, after engineering, was the hardest hit of the professions. As late as the 1935 academic year, 9,500 (25 percent) of the 38,000 students preparing for the law were Jewish.[53] Jewish aspirants negotiated the hurdles placed in their way only to discover there was little opportunity to earn a living. They had almost no hope of gaining a position in an established law firm, no matter how good their records. The average income for a lawyer in 1933 was less than $3,000, and one-third earned less than $2,000, hardly sufficient to support a family. In 1934, 1,500 lawyers took the pauper's oath in New York City in order to qualify for Works Progress Administration (WPA) employment. Some ultimately settled for positions in the government agencies of the expanding welfare state, where they were especially attracted to the new field of labor law. Others joined the not-for-profit sector, becoming legal counsels for unions, social work agencies, and civil rights organizations. But these were the fortunate few. An aspiring Jewish lawyer might have understood that the Depression was not a conspiracy against him personally, but restriction based on his religion could not easily be rationalized. It left an invisible scar.[54]

The general impact of the Depression was observed first by the community's welfare and fraternal agencies. A nationwide survey of thirty Jewish welfare agencies showed a 42.8 percent increase in relief recipients during the first nine months of 1931. In Baltimore and Minneapolis the rise in requests for assistance was over 75 percent. In Philadelphia the strain on the local federation was so great that by 1930 it had incurred a deficit of $320,000. Only a timely loan from the New York Federation staved off disaster. In Chicago, where by 1932 over 50,000 Jews were unemployed, there was a 200 percent increase in requests for welfare from Jewish agencies.[55] Unable to pay their dues, over 4,000 members of Workmen's Circle dropped their enrollment and benefits, so that by 1933 membership declined to its 1918 level and a special fund had to be established to tide the chapters over the crisis.[56]

One of the positive effects of the Depression was that it compelled Jewish social welfare and cultural agencies that depended on private philanthropy to consolidate their fund-raising efforts. The trend toward forming community federations accelerated during the crisis. Of the 145 Jewish federations in existence in 1936, 48 were established after 1931. In Philadelphia the federation joined parallel Protestant and nonsectarian groups in a joint campaign that laid the foundation for the United Way. Predictably, the boom in building synagogues, hospitals, and centers that had been a hallmark of the twenties came to a halt, often leaving individual congregations and local federations with mortgage payments they could no longer meet. In Boston, where the federation movement began in 1895, overbuilding of synagogues and hospitals threatened bankruptcy.[57]

The decline in fund-raising also heightened political tensions within the community, especially between Zionists and anti-Zionists. The portion of federation funds earmarked for overseas relief had to be severely curtailed as consolidated campaigns failed to meet their goals. Still reeling from the need for extra funds caused by the Arab riots of 1929 in Palestine, Zionists found their fund-raising drastically curtailed by the Depression. Bemoaning the "ignominious failure" of the still well-to-do Jews to put the Allied campaign of 1930 over the top, one Zionist observer decried the distribution formula that gave so little to the pioneers in Palestine.[58]

The federations, which during the twenties had used most of their resources for immigrant resettlement and adjustment, turned to relief of those in need after the economic collapse. But like all voluntary welfare agencies, they discovered that the problem was beyond their means and turned to the federal government for succor. The Depression thus undermined the self-imposed obligation, assumed by the first Jewish settlers after their landing in New Amsterdam, always to "take care of their own." The new, less Jewishly conscious social service professionals looked on the obligation as a holdover from earlier days that could no longer be justified. "We must have the courage to repudiate the alleged debt to Peter Stuyvesant," counseled one agency head who sought federal relief funds. By 1934,

70 to 90 percent of dependent Jewish families had been switched to public relief rolls.[59]

The economic crisis may have disrupted the Jewish drive to attain middle-class rank, but it could not dissipate the energy and resilience that fueled it, and they were now directed toward immediate survival. Coping strategies included everything from walking to work to a cheaper diet. The standard of living of second-generation Jews, which had risen steadily during the twenties, sank again during the Depression. There were some communal efforts to expand employment. The National Conference on Jewish Employment, organized through the initiative of the Anti-Defamation League, collected statistics on employment restriction but could do little to directly alleviate the problem. Mostly Jews relied on their own efforts to keep themselves afloat. "Passing" to get jobs posed a vexing problem for some families. To get a "good" position at an insurance company well known for its restrictive hiring policy, one young woman who did not have "typically Jewish features" received the required recommendation from an obliging minister and presented herself as an Episcopalian. Her proud unemployed father was chagrined, but her hard-pressed mother saw nothing wrong with circumventing an unfair system. "Would going around jobless and having to come to her father or mother for a dollar be better?" she queried the editor of the *Forward*.[60] Undoubtedly such "passing" occurred frequently, especially among highly secularized Jews who could not see why they should have to suffer for a religion they no longer practiced. Not until after Roosevelt's 1941 executive order established the Commission on Fair Labor Employment Practices and the international crisis generated a full economic recovery did employment discrimination against Jews decline.

For a few with strong Zionist commitment, the solution was to emigrate to Palestine. The years between 1927 and 1932 were the years of the highest American Jewish *aliyah* (immigration to Palestine). For members of Habonim, a Labor-Zionist youth organization, a little ditty expressed the same sentiment:

> Goodbye, America
> Goodbye, Yankee fashion
> I'm going to Palestine
> To hell with the Depression![61]

But most members of the second generation considered themselves American and could not conceive of resettling in an unknown place. Much to the chagrin of Zionists, more Jews chose to become farmers in America than in Palestine. By 1931 the minuscule Jewish agricultural sector had grown to 16,000 families. The retraining of potential farmers was supported by the Jewish Agricultural Society, which lent $6.5 million for that purpose in 1930 alone. But these Jews were not destined to be ordinary farmers: many turned to poultry farming and helped develop that industry in New Jersey. Requiring little acreage and start-up capital, such farming was in fact reminiscent of traditional Jewish small business. Unexpectedly, these ventures proved their practicality when Jewish welfare agencies were called on to find areas of the ethnic economy where Jewish refugees from the crisis in Europe could be absorbed. By 1941, 2,500 Jewish refugees had become chicken farmers. They aproached their new calling with "Teutonic thoroughness," and for a time poultry farming near the metropolitan market was a good business.[62]

The energy and skill that had contributed to the second generation's rapid mobility during the twenties now helped it withstand the shock of the Depression and to recover comparatively quickly. Better education and training had lifted many out of dead-end factory work; now they discovered that their higher-status jobs often offered more security. By and large, younger, better-educated Jews entering the labor market were generally more employable, especially in the public sector, which was just opening up to them. Moreover, despite its contraction, the Jewish ethnic economy still had comparatively greater depth than that of other groups and was able to absorb some of its own unemployed. As in all contracting job markets, those who gave evidence of trainability by their prior work or education record were the first to be rehired or to be considered for retraining. Even though 12 percent of the heads of Jewish households were unemployed and 50 percent of Jewish youths were seeking employment, Jews generally fared slightly better during the Depression than Italian-Americans, 21 percent of whose youths required welfare support compared with 12 percent for Jews.[63]

The Depression delayed but did not basically alter long-range economic trends established during the twenties and before. These were marked by a proportionately great investment in formal education and training for skill enhancement and a continued preference for small independent business ventures. But as the economy expanded after 1940, new sources of income generated by war work developed for heretofore unemployed professionals, especially engineers and lawyers, caused a notable improvement in per capita income. Small business continued to account for the largest percentage of Jewish income by the forties, but the percentage generated from professional occupations was increasing. In the postwar period that change became more marked and would have a considerable impact on fund-raising strategies. Professionals usually contributed less to philanthropy.

By 1941 the impact of investment in education and skill enhancement had become apparent. The second largest source of income after business was skilled work. Social workers had risen to 5 percent while civil service employees now accounted for 14.5 percent of the Jewish work force. Undoubtedly many of these were teachers. The proportion of Jews in the professions now stood at 10.5 percent, of which lawyers, doctors, and dentists composed 26 percent.[64] In a comparatively short period a combination of small business enterprise and investment in education and training had moved American Jewry into the American middle class. In the postwar years Jews would gain the top of that class.

In the interwar period Jews were more likely to be found as proprietors of small businesses than in the lockstep steady promotion ladder of the large corporation, to which they did not have access. But a large group of workers remained in the labor force, most employed in the ethnic economy. Yet the indications were that the Jewish sojourn in the working class would not last beyond the next generation. Neither, it seems, would their tenure as small businessmen. Most distinctive about the Jewish occupational profile during the twenties and thirties was the increase in the percentage of Jews finding a place in the professions. By 1945 the Jewish occupational profile had changed considerably from what it was in 1920. The foundation had been laid for a third commercial elite, based on the merchandising of professional skills. "Egghead millionaires" were chemists who manufactured plastics, engineers who installed air-conditioning systems, and accountants who managed estates and portfolios.

Embourgeoisement might have occurred earlier but for the Depression. Its effect on Jews was drastic, especially among the thousands of Jewish petty merchants and small manufacturers. Jewish economic difficulties were also exacerbated by the continued restriction of the job market. But by and large Jews endured the Depression comparatively well. The upgraded skills that partly account for their rapid rise during the twenties gave American Jews an extra measure of resilience, as did the existence of a well-developed ethnic economy.

We began our discussion in quest of some explanation for the comparatively rapid economic mobility of American Jewry during this period. No complete answer is yet available, but surely an important source of that remarkable leap to the middle class should be sought in the web of historical circumstances that fashioned the Jewish response to the American economic environment. For example, Jews were excluded from managerial positions in large corporations, from the professions, and from certain areas of the labor market. In response there arose Jewish strategies, undoubtedly drawn from historical experience, to circumvent these barriers. These restrictions may in fact have honed Jews' competitive spirit. There were opportunities, especially in marginal areas of the economy, for Jews to fulfill their traditional role as business pioneers. Sometimes, as in the film industry, these new ventures became major industries, but in most cases they remained marginal. Jews relied on kinship and brought their Old World entrepreneurial experience into play in the new. It is in their historical experience that we ultimately find the source of the rich network of family and communal linkages that permitted capital to be transferred from one generation to the next and from one subcommunity to another. There can be no capitalism without capital, and Jews, through their *aktsiyes* and loan societies, developed a practical instrument for raising and moving it. These intracommunal credit channels define the crucial relation between ethnicity and the remarkable Jewish economic performance from 1920 to 1945.

When we get away from the esoteric, sometimes ethnically prideful accounts of the Jewish success story, we are left with the fact that Jews were in the right place—the cities of America—at the right time—the prosperous twenties—with the right occupational profile and training. The last had not developed fortuitously; it required a leap of faith for a poor family to invest in a son's education. But the investment meant Jews were in effect priming themselves to operate efficiently in the emerging complex market economy. They located themselves in precisely those areas of the economy—urban small business and the professions—that would undergo accelerated growth.

What Jews did more and earlier than other groups was to invest in their own human capital. It was a sound investment, according to one researcher. Jews earned a 20 percent higher return from schooling than other groups, including a 16 percent higher earning capacity. Moreover, that enhancement eliminated the striking cultural divisions they had brought with them from Europe. Speaking of the uniformity of the economic ascendency, whether Jews stemmed from Galicia or Lithuania, the same researcher reports that "there [were] no systematic differences among Jews by parent's country of birth."[65]

In the last analysis it may be the realization of the potential of their human capital, rather than values embedded in their culture, that furnishes the best clue to the the remarkable leap Jews made during these years. Some may note that the idea that people are the primary source of productivity and wealth, inherent in the concept of human capital, is also intrinsic to Judaic culture.

CHAPTER SIX

ZIONISM AND THE RESTRUCTURING OF JEWISH POLITICAL LIFE

AFTER years of gathering statistics, in 1918 the New York Kehillah finally published the Jewish Communal Register. There were 3,997 Jewish organizations in the city, approximately one for every 375 Jews. Despite the decline of the immigrant ethnic culture, in the free atmosphere of America "associationism" flourished. From burial societies to elaborate federations, American Jews were creating every conceivable kind of organization.[1] There followed complex, sometimes bitter, intracommunal politics waged by these organizations, each with its own culture and program. On the surface the conflicts appeared to be rooted in ideology, but beneath lay the allocation of communal revenue. The politics were serious and intense, since Jews had developed fund-raising to an art, and millions of dollars were at stake. Jewish politics became budget politics, and few other ethnic communities had anything similar.

Strong leaders might have better managed the plethora of conflicting organizational interests, but during the twenties the golden age of American Jewish stewardship was drawing to a close. Jacob Schiff died in 1920, Oscar Straus in 1926, and Louis Marshall, who took the most active leadership role, in 1929. Their roots were in the German Jewish community, which had established itself during the nineteenth century. Its members were propertied, Jewishly educated, and committed, and they possessed a sense of service. Its leaders formed a patriciate whose role was recognized, albeit more and more reluctantly, by the immigrant masses and their second-generation successors.

But after World War I the German Jewish constituency was clearly overshadowed numerically by the Jews of eastern European descent, who had begun to arrive in mass after 1870. Those in the American Jewish Congress movement, who called for democracy in Jewish life and argued that the German *shtadlanim* (a comparison with the court Jews of the Middle Ages) represented a declining constituency, had a telling point. Members of the German Jewish patriciate, like Louis Marshall, who continued to lead found their position made increasingly difficult by raucous voices from "downtown." During the interwar years the Jewish threshold for governance, never notably high, appeared to vanish. No single voice seemed able to encompass the multiplicity of interests that characterized American Jewry. "We speak of leadership in American Jewry," complained a student of Jewish affairs, "but in reality there is no such leadership. There is no force, no authority . . . that can speak for the Jews of America."[2] Brandeis, Marshall, and Lipsky, the three Louises, who tried to lead at various times during the twenties, found they were no longer as acceptable as Jacob Schiff had been before the war. One scholar concluded that at least in the post–World War II period there existed a polity in American Jewry whose power was centered in the federations and the larger national organizations and that gave voice to the community's political agenda.[3] But if there was governance during the interwar years, there was no single communal leader that all recognized, and to whom second- and third-generation Jews paid heed. In a voluntaristic community there was in any case no way to enforce compliance. More than anything else, the absence of organizational unity accounts for American Jewry's ineffective response to the Holocaust. The seeds of that disunity were historical and came to fruition during the twenties.

Yet during that prosperous decade communal affairs were better managed than ever before. A professional civil service gradually replaced the volunteers who serviced community agencies and organizations. Its impact was felt first in the federations and then spread to the larger national organizations. Many were recruited from the cadre of Jewish social workers whose training had been initiated by the New York Kehillah through its School of Jewish Communal Work, which in 1925 became the Graduate School of Jewish Social Work.

The professionalization of Jewish organizational life proved a mixed blessing. The professionals were effective in meeting the myriad social service, educational, cultural, and religious needs of the community. But as they replaced volunteers, a way of keeping thousands of Jews involved in Jewish activities also diminished. The lay leaders continued to determine policy, but they came and went with each election while the professionals remained and represented organizational continuity. The organizations also became more formal, so that in the far-flung social service network assistance could no longer be claimed as a fraternal right, an extension of an obligation linked to kinship. Most important, the professionals, especially those involved in the federations and social work, were often militant secularists with little knowledge of Jewish traditions and values.[4] That change produced yet another source of disunity, an antagonism between the philanthropic and religious centers of American Jewry or, as in the Crimean resettlement project, with ideologically committed Zionists.

In 1927 the 4,228,000 Jews of America had 17,500 registered organizations to support their political, fraternal, welfare, defense, and economic needs. There were forty-nine different types of organizations, ranging from community service agencies like the now united Hebrew Immigrant Aid Society to multicountry agencies like the Joint Distribution Committee. Influence depended as much on the ability to raise money as on the size of membership. In the twenties, for example, the American Jewish Committee had sixty active members, and ten implemented its policies. Yet it carried considerable weight in the community. Eighteen percent of the organizations were associated with religious matters, while the new local federations comprised only 5 percent. But that comparatively small percentage gave no clue to the importance of the federations that controlled the crucial fund-raising apparatus.

Not all organizations were concerned with the American political scene or with community politics. Fraternal organizations like B'nai B'rith, which had about 150,000 members in 1940, and the Workmen's Circle, which had declined to about 75,000, boasted numbers but, by the nature of their role, took little direct interest in the power transactions that characterized Jewish politics. Similarly the landsmanshaftn, which had over a quarter of a million members, concerned themselves primarily with local affairs and social services. In 1938 only 15 percent of their members were native born, and 75 percent were classified as wage earners. Unable to attract the second and third generations and not having made the leap to the middle class, they were considered a "backward element" of American Jewish communal life.[5] I noted previously that the Jewish labor movement did not establish a full linkage to the Jewish communal world until the mid-thirties. Instead, it sponsored a panoply of secular Yiddish cultural and fraternal organizations destined to decline with the Yiddishist culture.[6] As subordinate units of national religious or fraternal organizations, Jewish women's organizations, which proliferated during the twenties, were also deflected from a separate political role. By 1926, for example, the National Federation of Temple Sisterhoods had grown from a handful of local sisterhoods to 317 chapters with a membership of 50,000, but it remained under the auspices of the Union of American Hebrew Congregations. The two exceptions were the National Council of Jewish Women, which in 1927 had 206 branches, and Hadassah, which by 1940 had grown to 843 chapters and acted independently of the Zionist Organization of America (ZOA), with which it was affiliated.[7]

On the national level the two primary defense organizations were the American Jewish Congress (AJCONG) and the American Jewish Committee (AJCOMM). Each represented a different constituency. The former began officially in 1918 as the culmination of a movement of "downtown" Jews to democratize Jewish organizational life. Its founders viewed it less as an organization than as a popular movement to unify American Jewry. But when it finally came into existence after a nationwide election in which 335,000 votes were cast, its founders agreed to stay organized only for a specific purpose—to represent Jewish interests at the Paris Peace Conference, after which it would dissolve itself. The movement to break that pledge, which developed in earnest after its final report had been received in 1919, emanated primarily from supporters of the ZOA, the large fraternal orders, and the Yiddish press, who viewed the ominous events in Europe as a portent of a permanent crisis. For the Zionist movement the reconstitution of the AJCONG represented an opportunity to establish an additional foothold in Jewish organizational life. It soon became evident that the new Zionist organizers had little interest in other aspects of communalism, such as education.[8] Despite some movement in that direction, there was little hope that the AJCONG would unify American Jewry as the original founders had hoped. Twenty-seven smaller national organizations became affiliated with the organization, but that included six Zionist organizations and twelve insurance-paying brotherhoods. None of the major rival organizations joined. The AJCONG thus failed to reflect, much less encompass, the entirety of Jewish organizational life. By the mid-twenties its grandiose schemes for unity had been abandoned, and it became merely another organization cluttering the Jewish political landscape. As early as 1925 and for three years thereafter, serious thought was given to dissolving the organization. Its budget from 1923 to 1927 was smaller than those of most of its constituent organizations. By 1928 it was operating at a deficit and having trouble finding a mission. Only thirty communities outside New York City bothered holding election conventions. "It didn't have the original swing, the original impetus, the original fervor, and we had to work hard to keep things going," according to Bernard Richards, who served as its executive head.[9] It was only when its leaders discovered the enthusiastic response of Jews to the protest rallies it organized to publicize the plight of the Jews of Romania, Poland, and Russia that it hit on the successful activist style that became its hallmark. It then gained a reputation as an energetic secular organization crusading for domestic reform and the defense of civil rights. Frustrated by a sense of powerlessness in the face of the Nazi threat, Jews perceived only that "at least Congress was trying to do something." Its militancy established the AJCONG's reputation but did not solve its budget problems.[10] Having neither the organizational apparatus nor the financial resources, it could do little more than protest. The progressive democratic model of community organization on which it was based was clearly not sufficient to sustain it. In a sense the reconstituted Congress was a victim of its own ideology.

Founded in 1906, the American Jewish Committee eschewed the notion of mass participation in Jewish life. The founders were convinced that public policy should be made by elites and influenced by other elites. It fancied itself one such. The Committee had two classes of members: sustaining members, who supported the agency financially but took little active part, and twenty corporate members who made and implemented policy. The AJCOMM's constituency was the wealthy stratum that stemmed primarily, though by the twenties no longer exclusively, from the nineteenth-century German Jewish migration. It was an "uptown" agency that, like the AJCONG, entertained notions of being the instrument by which Jewish communal life could be welded together. On the surface the conflict between the Committee and the Congress centered on the issue of nationalism represented by Zionism. The Congress had become unabashedly Zionistic while the Committee, like the Reform movement to which many of its members belonged, was moving gradually from anti-Zionism to non-Zionism or cultural Zionism. Led by Louis Marshall, it had approved the Balfour Declaration in 1917. Some of its leading members would be drawn into the expanded Jewish Agency for Palestine. But the ideological and cultural dissonance between the two agencies was not easily bridged. They disagreed fundamentally about how American Jewry should be organized and the role Jews should play in American society. Committee members were usually more concerned with their Americanism and viewed their Jewishness in religious rather than ethnic terms. They would have preferred to see the second generation meld as quickly as possible into the American mainstream.

During the twenties the AJCOMM too was compelled to alter its organizational culture and structure. It had earlier brought the New York Kehillah under its wing as a chapter.[11] Now its charter was changed to permit eleven national organizations to affiliate, in hopes that a broader membership base would disarm the charge that the Committee was an undemocratic oligarchy. But the growing crisis faced by European Jewry cast doubt on some of the AJCOMM's basic strategies. There was evidence that the national minority rights clauses on which its president, Louis Marshall, had staked so much at the Paris Peace Conference were not yielding the expected security for Polish and Romanian Jews. Legal instruments, so effective at home, did not produce the same results in nations that lacked an Anglo-American reverence for the law. Investigations by Ambassador Hugh Gibson and Henry Morgenthau had produced evidence of official anti-Semitism in Poland.[12] The successful court and public relations battle against Ford so impressed the AJCOMM's leaders that, like generals refighting their winning battles, they became convinced that the same tactics could be applied in Germany, where anti-Semitism had become virulent, and they so advised the leaders of German Jewry.[13]

The movement to reconvene the AJCONG in June 1921 came on top of these developments. What rankled was that the reconstitution of the Congress was so clearly a breach of trust. There had been an understanding that no resolution would be introduced involving its perpetuation. That had been circumvented by adjourning sine die, but the spirit of the agreement had been violated. The *American Hebrew,* which customarily saw eye-to-eye with the Committee, condemned it for creating the impresssion that there was to be a Jewish "state within a state."[14] More important, the reconstitution of the AJCONG was a signal that the second generation would no longer accept the leadership of the German Jewish patriciate as a matter of course.

But the Committee's financial condition was far superior to its rival's. Money from its well-to-do members permitted it to steer an independent course, and it did not yet have an expensive nationwide chapter network to administer. Through its close connection with the American Jewish Joint Distribution Committee (JDC), it had a kind of "power of the purse." The JDC, which disbursed philanthropic funds abroad, was nonpolitical, but since its establishment in 1914 the leadership strata of the two agencies had been almost identical. Of the JDC's forty-two directors in 1931, twenty-seven were on the AJCOMM's executive committee, and seventeen of these also served on the JDC's executive committee.[15] Its principal contributors were drawn from the same group.

Nevertheless, as the second-generation descendants of the eastern European immigrants came to the fore, it became clear that the AJCOMM was out of step, especially in its attitude toward the creation of a Jewish homeland in Palestine. Most of the children of eastern European immigrants had become secular, but they were less embarrassed by their ethnicity and less conservative in their political views. During the twenties that divergence was reflected in the conflict over two major issues—the Crimean resettlement project and the expansion of the Jewish Agency for Palestine. Realizing that some form of Zionism would become part of the American Jewish persona, the AJCOMM sought to adjust to it on its own terms. Eager to have the group on board, Zionists played down their nationalist rhetoric and focused on specific projects in Palestine to attract American Jewish capital. At the ZOA's 1920 convention, for example, mention of nationalist goals was carefully avoided, even though the Balfour Declaration had legitimized the Jewish settlement in Palestine. It was common interests that brought about the strange liaison between Louis Marshall and Chaim Weizmann. Both, we shall see, faced adamant opposition in their own camps, and both would discover that the conflict could not easily be circumvented. The Zionist movement in America, unlike the Congress or the Committee, was composed of organizations whose communalism and defense strategies were conceived in terms of Zionist ideology. A Jewish homeland, they were convinced, would strengthen the Jewish enterprise and shore up its security while invigorating its culture. Zionism was the way they expressed their Jewishness, and the two could not easily be separated.

We come next to the growth of the federation movement, a development that would alter the character of the Jewish organizational world by transforming the power relations that undergirded it. The need to finance a plethora of social service institutions, from orphanages to hospitals for the tubercular, had given fund-raising a special importance in the Jewish community. It was supported by a strong tradition of philanthropy based on the commandment for *tzedakah,* a Hebrew word that contains the root *tsedek,* which concerns justice. Jewish giving, then, is not charity, based on the Latin word *caritas,* which concerns love. What in the Christian world is given out of love, Jews are obliged to give to right the injustice of poverty. Giving is a matter of halakah, the law.[16] One researcher has called such Jewish givers a "philanthropic moral community," but giving among Jews clearly went beyond morality and law.[17] There had developed over the centuries a tradition of giving that even secularized Jews who cared little for Jewish law still adhered to. A "habit of giving" was ingrained and buttressed by the communal status system. The increase in the sums collected by organized Jewish philanthropy during the interwar period correlates most directly with an increase in disposable income rather than with a growth in morality.

The federations developed in the last third of the nineteenth century as part of the quest for order in the chaotic fund-raising arena, which paralleled an earlier rationalization of fund-raising among the Protestant denominations, sparked by the Social Gospel movement.[18] As early as 1864 the Jews of Memphis established a single umbrella organization for charitable activities. In 1895 Boston followed, actually using the term "federation," and a year later Cincinnati did the same. Other sizable Jewish communities followed suit. In some cases, such as Baltimore, two federations came into existence, one meeting the needs of German Jews and the other serving more recent arrivals. In 1900 the newly established National Conference of Jewish Charities held its first convention, with representatives from almost six hundred charitable societies. It did not take much to convince the German Jewish stewards, who were the targets of countless individual solicitations, that "order" had to be brought to Jewish philanthropy. Jacob Schiff had earlier started a precedent of accountability and sometimes required matching of funds for his grants. Ultimately the quest for efficiency would lead to a national federation and an agreed-on formula for disbursing funds after a single annual campaign.

By 1945 over 90 percent of all Jewish communities, covering 97 percent of all American Jews, had federations. The growth of local federations brought a steady growth in the sums raised, and there was a gradual change in allocation priorities. Before World War I much of the philanthropic dollar had been expended on the needs of the new immigrants, especially because of family desertion, dubbed "the poor man's divorce."[19] As immigration dwindled the focus shifted to relief needs abroad and cultural needs at home. The JDC assumed responsibility for the former and the federations for the latter.

Strategies to maximize giving were developed. Newly wealthy potential givers, desiring to belong to the "moral community," were attracted to the federation's social events. An invitation was taken as a sign of having arrived. In the process there arose a new generation of "philanthropoids," as givers were labeled by professional fund-raisers. Various grades of membership were established, each requiring a specific level of giving. Everyone knew not only what they were expected to give but how much others had given. The social pressure to make a "good" contribution was intense. To maximize collection, the campaign reached deep into the ethnic economy. In New York City a division head was assigned to each of 137 "trades" and 21 groups of "allied trades." At federation headquarters complete files were kept on each trade's previous contributions. It seemed the entire energy of the community was centered on the "campaign." An anxious watch was kept to see whether the "big givers" would come through so that the campaign could go "over the top." By such techniques between 1916 and 1921 the federations more than doubled the $10 million collected in the previous five years. It was that sharp increase in available funds that sparked the building boom to house Jewish social service and cultural agencies. In 1927 Detroit was the only city that could not boast one of the sixty-one hospitals the Jewish community built and supported in major urban centers. By 1940 there were in addition forty-six outpatient clinics, eighty-four family welfare agencies, fifty old-age homes, and dozens of other social welfare institutions.[20]

The building boom was brought to a halt by the stock market crash and the depression that followed. Between 1931 and 1934 collections dropped by 30 percent, while family dependency grew by leaps and bounds. There was a new urgency to streamline fund-raising; pressure grew to centralize the campaign and make it nationwide. In 1932 an organizational capstone was put in place: sixty-three local federations and five welfare funds joined to establish the Council of Jewish Federations and Welfare Funds (CJF). By the end of World War II virtually all federations had joined the umbrella organization. When it became apparent that fund allocation required accurate information, the CJF absorbed the Bureau of Jewish Social Research and the National Information Appeals Service. The latter agency provided data on those seeking support from federations, and the former provided general information about American Jewry that was necessary for long-range planning. Inevitably the CJF assumed a centralized policy-making role. It provided the local federations with know-how and trained professionals for organized fund-raising.

What began as a local coordinating mechanism had by the mid-thirties taken on a governmental character, with the annual campaign operating like a voluntary Internal Revenue Service. At the annual meeting of the CJF held in Chicago in 1934, basic decisions were made on community policy, such as emphasizing Jewish culture rather than direct relief. Like the JDC, the CJF provided a neutral, apolitical environment where the philanthropic agencies established by German Jews and by the descendants of eastern European Jews could operate unimpeded by the vitriolic communal politics that characterized American Jewish life. In 1944 the National Community Relations Advisory Council, an umbrella organization that included the AJCOMM, the AJCONG, and B'nai B'rith as well as fourteen local community relations councils, was established in an attempt to impose a parallel coherence on the chaotic world of the defense and social welfare agencies. But efforts in this area were less successful. Nevertheless, before World War II a two-tiered system was in place to fund the domestic and foreign obligations assumed by the community. Fund-raising and communalism were developing hand-in-hand.[21]

But on the question of how funds should be allocated, agreement eluded both the federations and the JDC. Neither could accommodate the long-standing conflict between Zionists and non-Zionists. Several times the conflict broke into the open over the allocation question. Zionist fund-raising was no match for the JDC, whose aims were broader and whose backers were richer. Between 1921 and 1925 the Zionist organizations launched four "appeals" but raised only $6 million compared with the JDC's $20.8 million. In 1925, led by Rabbi Stephen Wise, the newly organized United Palestine Appeal (UPA), composed of the Jewish National Fund, the Palestine Foundation Fund, and the campaigns of Hadassah and Mizrachi, attempted its own Zionist version of consolidated fund-raising. But again the campaign did not achieve its goal, $5 million, though it came close enough for campaign leaders to call it "an extraordinary accomplishment in these apathetic days."[22]

Only the simultaneous failure of the JDC-sponsored Crimean settlement project and the emergency created by the Arab riots of 1929 gave Zionists an opportunity to enlist non-Zionists with their superior fund-raising capacity, by welcoming them into the Jewish Agency for Palestine and by consolidating all fund-raising under the banner of the United Jewish Appeal (UJA). But such a consolidation would require the continuing pressure of the crisis faced by world Jewry after the advent of the National Socialist regime in Germany. Between 1925 and 1934, smarting at the policy of making Jews secure in place, the Zionist-sponsored UPA remained outside the consolidated fund-raising network. But after that year the Zionist position began to soften.

In 1935 the CJF too formulated new priorities. It would support only needs "so specifically Jewish that none but Jews can be expected to support them." That meant cultural activities and defense against anti-Semitism, but especially overseas needs, which included those of the Yishuv in Palestine. Between 1935 and 1946 the funds given for overseas needs increased by 60 percent, including 95 percent of the funds received by UJA.[23] But a unified fund-raising effort would not be achieved until the Zionization of American Jewry generated sufficient pressure on the JDC's "big givers" to increase their allocation for Palestine.

The refugee crisis of 1938, a clear portent of the mortal danger faced by the Jews of Germany and Austria, finally provided the circumstances for consolidation. On 18 January 1939 William Rosenwald, Jonah Wise, and Louis Lipsky signed the charter of the reconstituted UJA. The agreement was wrung from the reluctant contenders by the Council of Jewish Federations and marks its debut as the most powerful agency in American Jewish life. Interested in maximizing fund-raising, CJF suggested a new formula for a combined appeal to raise $20 million. Its strategy was to circumvent the conflict by raising enough money to satisfy the needs of both agencies. The allocation formula would be agreed on before the campaign, and any surfeit would be fairly distributed by a special committee. The CJF, whose constituent federations actually conducted the campaign in 225 communities, promised full mobilization. It was not an easy compromise, and the future of the UJA continued to be uncertain for several years. But the increase in collections was notable and went far to soothe ruffled feelings. The agreement was renewed for 1940, and the American Organization for Rehabilitation through Training (ORT) and the Hebrew Immigrant Aid Society were now included in the campaign. The goal was raised to $23 million.[24] The consolidation of fund-raising changed the character of Jewish intracommunal politics, but it could not by itself unify American Jewry during the years of the Holocaust.

Led by Rabbi Abba Hillel Silver, the UPA continued to test the waters for a separate campaign, and only the mediating role of the CJF prevented a renewed split. Gradually the allocation formula began to reflect the primacy Zionism had gained among American Jews. The UJA became the Jewish community's highly effective voluntary tax collector. Behind that were the federations, which had in fact become the organizational heart of American Jewry. Between 1939 and 1945 the UJA, held together only by a thread, raised $124 million—not enough considering the Jewish need in Europe and Palestine, but a truly remarkable feat compared with organized fund-raising in other areas of American society. It was the only example of Jewish organizational unity in the face of the Holocaust.

Scholars have pondered the remarkable fund-raising apparatus of American Jewry, noting the traditional "habit of giving" that was part of Jewish law and culture. But perhaps more important for the secularized Jews of the interwar period was a superior ability to give, rooted in their growing affluence. When these factors were combined with the desperate need stemming from the crisis of the thirties, the ingredients for successful appeals were in place. Moreover, when the Zionist impulse was added, the danger of the UJA's developing into a soulless apparatus was lessened. Talk of rebuilding the Jewish homeland and making the desert bloom stirred the souls as it loosened the purse strings of Jewish givers. Most important, the ability to raise large sums of money created a new power relationship within American Jewry and between it and the host culture. Like American politics, Jewish politics became increasingly concerned with "spoils," the "who gets what" question raised by the availability of large sums of money. That question lent a bitter flavor to the three primary issues that involved the Zionist movement during the twenties: the disposition of funds within the Zionist movement; the allocation of millions of dollars to resettle Jews in the Crimea; and the expansion of the Jewish Agency for Palestine to include non-Zionists.

In the interwar period the American Zionist movement acted as an agent of change for American Jewish politics. Though we refer to it as a movement, it was far from monolithic. Its leading adherents ranged from Judah Magnes, chancellor of Hebrew University in Jerusalem, who feared that the Balfour Declaration did not adequately protect the rights of the Arab population of Palestine, to cultural Zionists like Cyrus Adler, who saw the need for a new center of Judaic culture but strenuously opposed "political Zionism." There were also socialist Zionists who believed that in a Jewish homeland it would be possible to amend a faulty Jewish class structure. There were religious Zionists who saw an opportunity to send forth Torah (Jewish law) from a reconstituted Zion. There were a growing number of revisionist Zionists who, like their charismatic leader Vladimir Jabotinsky, preached a strident nationalism. The controlling center was occupied by ordinary American Jews who viewed the Jewish settlements in Palestine through the prism of their own middle-class lives. The Jewish homeland would, they hoped, become a liberal democracy like that in America, which would serve as a haven for Jews who needed it. They did not count themselves among them.

In 1914 the Federation of American Zionists, the umbrella organization for Zionist agencies, seized the opportunity to recruit the well known Boston "people's lawyer" Louis Brandeis to head the Provisional Zionist Executive Committee, which administered the World Zionist Organization (WZO) and had been transferred to the United States for the duration of the war. It was a coup because Brandeis's popularity was at its peak and would help legitimize Zionism, especially among more established Jews. Meanwhile the successful conclusion of the war presented the Zionist movement with new opportunities. The efforts of Stephen Wise and Louis Brandeis had wrung a confirmation of the Balfour Declaration from the Wilson administration. Zionists believed the declaration promised Jews a national home in Palestine. Now the former Ottoman province that included Palestine was cut loose and after considerable bickering had been assigned to Great Britain as a League of Nations mandate. The possibility of realizing Zionist goals had never seemed better.

Yet at that favorable historical juncture, the American Zionist movement virtually tore itself apart. By 1920 the welcome that rank-and-file Zionists, largely of eastern European descent, had given to Brandeis and his group had begun to wear thin. His relentless attention to organizational detail, his unwillingness to emerge from behind the scenes after his appointment to the Supreme Court in 1916, and his slogan for building the ZOA— "Men, Money, Discipline"—rankled. So did his placing a time clock in the Broadway ZOA headquarters. The staff considered themselves full-time Zionists on duty twenty-four hours a day, who required no time clock. They were not "logical Zionists" like Brandeis but "biological" ones who, according to Maurice Samuel, a staunch opponent of Brandeis in the forthcoming conflict, were the only ones suited to manage the Jewish interests.[25] The Cleveland convention of the ZOA, during which the final split of the movement occurred, marked the culmination of grievances that had been brewing since the end of the war.

The decade had begun hopefully. There would be some whittling down of the Zionist predominance before Great Britain's mandate would be ratified by the council of the League of Nations, but the Zionist ship was on course and there was much reason to rejoice. Within the movement, however, storm clouds were gathering. There was a growing tendency by the Brandeis leadership to act independently of the WZO, which was financially dependent on American Jewry. Brandeis's insistence on stewardship of funds threatened the well-being of the world Zionist enterprise. It was imperative that his hold on the purse strings be loosened.

That would not be an easy task. Brandeis was shocked at the inefficiency of Zionist administrative practices at home and abroad and became convinced that the WZO's budget for Palestine was wasteful. There were too many sinecures for party bureaucrats. The kibbutzim (Zionist-sponsored communal settlements) were impressive but, steeped in an ideology of agricultural fundamentalism, could not serve as the foundation of a modern economy that would also require private investment and small-scale industry. Too much money was being spent on propaganda and education and not enough on practical projects that could build Palestine's economy step by step. As in the colonization of America, which served as Brandeis's model, the settlements must show a profit, and labor should not be subsidized. He viewed as visionary the ideological conception that a Jewish homeland should be developed as a unified public effort of the Jewish people, with labor serving as the foundation of the society. Also impractical was talk of a five-year tithe on all Jews to raise $25 million. Palestine's economy would thrive only when it escaped from *schnorrerdom* (beggary), he insisted. The mixing of philanthropic and investment dollars in one fund, to be controlled by the newly established Keren Hayesod, the fund-raising arm of the Zionist movement, was an invitation to corruption. It gave the leaders of the WZO virtually total decision-making power over money they had not raised. Most important, American Jewry was bearing too heavy a share of the financial burden. It deserved a greater voice in the disposition of funds, since over 70 percent had been raised by American Jews, many of them non-Zionists.[26]

The conflict came to a head at the stormy London conference of the

WZO, held on 7 July 1920. Efforts to avoid an outright split between Brandeis and Weizmann, who headed the World Zionist executive, were futile. For Weizmann what was important was the degree and quality of commitment to Zionist ideology. Brandeis and his group, observed Weizmann, "made of Zionism simply a sociological plan . . . instead of the folk renaissance that it was."[27] When the leadership of the world movement was offered to Weizmann in 1919, commitment to Zionism took precedence over his professional career. He abandoned his academic position at the University of Manchester without hesitation. But Brandeis, heeding the counsel of Felix Frankfurter and others, continued to control the ZOA from behind the scenes and refused to give up his seat on the Supreme Court.

Louis Lipsky, who succeeded Julian Mack as president of the ZOA, observed "a visible change in Brandeis' demeanor" when he returned from London.[28] Orderly and controlled in his personal affairs, he was shocked by the disregard for parliamentary procedure and the long, vague discussions that never seemed to produce concrete results. Unaccustomed to the rough give-and-take of Zionist politics, Brandeis had been taken aback by the vitriolic attacks on him during the conference. He was apprehensive that the shoddiness of the WZO's accounting procedures would lead to misappropriation of funds. When Brandeis righteously declared that "a dollar wasted is a dollar stolen," he was dubbed a Puritan by opponents.[29] Gradually he became convinced that the only solution was to overhaul the leadership of the WZO and replace it with men of high moral stature and business experience. But his plan for better management was rejected because it would allow non-Zionists to control the settlements in Palestine. Convinced that American Jews lacked Jewish spirit, many eastern European Zionists viewed them simply as a source of funds. But Brandeis believed the American Jewish financial contribution warranted greater representation in the inner councils of the world Zionist movement. A deep cultural chasm separated the two groups. Like Weizmann, Brandeis may have concluded that no bridge was possible betweeen Washington and Pinsk.[30]

On 17 April 1920 the battle was joined. The conflict predictably came down to control of funds. Weizmann, bypassing the ZOA, issued a proclamation establishing the Keren Hayesod as the official fund-raising arm of the world Zionist movement in America. Brandeis supporters could not accept what they felt was an attempt by the Weizmann leadership to reach directly into the American Jewish till. In an effort to strengthen his position, Weizmann resolved his differences with the revisionist faction in October 1920 and allowed them to bring a small group onto the World Zionist executive. Frankfurter reminded Weizmann of his promise not to increase the size of that body. The maneuver smacked of betrayal, and the break was complete. For Brandeis the only answer was to steer a course independent of the WZO.

The Brandeis-Weizmann split served as a signal for rejoicing in the anti-Zionist camp. An editorial in the *American Hebrew* called on Jews to "Scrap Zionism—Build Palestine."[31] That is the path Brandeis seemed to be following. The ZOA budget of 1920 did not contain the usual $75,000 monthly subsidy for the WZO, and the 1921 budget allocated only $25,000, carefully earmarked for expenditure in Palestine only. Implementing a policy favoring investment over charity, Benjamin V. Cohen, who as financial secretary of the WZO served as Brandeis's eyes and ears in London, drew up plans to place the Zionist operation in Palestine on a sound business footing. In one year the staff of the London office of the world Zionist executive was reduced from 118 to 30. Within the ZOA, a Palestine Development Committee was established to handle investment in Palestine directly. At the same time the budgets of its cultural and propaganda departments were reduced from $20,000 to $6,000. In a word, the Brandeis faction was using the power of the purse to bring the WZO into line.

At the ZOA convention held in Buffalo in November 1920 Brandeis was received with "rejoicing and pride," and his program was confirmed. But many in the Zionist rank and file did not sympathize with his penchant for bookkeeping, which placed the WZO in financial straits. They demonstrated their strong support of Weizmann when he and Albert Einstein toured American Jewish communities in April 1921. Ostensibly undertaken to raise funds to develop a Hebrew university, the tour became a triumphal procession. "Weizmann is reinforced by the tremendous welcome in New York," wrote Stephen Wise to his daughter.[32] But Wise incorrectly attributed the crowds' enthusiasm to the popularity of Einstein and misunderstood the intense feelings of the aroused immigrant Jews who were the mainstay of the American Zionist movement.

With the approach of the ZOA convention, scheduled to be held in Cleveland in June, the lines were clearly drawn. On one side were Brandeis and his coterie, well-educated, successful public figures. Especially noteworthy was Felix Frankfurter, who had from his Harvard Law School position already earned a reputation as a legal scholar and an astute power broker. Horace Kallen, who also boasted a Harvard education, was the theoretician of the group, who conceived of the pluralistic, free-enterprise Zionism that had become its hallmark. Like Mordecai Kaplan, Kallen viewed Zionism instrumentally. He favored it because it would help keep Jews engaged at least culturally.[33] Stephen Wise, president of the American Jewish Congress, was the best known of the group because of his oratorical and public relations talent. He also possessed the best Zionist credentials and served as the link to the world Zionist movement. Julian Mack, a circuit court judge who served as the actual head of the ZOA for Brandeis, did much of the negotiating with the Weizmann faction. Bernard Flexner, Benjamin Cohen, Laurence Steinhardt, Eugene Meyer, Jr., Nathan Straus, and Louis Kirstein completed what was easily the most impressive cadre active in the Jewish community. All boasted credentials in either business or the professions, and all stood in awe of the austere Brandeis, whom Franklin Roosevelt later dubbed "Old Isaiah."

Nowhere near as prestigious but far closer to the eastern European heart of Zionism was the Weizmann faction, headed by Louis Lipsky, a journalist, critic, and Zionist activist since his youth in Rochester, New York.[34] Supporting him was a small group of acculturated eastern Jews headed by Emanuel Neumann, who had already built a reputation as a fund-raiser and who would head the UPA campaign in 1924. Elihu D. Stone and Bernard Rosenblatt, both long-term Zionists, made up the core of this leadership cadre. Their primary objective was to prevent the Brandeis group, whom they considered outsiders, from dominating the Zionist movement. Their belief that they had the votes to break the hold of the Brandeis faction in Cleveland turned out to be accurate.

Last-minute attempts to reconcile the differences, made by Walter Lippman and Samuel Untermeyer, came to naught. The Brandeis faction was defeated, and thirty-one of its members resigned from the executive committee to take their place as "humble soldiers in the ranks." Some suspected they would eventually be called back. In the interim they would make their contribution through the newly established investment fund, the Palestine Development Corporation.[35] A long-simmering revolution of the eastern European immigrants against the *yahudim,* those better-acculturated and established Jews who dominated Jewish organizational life, had come to a boil. The second generation, coming of age during the twenties, no longer required an acculturated leadership to mediate with the American political establishment. But in the Zionist movement it soon became clear that the resignation of the Brandeis group was a Pyrrhic victory. On its own Zionist fund-raising was insufficient for the group's grandiose plans. The control of much of the investment dollar, which might fill the vacuum left by philanthropic contributions, remained with Jews who were more comfortable with men like Brandeis than like Lipsky. That reality ultimately compelled Weizmann to fashion his own alliance with non-Zionist American Jews who, by the capital they possessed, held a key to the economic development of the yishuv. After it became clear that the American Zionist movement was in total disarray, he asked the Brandeis group to take the helm in 1927 and again in 1929. The link would be Louis Marshall, who it was rumored, after the Cleveland debacle, would assume the leadership formerly held by Brandeis.[36]

The decline of organized Zionism in America after the Cleveland convention goes beyond the resignation of the Brandeis group. Led by Benjamin Cohen, some former Brandeis adherents actually drifted back to the ZOA. Like other Americans during the twenties, the Jewish masses were distracted and steeped in privatism. The hedonistic spirit of the decade posed a challenge for other organized causes, including labor, whose membership also declined precipitously. Even the Ku Klux Klan, which had seemed vigorous in the early 1920s, experienced a decline in membership at the end. There was also less enthusiasm for idealistic causes among the rapidly acculturating Jews. It required a constant effort to keep the declining membership of Zionist organizations active. In 1918 the ZOA claimed 200,000 members. A decade later membership had reverted to what it was in 1916, about 22,000. In 1929, the year of the Arab riots in Palestine and the death of Louis Marshall, the ZOA's membership had declined to 13,000, and two years later the organization was virtually defunct, with only a few more than 8,000 dues-paying members.

If the Lipsky administration paid little heed to the details of bookkeeping, it was surprisingly effective at political lobbying. It achieved a political triumph with the passage in May 1922 of the Lodge-Fish resolution endorsing the Balfour Declaration. Enacted by the same Congress that had passed the restrictionist immigration law of 1921, the resolution was all the more remarkable because few of the Lipsky faction who testified in its favor possessed political influence comparable to that of the Brandeis supporters who had resigned from the ZOA. At the congressional hearings in April 1922, the testimony by Rabbis Morris Lazaron and David Philipson indicated that there still was powerful anti-Zionist sentiment, especially in the

Reform movement. But the lure of cheap political capital during a congressional election year proved irresistible for Senator Henry Cabot Lodge, then at the height of his political power, and Congressman Hamilton Fish.[37] The passage of the resolution also marks a change in political strategy for Zionists, who had preferred to work through the Oval Office. Time would show that the influence of Congress on foreign affairs was less effective, since it was the president who was constitutionally responsible for making foreign policy.

If the decline in membership and vitality was not sufficient to sadden committed Zionists, evidence developed that Brandeis's persistent fears regarding the mishandling of funds had some foundation. At the 1928 ZOA convention there were few who did not sense that Lipsky's management was inefficient and wasteful. The spirit of cronyism passing for fraternity that characterized his tenure was not unlike the opportunistic links one could find in any Tammany club. But few suspected outright misuse of funds. Those who dared mention the possibility were dismissed as "vengeful Brandeisists." Lipsky was elected for another term, and the "corruption" charge was never confronted. But by the following year the precipitous drop in membership and a growing deficit alerted even his most loyal supporters that something was amiss. An investigatory commission, stacked in Lipsky's favor, was appointed by Weizmann to investigate the charges of financial irregularity. What it discovered was not stealing on a grand scale but the kind of carelessness Brandeis had complained about. Clearly the financial shortfall was related more to the economic crash than to outright corruption. Lipsky had without authorization extended ZOA credit to a private person. He had high-handedly endorsed another's note. When faced with a shortage of money, he delayed transfer of funds to the Hebrew Trust. Without authorization, he guaranteed the $185,000 indebtedness of the American Zion Commonwealth. There was also evidence that the ZOA's books had been tampered with. But in no way had Lipsky enriched himself. The committee recommended that everyone involved resign, but Lipsky, who had at first offered to do so, stating that "these judges are just another bunch of Nordic Jews," outmaneuvered his opponents by disfranchising a large section of Hadassah through his control of the credentials committee. The charge of Lipsky's malfeasance was never fully investigated, since few of his followers would believe that a "Jewish Jew" could steal. Instead, his followers insisted that on balance the Lipsky administration had done more good than harm.[38] But the truth lies elsewhere. The internal check mechanism of the organization, so carefully put in place by Brandeis, had broken down. In terms of leadership and organization, the American Zionist movement clearly was not prepared to cope with the difficult challenges the thirties would bring.

By 1930 the ZOA was on the verge of collapse, and its leaders seemed unable to do anything about it. At the next convention, again held in Cleveland, the old Brandeis group was invited back by Rabbi James G. Heller, chairman of the ZOA executive committee. A memorandum stating the terms of the transfer of power, which had all the appearances of an ultimatum, was submitted by Julian Mack. The ZOA would have to agree to a complete reorganization along the lines originally suggested by Brandeis in 1921. Only then would an attempt be made to wipe out the deficit. The terms were accepted.

The priority the Zionist movement was compelled to give to fundraising diminished the ideological passions the eastern European membership fed on. A Zionist, a contemporary joke had it, was someone who solicited money from another person to send a third person to Palestine. And Jews so sent would not necessarily stay. By 1923 people stood in line all night outside the American consulate in Jerusalem to obtain return visas. The cherished objective of Zionist ideology—reestablishing a Jewish homeland in Palestine and making the neglected land flow with milk and honey—seemed more remote than ever during the final years of the twenties. Yet a decade later American Zionism would be on its way to organizing the most effective political interest group in the nation.[39]

The malaise of the world movement became especially clear in August 1929, when the Arab population of Palestine demonstrated its opposition to Jewish settlement through violent riots. It strengthened the hand of those who insisted all along that Palestine was not, as the founding myth of Zionist ideology would have it, "a land without people, for a people without a land." Even the assumption of labor Zionists that the Arab population would be integrated on equal terms by the development of Palestine's economy now seemed unrealistic. There was more doubt than ever that a Westernized Jewish population could be integrated into the Middle East.

The Jewish reaction to the riots was stormy. The nationalistic revisionists rallied at the Western Wall, where the riots had begun, and called for strong measures against Arab barbarism. But some, like Judah Magnes, saw moral failure in Zionists' blindness to the legitimate claims of the Arab population. They proposed that Zionist plans for Palestine should be scaled down and that there should be an acknowledgment that they could be realized only through a binational state. "If the only way of establishing the Jewish national Home is upon the bayonets of some empire," argued Magnes, "our whole enterprise is not worthwhile."⁴⁰ Most vexing was the role of the Jewish communists, who had been busily infiltrating the Jewish labor unions. After initially supporting the Jewish colonists against "British imperialism" and Arab effendis, the *Freiheit* slavishly followed the changed Party line dictated by Moscow. The Arab rioters now were pictured as "proletarian revolutionaries," and the Jews became "reactionary bourgeoisie."⁴¹

Already reeling from internal scandal and a drop in membership, the Zionist movement now had to counter evidence that its enterprise in Palestine was untenable. Arab leaders made their opposition to Zionist immigration and settlement known to American political leaders. On 30 August 1929 a protest rally advocating the Palestinian cause was held in New York City, the very heart of the American Jewish community.⁴² Jews too rallied to the cause in dozens of protest rallies. There was concern about the immediate danger to Jewish settlers. A delegation visited President Herbert Hoover and Secretary of State Henry L. Stimson to request not only a statement of support, but that the fleet be sent to the Middle East. It did not get much satisfaction. The policy of noninvolvement and acknowledgment of British predominance in the Middle East would not be altered even though eight American citizens had been killed in the bloody massacre at Hebron. The State Department gave credence to the dispatches of Consul Paul Knabeshue, who claimed the riots had been provoked by the Jews. That was also the conclusion of the British Shaw Commission of Inquiry.⁴³

The riots more than ever convinced Weizmann that incorporating non-Zionists into an extended Jewish Agency for Palestine was urgent. The role he envisaged for non-Zionists went beyond attracting investment capital to develop Palestine's economy. Their influence was needed to establish the legitimacy of the Jewish claim and to counter the growing anti-Zionism of key political leaders in the British government. Louis Marshall, the most prominent non-Zionist figure in the expansion, died shortly before the riots, and without men like him to take the lead that task would become more difficult.

But during the thirties the world Zionist movement remained divided, and its leaders were unable to convince the Roosevelt administration to pressure London to make Palestine accessible to Jews in need of haven.

That failure was a harbinger of the general failure to persuade Washington to play a more active role in rescuing Jews during the war years.

The general ineffectiveness of American Zionism during the twenties might have gone unnoticed had the movement been able to keep its coffers full. But it was in the area of finances that its weakness was most apparent. By the 1930 fiscal year the ZOA could no longer spare funds to shore up the settlements in Palestine, and in 1931 the UPA, its principal source of support, was able to transfer only $1,250,000 of a projected $3,500,000. Tracts of land bought on 20 percent margin were in danger of being lost. The Jewish Agency had failed to balance its budget twice despite drastic slashes. Without funds to subsidize immigrants, it could not even utilize the fifteen hundred Palestine certificates London was willing to make available. In Palestine the economy was in a depression and construction was at a standstill. The WZO had discharged dozens of employees, teachers' salaries had been cut, and all organizational and cultural activities had been suspended.

To realize its goals, the Zionist movement needed to claim a greater share of the American Jewish philanthropic dollar. One could talk about democracy, as Zionists did, but in American Jewish life the moneyed piper also called the tune. Zionists of all stripes were convinced that using these dollars to build the Jewish homeland would in the long run benefit all Jews, but wealthy American Jews did not yet see it that way and insisted that some form of control come with their investment. That was the position of the Brandeis faction. In 1930 Chaim Weizmann acknowledged that the movement had abused American Jewry as a "money-giving machine." But surely all could agree that it was better to invest in the Holy Land than in the Crimea, where the Joint Distribution Committee contemplated settling 200,000 Russian Jews.[44]

The Crimean project crystallized the conflict over fund-raising between Zionists and anti- or non-Zionists that had been brewing for years. To Zionists the dollars spent on the Crimean project represented Jewish assets that might finally have put the settlement in Palestine on a sound economic footing. They found the priorities of the JDC leadership difficult to understand. There was a long tradition of rehabilitating eastern European Jews in place, and few did not know of the yeoman work of the "Joint," which had spent millions to shore up communities first devastated by the war, then ravaged by the civil war in Russia, and finally left economically bereft and politically disfranchised by the anti–small business policies of the Soviet regime and the hostility of the new Polish government. The JDC had earned the praise of Herbert Hoover for its effectiveness during the American Relief Administration's operations in eastern Europe. In Poland it had established a network of loan and credit societies and cooperative associations to help put Jewish communities on their feet. It had financed trade schools, cultural institutions, and soup kitchens for the Jewish needy.[45] Jewish philanthropists took great pride in this work and planned to continue it in the Crimea by adding a social engineering dimension to its relief program.

In 1922 the plight of the *lichentsy,* the nearly one million Jewish petty merchants of the Pale, who had been turned into virtual outcasts by the Communist regime, drew the attention of the "Joint."[46] If the Jewish class profile could be changed by resettling some Jews on the land, argued Joseph Rosen, a persuasive agronomist once exiled by the Bolsheviks, Jewish civil rights would be restored as a matter of course and they would again become self-supporting. The JDC program could apply to hundreds of thousands and was far cheaper then settling them in Palestine, argued Rosen. Rehabilitation in place cost under $500 per settler, whereas resettlement in Palestine came to $5,000. Philanthropists like Julius Rosenwald, who promised to donate $3.6 million to the Crimean resettlement scheme, argued that both Palestine and the Crimea were needed, since the Palestine economy could not absorb all who needed help even in the unlikely case that Russian Jews could be convinced to settle there.[47] Over 5,000 families, totaling almost 31,000 persons, had been successfully resettled in Argentina by the Jewish Colonization Association, and 10,000 Jews had been resettled on the land in the United States. The Crimean plan would be far easier to implement than these projects, since the settlers would not have to be moved to another country. Most important, the Soviet government was eager to cooperate. Land, its main contribution, would cost it nothing, while JDC funds would bring needed foreign exchange.

For the leaders of the JDC, resettlement in the Crimea offered a practical solution for Russian Jewry that did not raise the question of dual loyalty. More important, it would let them move from mundane, stopgap relief efforts to grandiose, long-range schemes of social engineering. Russian Jews seemed eager to participate, and the plan gained the support of idealists and social planners, who abounded in the Jewish community. It was particularly popular among anti-Zionist Jews of the Left. A group of one hundred such Jews, mostly from New York City, had already formed a communal farm they called "the Herald," about thirty miles from Moscow. Magnes, perhaps aware that a *Hechalutz* (Zionist pioneer) training farm had been established in the Crimea in 1919, saw the possibility of "a genuine spiritual relationshp between our Palestine *halutsim* and the *halutsim* of Russia."[48] Aware that the success of the plan would also serve as an answer to Zionism by offering an alternative Jewish homeland in the USSR, Communist party ideologues lent support. From the vantage point of the new "social engineers," whose influence in the JDC was at its height, the plan seemed practical. But convinced neither that these were the real reasons for JDC's support of the project nor that the plan could be realized, most Zionists remained adamantly opposed to the scheme.

In 1925, over loud Zionist protest, a special campaign to raise the necessary capital was initiated, and the first $400,000 was committed. By May, 4,000 Russian Jews had been resettled, and applications were pouring in. As a goodwill gesture, Rosen donated enough seed corn to plant 2.7 million acres in the Ukraine. When the first tractors arrived, a JDC official, aware of the bitter case against Henry Ford then progressing in the courts, noted with glee, "Jewish boys running Ford tractors."[49] In March 1926, after James Rosenberg, vice chairman of the JDC, had conferred with Secretary of Commerce Herbert Hoover and received unofficial sanction from the former relief commissioner, the last important element for the officers of JDC was in place—the approval of the American government. It appeared the scheme would be an overwhelming success.

But all did not go smoothly. Within the Soviet Union there was opposition from the Jewish branch of the Communist party (Yevsetskia), which, having played little role in the negotiations, was eager to show its mettle and loyalty. All rumors that the project might culminate in a separate Jewish republic in the Crimea were squelched after it became clear that there was considerable opposition to the settlements among Ukrainians and Crimean Tatars.[50] From within the Russian Jewish community there rose complaints regarding the inadequate scale of the plan considering the Jewish unemployment problem in the Soviet Union. Others pointed out that it was foolish to retrain Jews for agricultural work while ignoring their strong tradition in the crafts. All over the world, agriculture had become a troubled economic enterprise. Yet based on an esoteric ideology that gave agriculture preeminence, the arrogant social engineers of Agro-Joint, the agricultural resettlement section of JCD, had undertaken a project to reshape Russian Jewry in their own image. They needed only to look at the failed agricultural settlements of the Baron de Hirsch Fund in the United States to learn how futile such attempts were. But such arguments availed little. The program went forward.

Predictably, the most adamant opposition emanated from the Zionist camp. Having witnessed the Soviet regime's breakup of Jewish communal and religious institutions and the disfranchisement of thousands of Jewish *lichentsy,* Zionists were hard pressed to understand how such settlements could be established on land "wet with Jewish blood." True, the settlement in Palestine might be more expensive, but at least there Jews would not be subject to the whims of a hostile regime. "In Russia the Jew goes to the land only because he must," argued one journalist; "in Palestine . . . there is the added zest of a poetic vision, an imagined future and an eternal hope."[51] One could perhaps save individual Jews in Russia, but not Judaism. Repeatedly Zionist spokesmen pointed out that hundreds of rabbis, Hebrew teachers, and Zionist leaders had been arrested, many never to be heard from again. Jewish schools had been closed, and worship was forbidden. The Soviet regime was "the biggest pogrom maker against the Jewish soul . . . so far." If the oligarchs proceeded unchallenged, everything that had been achieved in Jewish governance by the American Jewish Congress movement would be for naught, argued Stephen Wise. A plan involving millions of dollars that would profoundly affect the lives of thousands of Jews in Palestine and the Soviet Union was decided behind closed doors by twelve men. It was bitterly ironic, others pointed out, that the JDC was spending millions in the Soviet Union while domestic communists, under direct orders from Moscow, were devastating the Jewish labor movement. The settlement scheme represented an unholy alliance between Wall Street and Moscow in which the money invested in the Crimea and the Ukraine would surely be lost.[52]

A meeting between supporters and opponents of the project was convened in Philadelphia on 13 September 1925. The JDC stated its case with the help of Louis Marshall, who had donated $100,000 to the project. Marshall used the favorable report of Louis Fisher, whom the AJCONG had commissioned to investigate the resettlement scheme. A temporary compromise was reached that endorsed Crimean resettlement as a short-run solution but also promised more financial support to the settlement in Palestine. Over the next three years the JDC spent $4.5 million on the Crimean resettlement, while $1.56 million was to be invested in the Palestine

Economic Corporation. That reduced the amount targeted for the Crimea by 50 percent, a considerable victory for the Zionists, but opposition voices were not stilled. So irate did the leaders of the AJCONG become that, despite the poor Zionist showing in the 1924 fund-raising campaign, it was decided to mount a separate campaign again in 1925. The goal would be to raise $15 million for Jewish settlements in Palestine. The figure matched what Agro-Joint planned to spend in the Crimea. In July 1925, despite the concession made by the JDC, which gave Palestine one-third of all funds collected in the 1924–25 campaign, the AJCONG widely distributed the *Index,* which mustered all arguments against the settlements in the Crimea and those favoring settlement in Palestine.

As support for the scheme within the Soviet regime weakened, the JDC leaders were placed in a quandary. They would not, of course, acknowledge that the Zionist enterprise had a special claim on Jewish philanthropy. "If the Zionists will insist on preference for Palestine," cried Marshall, "we will have to insist on what we think is right."[53] Marshall had acknowledged that there was risk in investing in the Soviet Union, but Ford and the Rockefellers, he pointed out, were doing the same. The United States, it was true, did not yet recognize the Soviet Union, but considerable trade was being carried on. In 1921 the United States Congress had voted $20 million for Soviet relief. Surely that was some comfort. But Rosen, whose passion for the Soviet experiment resembled that of the Zionists for their kibbutzim, was intent on rebuilding Jewish character, not merely on rehabilitation. Farming, he felt, would correct a tendency among Jews to be "nervous, impatient, fidgety, restless, [and] eager."[54] It would help Jews assimilate into Soviet life and mitigate anti-Semitism, which, Rosen pointed out, had been made illegal in Russia. Thousands of Jews were finding places in the new government bureaus, and Jews were disproportionately members of the emerging educated elite. Supporters of the project pointed out that during the civil war it was the Red Army that had protected the Jews. Men like John D. Rockefeller had contributed to the project because they understood it was doing the greatest good for the greatest number, which should be the only standard of evaluation. Dozens of favorable personal testimonies were featured in the Anglo-Jewish press to buttress the JDC's case for the Crimea.

Ultimately it was internal developments in the Soviet Union rather than Zionist opposition that caused the collapse of the Crimean scheme. By 1927 there were signs of yet another change in Soviet economic policy. The project's planners began to suspect that Soviet officials looked on the scheme primarily as a means of earning foreign exchange. The chairman of the JDC, Felix Warburg, originally a staunch supporter of the project, now opposed recognizing the Soviet Union and was prepared to scale down funding for the settlements and to abandon plans for a separate $25 million campaign. Instead the project would be funded by a handful of "big givers" like Julius Rosenwald, who had become personally involved. The term "colonization" was abandoned in favor of the more neutral "settlement." In 1928 the JDC renamed the project the American Society for Jewish Farm Settlements. The gradual retreat of the stewards of philanthropy was a victory for the Zionists, who, we have seen, favored greater allocations for the settlements in Palestine.

The perception that Soviet authorities would remove their support from the Crimean settlements was accurate. By 1929, when the last contingent of 25,000 Jews was being settled, Soviet apprehension had grown regarding security in the Far East. More important, Stalin had embarked on his forced collectivization policy. Both developments placed the fate of the Crimean settlements in doubt. The Soviet government, which was already pressing the settlers to integrate non-Jews into the colonies, now began the forced collectivization of agriculture. The colonies were among the first to fall victim and were losing their Jewish character as well. Some settlers were expelled because they had so improved their conditions that they could be classified as kulaks (prosperous farmers). The promised independence for Agro-Joint officials also proved chimerical. The Jewish section of the Soviet Communist party pushed vigorously for an even more grandiose scheme, a Jewish autonomous area in Birobidzhan in the Soviet Far East, an arid, mosquito-infested remote land. But ignoring both schemes, thousands of Soviet Jews gravitated toward urban centers where there were more opportunities. Over half of the 1,000 Jewish colonists who settled in Birobidzhan had left by February 1929.

The leaders of JDC watched sadly as Soviet policymakers abandoned one plan for another. In 1929 two of its principal American backers, Julius Rosenwald and Louis Marshall, died. It was also the year of the stock market crash and of crop failures in the Crimea and Ukraine. In 1930 the pariah status of the *lichentsy* was officially abolished. The dire situation of Soviet Jewry was somewhat improved. It was an appropriate time to phase out the scheme, but the JDC, anxious to sustain its relief effort, was careful not to sever its links with the Soviet government. But by 1933 the Crimea project, which had begun with such high hopes, was dead. The leaders of the JDC never acknowledged that the $16 million invested in the scheme between 1924 and 1929 was a loss. The thousands of resettled Soviet Jews, they argued, had been nurtured, and the Soviet authorities had adhered to their part of the agreement, at least for a time. But the failure of the project was undeniable and marked the last hurrah for decision making by social engineers able to enlist the capital of wealthy Jewish philanthropists. Thereafter these funds became more subject to community control, which meant that more would be earmarked for the yishuv.

The Crimean project contained a lesson for Zionists too. Within less than five years Agro-Joint had settled almost 200,000 Jews on the land—the equivalent of the size of the entire agricultural sector of the yishuv that Zionists had been building since the turn of the century. Clearly idealism by itself was insufficient to develop a viable agricultural economy. That required millions of dollars. They saw more clearly than ever that the answer was, as Brandeis had foreseen, to build a bridge to those who possessed such capital. The enlargement of the Jewish Agency for Palestine, the governing agency of the yishuv, to include non-Zionists was part of that strategy.

The process was begun by Chaim Weizmann after the Cleveland ZOA convention in 1921. Aware of the importance of the support of wealthy non-Zionists, Brandeis had welcomed them to his group after 1917. He had defanged the vexing dual-loyalties question by denying that American Jews needed to resettle in Palestine to consider themselves Zionists. At the London conference of the WZO in 1920 he had pushed for a new leadership consisting of "established" Jews. But after the debacle of the Cleveland convention that link had been broken. Weizmann was aware that Louis Marshall, the non-Zionist president of the American Jewish Committee, might be convinced to offer his service as a substitute for Brandeis. At the Carlsbad conference of the actions committee of the WZO, convened in September 1922, he pushed through a resolution declaring that the Jewish Agency should represent the "whole Jewish people," which meant including non-Zionists. Timely support by the Mizrachi movement ensured passage by a vote of 164 to 87.[55] The bitterly contested resolution gave Weizmann bait to attract Marshall to the idea. Marshall's credentials for the bridging role were good. He had never opposed individual projects in the Holy Land and had brought the AJCOMM to support the Balfour Declaration. Under the impression that the expanded agency would supersede

Keren Hayesod, the Zionists' fund-raising agency, and finally put American investments in Palestine on a businesslike basis, Marshall allowed himself to be persuaded. He was also aware that article 4 of the League of Nations mandate called for an agency composed of all Jews, not only Zionists, who were interested in building up Palestine. Marshall considered himself such a Jew.

In February 1924, joined by Cyrus Adler, Horace Stern, and Herbert Lehman, Marshall convened a nonpartisan conference of 150 leading American non-Zionists at the Hotel Astor in New York. He told the delegates that indifference to the settlement in Palestine "would do a thousand times more harm than all the Ku Klux Klans and Henry Fords."[56] Weizmann extended his congratulations but continued to face adamant opposition from within the Zionist camp. Included in that opposition was Stephen Wise, who distrusted Weizmann and was particularly incensed at the Crimean scheme that Marshall supported. Not until March 1927 was the formal Marshall-Weizmann agreement, now called "A Union of All Jewish Forces for the Upbuilding of Palestine," sealed. The *American Hebrew,* a powerful advocate of Crimean settlement, could barely contain its joy: "We are happy to wipe out the bitterness and attend to the healing of the scars," declared an editorial.[57]

Two committees had been appointed, one to deal with the subject of the Jewish Agency and the second to organize an investment corporation, to be called the Palestine Economic Corporation (PEC). The PEC was established in 1925 with a capital of $3 million. The JDC, now under relentless attack by the Zionists because of the Crimean settlement, transferred $1.5 million, originally intended for the Crimea, to the PEC. Fueled by the new spirit of goodwill, Keren Hayesod and the JDC agreed to mount a joint campaign in 1925 with a percentage automatically going for Palestine. But to Zionists the knowledge that millions were being poured into the Soviet Union was so disturbing that they reneged on the plan. In the midst of it all Wise's declaration that one Haim Bialik, a much-loved Hebrew poet, was worth a thousand Felix Warburgs ruffled more feathers.[58] At the same time Wise's "Jesus" speech, mentioned earlier, caused such rancor among the Orthodox that it threatened to disrupt the fragile Zionist fund-raising apparatus by removing him as chairman of the UPA. There were Zionists who, convinced that the movement was selling its soul by admitting non-Zionists and capitalist assimilationists to its innermost recesses, opposed Weizmann's strategy of attracting wealthy non-Zionist Jews. Eventually the drastic downward spiral of remittances to Keren Hayesod persuaded the most adamant opponents that desperate measures were required. Such an alliance might be worth it if the non-Zionists would quickly come through with capital. "At best this is a mean business," observed one such at the Zurich conference of the WZO in 1929, "but if only there were a check on the table, at least it would be a business."[59]

In the bickering over the number of non-Zionists to be incorporated, Marshall was not averse to pointing out that their disproportionate monetary contribution warranted greater representation, if only because there needed to be "a reasonable relation between taxation and representation."[60] The "pact of glory," as the agreement came to be known, gave non-Zionists four seats on the Agency's governing council. Weizmann would serve as president of the Agency, and Marshall would be chairman of the 112 member council, 50 percent of which would represent Jewish communities outside Palestine. Forty percent of that number, forty-four non-Zionists in all, would represent American Jewry, and 10 percent, other Jewish communities. The non-Zionists thus posed a threat, since the Zionist movement was so badly fragmented that it could easily be outvoted in the council by a skillful practice of coalition politics. That realization triggered yet more vituperation.

In its early years the work of the expanded Jewish Agency went well. In December 1926, as part of the agreement with Marshall, a Joint Palestine Survey Commission, on which Felix Warburg represented the non-Zionists, had been established to produce a Palestine development program. The report, delivered to Marshall and Weizmann in London in June 1928, examined virtually every facet of the economy, from forestation to the enhancement of the water supply, to the possibility of developing a tourist industry. Surprisingly, it presented a vigorous defense of what had already been achieved but advocated apportioning state lands to the Jewish settlers.

But within two years it was clear that the expanded Jewish Agency would not work. As a device to mobilize more funds for the settlement in Palestine, its timing was wrong. The depression had created a vacuum in fund-raising that "capitalist" Jews seemed in no rush to fill. Between 1930 and 1938 the two fund-raising arms of the Zionist movement, Keren Kayemeth and Keren Hayesod, collected only $12,137,000, less than was collected in the nine years preceding the expansion of the Jewish Agency. The non-Zionists were usually unable to be present at the council meetings of the Jewish Agency held in Jerusalem and had to send substitutes. Absenteeism increased after Marshall's death and Weizmann's temporary removal from power in 1931. Predictably, many administrative positions of the Agency became sinecures apportioned among the various political factions of the Zionist movement. The Agency became highly politicized and increasingly ineffective. It did not succeed in muting the vituperation aimed at the non-Zionists by Zionist ideologues. Moses Leavitt, an assistant secretary of the JDC, felt himself subject to such uncivil behavior that he informed Cyrus Adler he would no longer attend meetings.[61]

For the stewards in the leadership of the AJCOMM and JDC, the final years of the twenties marked the end of their ability to shape the American Jewish future. Their social engineering scheme in the Crimea had come to nothing. But the Zionists who had warned that the scheme was bound to fail because it lacked not only Jewish control but Jewish content were in no position to gloat over their prescience, since after the riots of 1929 the settlement in Palestine seemed equally insecure. The Arab population was hostile, and British support for the yishuv had virtually disappeared. But as Germany began to eject its Jews, it became clear that there was nowhere else that Jews in need of a haven could go. Only the Jewish settlement in Palestine was eager to receive them. Most American Jews came to recognize that Palestine offered the most practical way of ensuring Jewish survival.

The Zionization of American Jewry developed gradually and not by design. After the Arab riots of 1936, UPA set itself a goal of $3.5 million but collected less than half that amount. The lack of development capital threatened to leave the Zionists in the most humiliating of all positions: a movement with grandiose goals of nation building but with neither the finances nor the organizational coherence to realize them. At the same time the bloody Arab riots demonstrated once again the difficulties faced by the Palestine enterprise.

Few foresaw the revitalization of the American Zionist movement that began in the mid-thirties. The dire developments in Europe would do for the Zionist movement what it had been unable to do for itself. It quickly developed from a passive presence to an activist, influential force on the American political scene. It was as if American Jewry had finally broken through a dam to achieve a Zionist consensus. The ZOA, virtually defunct in 1930, climbed to a membership of over 52,000 in 1939. Hadassah had 73,000 members in 1940, almost triple its 1925 membership. Sales of the shekel, a token payment that carried with it voting rights in the World Zionist Congress, the international organization of the Zionist movement, rose to almost a quarter of a million in 1938. Overnight the movement seemed transformed. The rabbinic bodies, including the formerly anti-Zionist Central Conference of American Rabbis (CCAR), became increasingly outspoken in supporting Zionist objectives. Even Cyrus Adler, passionately opposed to "political Zionism," came to favor a Jewish commonwealth in Palestine "if it can be done."[62] Like many other Jews, he came to realize that the crisis in Europe made the Zionist settlement in Palestine the most practical solution.

The elusive goal of penetrating the professional fund-raising apparatus, which had been dominated by the stewards, was achieved in 1939 when the JDC agreed to establish a joint fund-raising agency, the United Jewish Appeal (UJA). Thereafter, with the exception of 1940, the allocations assigned to the United Palestine Appeal (UPA) rose steadily every year. Finally a National Emergency Committee for Palestine, composed of most of the major organizations, was established in 1938. American Zionism finally had an address. In the next few years the Holocaust would radicalize the Zionist movement. But the process of energizing the movement was slow—too slow to make a difference for those destined for the death camps.

Behind its wartime militancy the old weaknesses of the movement persisted. Its leadership continued to be mediocre, possessing little of the vigor of the leaders of the Jewish labor movement or the commitment of European Zionist leadership.[63] Its internal rifts, especially between the Revisionist and Socialist Zionists, grew more intense. American Zionism was thus peculiarly ill equipped to assume the responsibilities that the coming crisis would thrust upon it. Only during the postwar decade did the movement enter a new, dynamic phase of its development. European Jewry had been destroyed, and the Jewish settlement in Palestine held out the promise that a new center of Judaism could be established to take its place. It took the catastrophic experience of European Jewry to convince American Jews of that. That tragedy reshaped American Jewish consciousness, creating Zionists of a distinctly American kind.

The proliferation of Jewish organizations during the interwar years reflected the economic, ideological, and social diversity of American Jewry. Each ideology, sometimes even a bare shadow of an ideology, produced its own organizational expression. The resulting multiplicity of organizations was not a sign that American Jewry was organized. On the contrary, the primary problem of those seeking to unify American Jewry during the Holocaust years was how to harmonize the different ideological voices represented by these organizations. That harmony was necessary if American Jewry was to effectively play the role assigned to it by history, that of advocate for world Jewry before the American government. The New York Kehillah, the American Jewish Congress, the American Jewish Committee, and the federation movement, each in its own way, offered a strategy to organize American Jewry nationally. There would be four additional attempts during the war, but none succeeded.

In the twenties the possibility of unity among the organizations was increased by the challenge Zionism posed. The Zionists spoke of "Jewish peoplehood" and "democracy" as essential requirements for a healthy communal life. But for the still-powerful anti-Zionists, the idea of Jewish nationalism remained unacceptable. Beyond the issue of nationalism there was the question of power, which in American Jewish life was linked to the large sums of money organized fund-raising was producing. Unable to penetrate the citadels of established Jewry, especially its developing fund-raising apparatus, the Zionist movement attempted unsuccessfully to build its own apparatus. But the UPA was only partially successful: it could never compete with the JDC and the federations. Jewish communal politics became budgetary politics. The split in the Zionist movement that occurred at the Cleveland convention of the ZOA in 1921 concerned, beyond anything else, control of funds. It came up again when the JDC embarked on a policy of resettling Russian Jews in the Crimea and the Ukraine. The allocation of philanthropic dollars to the project was bitterly contested by the Zionists. Finally, the money issue also lay behind Chaim Weizmann's desire to broaden the membership of the Jewish Agency for Palestine to include non-Zionists. The existence of large sums of money lent Jewish communal politics a weightiness not commonly found in the internal politics of other ethnic groups. So too did the serious approach to ideology.

The issues that preoccupied American Jews during the interwar period were those raised by Zionist ideology. They were relevant because they concerned Jewish survival, not merely the rehabilitation of Jews. That was the concern of the social service professionals and the "barons" who conceived of the Crimea project. It is in that sense that Zionism rejudaized the political culture of American Jewry.

We have examined separately the strands that composed the internal Jewish dialogue. But the conflicts that wracked Jewish life were occurring all at once, playing to an audience that was itself undergoing rapid change when it became aware of the crisis faced by Jews in Europe. The emerging individuated, secular American Jews could no longer be led in the same way as their forebears. The unresolved problem of American Jewish identity and leadership, which haunts Jews to this day, was but a reflection of that. The historian can hardly fail to detect a rudderless quality in American Jewish communal life during the twenties and thirties that goes beyond the failure to produce a leadership cadre to succeed the German Jewish stewards, which some will see as its greatest weakness. It is doubtful whether the more privately oriented Jews of the second and third generation would have followed such leaders: detribalized secular Jews required a new kind of leadership. Failure in the public sector of Jewish life stood in sharp contrast to the remarkable achievement of Jews in the private sector. It may well be that during the interwar period the best minds were still preoccupied with establishing themselves economically and professionally. Their energy was invested elsewhere. The result was a "lost generation" that proved unable to handle and in some cases even to recognize the enormous challenge to Jewish survival in the thirties and forties.

CHAPTER SEVEN

AMERICAN JEWISH POLITICAL BEHAVIOR DURING THE INTERWAR PERIOD

THE IDEA of a Jewish conspiracy to dominate the world—a mainstay of the anti-Semitic imagination—requires the assumption that Jews are bound together by a common ideology and political culture. From there the notion of a collective Jewish identity has overflowed into popular culture. We therefore need to exercise care lest we conceal the basic diversity of the American Jewish political voice. In their moment of testing during the years of the Holocaust, it was the inability of American Jews to speak with one voice that prevented them from adequately responding to the threat facing Jews in Europe. Jewish political diversity can in general be traced back to the way various segments of Jewry responded to emancipation. We learn in the following pages that forces at work in the free environment of America also weakened Jewry's historical corporate character.

Established Jews who traced their roots to the German Jewish migration of the nineteenth century often felt threatened by the idea of a specifically Jewish political identity and interest. They vehemently denied that there was, or should be, a separate Jewish interest expressed through the ballot. When Israel Zangwill suggested in an address to the AJCONG on 14 October 1923 that the absence of a Jewish vote was a "disgrace, not a policy to be commended," the leaders of the AJCOMM took umbrage. Louis Marshall, who opposed even the existence of an organization like the Jewish War Veterans, informed the president of the Hebrew American League of New Jersey that there was no such thing as a Jewish vote and that "it would be a misfortune if there were." He refused to lead a Jewish delegation to Marion, Ohio, after Warren G. Harding's victory in 1920. In 1928 Samuel Rosenman, a political adviser to Al Smith and a member of the executive committee of the AJCOMM, proposed a resolution that opposed ethnic voting as "contrary to American democracy."[1]

But much as it disturbed the patricians, by the twenties it was no longer possible to deny the existence of ethnic politics in America. The remarkable success of the city political machines had earlier convinced the leaders of both political parties to establish special foreign-language departments to mobilize the ethnic vote. In 1921 Bernard Richards, a founder of the AJCONG, directed that department for the Democrats. In 1944 the position was filled by David Niles. The heightened ethnic interest in politics that grew out of the war continued in the postwar era. A growing number of congressional resolutions reflected a continuing interest among ethnic voters in the welfare of their former homelands. Anxious to defeat Woodrow Wilson's League of Nations once and for all, Senator Henry Cabot Lodge had spared no effort to mobilize ethnic resentment among German-Americans during the "solemn referendum" campaign of 1920.[2] American Jews were in the forefront of this heightened ethnic activity. In 1917 they had wrung affirmation of the Balfour Declaration from the Wilson administration, and five years later the ZOA leadership enlisted Senator Lodge, then at the peak of his influence, to once again affirm support for the mandate. The result was the Lodge-Fish congressional resolution. Even Louis Marshall, who had counseled against establishing Jewish political clubs, testified against the restrictive immigration legislation, which he was convinced served neither Jewish nor American interests. Often the bitter ideological divisions within American Jewry interfered with projecting a coherent communal voice in the political arena. But we shall see that there were also instances where compelling need overcame these divisions.

Strangely, those Jews wishing to deny the existence of a recognizable Jewish political interest continually faced anti-Semitic elements that never doubted it. During the twenties, partly as a result of Ku Klux Klan actions, anti-Semitism, or at least some version of the Jewish question, played a role in virtually every major election and many local ones. In the heavily Jewish East Harlem Twentieth Congressional District, the campaign between Fiorello La Guardia and Henry Frank, a mediocre Jewish lawyer who was the Tammany candidate, became bitter when Frank accused La Guardia of anti-Semitism. The ability of the irrepressible La Guardia to address the charges in Yiddish helped him win the election. The issue of anti-Semitism resurfaced during the mayoral campaign of 1933, when La Guardia was again accused of it by "Holy Joe" McKee, running on an independent ticket.3 In the New York State gubernatorial campaign of 1928, the Jewish candidate, Albert Ottinger, a Republican running against Franklin Roosevelt, vainly tried to defend himself against charges that he was not Jewish enough.

Every federal election after 1936 featured some scurrilous anti-Semitic episode. During the campaign of 1940 there was fear that German funds supplied to domestic anti-Semitic groups would turn the campaign into an anti-Semitic crusade. In response, Roosevelt and Wendell Willkie stressed their support of religious tolerance. At a news conference at Hyde Park on 5 July Roosevelt included "freedom of religion" as one of the five freedoms requisite for international peace. A religious tolerance plank was included in the Democratic platform. It was also a note picked up in August 1941 when the Atlantic Charter embodying Allied war aims was proclaimed. Striving not to be outdone and aware that Nazi front organizations had come out in his favor, Wendell Willkie suggested that anti-Semitism ought to be considered a criminal offense, rejected an endorsement by Father Charles Coughlin, and denounced Nazi persecution of Jews in his speech accepting the Republican nomination on 17 August 1940. In March 1944 a special committee composed of Al Smith, Will Hays, and Joseph Proskauer was formed to combat racist propaganda during the forthcoming election. But again the campaign witnessed some anti-Semitic fallout. Both candidates were berated for their supposed links to Jews, but the brunt of the attack was again borne by those in Roosevelt's "Jew Deal," especially Sidney Hillman, whom anti-Semitic literature linked to William Z. Foster, chairman of the Communist party. One leaflet distributed in Stamford, Connecticut, accused Hillman of trying to become "the power behind the throne of a fourth term administration." Strangely, the usually inflammable Yiddish press, aware by then that victory in the war was assured, treated the Hillman matter calmly.4 The Republican candidate, Thomas Dewey, was variously accused of being secretly Jewish and of having sung in a synagogue ("Tommy the Cantor") while attending Columbia Law School and also of being connected with the Lehman international banking interest.5

The second generation was less prone to conceal its Jewish identity or its support of sectarian interests. The appointment of prominent Jews to the bench or to ambassadorial positions, or the election victory of a Jewish office seeker, was a source of pride for the Jewish voter as similar successes were for other ethnics. A candidate's position on an issue of Jewish concern such as immigration or anti-Semitism was openly discussed in the Jewish press. The 90 percent of the vote in heavily Jewish districts that Herbert Lehman garnered during his three gubernatorial campaigns was something special. Here Jewish support was not assured simply because the candidate was Jewish. Lehman captured the heart of Jewish voters when he contributed $50,000 to the troubled ILGWU after the 1926 strike. He was also a patrician and a liberal, an unbeatable combination in the Jewish community. Generally, however, Jewish voters were ethnic but rarely ethnocentric. The strong universalist strain in Jewish political culture blunted the parochial aspect of ethnicity but could not totally eliminate it. The growing number of high government officials who were Jewish, such as Eugene Meyer, Jr., a member of the Federal Farm Loan Board on whom Coolidge depended for advice on the depressed agricultural sector, and the Jewish advisers around Al Smith, became a source of pride for Jewish voters. Most important, there was visible proof of a Jewish presence in the Jewish congressional delegation and numerous local political offices, enumerated annually in the *American Jewish Yearbook* and the Anglo-Jewish press.[6] Jews were finally in the government: what greater sign of acceptance could one desire?

What gave American Jewry its strong ideological coloration was that the socialist element in the Jewish electorate made for an intensely activist constituency. During the twenties about a tenth of Jewish voters cast their ballots for Socialist candidates, and the number may have climbed to as high as 38 percent for the presidential candidacy of Eugene Debs in 1920. Socialists sometimes seemed to preempt the Jewish political voice even though the strength of the Socialist party declined in Jewish districts during the twenties. In 1922 the Lower East Side, which had sent the Socialist Meyer London to Congress, was gerrymandered out of existence, and Jewish socialist districts in Brooklyn's Brownsville and Williamsburg were disrupted by the split in the Socialist party. There remained a maverick reformist-universalist streak in the Jewish electorate, reflected in a tendency to veer off to third-party reformist candidates: 22 percent cast their ballots for the Progessive Robert La Follette in the election of 1924, far higher than among other ethnics.[7]

If the number of Jewish votes cast for Socialist candidates was comparatively small, most Jewish voters were usually found on the left end of the political spectrum, which ranged from communism at one extreme to a social democratic tendency—later to be known as liberalism—toward the center. One historian hypothesizes that the preference was based on an amorphous "constellation of values" blending notions of democratic social reform at home with international comity.[8] There is little agreement on why Jews in particular were so drawn to these humanistic values. In part, at least, it was a reaction to the nativism of the twenties. Jews considered intolerance the handmaiden of illiberalism. Having sensed the threat of the hooded Klan, Jews opted for pluralism and strict separation of church and state. Jewish voters joined the Progressive reformers in advocating regulation of the trusts even while their socialist brothers and sisters favored direct government ownership of industry. The synthesis was the mixed economy and the welfare statism of the New Deal, whose social security, housing, and health-care programs were first incubated in the Jewish labor movement.

Jewish voters resembled the Progressive reformers but came to reform from a different angle. They were, for example, more sensitive to the activities of the refurbished Ku Klux Klan, which they wanted declared illegal. Most Jewish voters also agreed with Felix Frankfurter that there had been a miscarriage of justice in the case of Sacco and Vanzetti. Considering themselves modern and secular, they viewed the Scopes trial as further evidence of the ascendency of fundamentalism, which concealed its "medievalism" under the cloak of religion. Predictably, secular Jewish voters favored openness and accessibility in all things, whether Harvard University or a liberal immigration policy.

It was in the neighborhoods of second-generation voters that politics was most immediate and earthy. Jews did not require the revelations of Lincoln Steffens to inform them of the corruption of the local political machine. They lived in an uneasy relationship with the Irish "bosses" who typically dominated the machines. That did not mean all Jews disdained the local political club. It was understood that the machine performed a service for immigrants. What nettled Jews, who idealized democracy more in the abstract than in concrete forms, were the low types it brought to the fore. The Jewish aspirant to a political career through machine auspices was not held in high esteem because he possessed none of the virtues Jews sought in leaders. When Congressman Sol Bloom candidly admitted that Tammany Hall had selected him to run for office because he was "amiable and solvent," he also revealed why most Jews found him lacking in stature even though they voted for him. He shared little of their inclination to seek transcendence through politics. Similarly, Samuel Dickstein was chosen by the "boss" of the Knickerbocker Club, between Pitt and Rivington Streets on New York's East Side, because as a Yiddish speaker he could be a viable opponent of the Jewish Socialist candidates. Dickstein remained throughout one of Tammany's boys and was recognized as such by his Jewish constituents.9 The local Jewish politicians were practical and burdened with little of the "idealism" that so attracted Jewish voters, who recognized the usefulness of these politicians but did not view them as their leaders. Sometimes they were an embarrassment, as in the case of the corruption scandal involving Judge Jesse Silverman, an appointee of the Flynn machine in the Bronx.

Jews were strangely unclubbable. As a group they had become less dependent than other immigrants on the largess of the political machine. By 1920 their general prosperity, rooted partly in their ethnic economy, took up some unemployment slack. A strong social service network went far to alleviate the condition of the very poor. At the same time the settlement houses served as a training school for second-generation reform-minded Jews who eschewed the sleazy politics of the political club. Henry Moskowitz, an early supporter of Al Smith, was associated with the Madison Street Settlement House. His wife, Belle Moskowitz, had been on the board of the Educational Alliance. Lillian Wald, Henry Morgenthau, Jr., and Sidney Hillman were associated with the Henry Street Settlement House. These Jews would help convert the socialist agenda to the reform program of Al Smith and the New Deal. In the process they also established a link to non-Jewish patrician reformers like Adolf Berle, Jr., Eleanor Roosevelt, and Harry Hopkins, who were also involved in the settlement house movement.

The Jewish electorate possessed an uncommonly broad interpretation of its group interest, and Jews repeatedly crossed ethnic and party lines to support the candidates they felt best upheld the values they cherished. That occurred in La Guardia's race in the East Harlem district in 1920 and in Franklin Roosevelt's gubernatorial race in 1928. In both cases a Jewish opponent was defeated with the help of the Jewish vote. It would be easy to attribute Jews' characteristic liberal political proclivities to values deeply embedded in Judaic religious culture. In the case of the Reform movement, sometimes called liberal or progressive Judaism, that was the rationale given for the positions taken. Reform leaders like Stephen Wise, Judah Magnes, and Abba Hillel Silver, who staunchly upheld the full liberal agenda, felt they were acting according to prophetic Judaism. A similar rationale permitted Jewish radicals in search of Judaic roots to argue that socialism was a secular version of the Judaic prophetic tradition. Chaim Zhitlovsky, a well-known voice who spoke for Jewish secular radicals, argued that the Jewish section of the newly established Communist International was "the only organization that seeks to realize the word of the prophets."[10] Many Jewish voters, in the process of abandoning their religious culture, were easily convinced that they were merely observing its basic tenets in a "modern" way.

Yet it was often precisely such radicals who were least knowledgeable and committed to the Judaism in which they imagined such values to be embedded. The more pious the Jewish voters, the less likely they were to be influenced by socialism or reformist tenets.[11] More likely the ideas associated with democratic socialism and liberalism, which so attracted Jewish voters, stemmed from the Enlightenment, which Jews favored because it granted them civil and political rights as part of being citizens of a modern nation-state. Like the political culture of all Western Jewries, that of American Jews was rooted in their postemancipation history.[12]

The Russian Revolution earned a special place among politically engaged Jews because it was considered part of the continuing emancipation then happening in Russia, a land to which many American Jews traced their ancestry. It held out the promise that Russia had finally embarked on the road to progress and modernity. The new Soviet regime seemed eager to recruit Jewish talent. To negate the revolution meant to abandon the hope that motivated Jewish political culture.

Nevertheless, by the mid-twenties much of the attraction the Russian Revolution held for Jews had dissipated. The wanton destruction of Jewish cultural and religious institutions and the imprisonment of thousands of Jewish leaders, coupled with the drive of American communists to co-opt Jewish unions and cultural institutions, cut through its mystique. By 1928 Jewish leaders of liberal or socialist persuasion, like Lillian Wald, Horace Kallen, and David Dubinsky, realized there were anti-Semites among the Stalinist heirs of Lenin's mantle. Socialists like Baruch Vladeck, managing editor of the *Forward,* and Morris Hillquit, head of the National Committee of the Socialist party, became so disaffected that they refused even to support extending diplomatic recognition to the Soviet Union, an issue that drew much Jewish interest in the twenties.[13]

There is an alternative explanation for the drawing power of left-wing ideologies among the second-generation. The political ideologies many second-generation Jews came to hold dear were not rooted in generational rebellion but were part of a normal socialization process. Their parents already favored these ideas. One noted radical recalls only a smooth entrance into radical politics. At Townsend Harris High School, from which Paul Jacobs graduated, everyone was stylishly radical; it was the norm. By the time he was ready to enroll at City College of New York, which by the thirties was a veritable finishing school for radical politics, "there was only one world into which [he] wanted to be taken and accepted."[14] The existence of a critical mass in certain Jewish neighborhoods generated not so much specifically liberal or socialist ideology as an urban ethnic culture in which possessing "humanistic" values believed to be associated with these ideologies was taken for granted. Whether one was a socialist or merely liberal depended on the degree of commitment, but few questioned whether these were the best values to uphold. A Jewish youth growing up heard them at home, in neighborhood discussions, at lectures at the Labor Temple on Fourteenth Street, or at Brownsville's Labor Lyceum. We should note, however, that the Jewish neighborhoods that generated the culture of the Left were more prevalent in New York, Philadelphia, and Boston than they were in the South and West. In Chicago, for example, Jewish radicalism was more muted, and the switchover to the Democratic party was also slower.[15]

But such neighborhood socialization did not necessarily lead to membership in the Communist party. Relatively few Jews became Party members, and those who did were often more attracted by the active social life than by the ideology. Eager to recruit mass support among Jews, the Communist party was particularly adept at organizing local social clubs, folk-dancing societies, even a mandolin orchestra and cheap vacation resorts. The talent and energy the Jewish Left expended for communalism was visible in every Jewish neighborhood. By 1931 there were in New York City two dozen neighborhood clubs of various types related to the Party. In 1926 the Party opened a Jewish Workers' University, which included in its curriculum courses in Yiddish literature and culture. For the lonely people who abound in cities, the communist fraternal network offered a ready-made social life. Once involved, it was but a short leap to political activism.

Having little historical experience in the exercise of power led Jews to fantasize about how society might be better organized. Such fantasizing could easily become the incubator for radical ideologies, which were characterized by utter rationality rather than by humanity. For Jewish radical intellectuals, theorizing about a just social order was the equivalent of a sport. It was reinforced by a high-status reward for idealism, or *ibergegebenkayt,* a Yiddish term suggesting commitment. For Jews idealism in itself was considered a virtue. When combined with oratorical ability, as in the case of Stephen Wise or Abba Hillel Silver, it was easily mistaken for *chochma,* or wisdom, the most highly cherished of all human attributes. That radical intellectuals like Abraham Cahan, Morris Hillquit, or Meyer London were chosen for political leadership struck other ethnics as odd. "We got our bookworms too," observed a Tammany leader, "but we don't make them district leaders, we keep them for ornament on parade day."[16]

In reality, by the twenties radical socialist intellectuals rarely occupied leadership positions in the American Jewish community. Unlike Europe, here radicals were compelled to leave the realm of theory and enter the relatively open political process, lest they lose credibility. The result was leader-activists who used politics to further their "program." Their presence was already making itself felt in the entourage of a young Tammany politician, Al Smith. Appointed to a special committee by the Women's Democratic Union, Lillian Wald and Belle Moskowitz pushed hard to get their ameliorative program in the areas of public health, housing, and education included in the Democratic platform of 1924. Stephen Wise was a leader in the unsuccessful drive to get an anti-Klan plank into that Democratic platform. Ideological commitment tended to activate new energies and talent that, in the political environment of the American city, could be released directly into the political process without danger. In the first generation there were those who sorely missed the risk of underground politics prevalent in prerevolutionary Russia—it had added an extra thrill to their lives. Perhaps it was the very accessibility of political life that turned them to dissidence.

Paradoxically, the same ideological commitment that produced political activists also led to an avoidance of the earthy quid pro quos of machine politics. A random sample of 1,500 Jewish families taken in 1925 showed that only 20 percent could be found on the election rolls, 10 percent higher than for Italian-Americans.[17] But the twenties was a general low point in enthusiasm for politics. In 1896, 82.8 percent of the electorate voted, but by 1924 the proportion had declined to 51.1 percent. The only legislation of real significance passed by Congress during the twenties was the restrictive immigration laws, and there the interest of Jews hardly seemed to matter. A greater percentage of Jewish voters were registered as Socialists and inde-pendents, and once involved they were more likely to vote, but generally Jews were not exempt from indifference to the passionless politics of the decade of privatism.

We delve next into remarkable change of Jewish party affiliation from Republican to Democrat during the twenties. It is through that change that the new sources of Jewish political behavior during the Depression decade may best be viewed. The conversion did not occur all at once, nor did it affect Jews alone. As late as the election of 1920, which Wilson intended to be a "solemn referendum" over the issue of joining the League of Nations, 43 percent of the Jewish vote was cast for the Republican candidate, Warren G. Harding. But four years later, despite the 22 percent drawn to the third-party candidacy of Robert La Follette, the march into the Democratic party was noteworthy. Davis received 51 percent of the Jewish vote. In the elec-tions that followed the percentage of Jewish votes for the Democrats grew steadily. In 1928 Jews cast 72 percent of their votes for Al Smith, and in 1932, when Franklin Roosevelt was the Democratic candidate, the number rose to 82 percent. The Jewish vote remained over 90 percent Democratic until the presidential campaign of 1948. The change in party affiliation of Jews elected to Congress was also apparent. In the seventy-fifth Congress (1937–39) there were nine Jewish Democrats in the House and one Jewish Republican, a complete reversal from the sixty-sixth Congress (1919–21), when there were five Jewish Republicans and only one Jewish Democrat.[18] By the 1930s Jews had become not merely regular Democrats, but the party's most loyal ethnic constituency.

Jewish voters were among several urban ethnic groups drawn to the new urban base of the Democrats. That movement was accelerated by Al Smith and by the Depression. Yet there is little in Smith's early political background to suggest that he would be drawn to second-generation Jewish social reformers, or they to him. Since the Mortara kidnapping case in 1858, Catholics and Jews were hardly on the best of terms. By the twenties it was clear that not only were the assumptions that informed Jewish political culture at loggerheads with those of Irish-Americans, but there was also a clash of interest at the clubhouse level and in the foreign-policy arena. As a quintessential Tammany machine politician of Irish Catholic background, Smith seemed an unlikely favorite for Jewish voters. But he spoke a few words of Yiddish, an asset for politicians who desired to build a career in New York City, where over 25 percent of the electorate was Jewish. He was also charming, buoyant, and from a Jewish perspective right on two issues: he favored a liberal immigration policy and had moved to outlaw the Klan in New York State.

The tensions between Jews and Catholics over the events in Mexico did not noticeably affect growing Jewish support for the Democrats, especially Al Smith. The attempt by the Calles regime (1924–34) to redefine the relationship of the Mexican government to the church had caused bitter resentment among American Catholics during the twenties. In Mexico, "Cristeros" retreated to the mountains to wage guerrilla warfare. Despite anti-Catholic feeling, American Catholic leaders called for government intercession. The conflict was temporarily resolved when Coolidge sent Dwight Murrow to Mexico to find a way out of the impasse, which also concerned the crucial issue of the expropriation of the subsoil rights of American oil companies. But as late as February 1933 the United States bishops issued another in a series of strong protests against Mexico's antichurch policies.

Jews were not directly involved in the Calles episode, but neither did they support the American church's pressure for intervention. The Jewish response was shaped more by an overriding concern for strict church-state separation than by anti-Catholicism. But socialist elements within the Jewish community had long before identified the church as "reactionary" and were oblivious to the aroused feelings within the immigrant Catholic community. Hostility had already been aroused by the continuing controversy regarding prayer in the schools. In the winter of 1926 the debate raged over reciting the Ten Commandments in public schools. Concerned about a "swelling tide of crime," several Catholic and Protestant clergymen advocated that the Decalogue be read in public schools each day. Jewish spokesmen, convinced there was no verbal cure-all for moral laxness, saw the move as a church attempt to gain a wedge for teaching religion in public schools and staunchly opposed the idea. For Catholics the Jewish position may have looked like yet another example of Jewish atheism and radicalism, but for the Reform rabbis who cautioned against the idea, the wall between church and state protected freedom of religion. By the mid-thirties the confrontation over government intervention in Mexico was escalated when the two groups found themselves supporting opposite sides in the Spanish civil war. For the Irish and other Catholics, Jews were supporters of "Godless communism," while Jews were aware that in few places did Father Coughlin find more enthusiastic listeners than Boston, a center of Irish Catholicism in America.[19]

We have noted that second-generation Jews were not reconciled to the continued dominance of the Irish-run political machines in Jewish districts. The political cultures of the two communities seemed constantly at loggerheads. For the Irish, politics was a profession in which one could perform well or badly; for Jews, who carried a heavy ideological freight into the political arena, it was an instrument for the "repair" *(tikkun)* of the world. That is what the transition from socialism to practical politics often came to. The Irish were puzzled by the central role Jews gave to ideology. The moral zeal Jews brought to practical politics aroused Irish wonder and sometimes ire, often making it impossible to carry on the normal political transactions of governance. Jews in their turn were repelled by the seeming corruption and self-aggrandizement of politics as practiced by the Irish. They had little idea that the Irish, despite their contempt for ethics-oriented politics, were the most liberal of the Catholic ethnics.

Had the cultural dissonance between Jews and Irish remained latent, it might eventually have been resolved as Jewish voters became more Americanized. Instead it was reinforced by a clash of interests concerning political "spoils" at the precinct level. The Irish-Americans had early on gained control of the political machines that governed American cities, and they proved reluctant to share power with other immigrant groups, whose growing numbers entitled them to party representation. Undoubtedly this was one of the reasons Jews and other hyphenates continued to be loyal to the Republican party. As late as 1936, of the ten Jews elected to the Massachusetts general court, eight were Republicans. By 1920 several factors, including a relative decline in numbers, weakened the Irish hold on city political machines. But having developed few alternative avenues of mobility in commerce, the Irish continued to view the machine and the jobs it provided as a clan preserve. During the 1930s, 30 percent of Tammany's members were Jewish, but only 10 percent of its leaders were. In 1923 there were no Jews among the eight associate school superintendents and only one among the thirty district superintendents in New York. In a city where Jewish students made up almost half the school population, only one of the thirty high-school principals was Jewish. Irish reluctance to share power became a source of Jewish resentment.[20] Jewish appointments to cabinet posts in city government occurred primarily when anti-Tammany Republican administrations or the fusion administrations of Mayors Seth Low, Purroy Mitchell, and Fiorello La Guardia were in power. During La Guardia's administration especially, the number of Jewish appointments rose sharply.

For Jews, who had built up their own businesses, the maldistribution of political spoils may not at first have caused great concern. They did not look to the political club for jobs. The confrontation resulted from the high priority Jewish reform leaders gave to the expansion of the civil service merit system. That stole the spoils from the clubhouse and gave an increasing proportion of jobs to Jews. During the La Guardia administration in New York the Jewish share of such positions rose from 55 to 74 percent. The club's lifeblood was its power to grant benefits to party loyalists, but the best positions were now distributed based on examination scores. There were complaints in the *Brooklyn Tablet,* a newspaper with a largely Catholic readership, about the paucity of Irish names on the civil service lists, but little could be done about it.

Not until 1923 did Brooklyn's Jews succeed in forming their own political club. It was first organized by Hymie Shorenstein, a shrewd, semiliterate "boss," in the almost all Jewish Brownsville election district. But Shorenstein's club hardly fit the machine mold. From its inception the club had a distinct ideological impulse that matched Brownsville's maverick streak and its socialist proclivity. Approximately a quarter of Brownsville's vote went to socialist mayority candidates, Norman Thomas in 1929 and Morris Hillquit in 1932. But it also led directly to the election of Emanuel Celler, who represented a step up from the mediocre clubhouse types Jewish districts usually sent to Congress. During the thirties more inroads were made into formerly Irish political preserves in places like New York, New Haven, and Providence. The growing social welfare role assumed by the federal government during the Depression delivered yet another blow to the influence of the political machine, so that by 1945 it had become a mere shadow of itself. Few Jewish voters mourned its passing.[21]

Although stemming from the clubhouse environment of Tammany, Al Smith came to represent the reform tendency within the weakened political machine. Some of his political problems stemmed from having to brave the opposition of Tammany stalwarts who resented his granting political spoils to other ethnics, especially Jews. What endeared him to the Jewish voters was that he was a shrewd machine politician who was nevertheless able to make the transition to a broader-based politics. But Smith was the exception. Differences between Jews and Irish persisted throughout the thirties. When the Jews required support of the Irish and the Catholic church, which their sons dominated, to pressure the Roosevelt administration for a more active rescue policy, the principal spokesman of the American church, Francis Cardinal Spellman, was as silent as the Jews had been when the church was under siege in Mexico.

It was Smith's reputation for intelligence and vision during his tenure as a New York State alderman in 1918 that first attracted a coterie of Jewish advisers. The most influential of these was Belle Moskowitz, whose first experience with social reform came through the settlement house movement and as a volunteer for the National Council of Jewish Women. She began with an interest in improving the condition of wayward girls, but like so many social workers she soon discovered that without supportive public policy, reformers were waging a losing battle. In 1918, together with her second husband, Henry Moskowitz, she joined the Democratic party to head the Independent Citizens' Committee for Alfred E. Smith. That committee developed into an independent political power base from which Smith could withstand the pressure of those Tammany leaders who viewed with fear and loathing the changes he advocated. The committee also served as the base of Belle Moskowitz's influence. Like Lillian Wald and others associated with the settlement house movement, she had come to understand the need to wed the reform program to the political process, but she nursed no personal political ambition. It may have been that plus her keen political sense and organizational ability that endeared her to Smith. She became known as "the woman behind Al Smith," writing his speeches, planning his legislative program, handling patronage and party matters, and helping to manage his campaigns for office. Most important, she developed the public relations skills required for the "Brown Derby" campaign of 1928.

There was good reason why Smith's Tammany cronies took a dim view of her role. The social welfare legislation she drafted tended to further weaken Tammany, which, like all city political machines, was fueled by the "favors" it performed for immigrant voters. After the campaign of 1918, in which she and Abraham Elkus played key roles, Moskowitz became convinced that the Democratic party could develop into a party of reform. It was not an opinion shared by other Jewish leaders, especially those of socialist persuasion, who were unable to understand what the Smith phenomenon was all about. It was primarily second-generation Jews who had gained some knowledge of American politics who became aware that before a reform program could be implemented an internal revolution had to be mounted within the Democratic party. The Jewish coterie around Smith was thus at the very heart of the developments that later produced the welfare state under the auspices of the Democrats.[22]

By 1924 the metamorphosis within New York's Democratic party was almost complete. Smith had successfully challenged the nomination of William Randolph Hearst for a Senate seat in 1922. After the death of Tammany sachem Charles F. Murphy, the party seemed unable to produce leaders of stature. In the gubernatorial campaign of 1928 Franklin Roosevelt, Democratic vice-presidential candidate in 1920, selected Herbert Lehman for the lieutenant governor's slot, over Tammany's opposition. He would succeed Roosevelt in 1932 and hold that office for three terms. By 1933 the Democratic party of New York State, now based on a broad ethnic coalition in which Jews were well represented, was dominated by reformers.

Belle Moskowitz was one of a group of Jewish and non-Jewish advisers associated with Smith whom the press soon dubbed the "war board." The Jews in the group were formally educated and native born, with only marginal ties to the organized Jewish community. But chagrined at the visible evidence of Jewish influence and the decline of their own, Tammany loyalists predictably objected to the "Moskies (Belle Moskowitz), Proskies (Joseph Proskauer) and Mo-o-o-ses (Robert Moses)."[23] The "war board," formed during Smith's tenure in the State Assembly, became well known to the public even though much of its activity remained behind the scenes. Jews were conspicuous in Smith's entourage but did not dominate it. Membership was based on skill and loyalty, not ethnicity, yet the Jewish electorate nevertheless viewed them with special pride. Like Theodore Roosevelt, Smith won the affection of the Jewish voter. He had recognized "Jewish brains," he spoke a little Yiddish, he was supportive during the Messina "blood libel" incident, he was one of the few Democratic leaders with courage to advocate an anti-KKK plank in the campaign of 1924, and he had helped engineer the appointment of Benjamin Cardozo as chief justice of the New York State court of appeals. Above all, he was a reformer and an intelligent legislator. What else could one ask for? Not surprisingly, during the election of 1924, Smith ran ahead of Coolidge and Davis in several Jewish election districts. When he ran for the presidency four years later, Jewish voters were ready to pull down the lever for the Democratic ticket.

It was Smith who brought Jews into the new Democratic party by offering them a role in the liberal urban ethnic coalition that buttressed it.[24] That is where Roosevelt found them in 1928 when he succeeded Smith in the

New York governor's mansion. But in 1928 the nation still hesitated to move completely from the country to the city. Hoover could boast a small-town Iowa boyhood that Smith, with his heavy New York accent, could never hope to claim. For many Americans the city remained the locus of an alien population "mixed in its origins, uncertain of its social status [and] rather vague about the moral code," noted Walter Lippmann.[25] The Klan, which articulated the fear of the city, had grown weaker by 1928, but the apprehension regarding the city and Catholicism remained latent and was reflected in the hostility to Smith's candidacy. American anti-Semitism often took the form of a displaced hatred of the city, with which Jews had cast their lot. During the populist period of the 1890s, Jews had been subjected to a calumny not unlike what Smith faced in 1928. In voting against a "wet" Catholic city dweller, Americans also revealed indirectly the fear that fed into the anti-Semitic imagination. The Catholic issue in the election of 1928 thus possessed a special significance for the Jewish voter.

The election of 1932 posed a difficult choice for many Jewish voters, who honored Hoover for his relief work in eastern Europe. The Jewish Republican candidate for the Senate, George Z. Medalie, supported Hoover, as did the Yiddish newspaper the *Jewish Morning Journal.* But the respect given to Hoover was insufficient to halt the march of Jewish voters to the Democratic party. For socialist-inclined Jews, the Depression was evidence that the "internal contradictions" Marxists had preached about had finally come to a head. Even nonsocialists, who had voted for Smith, now associated the Republican party with an economic system that no longer functioned. They increased their vote for the Democratic ticket by 10 percent and awarded Roosevelt a plurality of 900,000 votes in New York City. By the election of 1932 the Jewish voting preference had been completely reversed. Crossing a bridge created by the Smith wing of the party, Jews were now firmly in the Democratic column. Some, like Rabbi Abba Hillel Silver, would later observe that the very solidity of the commitment diminished their influence when they most needed it.[26] But it would be the Jews' love affair with Roosevelt that would have the most decisive influence on their political culture during the thirties.

Jews' interest in foreign affairs was more intense and enduring than that of other hyphenates. That interest could be partly attributed to the urbane, cosmopolitan character of their elites and partly to concern for the beleaguered Jewish communities in Europe and the Middle East. Undoubtedly the increasing level of formal education also counteracted parochialism, especially when it was superimposed on the idealism that was part of Jewish political culture. In the second generation, to be educated also meant to be engaged and informed, which translated into an interest in peace and world governance abroad and social welfare at home.

For most Jewish voters Woodrow Wilson embodied the irresistible combination of education and idealism they aspired to. He was educated, idealistic, and a reformer. His early reluctance to become involved in the war won their political hearts. How could it be a "war to make the world safe for democracy" if the czarist tyranny fought on the side of the Allies? In the election of 1916 Jews crossed party lines to give 55 percent of their votes to the candidate who promised to keep America out of war. Undismayed by his failure to do so, Jews were strong supporters of the League of Nations and furnished a disproportionate part of the membership of auxiliary voluntary support organizations like the Intergovernmental Union, which fought for America's entry into the League. The idea of national self-determination, mentioned in Wilson's Fourteen Points as requisite for lasting peace but imperfectly implemented in the Treaty of Versailles, gained strong support among Jews, especially after it was expanded to include support of a Jewish homeland in Palestine by the Lodge-Fish Resolution (1922). Had it not been for the siren call of the Socialist candidate Eugene V. Debs, James M. Cox might have received a far higher percentage of the Jewish vote in the election of 1920.

Similarly, the pacifist thrust of the Washington Disarmament Conference earned it Jewish support, especially after a rumor circulated that the Palestine question and the treatment of Jews in eastern Europe would be included on its agenda. The president of the Central Conference of American Rabbis (CCAR), Rabbi Edward N. Calish, urged American Jews to assume leadership in mobilizing public opinion for naval disarmament. Two years later, in July 1923, the CCAR was joined by the Rabbinic Assembly (RA) of the Conservative movement in passing resolutions in favor of "social justice in industry" and in supporting Harding's plan for a world court. A year later the CCAR urged adherence to the Permanent Court of International Justice and the Levinson-Borah plan for outlawing wars of aggression. The latter became the Kellogg-Briand pact (1928), which was expected to usher in an era of peace. After the Japanese invasion of Manchuria it was bitterly dubbed "the parchment peace."[27]

During the twenties the most persistent Jewish concern was generated by the failure of the National Minority Rights clauses that Poland, Romania, Czechoslovakia, and the Baltic nations had been compelled to add to their constitutions. With the exception of the Zionists, most Jews still hoped that Jewish communities would finally thrive in the protected atmosphere promised by the clauses. Louis Marshall had announced triumphantly that they would become the basis for Jewish emancipation in eastern and central Europe, but that hope proved forlorn. Reports from investigatory commissions to Poland and other nations confirmed the deterioration of the Jewish condition and the reluctance of recalcritant governments to grant the "guaranteed" rights. Part of their failure was attributable to the weakness of the League, which, with the Court of International Justice, adjudicated minority complaints. A Jewish-sponsored Minority Rights Congress, convened in Zurich in 1927, urged the League to be more forceful, but Poland and Romania denied its right to intervene. By 1933, as the security of German Jewry began to deteriorate, a League official reported candidly that "the Jews can no longer justify their hope of working out a common destiny with any people ruled by prejudice and active hatred."[28] But for American Jewry, whose leadership had placed such faith in legal devices and which preferred to protect Jews where they lived rather than undertake expensive resettlement, the failure of the national minority rights clauses was a special disappointment.

In the Yiddish press during the twenties attention was focused on the well-being of Jewish communities in eastern Europe and Palestine. When Sholem Schwartzbard, a Ukrainian Jewish watchmaker living in France, assassinated the *pogromchik* Symon Petlyura in 1926, the story received banner headlines. The hoped-for liberation from the Left also proved disappointing. The situation in the Soviet Union showed that regimes espousing socialist ideology could prove equally threatening to Jewish survival, though in a less physical way. Lenin had signed a decree ordering the "uprooting" of anti-Semitic movements that had left 75,000 Jews dead between 1918 and 1920. But Lenin's decree did not exempt the Jewish bourgeoisie from being considered "class enemies." As in Poland, the economic condition of Russian Jewry became desperate owing to the general antibourgeois, antireligious policies followed by the Soviet government. Jews seemed to have the misfortune of falling into despised categories no matter who held power. If it was not religion, then it was class.

The deterioration of the Jewish condition in postrevolutionary Russia had an impact on the American Jewish polity, since it focused attention on the crucial question whether the revolution in Russia could be considered a success. Socialists who still retained confidence in the Soviet experiment naturally argued that it could, pointing out that younger Jews were adapting to the new situation and that there was actually an improvement over the situation during the civil war. But for the sections of the community that viewed politics purely in terms of Jewish interests, the issue was whether a viable Jewish communal life could be maintained under communism. Increasingly, the notion that Judaism would somehow survive in the Soviet Union was open to doubt. There developed growing opposition to extending diplomatic recognition to the new Soviet regime. It was time to speak up and stop investing capital for resettlement of Jews in the Crimea. "Can American Jewry stand by and console itself with vague hopes while Russian Jewry is bleeding?" asked a speaker at the annual AJCONG convention in 1929.[29]

It had been the hope that the Russian Revolution would bring a "new day" that drew idealistic Jews. That idealism could also be seen in the strong Jewish support of the peace and disarmament movement in the interwar period. The most persistent advocate of the idea of making aggressive war illegal was Salmon O. Levinson, a well-known Chicago Jewish lawyer. The Kellogg-Briand Pact was eventually signed by thirty-two nations in a frenzy of international comity. By 1930, in the midst of the bloody campaign to liquidate the kulaks and collectivize agriculture, most Jewish social democrats had become convinced that the Stalinist system had become hopelessly tyrannical and opposed legitimizing it through recognition. The question of extending diplomatic recognition to the Soviet Union became a divisive issue among Jews and was not resolved by Roosevelt's agreement to exchange ambassadors in 1933. At the same time, an early awareness of the threat to Jewish security posed by the advent of National Socialism in Germany cast a different light on what was happening in the Soviet Union, where Jews were ostensibly not being persecuted as Jews. Stephen Wise's first public warning on the nascent Nazi party came as early as 1922. By the thirties Jewish agencies were in the forefront in warning against appeasement and the dangers of isolationism. After the outbreak of war in Europe, their outspoken stand in favor of American intervention became more manifest. In December 1940 the AJCONG established a National Committee on Jewish Aid to Great Britain. That direct interventionist posture distinguished Jews from other hyphenated groups like German-, Italian-, and Irish-Americans in the ethnic coalition of the Democratic party.

The Jewish dimension of the "great debate" that began with the outbreak of war in September 1939 is a minor theme in American foreign relations that exists only as a result of Berlin's fixation on what it called the Jewish question. But for American Jews, who were called on to respond to Nazi depredations against German Jewry, it became a major concern. Fear grew in Jewish circles that the isolationists would reveal their true anti-Semitic colors. The leaders of the AJCOMM had already noted that warnings regarding the threat posed by the developments in Germany, especially when they emanated from Jews, were viewed in some quarters of the foreign policy establishment as "excessively alarming, even fantastic."[30] For some the notion that isolationists would attempt to shore up their waning influence by resorting to anti-Semitism was confirmed by Charles Lindbergh's address in Des Moines on 11 September 1941. Linking Jews with Anglophiles and Roosevelt, Lindbergh cautioned Jews not to push their influence too far, because "they would be among the first to feel its consequences." This sounded like a threat rather than a warning, and Jews were heartened when 93 percent of the press condemned the speech.[31] But coming simultaneously with an investigation of the film industry by a subcommittee of the Senate's Interstate Commerce Committee and other signs in Congress that anti-Semitism was being "officialized," it increased apprehension among Jews. Yet though surveys continued to show a high level of anti-Semitism throughout the war period, the dreaded appearance of a "Jewish question" on the political agenda did not materialize.[32]

Paradoxically, Lindbergh probably overestimated the inclination of Roosevelt's Jewish advisers to openly advocate intervention. They were far more involved in domestic affairs and were apprehensive about taking an exposed position. He also overestimated the intensity of interventionist sentiment among American Jews. Jews generally perceived the threat emanating from Berlin earlier than other groups. The Jewish press featured detailed reporting on Nazi anti-Semitic machinations since the early twenties. But most Jews were more concerned with the domestic economic crisis and their daily bread than with events abroad. As with most Americans, the depression had a privatizing effect. Jews largely opposed the Ludlow amendment, which called for a national referendum before the United States could go to war. They opposed the neutrality laws, especially the 1936 version, which embargoed all military supplies to both sides in the Spanish civil war but left the loyalists whom the Jews supported vulnerable. They considered the Munich appeasement a grave miscalculation. After the outbreak of war, Jews favored the Neutrality Act of 1939, the destroyer-bases deal (September 1940), the Lend-Lease Act (March 1941), and convoying of leased equipment to Britain.[33]

Yet it is easy to make too much of Jewish interventionist sentiment, since the polling samples are too small to permit firm conclusions. Every one of the issues of the "great debate" drew a sizable Jewish minority that favored the isolationist position. Even though 35 to 40 percent of the volunteers for the ten-thousand-man Lincoln Brigade, the American contingent of the International Brigade, a military unit organized to support the loyalists, were estimated to be of Jewish origin, they rarely came from the mainstream of Jewish life.[34] Jews may have favored the loyalists in the Spanish civil war, but it took the form of opposing the arms embargo, not of physical intervention. After the fall of France, 32 percent of the Jewish respondents still felt it was more important to stay out of the war than to help Britain. After the initial defeat of the Soviet army in fall 1941, 46 percent of the Jewish respondents disapproved of convoying ships to the Soviet Union with lend-lease aid. Clearly out of step with American public opinion and Roosevelt's foreign policy on issues that might signal an interventionist passion, American Jewry and its leadership maintained a low profile.[35] Only after America was finally drawn into the war by the attack on Pearl Harbor and American Jewry no longer felt alone did its leaders feel secure enough to advocate total war against the Axis.

More courage was displayed on issues directly affecting Jews. Jews were unwavering in opposing American participation in the 1936 Olympic Games. Although not a matter requiring action by the administration, the question of American participation became important for its symbolism. Berlin's refusal to honor its pledge not to discriminate against Jewish athletes went beyond injury to Jewish pride; it involved the Olympic code of sportsmanship, which was what the games were all about. Jews perceived that by excluding Jews from the international sports arena, the Nazi government was subtly imposing its anti-Semitic norms on other nations. Such a deliberate humiliation could not be ignored. Much of the movement to change the location of the games, which first developed in 1933, emanated from the boycott movement, whose leaders placed much faith in the strategy of maintaining pressure on Berlin. Working through the Amateur Athletic Union, the AJCONG and other Jewish defense agencies strove to reverse the decision of the American Olympic Committee, whose president, Avery Brundage, was inclined to accept Berlin's assurances that all athletes would be treated equally. Congressman Emanuel Celler introduced a resolution prohibiting the use of public funds to defray the expenses of participating athletes. But those involved in the anti-Brundage campaign learned it was dangerous to raise matters of principle when the serious business of organized athletics was involved. There were warnings that Jews were "overplaying the Jewish hand in America as it was overplayed in Germany before the present suppression."[36]

The Jewish reaction to Kristallnacht (9 November 1938) was intense, but unlike the Olympic Games issue, where the general public favored American participation or was indifferent, the images of burning Jewish synagogues that the press featured prominently created a strong spectator sympathy in the American public. Paradoxically, bullying a minority and burning down its "churches" was considered more an example of poor sportsmanship than banning an athlete from competition. Berlin was shocked at the strong public reaction in Britain and the United States, which compelled the administration to recall Ambassador Hugh Wilson "for consultation" in order to "stay ahead" of public opinion.[37]

The Olympic Games debacle and the Kristallnacht incident took their place beside a series of minor confrontations that included the Treasury Department's refusal to issue a license to export helium as well as diplomatic protests when anti-Nazi comments were made by American politicians. It kept relations between Washington and Berlin in a state of tension. The activities of the "little flower," Mayor Fiorello La Guardia of New York, were especially satisfying for Jews, who historically placed great stock on resistance through humor. When in May 1933 La Guardia called Hitler a "perverted maniac" and earned a protest from Hans Luther, the German ambassador, he won the plaudits of the Jewish press. His roisterous speech at the mock trial of Hitler staged before an audience of 20,000 at Madison Square Garden on 7 March 1934 drew more kudos. La Guardia continued to earn the appreciation of Jewish voters when the city brought a libel suit against Robert Edmondson. And when in an address to an anti-Nazi rally delivered in March 1937 "His Honor" found Hitler not *satisfaktionfaehig,* he earned not only the appreciation but also the laughter of Jewish voters. The term, meaning not up to standard or unsatisfactory, was the same pejorative the Nazi propaganda machine used against Jews. It did not matter that the mayor of New York possessed no power over foreign policy. "I run the subways, and he [Cordell Hull] runs the State Department— except when I abrogate a treaty or something," La Guardia joked to a group of reporters. If the State Department was upset, all the better. Most

Jews suspected the Department of being anti-Semitic or at least unsympathetic to Jews, especially its top officers like William Phillips and Wilbur Carr.[38]

Barely had American Jews become Democrats when the ominous events in Germany compelled them to cash in their newly earned political chips. As with other ethnics, the Depression confronted Jews with serious economic problems, and like them they sought succor from the government. For Jews it was not an outlandish quest, since their political culture assumed that government should play such a role. But in the Jewish case the need for government action created by the economic crisis was compounded by the need to gain government intercession for Jews abroad. Their dependence on the goodwill of the Roosevelt administration went beyond that of other hyphenates. It lent a special urgency to Jewish politics.

For generations the mantle of Jewish leadership had been ensconced in Europe. American Jews had begun to play a part during World War I but had not been fully ready to lead. During the thirties leadership would be passed to them whether they were ready or not, as the only Jews who could act as advocates before the United States government, whose policy and power were central to Jewish security. Advocacy was not a new experience for American Jewish leaders, but it required political transactions that the maverick, sometimes dissident, Jewish electorate made it difficult to conduct. Some political capital had already been dissipated as a result of the reform activities of Stephen Wise. The most influential of Jewish leaders brought charges of civic corruption against the Jimmy Walker administration of New York City and asked Governor Roosevelt to remove him. Roosevelt, who needed the support of the Tammany machine to retain the ninety-four votes of the Democratic delegation to the convention and secure the 1932 presidential nomination, angrily lectured Wise and the Rev. John H. Holmes. They ought to pay more attention to religion and less to politics, he counseled. The result was that a crucial link to Roosevelt represented by Rabbi Wise could not be restored until the death of Louis Howe in 1935.[39]

Coming during an economic crisis at home and a developing security crisis abroad, the Jewish request for government intercession for German Jewry appeared like special pleading. How could Jewish refugees be admitted when there was severe unemployment? The quest required building coalitions with other ethnics, but that was no easy task given the resentment against Jews. Jewish leaders discovered that the responsibilities American Jewry had been compelled to assume were nowhere matched by its political power. As the Holocaust years drew closer, the possibility of meeting these responsibilities that history and kinship had assigned seemed remote.

Yet even a cursory glance at American Jewry during the Roosevelt years leaves the impression that its political influence was enhanced. It was based on the widely held belief that there existed a special link between the Jewish community and the New Deal, whose very name had been conceived by the Jewish journalist Samuel Untermeyer.[40] In every election after 1928 Jews awarded Roosevelt an ever greater percentage of their vote, even when the support of other ethnic blocs waned after the election of 1936. Surely such loyalty would earn a special reward. The breaking of the two-term precedent in 1940 was especially challenging for Roosevelt's campaign managers. The president seemed to have lost his usual sensitivity to ethnic sensibilities when he delivered his "hand that held the dagger" speech after the Italian invasion of France in April 1940. Earlier the court-packing scheme, combined with the downturn of the economy in 1937, seemed to have broken his magic hold on the electorate.

Predictably, in the 1940 election Roosevelt's heaviest losses occurred in Italian-American and German-American wards. In contrast, Jewish districts voted overwhelmingly for Roosevelt despite an appreciation of Wendell Willkie's internationalist sensibilities. Roosevelt's building of the welfare state seemed to count for much more with Jewish voters than his apparent failure to move energetically on the refugee issue. Huge pluralities in Jewish districts partly balanced the loss of other ethnic votes, giving Roosevelt the narrow margin to carry Illinois, Massachusetts, New Jersey, and Pennsylvania.[41] When informed on election night that the Jewish vote had held fast, Roosevelt expressed his gratitude. But his unspoken opposition to a change in immigration policy remained steadfast until 1944, when a symbolic group of fewer than one thousand refugees was allowed to enter the country and was sheltered in a camp near Oswego, New York. By the election of 1944 much of the remaining ethnic goodwill had vanished, and again large Jewish pluralities in Illinois, New York, and Pennsylvania were important in the Democratic victory. In some of New York City's Jewish election districts, so overwhelming had the commitment to the New Deal become that even the Republican poll watchers voted for Roosevelt. But that overwhelming support entailed a price. In one Connecticut town a campaign was conducted propagating the idea that Sidney Hillman would be "the power behind the throne" of a fourth-term administration.[42] Dewey carried most Italian and German districts.

A direct intrusion of a "Jewish" third party into the electoral process in New York State, a rare occurrence in ethnic politics, presents an opportunity to examine Jewish political culture directly. So strong was Roosevelt's hold on Jewish voters that even Jewish socialists were drawn to vote for him. The American Labor party was organized in New York State in 1936—as David Dubinsky, president of the ILGWU, explained to Labor Secretary Frances Perkins—to give Jewish socialists an opportunity to cast their ballots for Roosevelt without compromising their principles. Dubinsky, who resigned from the Socialist party in 1936, called on the leaders of the Jewish labor movement who had established the Jewish Labor Committee in 1934 to form such a third party. He hoped to loosen the hold of the waning Socialist party on the Jewish Left and strengthen the political leverage of the Jewish unions at the same time. After he was satisfied that such a party would help rather than hinder the New Deal in New York, Jim Farley, Roosevelt's principal political manager, cleared the legal roadblocks that had been in the way.

In the election of 1936 the new American Labor party (ALP) received 250,000 votes, which did not make a great deal of difference for Roosevelt but did help the New York gubernatorial candidate Herbert Lehman, who received over 30 percent of the Jewish vote on the ALP ticket. Norman Thomas, the Socialist candidate, received only 87,000 votes. Impressed with their showing, the handful of labor leaders decided to support La Guardia in his 1937 bid for the Mayor's office. This time the ALP's impact was crucial: 40 percent of the Jewish vote was cast on the ALP ticket, which meant in effect that the ALP not only had broken the hold of the Socialist party but had become a major player in New York State politics. The surest recognition of its success was that it became a target for Communist infiltration. By the election of 1944 the ALP was compelled to wage a two-front war, against the extreme Left on one side and against the Democratic machine on the other. In that election the ALP outpolled the Liberal party, which had been organized by Dubinsky when the Left, under the leadership of Sidney Hillman, gained control of the Socialist party. But both tickets were headed by Roosevelt, who retained his remarkable drawing power in all parts of the Jewish political spectrum.

The ALP is significant not for the additional votes it brought Roosevelt, but for the new operational dimension it contributed to the Jewish political culture of the Left. It separated the left-wing Jewish vote from the Socialist party, which meant that for the first time the Jewish Left was able to deal with American society not as it imagined it should be, but as it was. It redirected Jewish political energy, which had been activated by the Depression, into acceptable political channels. The long-range explanation for the ability to convert apocalyptic into reformist politics might be found in the higher level of education and Americanization of the second generation and the negative experience the leaders of the Jewish unions had with the revolutionary Left. Welfare statism had become the new ideology of the Jewish labor movement. The ALP took to calling itself "the party of the permanent New Deal."[43] It helped shed the distinct eastern European cast of Jewish political radicalism and served as a bridge for thousands of Jewish voters to enter mainstream American politics. That would not, however, have been possible without the New Deal welfare state program, which many Jewish voters believed was within acceptable striking distance of their own social democratic principles.

Retaining Roosevelt in power was virtually the only objective the strife-ridden Jewish community could agree on. More than anything else, the welfare state idea had come to embody most Jewish assumptions about the purpose of politics, which is the reason the Jewish "love affair" with Roosevelt assumed an almost religious cast. Rabbi William F. Rosenbloom of Temple Israel in New York City called him "the Messiah of America's tomorrow," while Stephen Wise hoped for his "immortality."[44] The "adoration" of Roosevelt was not so much for his person as for the political principles he was imagined to represent. For Emanuel Celler, a popular congressman from an all-Jewish election district in Brooklyn, it was not so much the president's humor or that he spoke to him without condescension as that he had political courage and "knew how to take risk."[45] Others shared the general belief that, although Roosevelt stemmed from "old wealth," he nevertheless had a deep compassion for the poor and "forgotten man," stemming from the crippling polio attack he had endured in August 1921. Transcending one's background to care for others is a cherished Judaic value. Yet the notion that there was a deepening of Roosevelt's character after the polio attack was characterized by his cousin, Alice Roosevelt Longworth, as an "absurd idea."[46] But few Jews doubted that Roosevelt possessed such a special compassion.

The image of a caring government in Washington served as a kind of bond between Jews and Roosevelt. Much of the New Deal's social welfare program, especially its social security, public housing, and labor legislation, had for years been part of the agenda of the Jewish labor movement and had also been advocated by Jewish social workers. When these programs were gradually implemented by the administration, Jews were convinced it was motivated by humanitarianism. That the administration's concern did not extend to the admission of Jewish refugees had no noticeable impact on Jewish loyalty to the Roosevelt administration. Jewish citizens were more preoccupied with the domestic crisis, where they were convinced that at least Roosevelt was trying to do something.

These strong ideological ties to the New Deal were reinforced by a political transaction that gave Jews, as members of the Roosevelt coalition, rewards for their loyalty. Of Roosevelt's 197 judicial appointments, 52 went to Catholics and 7 to Jews, which approximated the percentage of Jewish appointments to the bench in the three previous Republican administrations. Eager to maintain his links to the city machines, Jim Farley, who administered such appointments after the death of Louis Howe, usually followed the recommendations of the local bosses, at least until 1937. We have seen that they preferred to reward their own. Appointments of Catholics to the bench and to high positions within the administration predictably were proportionately higher than appointments of Jews. That was also true for appointments to new commissions and agencies, like the Securities and Exchange Commission, the National Labor Relations Board, and the Social Security Board, and to the numerous political jobs that had become available in the expanded bureaucracy of the welfare state. It is estimated that about 4 percent of these appointments went to Jews, slightly higher than their percentage of the general population but distinctly lower than their proportion of the educated stratum from which such appointments were drawn. Some departments, such as War, Navy, State, and Commerce, and certain agencies, such as the Federal Trade Commission, the Federal Reserve Board, the Tariff Commission, and the Board of Tax Appeals, were well known to be "off limits" to Jewish appointees. Nevertheless, a belief that a disproportionate share of political appointments had been awarded to Jews, and that their influence in Washington was pervasive, persisted throughout Roosevelt's tenure.

That impression may have been created because Jews were concentrated in the "friction" agencies, those that dealt directly with the public as representatives of government regulatory authority. The "Jew Deal" epithet, which subtly suggested that Jews were running the nation, surfaced during the 1936 campaign and remained a fixture of anti-Semitic rhetoric in subsequent campaigns. A pamphlet by Robert Edward Edmondson spoke of Roosevelt's "supreme council" and, under the symbol of the "seal of Solomon," depicted four leading Jews as controlling the Roosevelt administration. Bernard Baruch was labeled "unofficial president," Felix Frankfurter, "director of the New Deal," and Louis Brandeis "father of the New Deal." Edmondson charged Roosevelt with having brought "more Jewish revolutionary socialistic radicals" into key positions than had any president before him. The polls commissioned during the war years showed that the segment of the public who believed Jews had too much power ranged from 60 to 65 percent.[47]

It proved difficult for defense agencies like the AJCOMM to counteract the charge. The notion that Washington had been taken over by Jews was not limited to extremists. Adlai Stevenson, then a young lawyer in the capital and destined for an adulation by Jews like that given to Roosevelt, complained to a friend that Jews in Washington were too prominent and autocratic. Ironically, there is evidence that Roosevelt shared the apprehension that Jews were occupying too prominent a place in Washington and in Germany. When Harold Ickes informed Roosevelt that Joseph Kennedy, his ambassador in London, was telling the English that Jews controlled the American government, the president confided to Ickes that he shared Kennedy's assessment.[48] But from the present perspective it is difficult to avoid the conclusion that the New Deal was no "Jew Deal," nor did it deal especially benevolently with Jews, especially on the crucial refugee issue.

Anti-Semitic propagandists, in their efforts to affix the "Jew Deal" label to his administration, went as far as to suggest that Roosevelt himself was Jewish. But it was the highly visible presence of Jews among his coterie of advisers that lent credibility to the label. Most of Roosevelt's Jewish appointments were native-born Americans who incidentally happened to be Jewish, in some cases unhappily so. Usually they did not deny their Jewishness, but neither did they consider themselves merely Jewish spokesmen. They had, after all, achieved their positions not through a Jewish conduit, but through one of the nation's many private centers of power—the business community, organized labor, or the law establishment.

Of all the members of the "Jew Deal," Roosevelt formed the closest relationship with Henry Morgenthau, Jr., his secretary of the treasury. The friendship originated because the Morgenthaus, who were his neighbors in

Dutchess County, New York, had been generous contributors to his early campaigns. But the family bond in the Morgenthau case was exceptional. In most cases such positions went to Jews with special skills or connections. Samuel Rosenman was a gifted behind-the-scenes political manager and speech writer. All agreed that Benjamin Cohen was unequaled as a legislative craftsman. The same was true of Felix Frankfurter, whom *Fortune* magazine singled out as "the most influential single individual in the United States." William Randolph Hearst called him "the Iago of the administration," Calvert Magruder detected "Oriental guile," and Raymond Moley, a member of the "brain trust," saw Frankfurter as a "patriarchal sorcerer." None was able to determine the precise source of his influence.[49]

Ironically, Frankfurter, who more than other members of the "Jew Deal," acted as a lightning rod for anti-Semitic invective, was least willing to identify with Judaism. His Jewish identity had originally consisted of a part-time Zionism that had largely lapsed since his early association with his mentor, Louis Brandeis. He had done yeoman work for the Zionist movement after World War I, but unlike Brandeis, his interest in things Jewish was marginal after the Brandeis faction was deposed from the leadership of the ZOA in 1921. He saw Zionism merely as a way of giving himself "a fresh psychological relationship to other Jews and Gentiles." Palestine he viewed as a "small" problem, and the threat of Nazism, he felt, "far transcends ferocious anti-Semitism and fanatical racism."[50] He maintained almost no relationships with the Jewish friends of his youth. In 1940, when Jewish refugee children stranded in France were desperate for a haven, Frankfurter adopted two non-Jewish children, victims of the London blitz. When the Polish underground courier Jan Karski informed him of the actual workings of the "final solution," Frankfurter was so surprised at the revelations that he told Karski he could not believe them. Except for a few occasions when he acted as a liaison for Weizmann and David Ben-Gurion, he was more reluctant than Brandeis to press Jewish causes in the Oval Office. His primary interest was domestic legislation, such as the Social Security Act of 1935, which he helped draft.[51]

Yet Frankfurter was one of the most engaged figures in Washington. There were few issues on which he was not superbly informed and few policymakers he did not know. Not only did he possess a first-rate intelligence, but his position at Harvard Law School enabled him to become the nation's first broker of intelligence. He had been able to place his "happy hot dogs" in key positions in the administration. Men like Tom Corcoran and Ben Cohen gave Frankfurter a channel into the innermost recesses of the Roosevelt administration. He thus had a detailed knowledge of what was going on that perhaps was superior to Roosevelt's. It was he who brought the seventy-seven-year-old "Old Isaiah" (Brandeis) to reestablish his relationship with Roosevelt in 1933, and it was Frankfurter who most consistently advised him of the political shoals he faced in implementing specific policies. He continued to advise Roosevelt even after he was appointed to the court in 1939, but the appointment made him even less available as a Jewish channel to the Oval Office. Unlike Brandeis, who continued as a behind-the-scenes leader of the Zionist movement after his appointment to the court, Frankfurter virtually discontinued all contact with Jewish circles after 1939 when he assumed his court seat.[52]

We have noted that the practice of fully drawing on available Jewish political talent was established by Al Smith. Through Smith Roosevelt inherited Sam Rosenman, during his tenure as governor, and also became acquainted with most of the Jewish labor leaders, including David Dubinsky and Sidney Hillman. Felix Frankfurter and Bernard Baruch traced their acquaintance with the future president back to his days as assistant secretary of the navy in the Wilson administration. But most members of the "Jew Deal's" second tier, who served in the highest echelons of the bureaucracy, were newcomers to Washington. They included Abe Fortas, who began as chief legal adviser in the Securities and Exchange Commission (SEC) under the chairmanship of Joseph Kennedy and went on to become commissioner of manpower. Kennedy himself was replaced by Jerome Frank. Others were Nathan Margolin, a solicitor in the Department of Interior; Saul K. Padover, who was Harold Ickes's assistant; Michael W. Straus, director of the War Resource Council; Ernest Gruening, eventually governor of Alaska; and Felix Cohen, son of Morris Cohen, who, with Margolin and Fortas, wrote much of the new Indian policy into law. Also included in the group was Mordecai Ezekiel, in the Department of Agriculture; Charles Wyzanski, a solicitor for the Labor Department, where Isador Lubin headed the Bureau of Labor Statistics; David Niles, who became Roosevelt's expert on ethnic matters; and David Lilienthal, who headed the Tennessee Valley Authority. In reality, only a small number of Jews had actually gained a place in Roosevelt's inner circle, which was itself broad and everchanging. Most Jews who came to Washington occupied less exalted positions in the regulatory agencies and the upper grades of the federal civil service.

During the New Deal period Jews became acceptable in Washington, and in some rare instances desirable. A reputation for a sense of social justice expressed through social welfare legislation preceded Jews. It made them especially attractive to Secretary of Labor Frances Perkins, who had contact with what she fondly called the *Yiddish kopf* during her tenure as president of the Consumer Trade League. Ultimately she would pay a price for attracting a host of Jewish lawyers to the Department of Labor. In 1936 she spent much time denying that she herself was a covert Jew whose real name was Matilda Wutowski.[53] Roosevelt too was attracted to a socially conscious type that he imagined abounded in the Jewish community. "Dig me up fifteen or twenty youthful Abraham Lincolns from Manhattan and the Bronx to choose from," he instructed Charles Burlingham, "grand old man" of the New York Bar and an old chum from Harvard Crimson days. But he was quick to add that "they must have no social ambitions."[54]

Aware that such appointments entailed a political price, it seems unlikely that either Smith or Roosevelt set out to surround himself with Jews. With the exception of Morgenthau, most Jews in the inner circle possessed crucial legal or managerial skills or special talent as conceptualizers.[55] They stemmed from all sections of the Jewish community and, except for their ardent support of the New Deal, had little in common with each other. Honored to have been chosen to serve the nation, few Jewish appointees conceived of using their position for sectarian purposes.[56] Rabbi Stephen Wise, who frequently transmitted the Jewish concern to the administration, was exasperated by these "sha sha Jews," by which he meant Jews highly placed in the administration who were reluctant to speak of Jewish matters in the Oval Office. Eventually Wise came to understand that they were not Jewish men of influence, but rather men of influence who happened to be Jewish. Most were products of several generations of acculturation, during which ethnic and religious affiliation were muted in return for full access to the promise of America. Even when they could distinguish a Jewish interest, they would not jeopardize their hard-won positions to advocate it. The only exception to that proved to be Henry Morgenthau, Jr., who became convinced that the rescue of European Jewry was in consonance with American interests. Some like Benjamin Cohen and Frankfurter had been affiliated with the American Zionist movement, and Rosenman was a leading member of the AJCOMM, but these former connections seemed to have little influence once they attained power. Nevertheless, they became crucial players in the rescue drama of the thirties because of the positions they held near Roosevelt. Mobilizing such high-placed yet marginal Jews in the effort to rescue European Jewry became a major hurdle that rescue advocates could not negotiate during the years of the Holocaust. In some measure their inability to fully do so accounts for American Jewry's failing witness role.

A disproportionate number of the second-generation Jews who came to Washington during the Roosevelt era were lawyers. Some were excluded from the prestigious private law firms despite their class standing. In the spring of 1936, much to Frankfurter's chagrin, eight Jewish editors of the *Harvard Law Review* could not find positions in such law firms. Some of these rejectees, perhaps feeling resentful, sought employment in the government agencies of the expanded welfare state. From these government positions they were sometimes called on to do battle with their counterparts who easily slipped into positions in Wall Street law firms because they had the proper religious and social credentials. That silent struggle between outsiders, some of them Jews, and insiders within the government regulatory bureaus may have added fuel to the burning resentment the legal establishment felt toward the Roosevelt administration.

Beyond the coterie of Jewish lawyers in the administration and in the upper levels of the federal bureaucracy, Jewish social workers offered support for the New Deal and sometimes a direct channel of influence for welfare state ideas. We have noted the early contacts with Harry Hopkins, Eleanor Roosevelt, and Frances Perkins, in the Jewish settlement houses of the Lower East Side of New York City. A disproportionate number of the activist social workers were Jewish. As early as 1931 the National Conference of Jewish Social Service, which met in Minneapolis, passed a strong resolution urging the federal government to start large-scale emergency relief, including a public works and a social security program, for the victims of the Depression. By the mid-thirties the highly secularized Jewish social service establishment had produced a rationale for the welfare state that seemed to many more resonant of socialism than of traditional American laissez-faire values.57

The radicalization of second-generation Jews, despite evidence that their parents were doing comparatively well, should not come as a surprise. The depression went far to incubate a new generation of Jewish radicals who, when joined to the preexisting socialist and communist elements, composed a potentially powerful dissident force. Any examination of Jewish political culture during the Depression decade cannot ignore that radicalization.

During the twenties it was estimated that 15 percent of the members of the Communist party were Jewish. Abetted by the "united front" policy and a strategy of infiltrating Jewish organizations, the Communist party's Jewish membership climbed to an estimated 35 to 40 percent during the Depression. In some New York State districts the percentage was higher, and the proportion of Jews in the Party's leadership—its organizers, educational directors, and fund-raisers—was higher still. In addition, approximately 5,000 of the 13,000 members of the Young Communist League (YCL), were Jewish. The disproportionate Jewish representation was so conspicuous that the Party assigned noms de guerre to suggest native ancestry. In the New York metropolitan area membership in noncommunist left wing organizations was also disproportionately Jewish.[58] There was an unmistakable Jewish cast to the radical Left, and the strident rhetoric of the publicists of anti-Semitism spoke of "Judeobolshevism." The term, we shall note, became a buzzword of the Right in the interwar period.

Yet communism was overwhelmingly rejected by most American Jews, who fought to maintain the autonomy of organizations earmarked for penetration by the Communist party. In 1936 the AJCONG fought off a Communist attempt to infiltrate its governing council, and four years later Stephen Wise dissolved the youth division of the AJCONG when it rejected a request to withdraw from the Communist-dominated American Youth Congress.[59] Poale Zion (Labor Zionists) also withdrew from the American Youth Congress. Most rabbis resigned from the Jewish People's Committee for United Action against Fascism and Anti-Semitism after they learned it was a front organization. The stamp of "radicalism" was affixed by a comparatively small number who joined the Party or became hangers-on.

Considering that the Jewish community had been targeted for special attention by the Party, the results were relatively meager. Out of an estimated total 800,000 Jewish votes cast in New York State, only 50,000 went to communist candidates during the thirties, even though the Communist party mounted a union-organizing campaign in precisely those new employment areas—teaching, social work, department store sales, and government work—in which second generation Jews were concentrating. At the same time disaffected Jewish college students and intellectuals became prime recruits for the YCL or one of the Party's many front organizations. The new radicals were drawn from the second and third generations. One researcher estimates that from 10 to 20 percent of Jewish college students were radicalized during the thirties.[60] The Party tried to entrench itself in the Yiddish-speaking subculture by establishing the Jewish People's Fraternal Order. Under its umbrella a network of social programs, schools, summer camps, folk dancing and singing groups was organized. They fulfilled a fraternal and social function, and there was little revolutionary propaganda to be heard. Instead the Party's programs for Jews emphasized a secular version of Jewishness and skillfully muted the inherent conflict between Marxism and Judaism.

Most impressive for potential converts was the way communist propaganda spoke out vigorously against anti-Semitism. After Kristallnacht, Party activists distributed handbills in many Jewish neighborhoods reminding voters that no one fought Nazi anti-Jewish depredations as vigorously as the communists. The sinking of the "illegal" refugee ship the *Salvador* in the Sea of Marmora on 12 December 1940, with the loss of over two hundred Jewish refugees, produced handbills in Jewish neighborhoods accusing the British of mass murder.[61] But after the Non-Aggression Pact and the subsequent partition of Poland, warnings that the Communist party was an instrument of Moscow and was trying to mislead the Jewish community were widespread in the Jewish press. The *Reconstructionist,* one of the community's most influential journals, feared for the thousands of Jews who would be forced to join their fellow Jews in the camps of Siberia.[62] The pact undermined the little goodwill the Party had built up among some Jews. Earl Browder, chairman of the Communist party, sought to capitalize on Jewish fears by reminding Jews that five million of their fellows were secure and "building a happy prosperous life in the new socialist country" and that support of a second imperialist war would lead the Jewish people to "catastrophe." At the same time he issued a directive reminding the Party cadres of the need to regain the support of the "Jewish masses."[63]

But not until the German invasion of the Soviet Union in June 1941 did favorable circumstances again develop for the Party to rebuild its base in the Jewish community. Communist propagandists maintained a constant drumbeat, emphasizing that the Soviet Union was in the forefront of the struggle against fascism, the primary enemy of the Jewish people. Energetic efforts were made to enlist Jewish support for opening a second front, which at the instructions of Moscow had become the primary objective of communist propaganda.[64]

By 1943 it was clear that the Party was sparing no effort to enlist American Jewry to its cause. The Soviet government sent Solomon Michoels, director of the Moscow Jewish State Theater and chairman of the Jewish Anti-Fascist Committee in Kuibyshev, and Itzik Feffer, a poet who was also a lieutenant colonel in the Red Army, to tour American Jewish communities. They would be guests of the Jewish Council for Russian War Relief and the Committee for Jewish Writers, both Communist front organizations. Everywhere they spoke they were greeted by large Jewish audiences. But rather than garnering goodwill, the tour triggered acrimony in the Yiddish press. The Reform journal *Liberal Judaism* was hard pressed to understand the opposition, as was James Rosenberg, former director of Agro-Joint. But the *Yiddisher Kemfer,* the organ of the Labor Zionist movement, was suspicious of the purpose of the visit and the agencies that were sponsoring the tour. "American Jews do not need anti-Fascist propaganda," it pointed it out. "It is hard therefore to explain why, from all nationality groups, only the Jews were chosen."[65]

The Party never fully regained its influence among Jews after the purge trials and the Nazi-Soviet Non-Aggression Pact. Yet at its zenith its influence on significant elements within American Jewry exceeded anything experienced in other ethnic communities, with the possible exception of the American Finns. That influence rested partly on its ability to present poorly educated Jews with a coherent perspective on world events. Jews held scholars in uncritical esteem and were bound to be influenced when leading American intellectuals echoed the Party line. For others, Party membership offered "a privileged relationship to history," which they were told they were making. Many secular Jews were impressed that the Soviets had made anti-Semitism illegal and seemed unaware of their brutal suppression of Jewish culture and religion. Closer to home, the Communist party shrewdly exploited the panic many Jews felt as anti-Semitic spokesmen echoed the Nazi line. Cyrus Adler detected a "growing dread" among Jews "that something may happen to them like that which happened to the Jews of Germany."[66] Between December 1941, when America entered the war, and June 1944, when a second front was finally opened on the beaches of Normandy, Jews were gratified that only the Soviet Union, with enormous expenditure of lives, was fully resisting Nazi aggression. An enemy of their enemy became their friend, at least for the duration.

The Jewish affinity for radical politics did not come without cost. Throughout the interwar period one of the mainstays of anti-Semitic rhetoric was based on an imagined link between Jews and communism. During the twenties Jewish defense agencies expended considerable effort to counteract the charge. Literature was published by the AJCOMM to "prove" that only a small number of the rulers of Soviet Russia were Jews. But pushed by the Nazi propaganda machine, the term "Judeobolshevism" became common currency. The dozens of articles placed in the press denying the link seemed only to confirm it. "To the average American," complained one journalist, "an ending in 'off' or 'vitch' is conclusively Jewish. . . . That elects almost every Russian into Semitic membership."[67] On 29 May 1933 Congressman Louis McFadden rose on the floor of the House to again allege the existence of an international Jewish conspiracy. The AJCOMM requested that the statement be retracted. Instead McFadden rose again, this time to accuse Brandeis, Baruch, and Frankfurter of being "communist henchmen." McFadden was not returned to his seat in the next election, but the damage was done. Congressman Samuel Dickstein, who had proposed legislation to investigate both communist and fascist subversion, earned the displeasure of *Time* magazine for being too avid in "spreading the record of the plight of members of his own race in Germany."[68]

As citizens intensely concerned with world affairs, Jews were naturally drawn to the momentous issues concerning war and peace during the interwar period. But America's Palestine policy and its associated refugee policy, which barely created a stir on the world stage, were life and death matters for their survival as a people. Naturally it was the "plight of the race" issue that came to occupy center stage in Jewish politics during the thirties. Everywhere there were beleaguered Jewish communities in need of succor and the protective mantle of a benevolent democratic power. But in playing its role as advocate of world Jewry before the United States government, American Jewry found itself unable to speak with a single voice. Its disunity was exacerbated by hostility from the Right and manipulation from the Left. How the resultant lack of communal cohesiveness diminished its ability to play the role history assigned to it is the subject of the final chapter.

CHAPTER EIGHT

THE AMERICAN JEWISH
RESPONSE TO THE HOLOCAUST

W E COME finally to the subject that has aroused the most heated debate in American Jewish historiography: American Jewry's response to the Holocaust.[1] We cannot, of course, take sides in the controversy, because though history can throw light on the subject, the answer to whether American Jews did or did not do enough rests ultimately on factors beyond history, such as what one imagines American Jewry to have been during these unhappy years. One must also define sufficiency. What would have been enough, given a cataclysmic event like the Holocaust? Beyond that, after collecting the historical evidence on the American Jewish response, historians must still make judgments concerning Jewish power. We cannot, after all, assign responsibility until we know how much power was available to discharge it. But we do not know precisely what constitutes ethnic power or how to measure it or distinguish it from influence. Judeophobes persistently imagine that Jews have great power, but Jews often see themselves as powerless. Others mistake private power in the hands of individuals who happen to be Jewish for communal power. We have noted that the former may have increased in the interwar period, but in some important respects the latter was declining. We will note that it was private Jews, unable or unwilling to concern themselves with Jewish communal needs, who composed the "Jew Deal" of the Roosevelt administration. They had power, but it could rarely be enlisted to serve a specific Jewish need. And Jewish communal power was lacking during these critical years because the underlying cultural cohesiveness that might have lent coherence to Jews' political voice had diminished.

We have noted that American Jewry was so riven religiously and ideologically that there was little agreement among its various subcommunities about where the Jewish interest lay or how it was best served. As ominous portents appeared of the catastrophe about to befall European Jewry, a strife-ridden, often uncivil communal atmosphere prevailed. Jews could not agree on the nature of the Nazi threat, much less on how to respond to it. Disunity interfered with their historical advocacy before the United States government. Instead, American political leaders heard a cacophony from different Jewish constituencies, each separately pleading for the rescue of its clients, each proposing a different plan of action.

Preoccupied first with the Depression and then with the war, few in the Roosevelt administration bothered to listen. The special plight of European Jewry, which faced systematic slaughter, was never differentiated from the suffering of other residents of occupied countries under the Nazi heel. To be heard, the Jewish voice required not only coherence but amplification. Greater volume might have been achieved through the support of other ethnic and religious groups with which Jews were linked in the New Deal coalition, but we have already noted that such support was not forthcoming. The number of ethnic leaders who comprehended that it was not merely Jews but their own world, based on the Christian principles of Western civilization, that was being devoured in the death camps of Europe was very small. Instead, the Depression and the war heightened ethnic tensions. Subsidized by the Nazi government, anti-Semitism reached new heights during the thirties and forties, convincing Jews that what was happening in the Reich was about to happen here. American Jewry, no less than its European counterpart, felt it faced the murderous Nazi threat alone.

The National Socialist movement that came to power in Germany in January 1933 had at its ideological heart a desire to reverse the emancipation process by which Jews had gradually been granted full political and civil rights. The last step in that process had been put in place by the Weimar constitution in 1919. For National Socialists that was reason enough to condemn the Weimar Republic. When in 1935 the Nuremberg laws revoked Jewish rights of German citizenship, de-emancipation was complete. The Jews of Germany were now totally vulnerable. The period of calm that followed the enactment of the laws was temporary; soon a series of government edicts severely contracted German Jewish cultural and commercial activity.

Having preceded German settlement in some Rhineland communities, German Jewry was reluctant to take full measure of the threat it faced. But after Kristallnacht (November 1938), even the most patriotic German Jew could no longer believe that Jewish communal life was still tenable in Hitler's Reich. All who could now desperately sought to emigrate, only to discover few havens were available. As Germany turned eastward to annex the rump of Czechoslovakia (March 1939) and to attack Poland (September 1939), the much-desired goal of becoming *Judenrein* (free of Jews) slipped further from Berlin's grasp. The outbreak of war was a signal for more drastic anti-Jewish measures. Included were laws to identify Jews, which ultimately meant wearing the yellow star, the expropriation of Jewish property, the deportation of Jews for "settlement" in the East, the reghettoizing of Jews in the East, and finally, after the invasion of the Soviet Union in June 1941, their systematic annihilation.[2] The invasion of the Soviet Union marks the end of the refugee phase of the Holocaust, though thousands of Jews remained in the refugee stream.

Jews were not alone in being pushed out of Germany and its growing empire. Included also were political, labor, and religious leaders and sundry artists and writers who were no longer ideologically acceptable in the "new" Germany. But the Jews composed more than 70 percent of the exiles, the largest single group. Their condition was also more critical because the possibility of finding a haven was diminished by Berlin's policy of compelling them to leave Germany virtually penniless. Moreover, their occupational profile (they were concentrated in proprietary and management categories) and their age (70 percent were over forty) made them an undesirable population for absorption, particularly during a worldwide depression. Finding suitable asylum for a group that eventually might include over ten million souls posed insurmountable difficulties. It was the refugee crisis caused by the reluctance of potential receiving nations to take them in that first involved American Jewry.

Immigration policy was not a new concern for American Jewry. The most critical political issue it faced during the early twenties was America's immigration policy, which also seemed aimed at excluding Jews. The national origins idea that determined the immigration quotas was based on the notion of Nordic supremacy and bore an unmistakable resemblance to the Aryanism of Nazi ideology. The Reich was pushing Jews out for the same reason that America was reluctant to accept them. The refugee policy of the thirties seemed to be a replay of the restrictionism of the twenties, but this time the danger was more imminent, while the Depression created even greater reluctance to receive refugees. But for historical and economic reasons it was the United States that remained the preferred asylum for refugees to repair their disrupted lives. The refugee crisis thus placed a special burden on Jewish leaders, who were called on to use their influence to soften the administration of the restrictive immigration laws that not only placed Jews of eastern Europe in an unfavored category but made no distinction between refugees and normal immigrants.

In the face of the Depression, the number able to enter under the relevant quotas was diminished by a directive Herbert Hoover issued on 8 September 1930 calling for a strict enforcement of the "likely to become a public charge" (LPC) provision of the law. Reluctance to receive refugees was no less apparent in other potential receiving nations. The Arab riots of 1936 hastened a hardening of antisettlement policy by the British government, which culminated in another White Paper in May 1939 restricting immigration and land sale in Palestine. As the war approached, no nation welcomed Jewish refugees.

Aware that public opinion was opposed to the admission of refugees, Jewish leaders feared that an open campaign for liberalizing immigration policy would intensify anti-Semitism and boomerang into even more anti-alien legislation. As in the twenties, they approached the issue reluctantly and by indirection. Again their strategy was to humanize the administration of the laws rather than to change them. They pushed for a provision exempting relatives of alien residents from quota restrictions case by case. During the early months of the new administration Felix Frankfurter and Irving Lehman asked Roosevelt to revoke Hoover's LPC directive. They also tried to simplify the bureaucratic maze the refugees had to negotiate. As the crisis intensified, refugee advocates suggested special measures such as mortgaging future quotas or exempting refugee children. All were rejected by an administration sensitive that public opinion was overwhelmingly opposed to any form of immigration.

Clearly it would have required considerable political courage for the administration to contravene such an overwhelming public consensus, a quality not conspicuously present during either the refugee or the rescue phase of the crisis. There followed the predicted flood of antialien bills calling for the further curtailment of immigration and the registration of aliens.³ In 1935 the Alien Deportation and Exclusion League, one of dozens of such organizations, published *The Alien Menace to the U.S.*, a pamphlet that called for strict enforcement of the deportation provision of the law and a halt to all further immigration. A 1938 *Fortune* magazine poll indicated that 67.4 percent of the respondents approved of such a total ban. A year later 83 percent opposed admitting any refugees above the quota.⁴ Even a statement proposed by Jewish leaders concerning America's time-honored tradition of asylum, to be made by Roosevelt without mentioning Jews, was not forthcoming. But small administrative corrections were made to ease the plight of the penniless refugees. In 1938 they would be permitted to apply for visas wherever they were, and later the requirement that fleeing refugees obtain a clean bill of health from the German police was modified. Between 1933 and 1934 134 quota refugees were accepted, and during the next fiscal year the number rose by 700. In 1936 Roosevelt also instructed the State Department to extend "the most generous favorable treatment" to Jewish refugees. By 1937 the number allowed to enter rose to 11,352, four times as many as in 1933 but still considerably below the number who were legally qualifed under the relevant quotas. In fact, only in 1939 were the now-joined German and Austrian quotas filled. The number of refugees entering the country during the crisis was only 10 percent of those legally entitled to visas.

Those fortunate enough to obtain visas found a social service network ready to receive them but hard pressed for financing. In 1934 a group of twenty mostly Jewish agencies established the National Coordinating Committee (NCC), headed by Joseph Chamberlain, to handle the expected inflow. (It became the National Refugee Service in 1937.) Over the opposition of the Zionists, who argued that Palestine was absorbing a greater proportion of the refugees, the NCC became a claimant for Federation funds in 1935. Three years later the Anschluss increased the refugee pool by 180,000, while within the Reich the move to expel the Jews intensified. The refugee problem became the "refugee crisis."

It was at this juncture that Roosevelt issued his still unexplained invitation for a refugee conference to be held at Evian-les-Bains in France. Jewish leaders were so overjoyed at this development that few noted that the invitation to thirty-two nations was circumscribed so as not to conflict with the immigration laws of the participating nations. That preordained the conference to failure, since a hoped-for initiative from the Latin American republics, which the administration counted on, would not materialize.

Only the Dominican Republic made a sizable offer to admit "political refugees," the euphemism for Jews. After initial skepticism that 150,000 refugees could be absorbed in the Dominican Republic, the State Department accepted Rafael Trujillo's offer and made it the centerpiece of its refugee policy. A new agency, the Dominican Republic Settlement Association (DORSA), was established to implement the plan. Financed largely through the Joint Distribution Committee (JDC), which again called on Josef Rosen to administer the program, over five hundred refugees were settled on land near Puerto Plata on the northern coast of the island. Zionists, who considered Rosen anathema for the role he played in the Crimean resettlement scheme in the twenties, did not favor DORSA or the more than six hundred other resettlement schemes examined by the Roosevelt administration. They would have preferred to see such capital used to increase the absorption capacity of Palestine. Nevertheless Sosua, as the settlement came to be known, was the only successful resettlement scheme that the American government, working closely with the JDC, helped implement.[5] It was also the seedbed of the bitter conflict over rescue strategy between JDC and the world Zionist movement, represented by the World Jewish Congress, which persisted throughout the Holocaust years.

Predictably, the Evian conference did little to relieve the crisis, which worsened after Kristallnacht. The lines before the American consulates grew longer as German Jews sought desperately to find a way out of the hell the Reich had become for them. They found little to console them. American Jewry was emerging from the Depression comparatively early, but fundraising continued to lag. In 1939 the JDC allocated $20 million for overseas needs, barely sufficient to maintain its far-flung relief operation, which included resettlement in Palestine. Even after Kristallnacht most second-generation American Jews remained unaware of the dire situation of their coreligionists and were not enthusiastic about subsidizing the immigration of German Jews. The self-help network of organizations was barely able to handle the increased burden of dependency caused by the depression. Already overburdened, local Jewish communities where the refugees were sent sometimes rejected responsibility for their support.[6]

The Evian conference unexpectedly produced an opportunity for direct government intervention in the crisis. The new international refugee agency, the Intergovernmental Committee on Political Refugees established at Evian, had entered into direct negotiations with Berlin. In the skillful hands of George Rublee, an old crony of Roosevelt's, a "Statement of

Agreement" with Berlin was reached based on an elaboration of the "Transfer Agreement" the Reich maintained with the Anglo-Palestine Bank, representing the Jewish community of Palestine. It permitted circumvention of the principal roadblock to accepting refugees, the German insistence that they leave penniless. The agreement proposed to permit German Jews to remove a portion of their funds in the form of capital goods. The refugees would act as forced salesmen for German firms, shoring up the country's precarious exchange situation and incidentally financing Hermann Göring's four-year rearmament program. To allow the mass of now-impoverished Jews to leave, all remaining Jewish capital and property in Germany would be sequestered, and the Reichsbank would issue bonds using that capital as collateral. These bonds would then be purchased by "outside Jews," whom the Nazis envisaged as controlling the international banking system.

The plan placed American and British Jewish leaders in a quandary. Should they be parties to a plan that was in fact a ransom proposal? Would not Romania and Poland follow suit and try to "sell" their Jews? A plan for token compliance with the proposal triggered intense conflict. It was argued that such bonds backed by stolen property could not be legally handled on the international money market. Opponents of the plan could not be aware that in little over a year the alternative would be "resettlement in the East," a code name for the "final solution." Little came of the plan, since events in Germany were moving so rapidly that the three to five years required to implement the agreement could not in any case be assured, nor was there a place for the refugees to go. Later there were those who imagined that an opportunity to "save" German Jewry had been lost, but there was no way of knowing in 1939 that the alternative would be the "final solution."[7] It is unlikely that the Nazi leadership itself had yet decided on the ultimate disposition of the Jews. The offer to ransom German Jewry in 1939 and the infamous "blood for trucks" ransom proposal in 1944 serve as ghoulish bookends to the Holocaust. Both placed American Jewish leaders in a precarious position, since compliance required channeling money and military supplies to a hostile nation.

The adamant opposition to admitting Jewish refugees did not exempt Jewish refugee children. At the hearings of the Wagner-Rogers bill, which proposed to admit 20,000 such children, Jewish refugee advocates remained in the background in a vain effort to play down the Jewish aspect of the refugee problem. Only two of the thirty friendly witnesses testifying before the congressional committee were Jewish. Even so, the measure found little support in Congress, which rejected it by the simple device of restoring the quota provision. There was little support for the proposal from the Roosevelt administration.[8] Nevertheless, the effort to find asylum for refugees went forward after war had broken out. In June 1940 the President's Advisory Committee on Political Refugees (PACPR), which served as the umbrella organization for refugee agencies after the Evian conference, was authorized to draw up lists of prominent political and cultural figures who would be granted emergency visas. This permitted over 3,200 "culture carriers," many of them Jewish, to find refuge in the country. But by June 1941 the State Department, arguing that spies had infiltrated the refugee stream, succeeded in all but closing the gates by means of a directive to the consuls prohibiting them to issue visas to applicants who had "close relatives" in occupied Europe. Few refugees did not. Refugee admission, which had already declined by 60 percent after the outbreak of war, now virtually ceased, and no argument concerning the inhumanity of the policy made by James G. McDonald, chairman of the PACPR and former refugee commissioner for the League of Nations, moved State Department officials.[9]

Instead, the Roosevelt administration turned to the politically more palatable but far less feasible policy of mass resettlement outside the United States. Hundreds of likely areas were considered, including Mindanao in the Philippines and Baja California. But except for the DORSA project in the Dominican Republic, none came to fruition. Proposals were rejected for settling refugees in American territories like Alaska and the Virgin Islands. The denouement of the refugee drama came with the German invasion of the Soviet Union in June 1941 and America's entrance into the war six months later. The former led to a German order on 23 October 1941 forbidding all emigration from occupied Europe. It was an ominous signal that Berlin was turning to mass extermination, but few Allied leaders paid heed. At the same time the opportunity to save those Jews who had found a precarious safety in unoccupied France, Spain, Portugal, or Switzerland by bringing them to the United States all but vanished with America's entrance into the war.

As news of the actual operation of the "final solution" reached American Jewish leaders in August 1942, they desperately sought intercession from the Roosevelt administration. On 8 December 1942 a delegation visited the president in the Oval Office to urge him "to save those who may yet be saved." A memorandum pleaded for the president to "Speak the word! Institute the action!" But though Roosevelt was sympathetic and assured the delegation that the Nazis would be held to "strict accountability," there was no change in rescue policy.[10] Nine days after the meeting, the Allies issued their first warning on war crimes. It contained no clue that they were aware of the "final solution" or that there would be accountability for crimes against Jews.

The refugee issue was now overshadowed by the urgency of rescuing the potential victims of the extermination policy. Pressure stemmed from Jewish as well as non-Jewish sources. Hundreds of church sermons and newspaper stories informed Americans of the terrible slaughter.[11] A mass rally in Madison Square Garden in March 1943 recommended steps the administration could take to save lives. Included were war crimes warnings but no recommendation to bomb the death chambers or the rail lines leading to the death camps. In response to increased pressure, an Anglo-American conference on refugee and rescue efforts was convened on the inaccessible island of Bermuda. It met in April 1943 at the same time that the remnants of the Jewish population of the Warsaw ghetto mounted the first urban resistance of the war. When it became apparent that the conference was part of a joint State Department–British Foreign Office strategy to forestall a more active rescue effort, the conference was widely condemned as a "hollow mockery." The failure to implement a rescue plan raised the level of public agitation and identified those officials, such as Assistant Secretary of State Breckinridge Long, who were thwarting the rescue effort.[12] In November, hearings were held on a bipartisan resolution (S.R. 203 and H.R. 352) calling for the establishment of a rescue commission. But it was not until the recruitment of Henry Morgenthau, Jr., secretary of the treasury and the Jew closest to Roosevelt, that the War Refugee Board (WRB) was established, on 22 January 1944. Financed primarily with JDC funds, the WRB embarked on an effort to rescue the Jews of Hungary, the last sizable Jewish community surviving in Europe. On 12 June 1944 the immigration laws, thought by rescue advocates to be immutable, were also circumvented. The admission of over nine hundred primarily Jewish refugees, temporarily housed in an Army Relocation Authority camp in Oswego, New York, until they could be returned to Europe after the war, was supposed to serve as an example for other receiving countries to follow suit. Few did.[13]

In some measure the thousands of Hungarian Jews who survived the

Holocaust owe their lives to the American inititative. But the breakthrough, which occurred only after Nazi military power had been broken, came too late to save the millions. The rescue campaign was lost largely during the refugee phase of the Holocaust. Only about 500,000 refugees, a small fraction of Europe's Jewish population, found haven, about 157,000 of them in the United States. Of these perhaps 110,000 were Jewish. That meager record haunts American Jewry. Could more have been done to change administration policy so that more of their fellow Jews might have found shelter in this country? Could the hands of the murderers have been stayed? No balanced answer to these agonized queries can be attained without some knowledge of the historical processes that changed the traditional forms of Jewish communal identity and organization. I hope the foregoing chapters have given readers some knowledge of that complex process.

American Jewry was derived from Europe, much as was the larger American culture. In a sense its perplexity on how to respond to the Nazi threat paralleled the national confusion regarding Nazi aggression. But in the Jewish case it was compounded by the weaknesses of communal ties after decades of acculturation and secularization. American Jews never found a common basis for communal action. We have noted that there was virtual unanimity in the Jewish support of Roosevelt and the welfare state program. But when it came to their internal politics, there were few issues Jews could agree on. The dissonance was rooted in differing class backgrounds and patterns of acculturation that may for convenience be classified along the familar "downtown/uptown" axis.

We have already noted that the Jewish encounter with modernity generated remarkably diverse political ideologies, which in turn produced conflicting strategies on how to serve the Jewish interest. The more established "uptown" Jews, associated with the Reform movement and the AJCOMM, were usually further along the acculturation continuum. They continued to feel some concern for their "brethren" but it was less often reinforced by direct family ties than it was with "downtown" Jews, nor could they any longer identify with the all-encompassing ethnic Jewishness, the "tribalism" of European Jews. Zionism, the clearest manifestation of that ethnicity, was viewed by most uptowners as a nationalistic doctrine that embodied all those things they found objectionable. Most unacceptable was Zionism's basic conviction that ultimately Jews could find no security in the Diaspora, even though their seemingly safe status was evidence that it was possible provided they lived on religious rather than ethnic terms. Uptowners denied the effectiveness of the protest rallies, made into a virtual ritual by the AJCONG, the organization of second generation downtown Jews. Convinced that emancipation was irreversible, especially in "civilized" societies like Germany, they viewed Hitler's coming to power with less apprehension. The Germany of Goethe and Schiller, the real Germany, would surely reassert itself, they maintained. Failing that, the responsibilities of power would eventually tame Hitler. In contrast, downtown Jews and their second-generation descendants approached the Nazi threat more viscerally. The Jews of Europe were not merely coreligionists, they were kith and kin, part of the same people. Many had begun to sympathize with Zionism's insistence on the need for a Jewish homeland, not in classical terms of Zionist ideology, about which they understood little, but as a solution to the refugee problem. As early as 1933 Louis Brandeis had urged Jews to leave Germany for reasons of ethnic pride. "Let Germany share the fate of Spain," he urged.[14] Protest rallies and boycotts at least allowed Jews to feel they were doing something. Without them there was only silence.

The plan to organize a boycott of German goods, first suggested by the Jewish War Veterans in March 1933 and then organized worldwide by Samuel Untermeyer, demonstrates the complex basis of the communal conflict. Supporters of the boycott were convinced it could hurt the German economy, especially if it gained the support of non-Jewish opponents of Nazism. More important were its symbolic and therapeutic effects. It gave supporters the sense that Nazism could be opposed abroad much as anti-Semitism was at home—by fighting against it. The sheer exultation of hitting back fueled the growth of the boycott movement, which spread spontaneously to other organizations. A list of health resorts in America and Europe was published to help travelers avoid German resorts. A physicians' committee issued a pamphlet, "German Drugs and Their American Equivalents." Gradually large department stores and labor unions were persuaded to join. By 1935 there was a mood of triumph in the boycott movement, a belief that it could bring Hitler down.[15]

But Morris Waldman, president of the AJCOMM, characterized the boycott as "futile [and] possibly dangerous."[16] Not only would it confirm precisely what the anti-Semites had been claiming about the economic dominance of the Jews, but the economy's recovery from the Depression would be hampered, since Germany bought more from America than it sold there. In New York City a German-American counterboycott organization had distributed a leaflet stating that "the Jewish race has declared war" and urging shoppers not to buy from Jewish stores or deal with Jewish doctors, dentists, and lawyers, lest they be cheated. The AJCOMM feared forfeiting the friendship of Christians, who would "before long protect them [German Jews] from destruction."[17] Moreover, the boycott, it was argued, would not win friends in the Roosevelt administration, where the principle of free trade embodied in Secretary of State Cordell Hull's reciprocal tariff agreements was the central plank of the nation's overseas economic strategy. Some German Jewish leaders like Oskar Wasserman, director of the Deutsche Bank, had made known their opposition to the boycott. On 27 March 1939 the Zentralverein, the official agency that represented German Jewry, and three former presidents of the German Zionist Federation urged Wise to call off a scheduled boycott rally that they feared would boomerang. Armed with letters from "responsible" Jewish leaders in Germany, the AJCOMM's leaders had all along warned of the danger of retaliation. But the leaders of the AJCONG considered the Zentralverein no longer free and rejected the suggestion. Predictably Samuel Untermeyer, now at the helm of the World Non-Sectarian Anti-Nazi Council to Champion Human Rights, was convinced that the boycott was hurting Germany. Willy-nilly the boycott movement itself became a source of strife.[18]

The Joint Boycott Council, organized in 1936 as an umbrella organization for the boycott movement, failed to bring the Jewish organizations into line. The AJCOMM and B'nai B'rith never supported the movement. The AJCONG helped establish the council but found itself in a dilemma caused by its Zionist orientation. There was a threat that the counterboycott against Jewish businesses organized in Germany on 1 April 1933 might continue indefinitely if the anti-Nazi agitation did not cease. Beset by petty jealousies and pressure from within the organization and from the Tennenbaum group, the AJCONG could no longer hedge on the boycott issue. But even after Wise came out in support of the boycott on 14 August 1933, he tried vainly to convince the militants that boycotts should be "the last and not the first weapon of the Jewish people."[19]

During the same month, the Zionist movement approved an extension of the *ha'avara* (Transfer Agreement) that permitted German Jews to remove some of their funds from the Reich in the form of capital goods and resettle in Palestine. The Transfer Agreement held out the hope of becoming a financial and demographic boon to the hard-pressed yishuv. The choice Zionist leaders had to make was clear. A concrete tangible asset that would strengthen the economy was preferable to a dubious attempt to weaken the German economy. The Zionist movement became the principal breaker of the boycott. In the Jewish world there was outrage at what was considered a betrayal. Desperately, Wise spoke of a "moral boycott." The boycott, he observed, "is a weapon, but not *the* weapon." The organization of the AJCONG's boycott committee was delayed until February 1934, while focus on the less controversial mass protest rally strategy was intensified. On 7 March 1934 the AJCONG organized the successful "Case of Civilization against Hitler" rally, which was attended by thousands in Madison Square Garden and received wide press coverage. Not until February 1936 did the boycott committees of the AJCONG and the Jewish Labor Committee merge to form the Joint Boycott Council.

By that time the boycott movement was enmeshed in controversy. It had roused the opposition of the anti-Nazi Steuben Society and the State Department. Supporters pointed out that between 1932 and 1935 German exports had declined from 5.8 to 3.8 percent, to which boycott opponents responded that the decline was far greater between 1929 and 1932, before the boycott was organized. Most troubling, by the early months of 1939 the boycott movement clashed with the imagined opportunity to rescue German Jewry embodied in George Rublee's "Statement of Agreement" with the German government. The agreement, we have noted, was based on an extension of the Transfer Agreement, modified to bring foreign exchange to Germany, and would have required abandoning the boycott strategy. Predictably, boycott enthusiasts were the staunchest opponents of the agreement, which they viewed as a ransom proposal.

The conflict over the boycott highlighted the organizational disarray within the Jewish community. Not only were there differences in the estimation of the Nazi threat and how to counter it, but ideological and organizational interests were allowed to take precedence over the general interest, which in any case could not be determined.[20] Viewing the development of Palestine's economy as primary, the world Zionist movement adhered to its own interest, convinced that it was furthering the interest of all Jews. That posture of Zionist primacy would characterize all subsequent conflicts, whether they concerned the formation of a Jewish army, the solution to the refugee crisis, the formula for distributing philanthropic funds, or most important of all, the basis of Jewish unity. Plagued by disunity within its ranks and encumbered by its ideology, the American Zionist movement lacked the consensus and then the flexibility required to bring American Jews together.

That failure can best be seen in the bitter political wrangling that accompanied the four major attempts between 1933 and 1945 to set up a mechanism for unified action among the major Jewish organizations. The first occurred on 22 January 1933 when B'nai B'rith joined with the AJCOMM and the AJCONG to establish the Joint Consultive Council (JCC), a carefully constructed agency designed not to infringe on the organizational integrity of the three constituent organizations. Its activity was limited to providing a means of unified action in relation to the Jews of Germany. Since the AJCOMM leaders believed in 1933 that the situation would eventually resolve itself, the JCC would be temporary and provisional. The hope was that a permanent organization would be established when a clearer picture of the German Jewish condition emerged. In its early months the activities of the JCC looked promising. It successfully pressed the State and Labor Departments to simplify the system of obtaining visas. But behind the scenes there was tension. Convinced that the AJCONG was breaking the agreement for consultation by continually sponsoring "emotional" mass rallies, the leadership of the AJCOMM withdrew its support. Particularly nettlesome were Wise's continuing attempts to establish a World Jewish Congress. The notion of world Jewish governance, which they imagined would supersede existing Jewish organizations, was considered an ill-concealed conspiracy to achieve Zionist hegemony. To men like Cyrus Adler, Joseph Proskauer, and Louis Waldman it was simply not acceptable and itself became a source of divisiveness.[21]

By the final months of 1936 it was clear that the JCC had become a victim of the internal strife it was supposed to contain. The death blow came when the AJCONG insisted that the JCC's petition to the League of Nations on the mistreatment of German Jewry be delivered through the auspices of the World Jewish Congress. The AJCOMM left the JCC. A new consultative body, "the Committee on Cooperation," consisting of the AJCOMM, AJCONG, B'nai B'rith, the Anti-Defamation League, the Jewish War Veterans, and the newly organized Jewish Labor Committee (JLC), was hastily established. But it too soon foundered on the same shoals, a threat by the AJCONG to call for a nationwide election of delegates to form a conference that might legitimately speak for American Jewry.[22]

In an effort to forestall an unseemly nationwide ethnic election, the

AJCOMM and B'nai B'rith agreed to yet a third attempt at creating a mechanism for unified action. It led to the establishment of the General Jewish Council for Jewish Rights in June 1938. Composed of five delegates from each of the four major organizations, it was supposed to act as a clearinghouse. To avoid conflict, a two-thirds vote of the delegates was required for any step to be taken. The delegates were forbidden to encroach on "religious, racial, national, or economic philosophies" of the constituent organizations. That proved so constricting that, together with the refusal of the Council of Jewish Federations (CJF) to grant it operating funds, its demise three years later was inevitable.

In March 1943 yet another attempt to paper over the disunity between the major organizations was undertaken by creating the Joint Emergency Committee on European Jewish Affairs (JEC). It too began hopefully by attracting to its banner all major national organizations. In August 1942 confirmation of the operation of the "final solution" had been received through Gerhard Riegner, the agent of the World Jewish Congress (WJC) in Bern, Switzerland. Perhaps there would now be a sufficient sense of urgency to finally weld the organizations together in a common rescue effort. But strife between the Joint Distribution Committee (JDC) and WJC around the listening posts on the periphery of occupied Europe indicated that not even such dire news could bring the organizations together. The situation drew a scream of pain from Hayim Greenberg, editor of the *Jewish Frontier,* a Labor Zionist publication: "Of what value are all our differences of opinion, all our philosophies, . . . all our tragic-comically inflated prestige considerations, when the axe of the executioner hangs over the neck of nearly every other Jew in the world?"[23] But there was no response from Jewish leaders. Six months after it was established the JEC fell victim to a renewed Zionist effort to unify American Jewry under its auspices. The AJCONG called for a nationwide election to finally pave the way for a representative American Jewish assembly, ultimately to be known as the American Jewish Conference. It would be the most ambitious attempt yet to bring organizational unity to American Jewry and also its most drastic failure.

These efforts indicate that American Jewry realized the need to unify itself in the face of the crisis but that there was no single organization powerful enough to impose such unity. The most likely candidate for such a role was the Zionist movement. It had gained in numbers and influence during the crisis, but its radicalization made it unacceptable to non-Zionist philanthropists, whose resources continued to play a crucial role in Jewish life.

Louis Brandeis had long since eliminated the ideological imperative that American Jews settle in a Jewish state. That made it possible for most second-generation American Jews, convinced that Jewish refugees needed a haven, to flock to the Zionist banner. It was the refugee crisis of the thirties rather than Zionist ideology that finally earned Zionism a measure of acceptance among American Jews. Nevertheless, the elimination of the settlement imperative and the growing influence of the less demanding cultural Zionism did not fully resolve the problem posed by "political Zionism." Conflict stemmed from the two primary roles the American Zionist movement tried to fill. The first, we have seen, was garnering a larger share of the money being collected from the annual fund-raising drives conducted by the local federations. The second was advocacy before the American government.

The surest sign of the new strength of American Zionism was its ability to claim a greater share of the philanthropic dollar. But behind its glow of health American Zionism remained what it had always been—divided, uncertain of its direction, and beset with strife among its leaders. Its vigor was due less to its ability to tap its internal resources than to the popular support brought by the crisis facing European Jewry. That support enabled it to neutralize its opposition. The largest fraternal order, B'nai B'rith, which had until 1935 maintained a neutral position under the leadership of Henry Monsky, now supported Zionism. The strong non-Zionist proclivities of organizations like the AJCOMM and the National Council of Jewish Women, could not be changed overnight, but their leaders and wealthy supporters could often be convinced to support key parts of the Zionist program in the cultural and welfare sphere. Except for the idea of a national state, much of the Zionist program gradually became acceptable.[24]

But it would take time to translate the new consensus into action. In October 1938 an agency to mobilize public opinion, the National Emergency Committee for Zionist Affairs, was established. But not until August 1943, when it was reorganized and renamed the American Zionist Emergency Committee (AZEC), was a political pressure apparatus, based on over four hundred local emergency committees, fully in place. It was remarkably effective: in a matter of hours the AZEC could deluge the White

House or Congress with ten thousand cables. Under the management of Emanuel Neumann, the AZEC's public relations and political action department had become particularly successful at enlisting Christian clergy and lay leaders for the Zionist cause. It could duplicate the protest rally strategy almost anyplace in the nation. The AZEC, which became the political arm of American Zionism, was on the way to becoming the strongest pressure group in American history.[25] The Zionists were also changing the character of Jewish political activity from behind-the-scenes influence to direct political pressure. After 1939 there were few in the Jewish community who would deny that the internal political dialogue was now dominated by the Zionists. The new Jewish style also became familiar to the nation's political leaders, who would learn to respect its power.

That did not yet mean that Zionist demands would be acceded to. Special-interest pleading ran the risk of being considered unpatriotic during a national emergency and often went unheard. More important, Zionists could deal with the crucial question of rescue only within their limited frame of reference. They insisted that the logical place for Jewish refugees to settle was in Palestine, the only community that wanted them. Much of their energy was thus spent in a futile effort to undo the restrictionist immigration and land sales policy embodied in the 1939 White Paper. What London had denied to Jews by political fiat, the Zionists would regain by political counterpressure. But from the beginning this strategy placed the Zionist movement in an uneven contest where the British government held all the cards. There had been a considerable diminution of Jewish power, real and imagined, in the interwar period. Unlike the situation during World War I, when both sides were eager to earn the goodwill of American Jewry, during World War II there was murderous intent on the part of the Axis and only indifference from the Allies.

Moreover, the relentless protest against the White Paper, charging Britain with perfidy, confused many patriotic Jews. During the "Battle for Britain" the image of a gallant island people was reflected in a veritable craze to support Britain. There were "bundles for Britain" campaigns, and British children, victims of the blitz, were readily granted the havens not offered to Jewish refugee children. American Jews were not exempt from the intense Anglophilia that swept the nation in 1940. It was intensified by gratitude felt for the only nation still resisting the Nazis. In Palestine Ben-Gurion, leader of the Labor party, had solved the dilemma by promising to fight the White Paper as if there were no war and the war as if there were no

White Paper. But that was not a realistic policy for many American Jews, who did not yet fully link the rescue of European Jewry to the establishment of a Jewish homeland. If Jews could temporarily be settled in British Guiana or the Dominican Republic or any of the countless places being considered, then so be it.[26] Aware that they deflected money and human resources from the Jewish settlement in Palestine, most Zionists did not lend their support to alternative resettlement schemes like Sosua and British Guiana. As with Zionist opposition to the boycott, the needs of the yishuv came first. At the Evian and Bermuda conferences they insisted that their campaign against the White Paper be given priority. But Britain attended such conferences only on condition that the Palestine question not appear on the agenda. For those anxious simply to get the Jews out of Europe, the Zionist approach to rescue thus seemed strangely ineffective because of its narrowness.

Conflict between the various factions within the Zionist movement did not magically vanish as the crisis unfolded. After Vladimir Jabotinsky split off from the Zionist movement in 1926, the American revisionists languished. But the outbreak of the war brought to the United States a group of Palestinians associated with the Irgun Z'vai Leumi, the fighting arm of the revisionist movement. Led by Peter Bergson (Hillel Kook), Samuel Merlin, and Eri Jabotinsky, son of the founder, the group utilized public relations techniques with great skill and energy and soon became a thorn in the side of the mainline Zionist organizations. The group drew media attention with dramatic full-page newspaper advertisements and pageants like "We Shall Never Die," which attracted huge audiences wherever it appeared. Calling themselves by various names, such as American Friends of Jewish Palestine and the Emergency Committee to Save the Jews of Europe, they saw to it that the absence of a popular mandate and roots in American Jewry were all but forgotten.

Their earliest success came through their skillful exploitation of the Jewish army issue. In August 1940, during his last visit to the United States shortly before his death, Vladimir Jabotinsky, at a stormy meeting in New York's Manhattan Center, again advocated organizing such an army. The issue became one of the most divisive in American Jewish politics.[27] Now calling itself the Committee for a Jewish Army, the Bergson group attracted money and famous names, including well-known political leaders. Its militancy was particularly attractive to assimilated Jews, like the playwright and journalist Ben Hecht, who had been brought up short by the virulence of domestic anti-Semitism and the events in Europe.[28] In December 1941 a "Hebrew embassy" was established in Washington to bring the Revisionist program directly to the Roosevelt administration. The "embassy" was particularly embarrassing to the mainline Zionists, who, much to the chagrin of Nahum Goldmann, the representative of the Jewish Agency for Palestine, did not even maintain an office in Washington. The following month the Bergson group placed a full-page advertisement in major newspapers: "Jews Fight for the Right to Fight." Bergson also organized a Jewish Army Committee chaired by the immensely popular Senator Robert F. Wagner, which included on its roster Harold Ickes, Wendell Willkie, Al Smith, and William A. White, as well as numerous governors and university presidents. To bring themselves to the fore, the Bergson group skillfully exploited the Jewish army issue, which appealed to the desire of many Jews to strike back.

A belated effort to neutralize the group in May 1941 failed when Bergson rejected Wise's offer of recognition in return for accepting organizational discipline. For the mainline organizations the Jewish army issue exposed Jewish powerlessness. Aware of the issue's potential for harm, Wise asked Roosevelt to intercede with the British government in June 1941. But sensitive to Arab feeling, the British demurred, citing "technical difficulties" and supply shortages. Instead they assigned Jewish volunteers to service units and limited their recruitment to 5,000 out of a potential pool of 150,000 men. When Rommel's threat to the security of Palestine developed in spring 1942, the figure rose to 10,000.[29]

Lack of power to compel Britain to do its bidding on the question of a Jewish army doomed the Zionist effort to failure, but that seemed only to intensify communal conflict. So attractive was the image of a fighting Jew that the AZEC had taken to using it in its literature. The Reform movement's Central Conference of American Rabbis (CCAR) which had been moving steadily toward accepting Zionism after the Columbus platform, was thrown into turmoil by the Jewish army issue. At the annual meeting of the CCAR in June 1942, a resolution in support of a separate Jewish army proved too much for a group of hard-core anti-Zionist Reform rabbis. It precipitated the establishment of the staunchly anti-Zionist American Council for Judaism (ACFJ), led by Rabbi Morris S. Lazaron, well known for opposing Zionism. For a time it was able to raise a voice belying its small number of adherents.[30]

Last-ditch opposition to Zionist militancy at home occurred simultaneously with physical intercession to prevent Jews from reaching Palestine. The first shots British soldiers fired in World War II were not at German soldiers but at Jewish refugees illegally trying to enter Palestine.[31] On 25 November 1940 news of the accidental sinking of the refugee ship S.S. *Patria*, with the loss of two hundred lives, brought home again how inhumanly political London's policy was. Based on the growing evidence that European Jewry was being ground to dust between the millstones of murderous Nazis and callous Allies, a bitter edge entered the protest ritual. A new note also crept into the agendas of local Zionist conventions, consideration of the heretofore taboo idea that the answer to the Jewish dilemma was an independent Jewish commonwealth in Palestine. That was the gist of a resolution passed at the convention of the religious Zionists, Mizrachi, in May 1941. By September the commonwealth idea was included in every public declaration of the Emergency Committee.

The radicalization was hastened by the heartless loss of a second refugee ship on 24 February 1942. The S.S. *Struma,* one of the many illegal tramp steamers of Aliyah Beth, the illegal immigration organized by the yishuv, had barely limped into the harbor at Istanbul. It mysteriously exploded after the Turkish authorities towed it out to sea. Only 2 of the 750 illegals aboard were saved. For Jews it was further proof that the only hope of survival was to take their fate into their own hands. The commonwealth idea was part of that conviction and became standard currency among "downtown" Jews before the ZOA's Biltmore convention adopted it in May 1942. The delegates nodded in approval when David Ben-Gurion, leader of the Labor Zionists, told them that "Palestine will be as Jewish as the Jews will make it."[32] The confirmation of the news of the "final solution" in November 1942 led inevitably to the radicalization of American Zionism. Neglected was Wise's cautionary warning that the commonwealth issue could divide the community beyond repair.

Opposition to the commonwealth idea was not limited to knee-jerk anti-Zionists. Many rescue advocates believed that an obsession with the messianic vision of a Jewish state would militate against a broad effort to rescue European Jewry. Zionist leaders seemed reluctant to believe that unless a collective effort to rescue European Jewry was mobilized while there was still time, few European Jews would survive to populate such a state. The commonwealth resolution, they argued, bore little relation to the need to rescue European Jewry and was creating a suspicion that Zionists were unwilling to confront the rescue issue directly. The crisis was bringing mainline Zionists uncomfortably close to the extreme nationalist position of the Revisionists. So argued Tamar de Sola Pool, Judah Magnes, and others on the left end of the political spectrum, who were concerned about the rights of the Arab population of Palestine. Outside the Zionist fold the commonwealth resolution tended to undermine all hope that Zionists and non-Zionists might find a common ground on which American Jewry could act together for limited ends. An early consequence of the radicalization was the March 1943 resignation of the moderate Chaim Weizmann from all matters concerning foreign affairs.

In that year, when European Jewry was being devoured by the fires of the Holocaust, American Jews remained divided. When war came to Europe the leadership of world Jewry had naturally passed to Americans, but Zionism, now the only movement strong enough to bring American Jews together, was itself hopelessly divided between conciliators and maximalists. On one extreme was the Bergson group, now calling for the separation of the homeland from the rescue goal.[33] On the other were those who viewed Palestine merely as a cultural center for Judaism or a national home rather than a sovereign commonwealth. At the same time, the mobilization efforts of the Zionist Emergency Committee had become hopelessly mired in interpersonal strife between Rabbi Stephen Wise and Rabbi Abba Hillel Silver.[34]

That was the situation when the call for yet another effort to unify American Jewry was issued by Henry Monsky, president of B'nai B'rith. In June 1943 Americans witnessed a remarkable sight as thousands of Jews voted in a communal election to choose 377 convention delegates. Held at the Waldorf-Astoria between 29 August and 2 September 1943, its chances for success were slim despite the thirty-four organizations that responded to the invitation. It was only the second ethnic election held in the Jewish community since the American Jewish Congress election in 1918. There would also be 125 delegates appointed by the sixty-five national organizations representing approximately 1,500,000 affiliated Jews. That the delegates would be largely Zionist oriented was assumed. By 1943 most affiliated Jews had become Zionists of one sort or another, but that emerging consensus did not yet encompass the entire Jewish community. To prevent a breakup before the conference could get under way, a preliminary agreement to avoid divisive issues like the commonwealth resolution of the Biltmore convention was concluded with the non-Zionist leadership of the AJCOMM and the JLC. The focus of the program would be postwar planning and foreign affairs. It was only shortly before the conference was to convene that the missing rescue issue was added to the agenda.

For the first two days the preconference agreement was adhered to, but on the third day the conciliators lost control of the convention. Abba Hillel Silver, who had become the voice of the maximalists and for that reason had been excluded from the speakers' list, gained access to the rostrum. The searing address he delivered electrified the audience and stampeded the delegates to confirm the commonwealth resolution by a vote of 480 to 16. Joseph Proskauer's warning that the AJCOMM would not be bound by the vote was ignored. A few weeks later he led the AJCOMM out of the conference. The JLC followed suit.

Zionism had come to dominate American Jewry, but at the price of seemingly permanent internal division. Extremist organizations like the ACFJ, the Revisionist Zionists, and the Union of Orthodox Rabbis had repudiated the conference even before it got under way. But for most committed Zionists the commonwealth idea no longer seemed radical. Marie Syrkin, a well-known Labor Zionist writer, saw Silver's speech as a "moment of illumination and decision." A Jewish commonwealth had become the "only possible answer." But Judah Magnes, rector of the Hebrew University with ties to the "uptown" leadership, warned that the Jewish state resolution was "a declaration of war by Jews on the Arabs."[35] Similarly, Joshua Trachtenberg, an ordinary delegate representing the Jews of Easton, Pennsylvania, found the conference "bitterly disappointing." There continued to be dissenters within the mainline Zionist organizations like Hadassah and Poale Zion (Labor Zionists).[36]

Armed with a mandate based on an election, the radicalized Zionist movement set out to realize its objective. The first order of business was to undo the British White Paper. The assumption that pressure could alter the policy of a major power was based on Ben-Gurion's opinion that "the English people have not spoken yet" and that the White Paper was "not irreversible."[37] But he underestimated the difficulty of changing policy during wartime. Events were flowing away from the realization of Zionist goals, and Britain did not relax its opposition to Jewish refugees' entering Palestine. Heeding the advice of Harold P. Hoskins and General Patrick Hurley, who had separately prepared reports on the Palestine situation, Roosevelt was not prepared to challenge British Middle East policy during the war. Instead he moved toward freezing the situation until the war was over. That policy was confirmed by the Anglo-American Declaration of

June 1943, which cautioned that the continued Zionist pressure posed a "serious distraction from the war effort."[38]

It was thus not a propitious moment for the Zionists to gear up their now formidable organizational apparatus to gain government support for the commonwealth idea. But 1944 was an election year, and Roosevelt needed the support of his most loyal constituency in his campaign for a fourth term. He may have been aware that the Zionists were not strong enough to deny him the Jewish vote, however. The reorganized American Zionist Emergency Committee, now chaired jointly by Wise and Silver, switched its efforts from the White House to Congress. By October 1944 the "bottom up" pressure organized by Silver and Henry Montor, the skillful administrator of AZEC, had produced results. Of the 535 members of the seventy-eighth Congress, 411 had endorsed the commonwealth resolution. But as Wise and Nahum Goldmann, representative of the Jewish Agency in Washington, had cautioned, foreign policy was made in the White House, where the reluctance to challenge Britain's dominance in the Middle East during wartime continued. With the help of Congressman Sol Bloom, Jewish chairman of the House Foreign Affairs Committee, who had cleared it with the White House, the Wright-Compton resolution (H.R. 418) was introduced into the House and the identically worded Wagner-Taft resolution (S.R. 247) into the Senate.

The vaguely worded resolutions called for the United States "to use its good offices" to promote free entry of Jews into Palestine "so that the Jewish people may ultimately reconstitute Palestine as a free and democratic Jewish commonwealth." There was strong congressional support for the resolution, but during the February hearings the divisions within the Jewish community became apparent for all to see. Testifying on 8 February, Silver reminded the committee of the nation's historical responsibility for the mandate and pointed out that the White Paper had in fact not succeeded in winning the loyalty of the Arab nations. If sufficient force was shown, Silver maintained, the Arabs would fall into line. But that was not the opinion of Philip K. Hitti, a spokesman for the Arab cause, who cited the Atlantic Charter in support of his argument that Palestinians too deserved national self-determination. Lessing Rosenwald, speaking against the resolution for the American Council for Judaism and the testimony of the AJCOMM spokesman in favor of a United Nations trusteeship, demonstrated that even within the Jewish community there was no consensus.[39]

Finally, in private session General George Marshall, commander of the

Joint Chiefs of Staff, supported by a letter from Secretary of War Henry L. Stimson and his assistant John J. McCloy, argued that the resolution would be "prejudicial to the war effort" and requested that action on the resolution be deferred. The opposition of the oil interests and the exigencies of war had easily parried the Zionist thrust. Roosevelt understood little of the special value Jews had come to place on a national home. Like his vice president Henry Wallace, he thought of Jewish entrepreneurial energy as serving the needs of the nations where Jews settled.[40] His annoyance at the timing of the resolution doomed it from the outset.

The failure of the commonwealth resolution required damage control lest the Zionist cause lose momentum. On 9 March Roosevelt received a saddened Wise and a defiant Silver in the Oval Office. The press release of the meeting assured the public that the United States had never supported the White Paper and that at the proper time Jewish and Arab leaders would be consulted on the disposition of Palestine. That fell considerably short of the commonwealth idea and made the maximalists more determined to wring some concessions from the Roosevelt administration. The forthcoming election campaign offered an opportunity to do so. Wise's stirring address at the Democratic convention produced a pro-commonwealth plank for the Democratic campaign platform. Silver, who was not a registered Republican but had been a strong supporter of Senator Robert Taft (Ohio) and an opponent of a third term for Roosevelt, achieved the same at the Republican convention in Chicago. It was the first time Zionists had garnered bi-partisan support, a sign that there was awareness of their growing influence. But that new power would not produce results until 1948, too late for the Jews of Europe.

The Zionist failure was balanced by progress on the rescue front, reflected in the establishment of the War Refugee Board (WRB), followed by the administration's implementation of the "freeport" idea. The former finally established a government agency specifically for the rescue of Jews, and the latter marked a symbolic circumvention of the immigration laws that had been thought immutable. They marked the high point of the administration's rescue effort. Nevertheless, over half of Hungary's almost one million Jews and the surviving Jews of Slovakia went to the slaughter. The reversal of policy had come too late. As the war drew to a close, the catastrophe that had befallen European Jewry was graphically revealed in photographs and film. These images, continually reinforced by the sermons of their rabbis, many of whom had rushed to Europe to help the survivors, and finally the appearance of the first survivors in their communities, seared the Holocaust into the memory of American Jews. The feeling that they did not do enough has influenced their political culture ever since.

Yet clearly the notion of community failure is based more on guilt and sorrow than on a realistic estimate of Jews' power to influence government policy. The assumption that there was a single community, able to respond to a crisis of this scale, is not borne out by the factionalized condition of American Jewry. The best hope for uniting American Jewry lay with the Zionist movement, which we have seen was itself so divided that it could not impose its will. Ironically, those whose ideology warned that Jewish life in the Diaspora was untenable found themselves totally unprepared when the crisis came. Ultimately the Zionist movement would develop into the strongest single influence on the American Jewish scene. But the years the movement required to transform itself from a loosely organized group devoted to philanthropy into a political force were precisely the years needed to mobilize American Jewry for rescue. In some measure the weak response of American Jews to the Holocaust can be traced to the fragmentation of the American Zionist movement, but it is only one of the many signs of weakened communalism that became manifest during the interwar years.

The failure of Zionist leadership to appreciably influence the administration was illustrated again during Roosevelt's meeting with King Saud of Arabia on his return from the Yalta conference. The president seemed totally won over by Saud's presentation of the Arab cause. The Saud episode was an aberration based, Wise thought, on "poor advice of some counselors in our State Department and in the Colonial Office of England."[41] But the image of a preoccupied president accepting the advice of those who saw him last is too simple to explain Roosevelt's complex relationship to his Jewish constituency. Roosevelt had to withstand Jewish demands while retaining Jewish loyalty. He did so by successfully manipulating Jewish leaders, and often that required telling them only part of the truth. In retrospect his administration's seeming concern for the "forgotten man," which so won the hearts of Jewish voters, did not extend to the doomed Jews of Europe, whose plight Roosevelt never fully fathomed. "His currency was people and politics, not pain."[42]

The inability of American Jewry to convince Roosevelt to act more energetically on the rescue front also related to conditions stemming from the war. The rescue problem entailed important factors that it was beyond the power of American Jewry to affect. The horrendous character of the news about the "final solution" created a credibility problem. Few would believe such gruesome stories. Many Americans who regretted America's entrance into World War I came to believe that the nation was being duped by clever propaganda and were determined not to let it happen again.[43] Rescue advocates and their allies in the liberal community never succeeded in convincing a preoccupied president and the American public of the significance Auschwitz held for their time in history. For Roosevelt and most Americans, the processed mass murder in the death camps became merely another atrocity in a particularly cruel war that had seen Lidice, the Bataan death march, Katyn, and in December 1944, the Malmédy massacre. For many, Auschwitz was not even included in the catalog of war crimes. It was part of "Jewish wailing," an unseemly tendency for Jews to mourn publicly.[44]

Beyond that there existed little precedent for ethnic groups to pull foreign policy away from its perceived national self-interest, and none during wartime. Irish-Americans had not prevented the building of an unspoken Anglo-American alliance that dominated international relations during the first half of the twentieth century. German-Americans, some of whom switched their traditional Republican vote to Wilson in 1916 when he ran on the slogan "He kept us out of war," discovered the fate Americans held out for those who dared to be out of step during wartime. They could not prevent America's declaration of war on the "fatherland" in April 1917. In 1945 Polish-Americans could do little to prevent the "Crime of Crimea," the ceding of part of Poland to the Soviet Union at the Yalta conference. In the context of American ethnic history, the Jewish failure to appreciably change wartime priorities to include the rescue of European Jewry and the opening of Palestine for Jewish settlement hardly seems surprising.

Roosevelt's anti-refugee policy was based on a broad popular consensus. Most Americans did not believe that admitting refugees served the national interest during a depression. Certainly no ethnic group could hope to change immigration policy without a broad political coalition to amplify its voice. The liberal-ethnic-urban coalition that buttressed the New Deal seemed ready made to play such a role, but the virulent anti-Semitism during the thirties as well as the Depression itself aggravated interethnic tensions and prevented the building of such a coalition. Jews remained virtually alone in trying to make their case for refugees and for rescue.

The indications of a renewed growth of anti-Semitism during the thirties were clear. There were more than 120 organized hate groups exclusively devoted to preaching anti-Semitism. In the two years between 1942 and 1944 the percentage of respondents who thought Jews had too much power and wealth rose from 52 to 65 percent. On a preference list of ethnic groups, Jews consistently ranked last or next to last.[45] Yet there may have been less there than meets the eye. The survey data were often internally inconsistent. As news of the "final solution" began to filter through to the American public, polls commissioned by the AJCOMM in 1942 and 1944 found only 12 percent of the respondents classifiable as anti-Semitic.[46] Much depended on how the survey questions were worded and how anti-Semitism was defined. Most important, the surveys did not address two important questions: To what extent was public policy actually influenced by anti-Semitism? And how did American Jewry perceive it? The latter question especially is crucial to understanding the American Jewish response to the crisis.

During the thirties Jews were so traumatized by the specter of anti-Semitism that the editors of the well-known 1936 *Fortune* magazine study recommended, as the first order of business, "the quieting of Jewish apprehensiveness." One Jewish observer characterized the community as being in a "state of fear, anxiety and constant alarm."[47] For Jews there was something new, but not in the "biologism" of Nazi anti-Semitism. They had, after, all witnessed evidence of a similar ideology in 1921 and 1924, when restrictionists spoke of "Nordic supremacy." What frightened them was the sight of a modern state, driven by a racialist ideology, prepared to devote its resources to convert the world to anti-Semitism in the name of a "higher form of consciousness." They saw that American anti-Semitism in the thirties was energized and financed from the outside by the German diplomatic staff and through other conduits. Funds and literature from abroad were delivered to anti-Semitic groups headed by Charles Sylvester, Gerald L. K. Smith, Gerald Winrod, and particularly Fritz Kuhn, the *Führer* of the German-American Bund. A successor organization to the "Friends of the New Germany" organized in 1934, the Bund boasted 25,000 members, four newspapers, and twenty-two summer camps.[48] Jews were shocked by the sight of Nazilike histrionics complete with familiar uniforms and symbols. The massive Bund rally held in Madison Square Garden on Washington's Birthday in February 1939 appeared so Nazilike that it might have taken place in Nuremberg. During the twenties Jewish defense agencies had effectively counteracted hate groups like the Ku Klux Klan and had witnessed the decline of domestic nativism. Now anti-Semitism appeared in even more virulent form supported by foreign sponsors. More troubling was the size of the audience reached through the airwaves. It was rumored that the radio preacher Charles Coughlin was heard by fourteen million American listeners. It seemed that a Nazilike movement, including its anti-Semitic component, might triumph here too.

Yet by any objective measure the anti-Semitic demagogues of the thirties were not an impressive lot able to fit comfortably into the mainstream of American politics. When Berlin became fully aware of Fritz Kuhn's machinations in 1938, it withdrew support. He was imprisoned for embezzlement in 1939. Huey Long's "share our wealth" movement became anti-Semitic only after his assassination in 1935, when Gerald Smith became its national coordinator. William Dudley Pelley's ambitions outpaced his talent, and the Silvershirts remained dependent on outside funding. Coughlin was restricted from entering politics by his priestly vows and by a persistence of anti-Catholicism. He remained a "closet anti-Semite" until 1938 when, under the influence of Congressman Louis McFadden and of Dennis Fahey, a professor of philosophy in Dublin's Holy Ghost Missionary College, he joined the chorus of anti-Semites.[49] He never seized the opportunity to gain a national base by succeeding Huey Long or Charles Townsend. Ultimately he was compelled to repudiate the violence of his Christian Front platoons. Gerald Winrod and Robert Edmondson were simply in the business of anti-Semitism and never achieved national stature.

The actual influence of these extremist organizations was somewhat less than perceived by the apprehensive Jewish community. Of the respondents to a Gallup poll taken in 1933, 94 percent disapproved of Nazi treatment of Jews. After Kristallnacht a strong "spectator sympathy" in Britain and the United States for German Jewry became a cause for concern in Berlin.[50] American ethnic communities and the general public may have rejected the admission of Jewish refugees, but they also proved a weak base from which to launch an organized mass movement based on anti-Semitism. As measured by number of organizations, size of membership, and readership of the ethnic press, the influence of hyphenates like German-Americans and Italian-Americans who might have lent themselves to the designs of their former homelands had declined markedly from its peak years between 1914 and 1917.[51] When the Depression struck the level of anti-Semitism was receding, and though it rose again during the thirties, a "Jewish question" showed little sign of entering the political dialogue. Unlike Germany, where the movement was supported by government policy, in the United States anti-Semitism remained an incoherent, isolated force. As the war approached the strident anti-Semitism preached by hate groups may actually have had a boomerang effect, especially among opinion-making elites who later became the mainstay of the civil rights movement.[52] America's entry into the war ultimately militated against a racist worldview. It was the German enemy that advocated racial hatred.

That the Jews of the thirties perceived a greater threat from anti-Semitism than existed in reality is not as puzzling as it may seem. The Jewish reaction was shaped by the exclusion experience of the twenties and the news of what was happening in Europe. These influences were reinforced by daily slights, especially in the area of employment. For Jews the heightened interethnic tensions looked like anti-Semitism. There was no way to oppose the Jewish interest in admitting refugees, for example, without appearing anti-Semitic. In the case of German- and Italian-Americans, the support Rome and Berlin gave these groups made Jews fear a transfer of the dreaded malady from Europe. "Italian consuls do nearly everything but administer the fascist oath to Italo-Americans," wrote one observer.[53] When after 1938 Mussolini adopted German anti-Semitism, the Italian-American press, especially *Grido della Stirpe* (The cry of the race) and to a lesser extent the papers dominated by Genoroso Pope, adopted a fascist line. Despite efforts to counteract it made by organizations like the Sons of Italy, anti-Semitism, fueled by resentment of Jewish economic and political advancement, grew in Italian neighborhoods.[54] When Italian Blackshirts joined Bundists in a well-publicized joint meeting at Camp Yaphank on 4 July 1937, it sent shivers down Jewish spines.

The threat from German-Americans seemed even clearer. To those haunted by memories of the anti-German panic during and after World War I, the pull of the "new Germany" seemed irresistible, especially if they had arrived after the war. By 1934 most of the anti-Nazi elements in the German-American community had been silenced or pushed to the periphery. During the twenties relations between American Jews and American Germans had been civil, although newspapers like the Milwaukee *Sonntagspost,* the Illinois *Staats Zeitung,* and the Chicago *Abendpost* often echoed the strident nationalism heard in the speeches of Erich Ludendorff and Gregor Strasser. The linkage of the Nazi party's overseas affairs bureau and Fritz Kuhn's German-American Bund, organized in 1935, followed as a matter of course. For American Jews it was a voice that came directly from Berlin. [55]

We have already noted the foreign policy and domestic roots of Jewish-Irish dissonance. Irish dominance of the Catholic church, whose influence would have helped in the refugee relief operation of the thirties, lent that relationship a special urgency. But except for some Catholic officials like George Cardinal Mundelein of Milwaukee, little help came from the church, though there was a high Catholic representation in the refugee stream.[56] The church's principal American prince, Francis Cardinal Spellman, had gained a reputation for being "unfriendly" toward Jews. Unfamiliar with the actual workings of the church, few Jews could understand why Coughlin's superior, Detroit's Bishop Michael Gallager, did not silence him. By the time Coughlin was compelled to give up his radio program in October 1940, much damage had already been done.

Although African-Americans were politically too weak to be of much help in a coalition for rescue, the strident anti-Semitism among urban ghetto blacks became a source of concern. Jewish philanthropists like Julius Rosenwald had helped to establish the National Association for the Advancement of Colored People (NAACP), the first Negro defense agency. Jewish legal talent—Arthur Spingarn, Milton Konvitz, Jack Greenberg, and others—helped found the Legal Defense Fund, which split off from the NAACP in 1939. They were the first to mount a legal challenge to segregation. It was Samuel Leibowitz who helped get the Scottsboro boys' rape conviction reversed by the Supreme Court in 1932, after the case had been exploited by the Communist party. On the level of popular culture, Jewish musicians like Benny Goodman were the first to interact and record with black singers like Billie Holiday. Jewish impressarios contributed disproportionately to bringing Negro "rhythm and blues" into the mainstream of American culture. Louis Marshall and his son were behind the unsuccessful effort to get an antilynching law on the books in New York State. And Philip Randolph, head of the Sleeping Car Porters Union, whose threat to organize a "march on Washington" led Roosevelt to issue "fair employment" executive order 8802, worked closely with Jewish labor leaders like Jacob Potofsky and Joseph Schlossberg. It was the Jewish labor movement that gave Randolph his friendliest reception. Complementing the philanthropic and cultural connection, political teamwork between blacks and Jews had developed in the thirties. Together they became Roosevelt's most loyal constituency.[57]

Whether that special relationship was based on a Jewish sensitivity to injustice and a common sense of victimization or whether it developed as part of a strategy that permitted Jews to air grievances regarding exclusion without constantly speaking of anti-Semitism is difficult to say.[58] What is clear is that by the late twenties all was not well in the relationship. Black resentment of rapid Jewish mobility was fueled by charges of mistreatment of black domestics by Jewish housewives and charges of price gouging and discrimination by Jewish storeowners in the ghettos. In politics there developed a conflicting interest concerning participation in the 1936 Olympic Games and black opposition to the entrance of Jewish refugees. In the case of the latter the *Amsterdam News* observed that "everyone knows the Jews own Harlem and they're doing to us what they did to the Germans. But at least Hitler is throwing them out."[59] Black street-corner orators, many of them former Garveyites, pointed out that the refugees would soon be better off than the people of the ghetto. Sufi Abdul Hamid, one of the most flamboyant of the orators, who earned the title "black Hitler," preached for a "jihad" against "Jewish exploiters."

By 1935 tensions between blacks and Jews ran high in major cities, especially New York, Baltimore, and Saint Louis. The following summer, sparked by the arrest of a shoplifter, a serious riot broke out in New York in which Jewish stores were singled out for looting. Efforts by the NAACP, the Urban League, the AJCOMM, and representatives of the black and Jewish press to lessen tensions were of little avail. By the outbreak of war, Jews saw Harlem and other urban ghettos as seething caldrons of anti-Semitism. After the attack on Pearl Harbor, the patriotism generated by war, which also siphoned off young unemployed men from the ghetto streets, momentarily cooled passions. But in June 1943 in Detroit, and two months later in Harlem, a new wave of rioting broke out in which Jewish-owned stores were again singled out for looting. The Jewish press, which had for years downplayed black anti-Semitism, now broke its silence. The liberal CCAR passed a resolution condemning the Detroit riot as a "triumph of Hitlerism." The disruption of a relationship in which Jews had invested so much during a period when they felt the world conspired against them did much to dampen the hope that democracy and pluralism offered the best defense against anti-Semitism. It seemed that American Jewry would not be immune from Nazilike depredations.

Jews did not come to the battle against anti-Semitism bereft of defense strategies. The Anti-Defamation League (ADL), established in 1913, had developed instruments to monitor its progress as if it were an epidemic. Its files were made available to the Federal Bureau of Investigation to document the Nazi infiltration of domestic anti-Semitic groups. Jews had also learned during the twenties that anti-Semitism declined as the level of education increased. Accordingly, Jewish defense agencies sponsored "public education" campaigns and made "tolerance" curricula available to the schools. Innumerable "fireside discussion groups," roundtables featuring experts on Judaism and clergy of all faiths, were deployed, frequently using radio air time, to get the tolerance message across. A deluge of "tolerance" literature was produced and distributed. An article in the *Saturday Evening Post* began with the words: "Stirred by the ill-winds of intolerance and persecution and unbelief, Protestants, Catholics and Jews in the United States have begun to make common cause against their common enemies." Interfaith stories were "planted" in the ethnic press linking tolerance to democracy and contrasting it with the hatred generated by Nazism. The ill effects of anti-Semitism became a standard topic for forums addressing the nation's educated elite, such as the University of Chicago's Roundtable of the Air. The interfaith movements established during the twenties were also called into play. In 1939 the school system of Springfield, Massachusetts, was selected for an experiment in teaching "mutual acceptance." Touted as a success, the Springfield program was introduced into the curricula of other middle-sized cities.[60] Perhaps the most successful of these educational efforts was initiated in 1944 by John Slawson, executive director of the AJCOMM. He commissioned the refugee scholar Max Horkheimer to produce a five-volume "scientific" study of anti-Semitism. One of the volumes in *Studies in Prejudice* was Theodor Adorno's *The Authoritarian Personality,* which went far to make tolerance appear normal and anti-Semitism seem a mental disorder. That classification may not have served the cause of truth, but it was a great asset in a nation where being "normal" was given the highest priority.

Interestingly enough, "Jewish" Hollywood, which frequently bore the brunt of anti-Jewish hysteria, was little interested in the group prejudice theme. Between 1933 and 1940, few films about prejudice or Jewish life were produced. When Germany, which composed 10 percent of the film industry's export market, banned films featuring the names of prominent Jewish actors, studios simply changed such names or omitted them. A shift to portraying the dark side of fascism began in 1938 with the release of *Three Comrades* and *Confessions of a Nazi Spy.* Even here references to anti-Semitism remained oblique. Not until the release of Charles Chaplin's

The Great Dictator in 1940 was the connection between Nazism and anti-Semitism dealt with directly. "I did this picture for the Jews of the world," said Chaplin. The film was enormously popular, "worth at least three divisions," according to one savant.[61]

Resorting to the judicial system to fight anti-Semitism proved troublesome for Jewish defense agencies. There had always been a conflict between those who favored direct confrontation with anti-Semitism in the public arena and those who advocated "soft," long-range strategies that relied on "education" and the natural sense of fair play assumed to be inherent in democratic societies. The increased activities of formal anti-Semitic organizations, especially the German-American Bund, brought the issue to a head. Through infiltration, the ADL had developed information on the link between the Bund and the overseas bureau of the Nazi party. But Congressman Dickstein's campaign as vice chairman of the House Un-American Activities Committee, which in 1934 and 1935 produced volumes of testimony on the "subversive" intent of the Bund and other "extremist" organizations, alarmed civil liberties organizations, whose ranks were disproportionately composed of Jews. They feared that the ill-defined line between subversion and legitimate dissent would limit free speech. Jews, argued one civil libertarian, must take great care in their battle against anti-Semitism not to quench "the flame of reason." But another voice, convinced that the propaganda and lies of the anti-Semites were "poisoning the minds of the people," thought the rhetoric was "beyond the limits of tolerance" and should be censored. Between stood Rabbi Robert Gordis of the Conservative movement, who argued for a fuller use of the slander and libel laws rather than for censorship and banning of subversive organizations, because "the remedy is all but worse than the disease."[62] But few Jews complained when, four days after Pearl Harbor, the offices and newspapers of the Bund were closed by the Treasury Department.

With the outbreak of war in September 1939 Jewish apprehension regarding domestic anti-Semitism was somewhat relieved. Unlike the situation between 1914 and 1917, when Wilson asked Americans to be neutral in mind and heart, between 1939 and 1941 most Americans came to view Hitler's Reich as a malevolent force and the war as a just one. The fear now became that the war itself would bring out the familiar charges of war profiteering and draft dodging. By 1941 anti-Semitic propagandists were enjoying a field day projecting an unpatriotic image of Jews. When gas rationing was introduced, one broadside read:

First man killed—Mike Murphy
First man to sink a Jap warship—Colin Kelly
First man to down five Jap planes—Eddie O'Hara
First man to get four new tires—Abie Cohen[63]

There was suspicion that the alarming increase in anti-Semitism and the rumor campaign that accompanied it had their roots in Berlin. The charge of war profiteering, which was its mainstay, was bitterly ironic for Jews, since the shift to wartime production severely affected the luxury-item businesses in which Jews were disproportionately represented. After 1940, in the midst of general expanding employment, the unemployment rate for Jews rose.[64]

To plan a counterstrategy, Jewish defense organizations held a series of meetings in 1940. The key, it was decided, was to get out information to the general public demonstrating that Jews were doing their part for the war effort. Accordingly, in October 1941 the Jewish Welfare Board (JWB) established a Bureau of War Records to collect and disseminate accurate information on the Jewish contribution. Its operation was based on a network of two hundred local volunteer war record committees who would filter information on recruitment, casualties, and citations to the clearinghouse in New York, which would then publicize it. Throughout the war a steady flow of information on Jewish contributions to the war effort was collected and disseminated. By 1945 the bureau had informed the nation that 550,000 Jewish men served in the armed forces, 8 percent beyond their proportion of the population, that the Jewish community had suffered 40,000 casualties, including over 8,000 killed in action, and that 36,000 Jewish servicemen had received 61,448 medals, including one Medal of Honor and 74 Distinguished Service Crosses. Jews, the public was informed, served in every branch of the armed forces and had attained almost every rank. The JWB data were supplemented by several private efforts to publicize the Jewish role in the war.[65]

To counteract the slanderous "first" jokes, a series of "First for Freedom" stories, in which Jews were the heroes, were given wide publicity by B'nai B'rith's news service. There was the story of Frances Langer, the first nurse killed, the story of Sgt. Irving Strobing, who tapped out the last coded message before the fall of Corregidor, the story of Sgt. Meyer Levin, Captain Colin Kelly's Jewish bombardier, and tales of heroic exploits by dozens of other "Jewish heroes." Among them was the story of "Two-Gun Cohen," a Jew serving in the Chinese army, and accounts of the Jewish uprising in the Warsaw ghetto.[66]

The greatest propaganda coup occurred as a result of the sinking of the troopship S.S. *Dorchester* off Greenland in February 1943 with the loss of 678 servicemen. Among them were three Christian chaplains and one Jewish chaplain, Rabbi Alexander D. Goode. As the story was pieced together by the JWB's Bureau of War Records, the chaplains had supposedly given up their life vests so others could survive. A last letter from Rabbi Goode to his wife added a poignant touch. Posters of the four chaplains holding hands on the flooded deck of the sinking ship were widely distributed. The four chaplains scene, which effectively transmitted the interfaith message, became one of the most familiar images of the war, especially after it was reproduced on a postage stamp. It also gave rise to a series of stories stressing the interdenominational theme. The best known, *Three Pals, Comrades in Life and Death,* is the story of three friends, Protestant, Catholic, and Jew, who stemmed from the same town, together attended high school and played football, and subsequently fell together on the field of battle. As the war progressed a growing number of gold stars appeared in the windows of Jewish homes to buttress the case that Jews were sharing fully in the cost of the war.

But it is difficult to determine how effective these efforts were in counteracting anti-Semitism, which reached a high point in 1944 and declined thereafter. Undoubtedly the first gruesome photos of the death camps encountered by the advancing Allied armies, which served as evidence of what anti-Semitism brought in its wake, also contributed to its postwar decline, as did the euphoria of victory. But after the Holocaust few Jews could convince themselves that anti-Semitism had simply vanished. It could blossom again at the slightest sign of social crisis. Apprehension about its existence remained a persistent characteristic of postwar American Jewry. During the thirties and forties the actual threat it posed may have been overestimated, but few Jews doubted its pervasiveness. One of the reasons for overestimating the strength of anti-Semitism stemmed from the difficulty of differentiating it from "normal" intergroup tensions, which had reached a high level during the depression. From a Jewish perspective they seemed the same.[67] Most important, the Holocaust made it difficult to view even latent anti-Semitism with equanimity.

The American Jewish response to the Holocaust cannot be understood without an awareness of the prevalence of despair. American Jews felt so vulnerable that it may have been partly their apprehension regarding domestic anti-Semitism that muted their appeal for help, which during the war could be mistaken for special-interest pleading. In 1940 American Jews were aware that their fellows under the Nazi heel were experiencing incredible cruelty and deprivation and random killing, but early rumors concerning their fate spoke of resettlement, not annihilation. It was still possible to hope that Jews might find security where they were. Even after news of the "final solution" was confirmed in fall 1942, their imagination was slow, perhaps unwilling, to comprehend that the Reich had embarked on a program of total liquidation. It boggled the imagination. At first they spoke of American Jewry's need to assume the leadership of world Jewry, which for centuries had been ensconced in Europe. "If in the last war American Jewry came to maturity," wrote the noted historian Salo Baron in 1940, "the present war has placed in its hand undisputed leadership of world Jewry."[68] Even Baron had not yet fathomed the depth of the crisis and still assumed there would be a Jewry to lead. Optimistically, Jews began to talk and plan for the postwar world. As late as 1943 the American Jewish Conference (AJCONF), the most formidable of the four efforts to unify American Jewry during the crisis, began with postwar planning and established a rescue commission only as an afterthought. Zionist organizations too assumed there would be a European Jewry to settle the Jewish commonwealth they hoped to establish. So incredible was the fact of genocide that Jewish leaders seemed unable to absorb it. Only gradually did an awareness grow that European Jews might not survive the war. That awareness triggered a new wave of militant protest in spring 1943, which culminated in the Bermuda conference in April. Even then some cautioned against evacuating Jews from Europe lest the end of European Jewish civilization be hastened.[69]

There may be an alternative explanation for the unseemly planning for the postwar world while the destruction of European Jewry proceeded apace. Most steps suggested by rescue advocates had been precluded by Allied governments. Bombing the rail lines and gas chambers was merely one of several rescue proposals submitted by Jewish leaders. All were rejected on the grounds that they required reordering war priorities. Short of physical intervention, there was little else that could be done aside from hoping for the best. Bereft of sovereign power, Jews possessed no armed force that might pluck European Jews from the death chambers. They could only hope to convince Allied leaders to use their armed forces for that purpose. But no Allied power was willing to do so. The fate of the Jews of Europe was never on the agenda of the conferences the Allies held to determine wartime strategy.

The noted Protestant theologian Reinhold Niebuhr wondered about the early Jewish reaction to the news from Europe. He may have been close to the mark when he noted that Jewish liberal humanitarians had difficulty coming to grips with the existence of an evil so dark that it could "undermine the characteristic credos of the democratic world."[70] He attributed the disbelief to the lack of a sense of original sin. So confident had Jews become that there was a "spirit of civilization" in the world—perhaps housed in the Oval Office, the League of Nations, or the Vatican—that would intercede for Jews that they could not believe "the world" would let it happen. Those few, like Niebuhr, who foresaw that this would not be the case and warned Jewish leaders to abandon their "revolutionary optimism" were hardly heard. Instead, Jewish organizations reacted with their normal strategy of amelioration through philanthropy and postwar planning.[71] They did what they knew how to do. The only Jewish agency to consolidate its efforts during the crisis (1939) was the United Jewish Appeal (UJA), the major fund-raiser.

By 1941 and the early months of 1942 most national Jewish agencies had established departments to plan for the postwar world. The AJCONG and its affiliate the World Jewish Congress created a postwar planning body, the Institute on Jewish Affairs, in February 1941. After the news of the Holocaust has been confirmed, the AJCOMM, having rejected an offer to work jointly with AJCONG, established its own Institute on Peace and Post-war Problems. The Jewish Labor Committee (JLC) followed suit with its Research Institute for Jewish Post-war Problems. In addition, many smaller organizations published pamphlets and established committees devoted to postwar planning. But not until the victory at Stalingrad (March 1943), when it was finally possible to see the light at the end of the tunnel, did such planning assume an air of reality.

Jewish organizations turned to the treatment of Germany and the question of war guilt and reparations. The first reaction was to urge harsh treatment of the Reich. Morgenthau's "hard" plan for the "pastoralization" of Germany was preceded by warnings in some Jewish publications that Germany must not be allowed to take its place in a federated Europe, which it would naturally dominate. Morgenthau, whose staff wrote the first government plan for the treatment of Germany, denied being motivated by "racial vengeance," but there could be little doubt that the news of the death camps had affected him. Faced with the accusation that he was motivated by ethnic rather than national interest, he acknowledged that his plan seemed inhumane and cruel, but he added, "We didn't ask for this war; we didn't put millions of people through gas chambers. . . . They have asked for it."[72] But while many Jews had been radicalized by the Holocaust, the posture of the AJCOMM remained legalistic and moderate. When Joseph Proskauer met with Roosevelt to offer suggestions for the forthcoming San Francisco conference, he explained to the president that Jews saw themselves as "the principal victims of the persecution that has sprung from the Hitler tyranny" but acknowledged that they were not the only victims. The AJCOMM recommended "special treatment" for Jews "only insofar as necessary to meet their special needs." Proskauer's major suggestion was to create a United Nations commission to promulgate an international bill of rights. The organizational culture of the AJCOMM had not appreciably changed since World War I, when Louis Marshall had placed much faith in another legal device, the national minority rights clauses.[73] A joint proposal for an international bill of rights submitted by the AJCONF, AJCONG, and the British Board of Deputies was rejected at the San Francisco conference.

Zionist organizations similarly held to their distinctive worldview, which now called for the establishment of a Jewish commonwealth in Palestine. Their proposal gave priority to free immigration to Palestine in preparation for a Jewish national home. There was general agreement that there should be trials for war criminals, but regarding the collective guilt of the German people there was a conflict of opinion. On the left end of the political spectrum were those, like Hannah Arendt, who cautioned that a distinction must be maintained between the German people and the Nazis. They proposed that a world tribunal punish those responsible for war crimes.[74]

The most comprehensive plan was prepared by the Institute of Jewish Affairs of the AJCONG. A careful researcher, Jacob Robinson, chairman of the Institute, began by gathering as much information as was available on the surviving Jews of Europe. The document that emerged touched on virtually every aspect of the postwar question. Included was an eleven point program for the trial and punishment of war criminals, a plan for compensation and reparations for survivors, a proposal to outlaw anti-Semitism, and finally a plan to create a Jewish commonwealth in Palestine. The work of the Institute provided the basis of the postwar claims submitted to the War Emergency Conference of the World Jewish Congress, held in Atlantic City in November 1944. Five years later the claims were formally submitted to the West German government and were enacted into law by the Adenauer government in 1952. It was also that conference, composed of 270 delegates representing Jewish communities in forty countries, that created the "Basic Program for Jewish Survival in the Post-war World."[75]

What we have seen in the foregoing pages is that during the interwar years the term community no longer adequately described American Jewry. Few of the commonalities that communalism was based on were present. The religious bond no longer unified, and the ethnic bond, based on a Yiddish-speaking culture, was on the wane. A new tie based on common Americanness had not yet developed. Paradoxically, only in the anti-Semitic imagination were Jews a unified and conspiratorial tribe. In reality American Jews were never able to speak in unison to the Roosevelt administration and therefore never fully played the advocacy role before the American seat of power that kinship and history had assigned them. The Zionist movement, which might have imposed unity based on the consensus it had achieved, was itself riven by factional strife among its leaders. Moreover, its ideology permitted it to support only a single narrow strategy for rescuing European Jews—to compel Britain to open the gates of Palestine. Unfortunately, during the war it was a goal far beyond its power.

Had it achieved unity, there is still no assurance that American Jewry would have been more effective in convincing the government to embark on a more active rescue policy. It is doubtful whether even a unified Jewry could have persuaded Roosevelt to risk seeing the war against Germany as a war to save the Jews. Until the spring of 1943, Allied leaders could not be certain their cause would triumph. The Jewish task was thus difficult, perhaps impossible, to perform. It required first that Jews persuade the American people to change their restrictive immigration policy in the midst of a severe depression and then, during a bloody war for survival, to alter wartime priorities to permit the rescue of European Jews. It is difficult to imagine that a group not winning medals for popularity could have managed such an achievement. Jews' perception of the dangers posed by domestic anti-Semitism may not have been fully grounded in reality, but anti-Semitism there was. It created enormous apprehension, perhaps even paralysis, in certain quarters of the community.

At the heart of this book is an examination of the historical forces that shaped American Jewry in the two decades preceding the Holocaust. Included are the transformation of its religious and ethnic culture, the growth of an elaborate organizational structure, its ideological and political conflicts, and the effect of anti-Semitism on Jews' mental set and their drive to attain middle-class status. In the impact of these events and processes are contained the answers to the questions raised by the debate over the adequacy of the American Jewish response to the Holocaust.

Historians can help us achieve a balanced judgment about what could reasonably have been expected from American Jewry, given what it had become. But they have no answer for those who are convinced that American Jewry was not what it should be. For them, enough could never have been done. We learn that during the interwar years Jews achieved remarkable progress in many areas of American life—but at a price. The individuation and secularization that promote individual achievement adversely affected Jews' ability to act collectively—they had first to be drawn away from their private search for self-realization. Undoubtedly the Depression itself intensified the privatizing effect. Jewish parents sought first to feed their families; only secondarily could they muster concern for the well-being of the Jews of Europe. Subject to these historical forces, both Judaism, the binding religious culture, and Jewishness, the secular ethnic culture of the immigrant generation, lost much of their power to reinforce communal cohesiveness. That loss fed the communal fragmentation that follows everywhere in the wake of modernization. The breakdown spawned ideological and political conflicts that, underneath it all, concerned how American Jewry could best survive when the traditional bonds holding it together had been eroded. Jews were converting to more than American language and mores. They were converting to a culture where modernization was accelerated. American Jews wanted to be part of that culture, but they also wanted to retain their Jewishness. In 1940 they had not yet developed a formula for doing both.

Clearly, the assumption that on the eve of the Holocaust there still existed a community of American Jews bound together by a common culture and purpose is not supportable. Rather, there were several Jewish communities that lived in an uneasy relationship, and leaders discovered that it was impossible to fully mobilize communal resources for rescue. Despite the desperate need, every attempt to achieve unity failed, and American Jews faced the Holocaust as a riven, fearful people.

Some indict American Jewry for that failure. They fault it for no longer being the unified, single-minded community they imagine it once was. But in doing so they enter into an argument with history. What they call for is an American Jewry willing and able to halt, or at least mitigate, the historical forces that were transforming it. They require it to step out of its history. But though inexorable historical processes may sometimes be slowed, in no recorded instance have they been reversed to meet the needs of the moment.

American Jewry has been unable to reconcile itself to the loss of its European parent community. The ties of kinship were close, and Jews find its bloody end too terrible to contemplate. That abiding sense of loss and guilt has shaped much of its contemporary sensibility. When people assume responsibility they do not have the power to discharge, it leads to endless guilt about not doing enough. Yet that American Jews still felt connected enough to assume such a responsibility can be taken as a sign that modernization had not totally destroyed their sense of peoplehood.

In the final volume of this series, *A Time for Healing*, we learn that the loss of communal cohesiveness and the weakening of identity were balanced in the postwar decades by a remarkable success story written mostly in secular terms. The number of American Jews prominent in the public arena and in the operational elites that manage this complex society, their firm anchorage in the professional middle class, and the effectiveness of their advocacy before the American seat of power all reached undreamed-of heights. American Jewry ultimately did assume the leadership it could not attain during the years of the Holocaust. That cannot of course compensate for the loss of the six million, but it does raise hope regarding the continued vitality of American Jewry. There are few on either side of the debate who would deny that the ability to muster such hope has played a major role in the Jews' millennial survival.

NOTES

Abbreviations

AH	*American Hebrew*
AJC	American Jewish Committee
AJH	*American Jewish History*
AJHQ	*American Jewish Historical Quarterly*
AJYB	*American Jewish Yearbook*
CJR	*Contemporary Jewish Record*
JSS	*Jewish Social Studies*
MJ	*Menorah Journal*
PAJHS	*Publications of the American Jewish Historical Society*
SUNY	State University of New York

Chapter One. Signals of Unwelcome

1. Ralph P. Boas, "Jew Baiting in America," *Atlantic Monthly* 21 (May 1921): 658–65.

2. John Higham, *Send These to Me: Jews and Other Immigrants in Urban America* (New York: Atheneum, 1975), 278; Judd L. Teller, *Strangers and Natives: The Evolution of the American Jew from 1921 to the Present* (New York: Delacorte [Delta], 1968), 96; Elliot E. Cohen, "Notes for a Modern History of the Jews," *MJ* 13 (November 1927): 511.

3. Robert P. Ingalls, *Hoods: The Story of the Ku Klux Klan* (New York: G. P. Putnam, 1979), 70 ff.; *AH,* 14 December 1923, 165.

4. D. Burner, "The Democratic Party in the Election of 1924," *Mid-America* 46 (April 1964): 17; See also David M. Chalmers, *Hooded America* (New York: Quadrangle, 1968), for general background.

5. Harold Quinley and Charles Glock, *Anti-Semitism in America* (New Brunswick, N.J.: Transaction Books, 1983), 65–66; William R. Glass, "Fundamentalism's Prophetic Vision of the Jews: The 1930's," *JSS* 47 (Winter 1985): 63–67.

6. Morton Borden, *Jews, Turks, and Infidels* (Chapel Hill: University of North

Carolina Press, 1984), 110; Jonathan D. Sarna, *Jacksonian Jew: The Two Worlds of Mordecai Noah* (New York: Holmes and Meier, 1981), 134.

7. Quoted in Borden, *Jews, Turks, and Infidels,* 120.

8. Benjamin K. Hunnicut, "The Jewish Sabbath Movement in the Early Twentieth Century," *AJH* 69 (December 1979): 198–215.

9. Charles Reznikoff, ed., *Louis Marshall, Champion of Liberty: Selected Papers and Addresses,* 2 vols. (Philadelphia: Jewish Publication Society, 1957), 1:419–22 (Marshall to Mayor of Messina, 1 October, 1928; Marshall to Brennglass, 20 October 1928); Teller, *Strangers and Natives,* 95. In 1976, after a highly dramatized reconstruction was published (Saul Friedman, *The Incident at Massena: The Blood Libel in America* [New York: Stein and Day, 1978]), it again became a problem for some members of that community, who felt that Friedman had blown the incident out of proportion.

10. *AJYB* 27 (1925–26): 450–55; Teller, *Strangers and Natives,* 44; *New York Times,* 17 October 1924.

11. Josef Bord, "Why Europe Dislikes the Jews," *Harper's* (March 1927), quoted in *AH,* 4 March 1927, 557; Lewis S. Gannet, "Is America Anti-Semitic?" *Nation,* 21 March 1923, 330–32.

12. Jerry Z. Muller, "Communism, Anti-Semitism and the Jews," *Commentary* 86 (August 1988): 28–31; Zosa Szajkowski, *Jews, Wars and Communism,* vol. 1, *The Russian Revolution, 1917* (New York: Ktav, 1972), 283–84, 292–94; Melech Epstein, *The Jew and Communism: The Story of Early Communist Victories and Ultimate Defeats in the Jewish Community, USA, 1919–1941* (New York: Trade Union Sponsoring Committee, 1959), 42, 177–79. After 1924, when recruitment for the Crimean resettlement venture and, after 1928, for the Birobidzhan project was undertaken, the stream of Jewish emigrants from America increased. It came to a halt at the time of the 1936 purge trials.

13. Reznikoff, *Marshall,* 1, 328–29 (12 April 1920, Marshall to Oscar R. Straus); Naomi Cohen, *Not Free to Desist: The American Jewish Committee, 1906–1972* (Philadelphia: Jewish Publication Society, 1972), 125–26.

14. Robert Singerman, "The American Career of the Protocols of the Elders of Zion," *AJH* 71 (September 1981): 67–68.

15. Burton J. Hendrick, "The Jews in America: How They Came to This Country," *World's Work* 65 (December 1922): 144–61; "Menace of the Polish Jew," February 1923, 366–77; Burton J. Hendrick, *The Jews in America* (Garden City, N.Y.: Macmillan, 1923).

16. E. E. Cohen, "Notes for a Modern History of the Jews," *MJ* 12 (26 December 1926), 633.

17. Reznikoff, *Marshall,* 1:406–7 (Marshall to F. Doubleday, 21 February 1923).

18. Reznikoff, *Marshall,* 1:322 (Marshall to David Brown, n.d.); Michael Dobkowski, *The Tarnished Dream* (Westport, Conn.: Greenwood, 1979), 197–200; Cohen, *Not Free,* 133.

19. Leo P. Ribuffo, "Henry Ford and the International Jew," *AJH* 69 (June 1980): 437–77. See also Alan Nevins and Frank E. Hill, *Ford, Expansion and Challenge, 1915–1933* (New York: Scribner's, 1957), and Anne Jardin, *The First Henry Ford: A Study in Personality and Business Leadership* (Cambridge: MIT Press, 1970).

20. Reznikoff, *Marshall,* 1:392 (Marshall to Ford, 3 June 1920). The exchange of correspondence is also reproduced in *AJYB* 23 (1921–22), 315–16.

21. Reznikoff, *Marshall,* 1:361–63 (Marshall to Harding, 25 July 1921).

22. AJC file, Anti-Semitism, 1914–, "An Address to Their Fellow Citizens by American Jewish Organizations," 1 December 1920 (typed); William E. Leuchtenberg, *The Perils of Prosperity, 1914–1932* (Chicago: University of Chicago Press, 1958), 10; Keith Sward, *The Legend of Henry Ford* (New York: Rinehart, 1948), 150.

23. Reznikoff, *Marshall,* 1:376 (Marshall to Sam Untermeyer, n.d.).

24. Ibid., 380–83 (Marshall to Ford, 5 July 1927; Marshall to H. I. Phillips [columnist for the *New York Sun*], 22 July 1927).

25. Carl H. Voss, *Rabbi and Minister: The Friendship of Stephen S. Wise and John Haynes Holmes* (New York: World, 1964), 239–40.

26. Editorial, *AH,* 7 July 1927, 191.

27. Henry L. Feingold, "Anti-Semitism and the Anti-Semitic Imagination in America: A Case Study, the 1920s," in *A Midrash on American Jewish History* (Albany: SUNY Press, 1983), 177–91.

28. Quoted in Alexander Bloom, *Prodigal Son: The New York Intellectuals and Their World* (New York: Oxford University Press, 1986), 29–30.

29. Nathan Glazer, *American Judaism* (Chicago: University of Chicago Press, 1972), 81. One researcher finds that small business was more significant before 1920. See Selma Berrol, "Education and Economic Mobility: The Jewish Experience in New York City, 1880–1920," *AJHQ* 65 (March 1976): 251–71. See also Henry Feingold, "Investing in Themselves: The Harvard Case and the Origins of the Third American-Jewish Commercial Elite," *AJH* 77 (June 1988): 530–53; Barry R. Chiswick, "The Earning and Human Capital of American Jews," *Journal of Human Resources,* 17 (Summer 1983): 313–36; Alan Wiedner, "Immigration, the Public School and the Twentieth Century American Ethos: The Jewish Immigrant as a Case Study" (Ph.D. diss., Ohio State University, 1977).

30. Harold S. Wechsler, *The Qualified Student: A History of Selective College Admission in America* (New York: Wiley, 1977), 645. See also Stephen Steinberg, "How Jewish Quotas Began," *Commentary* 52 (September 1971): 67–76

31. Felix Morrow, "Higher Learning on Washington Square: Some Notes on N.Y.U.," *MJ* 18 (Autumn 1940): 346–57; Stephen Steinberg, *The Academic Melting Pot: Catholics and Jews in American Higher Education* (New York: McGraw-Hill, 1974), 20; Nathan Belth, *A Promise to Keep* (New York: New York Times Books, 1979), 96–99; *AH,* 2 July 1926, 225.

32. Samuel E. Morison, *Three Centuries of Harvard* (Boston: Harvard University Press, 1936), 147.

33. For a description of campus attitudes see Marcia G. Synnott, *The Half-Opened Door: Discrimination and Admissions at Harvard, Yale, and Princeton, 1900–1970* (Westport, Conn.: Greenwood, 1979).

34. Steinberg, *Academic Melting Pot,* 28 ff., 101–2; Philip Slemovitz, "Recalling the 'Harvard Scandal': Lowell's False Prophecy Twenty Years Ago," *Congress Weekly* 10 (26 February 1943): 12–13.

35. Harry Starr, "The Affair at Harvard: What the Students Did," *MJ* 8 (October 1922): 266.

36. *New York Times,* 26 January 1923, 23; Victor A. Kramer, "What Lowell Said: A First-hand Report of a Significant Conversation with Harvard's Head," *AH,* 26 January 1923, 391, 394; Belth, *Promise to Keep,* 110.

37. Synnott, *Half-Opened Door,* 96 ff.; Nitza Rosovsky, *The Jewish Experience at*

Harvard and Radcliffe (Cambridge: Harvard University Press, 1986), 21; *AH,* 13 April 1923, 744.

38. Reznikoff, *Marshall,* 1:268 (Marshall to James Marshall, 10 August 1922).

39. *AH,* 22 September 1922, 447.

40. *AH,* 28 July 1922, 258. A reprint of a letter that appeared first in the *Exponent,* written by Maurice Stern, a Harvard alumnus, class of 1922.

41. *AH,* 29 October 1922, 733, 796.

42. Synnott, *Half-Opened Door,* 23–24; Dan A. Oren, *Joining the Club: A History of the Jews at Yale* (New Haven: Yale University Press, 1987), 43–44.

43. William T. Ham, "Harvard Students on the Jewish Question," *AH,* 15 September 1922, 406; *AH,* 9 June 1922, 116.

44. *AJYB* 31 (1929–30): 141–43, 243–46; Oren, *Joining the Club,* 51–52.

45. *AH,* 22 September 1922, 537; Oren, *Joining the Club,* 43; M. G. Torch, "The Spirit of Morningside: Some Notes on Columbia University," *MJ* 18 (March 1930): 254.

46. Morris R. Cohen, *A Dreamer's Journey* (Boston: Beacon, 1949), 224. See also Sherry Gorelick, *City College and the Jewish Poor: Education in New York, 1880–1924* (New Brunswick, N.J.: Rutgers University Press, 1981), 151–70.

47. *AH,* 12 January 1922, 63; editorial, "On the Gridiron," *AH,* 13 November 1925, 8; *AH,* 19 December 1922, 207; see also Michele H. Pavin, "Sports and Leisure of the American Jewish Community, 1848–1976" (Ph.D. diss., Ohio State University, 1981).

48. *AH,* 8 July 1921, 193; Teller, *Strangers and Natives,* 90.

49. Walter P. Eaton, "Jews in the American Theater," *AH,* 22 September 1922, 464.

50. Steinberg, *Academic Melting Pot,* 16, 24, 28; *AH;* 29 September 1922, 530.

51. Cohen, *Dreamer's Journey,* 150 ff.

52. Irving Howe, *World of Our Fathers* (New York: Simon and Schuster, 1976), 412.

53. Morrow, "Higher Learning," 349.

54. Elisha M. Friedman, "The Challenge of Anti-Semitism," *MJ* 7 (February 1922): 16; *AH,* 24 March 1922, 497.

55. *AH,* 13 October 1922, 593 (letter to the editor); editorial, *AH,* 13 July 1923, 171; Paul E. Anderson, "Are Jewish Children Brighter?" *AH,* 17 May 1926, 886, 911; Oren, *Joining the Club,* 43 ff.

56. *AH,* 30 June 1922, 169, 176; Jacob Weinstein, "Jewish Students at Columbia," *MJ* 22 (April–June 1934): 47–56.

57. Wechsler, *Qualified Student,* 659 ff.

58. Feingold, "Investing in Themselves," 552–53; editorial, *AH,* 9 March 1923; 521; Aviva L. Dekel, "The Idea of a Jewish University" (Ph.D. diss., George Peabody College for Teachers, Vanderbilt University, 1984).

59. James G. Heller, "Americanizing Our Universities," *AH,* 10 October 1922, 636; *AH,* 20 April 1923, 754.

60. Higham, *Send These to Me,* 170.

61. David H. Bennett, *The Party of Fear: From Nativist Movement to the New Right in American History* (Chapel Hill: University of North Carolina Press, 1988), 73 ff.; Leuchtenberg, *Perils,* 206.

62. House Committee on Immigration and Naturalization, *Restriction of Immigration,* H.R. 5, 101, 561, 68th Cong., 1st sess., 3 January 1924, 388–89.

63. Sydney E. Ahlstrom, *A Religious History of the American People* (New Haven: Yale University Press, 1972), 900.

64. Reznikoff, *Marshall,* 1:174–75 (Marshall to C. E. Hughes, 27 April 1921); *AJYB* 24 (1922–23): 355–56.

65. Higham, *Send These to Me,* 49; *AH,* 18 February 1921, 411.

66. John Higham, *Strangers in the Land: Patterns of American Nativism* (New York: Atheneum, 1968), 308.

67. House Committee on Immigration and Naturalization, *A Bill to Provide for the Protection of the Citizens of the U.S.* (H.R. 14461, 67th Cong., 3d sess.), 5 January 1921, 149–50, 170.

68. Ibid., 139 ff., 429 (testimony of John L. Bernstein); Sheldon M. Neuringer, "American Jewry and U.S Immigration Policy, 1881–1953" (Ph.D. diss., University of Wisconsin, 1971), 134.

69. Edward Bristow, *The Jewish Fight against White Slavery, 1870–1939* (New York: Schocken, 1983), 184, 190–295.

70. Emanuel Celler, *You Never Leave Brooklyn: The Autobiography of Emanuel Celler* (New York: Day, 1953), 81.

71. House Committee on Immigration and Naturalization, *Restriction of Immigration,* 293 (Marshall testimony).

72. *AJYB* 40 (1938–39): 561; Milton Plesur, *Jewish Life in Twentieth Century America: Challenge and Accommodation* (Chicago: Nelson-Hall, 1982), 51.

73. *AH,* 19 November 1920, 23

74. House Committee on Immigration and Naturalization, *Restriction of Immigration,* 288–89 (Marshall testimony).

75. Neuringer, "American Jewry and U.S. Immigration," 140.

76. Higham, *Strangers in the Land,* 188; Reznikoff, *Marshall,* 1:205 (Marshall to Abraham Cahan, 11 January 1923).

77. Belth, *Promise to Keep,* 91 ff.; Neuringer, "American Jewry and U.S. Immigration," 161, 167, 171.

78. House Committee on Immigration and Naturalization, *Restriction of Immigration,* 293; Teller, *Strangers and Natives,* 100.

79. *AH,* 25 April 1924, 753.

80. *AH,* 27 June 1944, 219. Rabbi Barnett Brickner's address before the National Conference of Jewish Social Service.

81. *AH,* 26 September 1924, 30.

82. George Barton, "Dying Embers of Bigotry in America," *Current History,* March 1926, quoted in editorial, *AH,* 19 March 1926, 557.

Chapter Two. Acculturation and Its Discontents

1. Editorial, *AH,* 24 August 1923, 305.

2. Quoted in Stanley Feldstein and Lawrence Costello, eds., *The Ordeal of Assimilation: A Documentary History of the White Working Class, 1830–1970s* (New York: Anchor, 1974), 368–69.

3. Konrad Bercovici, "The Greatest Jewish City in the World," *Nation,* 12 September 1923, 261.

4. Quoted in Alexander Bloom, *Prodigal Son: The New York Intellectuals and Their World* (New York: Oxford University Press, 1986), 22.

5. *AJYB* 23 (1921–22): 84–111.

6. *AH*, 23 May 1924, 34.

7. Sidney Goldstein and Calvin Goldscheider, *Jewish Americans: Three Generations in a Jewish Community* (Englewood Cliffs, N.J.: Prentice-Hall, 1968), 8; Roderick W. Nash, *The Nervous Generation: American Thought, 1917–1930* (Chicago: Rand McNally, n.d.), 1–4.

8. Harold S. Wechsler, *The Qualified Student: A History of Selective College Admission in America* (New York: Wiley, 1977), 119–23.

9. *AH*, 1 April 1927, 735; I. Montefiore Levy, "The Despair of Youth," *AH*, 20 May 1927, 735.

10. Arthur Goren, *New York Jews and the Quest for Community: The Kehillah Experiment, 1908–1922* (New York: Columbia University Press, 1970), 159 ff.

11. Ari Lloyd Fridkis, "Desertion in the American Jewish Immigrant Family: The Work of the National Desertion Bureau in Cooperation with the Industrial Removal Office," *AJH* 81 (December 1981): 285–99; Charles Zunser, "The Problem of the Wife Deserter," *AH*, 13 July 1923, 178, 186; *AH*, 7 November 1924, 833; *AJYB* 22 (1920–21), 42 ff.

12. Judd L. Teller, *Strangers and Natives: The Evolution of the American Jew from 1921 to the Present* (New York: Delacorte [Delta], 1968), 4.

13. Frederick L. Allen, *Only Yesterday* (New York: Harper and Row, 1959), 90; John D'Emelio and Estelle B. Friedman, *Intimate Matters: A History of Sexuality in America* (New York: Harper, 1988), quoted in *New York Times Book Review*, 24 April 1988, 32–33.

14. Mark Zborowski and Elizabeth Herzog, *Life Is with People: The Culture of the Shtetl* (New York: Schocken, 1952), 269–90; Rudolf Glanz, *The Jewish Women in America: Two Generations*, vol. 2, *The German Jewish Women* (New York: Ktav, 1976), 74–79.

15. Isaac Metzker, *A Bintel Brief: Sixty Years of Letters from the Lower East Side to the Jewish Daily Forward* (New York: Doubleday, 1971), 150–51.

16. Anzia Yezierska, *Hungry Hearts* (Boston, 1920), 15, quoted in Glanz, *Jewish Women*, 2:176, n. 48.

17. Glanz, *Jewish Women*, 2:74; "The Plight of the Educated Jewish Girl," *Jewish Courier*, 14 and 30 November 1920, cited in Jacob R. Marcus, *The American Jewish Woman: A Documentary History* (New York: Ktav, 1981), 74.

18. Quoted in Phyllis Deutsch, "Theater of Mating: Jewish Summer Camps and Cultural Transformation," *AJH* 75 (March 1986): 313–14. See also Stefan Kanfer, *A Summer World* (New York: Farrar, Straus, and Giroux, 1989), 133–57.

19. Deutsch, "Theater of Mating," 308–20; Glanz, *Jewish Women*, 2:80–82.

20. Glanz, *Jewish Women*, 2:92–94; Elinor Lerner, "Jewish Involvement in the New York City Woman Suffrage," *AJH* 70 (June 1981): 442–61; *AH*, 17 July 1925, 328.

21. Glanz, *Jewish Women*, 1:16, 18–23; Nancy S. Dye, *As Equals and as Sisters: Feminism, the Labor Movement, and the Women's Trade Union League of New York* (Columbus: University of Missouri Press, 1980), 27.

22. Irene D. Neu, "The Jewish Businesswoman in America," *AJHQ* 66 (September 1976): 137–54.

23. Lilian Benedict, "What Does a Home Mean to Women of Independent Income? Have Husbands Reason to Tremble at the New Guise of *Das Ewige Weibliche*?" *AH*, 1 October 1926, 656–57, 697.

24. Ibid.; *AH,* 30 June 1922, 184.

25. Glanz, *Jewish Women,* 2:ix–xii, 41 ff.

26. June Sochen, "Some Observations on the Role of American Jewish Women as Communal Volunteers," *AJH* 70 (September 1980): 23–34; Rachel C. Schlesinger, "Jewish Women in Transition: Delayed Entry into the Workforce" (Ph.D. diss., University of Toronto, 1983).

27. Ibid., Sochen; Glanz, *Jewish Women,* 2:41 ff.; Rebecca Kohut, "Jewish Women's Organizations," *AJYB* 33 (1931–32): 165–202; Deborah Golomb, "The Origins of American Jewish Women's Organizations" (Ph.D. diss., Ohio State University, 1978).

28. Marcus, *American Jewish Woman,* 664; Michael N. Dobkowski, *Jewish American Voluntary Organizations* (Westport, Conn.: Greenwood, 1986), 343–45; Jena W. Joselit, "The Sphere of the Middle Class American Jewish Women: The Synagogue Sisterhood, 1890–1940," in *The American Synagogue: A Sanctuary Transferred,* ed. Jack Wertheimer (New York: Cambridge University Press, 1987), 206–30.

29. "Three Clubs Worth Knowing," *AH,* 11 June 1925, 814; Charlotte Baum et al., *The Jewish Woman in America* (New York: Dial, 1976), 46 ff.; Beth S. Wenger, "Jewish Women of the Club: The Changing Public Role of Atlanta's Jewish Women (1870–1930)," *AJH* 76 (March 1987): 311–33; Norma F. Pratt, "Transitions in Judaism: The Jewish American Women through the 1930s," *American Quarterly* 30 (Winter 1978): 681–702.

30. Norma F. Pratt, "Culture and Radical Politics: Yiddish Women Writers, 1890–1940," *AJH* 70 (September 1980): 69–86; Alice Kessler Harris, "Organizing the Unorganizable: Three Jewish Women and Their Union," *Labor History* 17 (Winter 1976): 5–14; Sally M. Miller, "From Sweatshop Worker to Labor Leader: Theresa Malkiel, a Case Study," *AJH* 68 (December 1978): 189–205.

31. Glanz, *Jewish Women,* 2:102–31; U. Z. Engelman, "Medurbia: The Community," *Contemporary Jewish Record* 4 (October 1941): 511–21; U. Z. Engelman, "Jewish Statistics in the U.S. Census of Religious Bodies (1850–1936)," *Jewish Social Studies* 9 (April 1947): 127–74.

32. Harold P. Gastwirt, *Fraud, Corruption and Holiness: The Controversy over the Supervision of Jewish Dietary Practices in New York City* (New York: Kennicat, 1974), 5–11; Jena Joselit, *Our Gang: Jewish Crime and the New York Jewish Community, 1900–1940* (Bloomington: University of Indiana Press, 1983), 7; Albert Fried, *The Rise and Fall of the Jewish Gangster in America* (New York: Holt, Rinehart and Winston, 1980).

33. Goren, *Quest for Community,* 159–85.

34. Fried, *Jewish Gangster,* 92; Joselit, *Our Gang,* 11, 157.

35. Edward Bristow, *The Jewish Fight against White Slavery, 1870–1939* (New York: Schocken, 1983), 283; *AH,* 15 September 1922, 414.

36. Joselit, *Our Gang,* 97; Fried, *Jewish Gangster,* 111–15.

37. Fried, *Jewish Gangster,* 92 ff.; Joselit, *Our Gang,* 94; Leo R. Sack, "The Sacramental Wine Scandal: How the Privilege Accorded by Congress for Jewish Ceremonial Observance Is Abused," *AH,* 20 March 1925, 571, 579, 588.

38. Cyrus Adler, *Selected Letters,* ed. Ira Robinson (Philadelphia: Jewish Publication Society, 1985), 2:46 (Adler to Samuel Cohen, 3 January 1922).

39. *AJYB* 24 (1922–23): 23–25.

40. Sarah C. Schack, "The Kosher Chicken Racket," *MJ* 18 (February 1930): 148–58 (Chronicles); Gastwirt, *Fraud, Corruption and Holiness,* 44–49.

41. Alter F. Landesman, *Brownsville: The Birth, Development and Passing of a Jewish Community in New York* (New York: Bloch, 1969), 330; Fried, *Jewish Gangster,* 202; Joselit, *Our Gang,* 147–49.

42. Joselit, *Our Gang,* 11.

43. Daniel Bell, "Crime as an American Way of Life: A Queer Ladder of Mobility," in *The End of Ideology* (New York: Collier, 1962), 149–50.

44. In that year only 488 Jews graduated from the five high schools in Manhattan and the Bronx. Estelle Gilson, "Schooling in New York: Then and Now," *Congress Monthly* 54 (February 1987): 10; Selma C. Berrol, "Education and Economic Mobility: The Jewish Experience in New York City, 1880-1920," *AJHQ* 65 (March 1976): 257–71; Joel Perlmann, *Ethnic Differences, Schooling and Social Structure among the Irish, Jews and Blacks in an American City, 1885-1935* (New York: Cambridge University Press, 1988), 122–62.

45. It took years of agitation by Jewish community agencies to get Thomas Jefferson High School included in the budget. See editorial, *AH,* 2 June 1922, 108; *AH,* 19 September 1924, 485; see also Deborah D. Moore, *At Home in America: Second Generation New York Jews* (New York: Columbia University Press, 1981), 95–97; Joshua A. Fishman, "Language Maintenance and Language Shift: Yiddish and Other Immigrant Languages in the U.S.," *YIVO Annual of Jewish Social Science* 14 (1969): 12–26.

46. Editorial, *AH,* 18 August 1922, 321; Moore, *At Home in America,* 91 ff.

47. Quoted in *AH,* 8 May 1925, 831. See also William N. Greenbaum, "The Idea of Cultural Pluralism in the U.S." (Ph.D. diss., Harvard University, 1978).

48. Deborah D. Moore, "Jewish Ethnicity and Acculturation in the 1920's: Public Education in New York City," *Jewish Journal of Sociology* 18 (December 1976): 96–104; Nathan H. Winter, *Jewish Education in a Pluralist Society: Samson Benderly and Jewish Education in the U.S.* (New York: New York University Press, 1966).

49. Uriah Z. Engelman, "The Strength of Hebrew in America," *MJ* 16 (March 1929): 230–42.

50. Mordecai H. Lewittes, "Hebrew Enters New York High Schools," *MJ* 16 (April–June 1938): 234–43; Moore, "Jewish Ethnicity," 96–104; Lloyd P. Gartner, *Jewish Education in the U.S.: A Documentary History* (New York: Columbia Teachers College Press, 1969), 1–40 (introduction); Abraham S. Halkin, "Hebrew in Jewish Culture," in *The American Jew: A Composite Portrait,* ed. Oscar Janowsky (New York: Harper, 1942), 122–33.

51. Moore, *At Home in America,* 64–65.

52. Ronald Sanders, *Reflections on a Teapot: The Personal History of a Time* (New York: Harper, 1972), 53 ff.

53. Daniel Soyer, "Between Two Worlds: The Jewish Landsmanshaften and Questions of Immigrant Identity," *AJH* 76 (September 1986): 7–8.

54. Hannah Kliger, "Tradition of Grass Roots Organization and Leadership: The Continuity of Landsmanshaften in New York," *AJH* 76 (September 1986): 25–39; I. E. Rontch, "The Present State of the Landsmanschaften," *Jewish Social Service Quarterly* 15 (June 1939): 360–78.

55. For a complete listing and photographs of their often magnificent settings, see *AH,* 6 February 1925, 381; *AH,* 6 June 1924, 121, 122–23.

56. Teller, *Strangers and Natives,* 18, 89–90; *AH,* 24 August 1924, 418. Harold U. Ribalow and Meir Z. Ribalow, *The Jew in American Sports* (New York: Hippocrene, 1966), xiii–xv, 3–6.

57. Editorial, *AH,* 4 May 1923, 789; "The Champion Hakoah Team," *AH,* 23 April 1926, 802.

Chapter Three. The Contentment of Culture

1. Elliot Cohen, "Cultural Creativity and the Jewish Community," address delivered on the occasion of the founding of the Jewish Museum, 26 May 1948, 26, AJC file, Jews in the United States, Cultural Life.

2. Ibid.

3. Maurice Samuel, "The Quest for Culture," *MJ* 12 (February 1926): 339–40.

4. Salo W. Baron, "Can American Jewry Be Culturally Creative?" in *Steeled by Adversity: Essays and Addresses on American Jewish Life,* ed. Salo Baron and Jeanette Baron (Philadelphia: Jewish Publication Society, 1971), 548.

5. Nahama Sandrow, *Vagabond Stars: A World History of Yiddish Theater* (New York: Harper, 1977), 1–20.

6. Jean Benedetti, *Stanislavski* (New York: Routledge, 1989), chap. 4.

7. Sandrow, *Vagabond Stars,* 94.

8. David A. Lifson, *The Yiddish Theater in America* (New York: Yoseloff, 1965), 47–48; Sandrow, *Vagabond Stars,* 260.

9. Irving Howe, *World of Our Fathers* (New York: Simon and Schuster, 1976), 488; Sandrow, *Vagabond Stars,* 261–74.

10. Lifson, *Yiddish Theater in America,* 284–301; Judd L. Teller, *Strangers and Natives: The Evolution of the American Jew from 1921 to the Present* (New York: Delacorte [Delta], 1968), 21.

11. Lifson, *Yiddish Theater in America,* 64–65; Teller, *Strangers and Natives,* 140–43.

12. Howe, *Life of Our Fathers,* 489–90; Teller, *Strangers and Natives,* 12–13; Sandrow, *Vagabond Stars,* 281–83.

13. Lifson, *Yiddish Theater,* 548.

14. In 1927 there were 111 Jewish periodicals in Yiddish, English, and Hebrew. Included were 9 Yiddish dailies, including 5 in New York City alone, with a circulation of 536,364, 68 weeklies, 18 monthlies, 5 bimonthlies, 8 quarterlies, and 3 yearbooks. Harry S. Linfield, "The Communal Organization of Jews in the U.S., 1927" (Pamphlet, AJCOMM, 1930), 78; *AJYB* 23 (1921–22): 270–76.

15. The survey found that over 87.7 percent of the workers read the editorial page, compared with 50 percent of the general Jewish reading public. Mordecai Soltes, "The Yiddish Press: An Americanizing Agency," *AJYB* 26 (1924–25): 167–81, 214.

16. Figures from *Tikkun,* July–August 1987, 78–79. The best description of the influence of Cahan and the *Forward* is in *Grandma Never Lived in America,* ed. Moses Rischin (Bloomington: Indiana University Press, 1985).

17. *AJYB* 21 (1919–20): 571–82, 587–88.

18. Cyrus Adler, *Selected Letters,* ed. Ira Robinson (Philadelphia: Jewish Publication Society, 1985), 2:145–46 (Adler to Jacob Landau, 19 July 1927).

19. Clarence I. Freed, "Press Gallery Notables: Personalities Who Contribute to the Prestige of American Journalism," *AH* 4 (September 1925): 475; Jonathan D. Sarna, *Jacksonian Jew: The Two Worlds of Mordecai Noah* (New York: Holmes and Meier, 1981); Stephen J. Whitfield, *Voices of Jacob, Hands of Esau: Jews in American Life and Thought* (Hamden, Conn.: Archon, 1984), 183–85.

20. Stephen J. Whitfield, "The American Jew as Journalist," in *Studies in Contemporary Jewry,* ed. Ezra Mendelsohn (New York: Oxford University Press, 1987), 3:162 ff.

21. Silas Bent, "Mr. Ochs's Times," *MJ* 14 (May 1928): 435–44; Whitfield, *Voices of Jacob,* 184; Gay Talese, *The Kingdom and the Power* (Cleveland: World, 1969), 91–93.

22. Ronald Steel, *Walter Lippmann and the American Century* (New York: Vintage, 1981), 189–96, 372–74; Whitfield, *Voices of Jacob,* 189–90.

23. Howe, *World of Our Fathers,* 429.

24. Teller, *Strangers and Natives,* 48–49; Charles A. Madison, *Jewish Publishing in America: The Impact of Jewish Writing on American Culture* (New York: Sanhedrin, 1976), preface.

25. Uriah Z. Engelman, "The Strength of Hebrew in America," *MJ* 16 (March 1929): 230–42; Abraham S. Halkin, "Hebrew in Jewish Culture," in *The American Jew: A Composite Portrait,* ed. Oscar Janowsky (New York: Harper, 1942), 127.

26. Halkin, "Hebrew in Jewish Culture," 127.

27. *AJYB* 33 (1921–22): 270–76; Uriah Z. Engelman, "The Fate of Yiddish in America," *MJ* 15 (1934): 22–32; Samuel Halperin, *The Political World of American Zionism* (Detroit: Wayne State University Press, 1961), 56.

28. Editorial, *AH,* 18 June 1926, 177.

29. Hartley B. Alexander, "The Hebrew Contribution to the Americanism of the Future," *MJ* 6 (February 1920): 9.

30. Israel Cohen, "The Realities of Zionism," *MJ* 19 (1939): 401–15.

31. Alan M. Wald, "The Menorah Group Moves Left," *JSS* 38 (January 1976): 293–318. See also his *The New York Intellectuals: The Rise and Decline of the Anti-Stalinist Left from the 1930s to the 1980s* (Chapel Hill: University of North Carolina Press, 1987).

32. Alexander Bloom, *Prodigal Son: The New York Intellectuals and Their World* (New York: Oxford University Press, 1986), 29, 35.

33. Martin Jay, *The Dialectical Imagination: A History of the Frankfurt School and the Institute of Social Research, 1923-1950 (Boston: Little, Brown, 1973).*

34. Bloom, *Prodigal Son,* 54.

35. Howe, *World of Our Fathers,* 600–601; Bloom, *Prodigal Son,* 6; see also Irving Howe, "The New York Intellectuals: A Chronicle and a Critique," *Commentary* 46 (October 1968): 29–51.

36. Bloom, *Prodigal Son,* 3–4; Charles Kadushin, *The American Intellectual Elite* (Boston: Little, Brown, 1974), 334–56; William Barrett, *The Truants: Adventures among the Intellectuals* (New York: Doubleday, 1982); also Ruth R. Wisse, "The New York (Jewish) Intellectuals," *Commentary* 84 (November 1987): 28–38.

37. Quoted in John Higham, *Send These to Me: Jews and Other Immigrants in Urban America* (New York: Atheneum, 1975), 16 ff.

38. Editorial, *AH,* 4 August 1922, 279, 293.

39. Hasye Cooperman, "Yiddish Literature in the U.S.," in *The American Jew: A Composite Portrait,* ed. Oscar Janowsky (Philadelphia: Jewish Publication Society, 1964), 193–209; Teller, *Strangers and Natives,* 147–50.

40. Marie Syrkin, "The Literature of American Jewry," in Janowsky, *American Jew,* 106; David Singer, "Ludwig Lewisohn: The Making of an Anti-Communist," *American Quarterly* 23 (1971): 738–48; Teller, *Strangers and Natives,* 150.

41. Gilbert Seldes, "Jewish Plays and Jew Plays in New York," *MJ* 8 (August 1922): 236–40. Syrkin, "Literature of American Jewry," 94.

42. Isabel Paterson, "Notes on American Jewish Writers," *MJ* 10 (February 1924): 35.

43. Jonathan D. Sarna, *JPS: The Americanization of Jewish Culture, 1888–1988* (Philadelphia: Jewish Publication Society, 1989), 13–27; Charles A. Madison, *Jewish Publishing in America: The Impact of Jewish Writing on American Culture* (New York: Sanhedrin, 1976), 252–53, 257–74.

44. Editors of *Fortune, Jews in America* (New York, 1936), 11; Arthur S. Link, *American Epoch* (New York: Knopf, 1955), 310–11; William Paley, *As It Happened* (New York: Doubleday, 1979); Richard S. Tedlow and Henry L. Feingold, "Interview with Leonard Goldenson, Chairman of the Board of the American Broadcasting Company" (21 March 1981), *AJH* 72 (September 1982): 108–21.

45. Editors of *Fortune, Jews in America*, 11.

46. Ibid.

47. Quoted by Peter Biskind, "Hollywood," *Tikkun* 2 (July–August 1987): 82–83.

48. Tedlow and Feingold, "Interview with Leonard Goldenson," 121.

49. *AH*, 25 March 1921, 533.

50. Walter P. Eaton, "Jews in the American Theater," *AH*, 22 September 1922, 464.

51. *AH*, 13 October 1922, 591.

52. Quoted in Edyth H. Browne, "Ghetto Queen Discovers New Language," *AH*, 5 August 1921, 279; *AH*, 25 August 1922, 354.

53. Patricia Erens, *The Jew in American Cinema* (Bloomington: Indiana University Press, 1984), 104–5.

54. Erens, *Jew in American Cinema*, 76–81, 101; Lester D. Friedman, *Hollywood's Image of the Jew* (New York: Unger, 1982), 55–85.

55. Editorial, "Landlocked in America," *AH*, 26 September 1924, 521.

56. Charles Reznikoff, ed., *Louis Marshall, Champion of Liberty: Selected Papers and Addresses*, 2 vols. (Philadelphia: Jewish Publication Society, 1957), 2:807–9 (Marshall to Louis M. Cole, 12 May 1922).

57. I. Steinbaum, "A Study of Jewishness of Twenty New York Families," *YIVO Annual of Jewish Social Science* 5 (1942): 232–55.

Chapter Four. Crisis of Faith

1. H. S. Linfield, "Jewish Congregations in the U.S. of A.: Preliminary Statement," *AJYB* 30 (1928–29): 199–201; Wolfe Kelman, "The Synagogue in America," in *Understanding American Judaism*, vol. 1, *The Rabbi and the Synagogue*, ed. Jacob Neusner (New York: Ktav, 1975), 71; Arnold M. Eisen, *The Chosen People in America: A Study in Jewish Religious Ideology* (Bloomington: Indiana University Press, 1983), 31.

2. Linfield, "Jewish Congregations," 200; *AH*, 6 May 1927, 929; Deborah D. Moore, *At Home in America: Second Generation New York Jews* (New York: Columbia University Press, 1981), 135.

3. Michael Meyer, *Response to Modernity: A History of the Reform Movement in Judaism* (New York: Oxford University Press, 1988), 307; *AH*, 28 November 1924, 49.

4. *AH*, 20 February 1925, 14 (salaries); Cyrus Adler, *Selected Letters*, ed. Ira Robinson (Philadelphia: Jewish Publication Society, 1985), 2:14 (Adler to M. B. Friedman, 16 July 1920). By 1937 average salaries had risen to $3,700 annually, and 64 percent of candidates for the rabbinate had earned B.A. degrees; Eisen, *Chosen People*, 31.

5. Charles S. Liebman, "The Training of American Rabbis," in Neusner, *Understanding American Judaism,* 1: 219–65; Charles S. Liebman, "The Religion of American Jews," in ibid., 1:27–28; Jerome E. Carlin and Saul H. Mendlovitz, "The American Rabbi: A Religious Specialist Responds to Loss of Authority," in ibid., 165–244; Abraham J. Feldman, "The Changing Function of the Synagogue and the Rabbi," in ibid., 103–7.

6. *AH,* 29 May 1925, 100; *AH,* 7 October 1921, 553; editorial, *AH,* 25 November 1929. Frequently the accommodation was made by hiring a hall for the High Holy Days. A survey done in 1935 indicates that 78 percent of Jewish men had not attended services for a year. Sydney E. Ahlstrom, *A Religious History of the American People* (New Haven: Yale University Press, 1972), 972.

7. Harold P. Gastwirt, *Fraud, Corruption and Holiness: The Controversy over the Supervision of Jewish Dietary Practices in New York City* (New York: Kennicat, 1974), 7–10, 29; I. Steinbaum, "A Study of the Jewishness of Twenty New York Families," *YIVO Annual of Jewish Social Science* 5 (September 1942): 252.

8. Meyer, *Response to Modernity,* 307; Abraham J. Karp, *A History of the United Synagogue of America, 1913–1964* (New York: United Synagogue of America, 1964), 47; Deborah D. Moore, *B'nai B'rith and the Challenge of Ethnic Leadership* (Albany: SUNY Press, 1981), 141–42; Allon Gal, "Israel in the Mind of B'nai B'rith (1938–1958)," *AJH* 77 (June 1988): 554–71; E. E. Cohen, "Notes for a Modern History of the Jews," *MJ* 13 (February 1927): 78, quoted from the *Jewish Tribune,* n.d.

9. *AH,* 31 December 1926, 281; *AH,* 18 September 1925, 543; *AH,* 16 August 1927, 493; *AH,* 4 August 1922, 287. Jonathan D. Sarna, "Jewish-Christian Hostility in the U.S.: Perceptions from a Jewish Point of View," in *Uncivil Religion: Interreligious Hostility in America,* ed. Robert N. Bellah and Frederick G. Greenspahn (New York: Crossroad, 1987), 9.

10. *AH,* 15 October 1926, 735; Mordecai M. Kaplan, "A Program for the Reconstruction of Judaism," *MJ* 6 (August 1920): 182; Melvin Scult, "Mordecai M. Kaplan: Challenges and Conflicts in the Twenties," *AJHQ* 76 (March 1977): 401–16.

11. "Are Jews Losing Their Religion?" series in *AH,* 1 October 1926, 652; 15 October 1926, 735, 746; 22 October 1926, 759, 768; 5 November 1926, 831; 12 November 1926, 16, 42; 19 November 1926, 60; 26 November 1926, 80; 3 December 1926, 150.

12. *AH,* 14 October 1921, 598; *AH,* 11 November 1921, 712. The *American Hebrew* carried a weekly record of sermons delivered in major congregations.

13. Quoted in Erna F. Asher, "Why Are Our Synagogues Empty?" *AH,* 31 December 1926, 278.

14. "Are Young People Turning from Religion?" *AH,* 23 April 1926, 803; Lucy S. Dawidowicz, *On Equal Terms: Jews in America, 1881–1891* (New York: Holt, Rinehart and Winston, 1982), 96.

15. Mordecai M. Kaplan, "Toward a Reconstruction of Judaism," *MJ* 13 (April 1147): 113; Horace M. Kallen, "Can Judaism Survive in the United States?" *MJ* 11 (December 1925): 545.

16. Editorial, *AH,* 4 February 1927, 429.

17. Mordecai M. Kaplan, *Judaism in Transition* (New York: Behrman, 1941), xvi; Robert N. Bellah, "The New Consciousness and the Crisis in Modernity," in *The New Religious Consciousness,* ed. Charles Glock and Robert N. Bellah (Berkeley: University of California Press, 1976), 335; Joseph L. Blau, *Judaism in America: From Curiosity to Third Faith* (Chicago: University of Chicago Press, 1976), 83–87.

18. Blau, *Judaism in America,* 11; *AH,* 4 March 1927, 557, published in its newspaper, the *Chronicle.*

19. Robert N. Bellah, "Civil Religion in America," in *The Religious Situation, 1968,* ed. Donald R. Cutler (Boston: Beacon, 1968), 331–56; Jonathan Woocher, *Sacred Survival: The Civil Religion of American Jews* (Bloomington: Indiana University Press, 1987); Will Herberg, *Protestant, Catholic, Jew: An Essay in American Religious Sociology* (Garden City, N.Y.: Doubleday, 1955); Blau, *Judaism in America,* 8.

20. Charles Reznikoff, ed., *Louis Marshall, Champion of Liberty: Selected Papers and Addresses,* 2 vols. (Philadelphia: Jewish Publication Society, 1957), 2:911–13 (Marshall to Judah Magnes, 7 June 1923); editorial, *AH,* 23 November 1923, 25.

21. Stephen Wise, *Challenging Years: The Autobiography of Stephen Wise* (New York: Putnam, 1949), 129–32; Stephen Wise, *The Personal Letters of Stephen Wise,* ed. J. W. Polier and J. W. Wise (Boston: Beacon, 1956), 207 (Wise to Justine Polier, 1926); Carl H. Voss, ed., *Stephen S. Wise, Servant of the People: Selected Letters* (Philadelphia: Jewish Publication Society, 1969), 109–10 (Wise to M. Heller, 20 March 1922); Adler, *Selected Letters,* 2:50 (Adler to Marshall, 19 June 1922); Reznikoff, *Marshall,* 2:888–89 (Marshall to Rabbi Solomon Grandz, 3 December 1928).

22. Meyer, *Response to Modernity,* iii, 346 (Orthodoxy); Michael I. Harrison, "Do Denominations Matter?" *American Journal of Sociology* 82 (September 1982): 356–77; Eisen, *Chosen People,* 27; Sidney Goldstein, "Socioeconomic Differentiation among Religious Groups in the U.S.," *American Journal of Sociology* 74 (May 1969): 612–31; Galen L. Gockel, "Income and Religious Affiliation: A Regression Analysis," *American Journal of Sociology* 74 (May 1969): 632–46.

23. Jacob B. Agus, "The Reform Movement," in Neusner, *Understanding American Judaism,* 1: 13; Felix Morrow, "Reform Judaism Looks Ahead," *MJ* 19 (March 1931): 283–85; Meyer, *Response to Modernity,* 293.

24. For the overseas expansion of the Reform movement and the conversion of prophetic Judaism to social action, see Meyer, *Response to Modernity,* 335–46, 286–89; editorial, *AH,* 23 November 1923, 25.

25. *AH,* 23 July 1926, 312; Reznikoff, *Marshall,* 2:881–82 (Marshall to Julius Rosenwald, 27 June 1921).

26. Leonard J. Fein, "Reform Is a Verb," in Neusner, *Understanding American Judaism,* 1: 85–89; Richard N. Levy, "The Reform Synagogue: Plight and Possibility," in ibid., 1:64.

27. Morrow, "Reform Judaism," 291–93; Theodore Lenn, "The Reform Rabbi," in Neusner, *Understanding American Judaism, 1:33; Judd L. Teller, Strangers and Natives: The Evolution of the American Jew from 1921 to the Present* (New York: Delacorte [Delta], 1968), 162.

28. Samuel Halperin, *The Political World of American Zionism* (Detroit: Wayne State University Press, 1961), 201–13; Naomi W. Cohen, "The Reaction of Reform Judaism to Political Zionism (1897–1922)," *PAJHS* 40 (June 1951): 361–94; David Polish, *Renew Our Days: The Zionist Issue in Reform Judaism* (New York: World Union for Progressive Judaism, 1976), 138 ff., 163; Meyer, *Response to Modernity,* 302–3, 326–34; Howard R. Greenstein, *Turning Point: Zionism and Reform Judaism* (Chico, Calif.: Scholars' Press, 1981), 9–11.

29. Polish, *Renew Our Days,* 7. Meyer simply calls it a "sharp departure from its Pittsburgh predecessor"; Meyer, *Response to Modernity,* 319.

30. Solomon B. Freehof, "Reform Judaism and Zionism: A Clarification," *MJ* 32 (April–June 1944): 26–41.

31. Maurice Samuel, "The Quest for Culture," *MJ* 12 (August–September 1926): 343.

32. Eisen, *Chosen People*, 41, 55; Morrow, "Reform Judaism," 293–94; Maurice Samuel, quoted in Jacob J. Petuchowski, "The Limits of Liberal Judaism," in Neusner, *Understanding American Judaism*, vol. 2, *Sectors of American Judaism*, 51–52; Emil G. Hirsch, *My Religion* (New York, 1925), 220; Benny Kraut, *From Reform Judaism to Ethical Culture: The Religious Evolution of Felix Adler* (Cincinnati: Hebrew Union College, 1979).

33. Norman Podhoretz, *Making It* (New York: Random House, 1967), 28–32.

34. Sidney H. Schwartz, "Law and Legitimacy: An Intellectual History of Conservative Judaism, 1902–1973" (Ph.D diss., Temple University, 1982), 406–9; Mordecai Waxman, "The Ideology of the Conservative Movement," in Neusner, *Understanding American Judaism*, 2:247–49; Marshall Sklare, *Conservative Judaism: An American Religious Movement* (New York: Schocken, 1972); Elliot N. Dorf, "The Ideology of Conservative Judaism," *AJH* 74 (December 1984): 102–17; Moshe Davis, *The Emergence of Conservative Judaism* (Philadelphia: Jewish Publication Society, 1963).

35. Schwartz, "Law and Legitimacy," 411–21; Simon, quoted in Marshall Sklare, "Recent Developments in Conservative Judaism," in Neusner, *Understanding American Judaism*, 2:289–90.

36. David de Sola Pool, "Judaism and the Synagogue," in *The American Jew: A Composite Portrait*, ed. Oscar Janowsky (New York: Harper, 1942), 28–55; Egon Mayer, "Modern Jewish Orthodoxy in Post-modern America: A Case Study of the Jewish Community in Boro Park" (Ph.D. diss., Rutgers University, 1975).

37. *AH*, 29 January 1926, 371; Oscar Z. Fasman, "After Years, an Optimist," *AJH* 69 (December 1979): 161–62; Jacob B. Agus, "The Orthodox Stream," in Neusner, *Understanding American Judaism*, 2:108, 124–28; Louis Bernstein, "Generational Conflict in Orthodoxy: The Rabbinical Council of America," *AJH* 69 (December 1979): 36, 78 ff.; Gilbert Klaperman, *The Story of Yeshiva University* (New York: Ktav, 1969).

38. Charles Liebman, "A Sociological Analysis of Contemporary Orthodoxy," in Neusner, *Understanding American Judaism*, 2:141–43; Charles S. Liebman, "Orthodox Sectarians," in ibid., 2:155–74; Arthur A. Cohen, *A People Apart: Hasidism in America* (New York: Dutton, 1970); William B. Helmreich, "Old Wine in New Bottles: Advanced Yeshivot in the U.S.," *AJH* 69 (December 1979): 234–56.

39. Arthur Hertzberg, "The American Jew and His Religion," in Neusner, *Understanding American Judaism*, 1:17–18; Jacob Agus, "The Conservative Movement: Recontructionism," in ibid., 2:213; Charles Liebman, "Reconstructionism in American Jewish Life," in ibid., 2:220; Kaplan, *Judaism in Transition*, xiii–xvi, Blau, *Judaism in America*, 65; Eisen, *Chosen People*, 48–49.

40. Kaplan, "Program for the Reconstruction of Judaism," 182–83; Kaplan, *Judaism in Transition*, x.

41. Adler, *Selected Letters*, 2:139, 79–81 (Adler to Racie Adler, 23 February 1927; Adler to Kaplan, 21 September 1923); Scult, "Kaplan: Challenges and Conflicts," 401–16.

42. Quoted in Kaplan, "Program for the Reconstruction of Judaism," 189; Eisner, *Chosen People*, 77, 82.

43. Mordecai Kaplan, *Judaism as a Civilization: Towards a Reconstruction of*

American Jewish Life (New York: Macmillan, 1934), 340–45; Kaplan, "Toward a Reconstruction of Judaism," 113–30.

44. J. Kaplan, *The Meaning of God in Modern Jewish Religion* (New York: Behrman, 1937), viii (for God as process, etc.); Eisen, *Chosen People,* 48–49, 73–84; Agus, "The Conservative Movement," 212–18.

45. De Sola Pool, "Judaism and the Synagogue," 49.

46. Quoted in Liebman, "Reconstructionism," 230–31.

47. *AH,* 14 October 1927, 809; Meyer, *Response to Modernity,* 49–50.

48. Arthur A. Goren, *Dissenter in Zion* (Cambridge: Harvard University Press, 1982), 195 (Magnes to Kaplan, 14 January 1921).

49. Quoted in Liebman, "Reconstructionism," 227–28.

50. Quoted in Moore, *At Home in America,* 131; Horace Stern, "The Synagogue and Jewish Communal Activities," *AJYB* 35 (1933–34): 157–70.

51. Abraham J. Feldman, "The Changing Function of the Synagogue and the Rabbi," in Neusner, *Understanding American Judaism,* 1:106–7; Moore, *At Home in America,* 129–30, 146; De Sola Pool, "Judaism and the Synagogue," 54.

52. AJC file, Jews in the United States; Morris Engelman, "A Plan to Stabilize Jewish Communal Life," quoted from address delivered 4 February 1931.

53. Reznikoff, *Marshall,* 1:45–46 (Marshall to Herbert Lehman, 27 April 1920); editorial, *AH,* 26 October 1923, 609.

54. On the communal approach see Melvin Scult, "Mordecai Kaplan, the Teachers Institute and the Formation of Jewish Education In America," *American Jewish Archives* 38 (April 1986): 78 ff.; Nathan H. Winter, *Jewish Education in a Pluralist Society: Samson Benderly and Jewish Education in the U.S.* (New York: New York University Press, 1966), 65 ff., 113–18; Harry S. Linfield, *The Communal Organization of Jews in the United States* (New York: American Jewish Committee, 1930), 51.

55. I. L. Kandel, "Two Views of Jewish Education," *MJ* 6 (April 1920): 112.

56. Linfield, *Communal Organization,* 51; Isaac B. Berkson, "Jewish Education—Achievements and Needs," in Janowsky, *American Jew,* 62–70; Lloyd P. Gartner, *Jewish Education in the U.S.: A Documentary History* (New York: Columbia Teachers College Press, 1969), 16.

57. Berkson, "Jewish Education," 71 ff.; Arthur Goren, *New York Jews and the Quest for Community: The Kehillah Experiment, 1908–1922* (New York: Columbia University Press, 1970), 132–33.

58. Morris Fine, "The Released Time Plan of Religious Education," *Contemporary Jewish Record* 4 (February 1941): 13–24; editorial, *AH,* 5 March 1926, 505.

59. Fine, "Released Time"; Benjamin Fine, "Religion and the Public Schools," *MJ* 32 (April–June 1944): 93–101.

60. Reprinted in Horace Kallen, "Democracy versus the Melting Pot," in *Culture and Democracy in the United States* (New York: Boni and Liveright, 1924), 144–55. See also Eisen, *Chosen People,* 36, 45; Robert Bellah, "Civil Religion in America," in *The Religious Situation,* ed. Donald R. Cutler et al. (Boston: Beacon, 1968), 331–56.

61. Benny Kraut, "Towards the Establishment of the National Council of Christians and Jews: The Tenuous Road to Religious Goodwill in the 1920s," *AJH* 77 (March 1988): 390–91; Lance J. Sussman, "Toward Better Understanding: The Rise of the Interfaith Movement in America and the Role of Rabbi Isaac Landman," *American Jewish Archives* 34 (April 1982) 41–58; Meyer, *Response to Modernity,* 289.

62. Eisen, *Chosen People,* 176.

63. Adler, *Letters,* 2:126–27 (Adler to Magnes, 7 April 1926); Teller, *Strangers and Natives,* 77–78; *AH,* 1 January 1926, 256; Julius Haber, *The Odyssey of an American Zionist: Fifty Years of Zionist History* (New York: Twayne, 1956), 213–14.

64. Herberg, *Protestant, Catholic, Jew,* preface.

Chapter Five. From Class Struggle to Struggle for Class

1. Nathan Glazer, *American Judaism* (Chicago: University of Chicago Press, 1972), 80–81; I. M. Rubinow, "The Economic and Industrial Status of American Jewry," in *Proceedings of the National Conference of Jewish Social Service* (Philadelphia: NCJSS, 1932), p.3, 4. The term "egghead millionaires" first appeared in the article "The Egghead Millionaires," *Fortune,* September 1960, 172. From there it found its way into Nathan Glazer and Daniel Moynihan, *Beyond the Melting Pot* (Cambridge: MIT Press, 1963), 155.

2. William E. Leuchtenberg, *The Perils of Prosperity, 1914–1932* (Chicago: University of Chicago Press, 1958), 178–203; Arthur S. Link, *American Epoch* (New York: Knopf, 1955), 300–306; James W. Prothro, *The Dollar Decade: Business Ideas of the 1920's* (Baton Rouge: Louisiana State University Press, 1954), 60–76.

3. Hyman Kaplan, "The Passing of Poverty," *MJ* 14 (January 1928): 65–75.

4. *AH,* 14 October 1921, 597; Abraham K. Korman, *The Outsiders: Jews and Corporate America* (Lexington, Mass.: Lexington Books, 1988), 44–45. The term "courageous enterprisers" was employed by Jacob Marcus to describe the tendency of the Sephardic commercial elite to develop riskier areas of the colonial economy, such as ocean commerce; see Jacob R. Marcus, *Early American Jewry* (Philadelphia: Jewish Publication Society, 1953), 530.

5. Nathan Reich, "The Role of the Jews in the American Economy," *YIVO Annual of Jewish Social Science* 5 (1950): 198–202; Ronald Bayor, "Italians, Jews and Ethnic Conflict," *International Migration Review* 6 (Winter 1972): 379–80; Jacob Letchinsky, "The Position of Jews in the Economic Life of America," in *Jews in a Gentile World,* ed. I. Graeber and S. H. Britt (New York: Macmillan, 1942), 406–15; Thomas Kessner, *The Golden Door: Italian and Jewish Immigrant Mobility in New York City, 1880–1915* (New York: Oxford University Press, 1977), xi–xvii; Nathan Goldberg, "Economic Trends among American Jews," *Jewish Affairs,* 1 (1 October 1946): 11–16; Deborah D. Moore, *At Home in America: Second Generation New York Jews* (New York: Columbia University Press, 1981), 51.

6. Goldberg, "Economic Trends," 11 ff.; Nathan Reich, "Economic Trends," in *The American Jew: A Composite Portrait,* ed. Oscar Janowsky (New York: Harper, 1942), 161–70.

7. Thomas Kessner, "Jobs, Ghettoes and the Urban Economy, 1880–1935," *AJH* 71 (December 1981): 228–36; Bayor, "Italians, Jews and Ethnic Conflict," 379–80; Letchinsky, "Position of Jews," 414.

8. E. Rosenbaum and A. J. Sherman, *M. M. Warburg and Co., 1798–1938* (London: Hurst, 1976), 129, 135; Editors of *Fortune, Jews in America* (New York, 1936), 15; Vincent P. Carosso, "A Financial Elite: New York's German Jewish Investment Bankers," *AJHQ* 66 (September 1976): 84–87.

9. Leon Harris, *Merchant Princes: An Intimate History of Jewish Families Who Built Great Department Stores* (New York: Harper, 1979), xv.

10. Rubinow, "Economic and Industrial Status," 8; Lawrence P. Bachman, "Julius Rosenwald," *AJHQ* 66 (September 1976): 96–97.

11. Ande Manners, *Poor Cousins* (New York: Coward, 1972), 298; Editors of *Fortune, Jews in America*, 9.

12. Harold P. Gastwirt, *Fraud, Corruption and Holiness: The Controversy over the Supervision of Jewish Dietary Practices in New York City* (New York: Kennicat, 1974), 7–9; Rubinow, "Economic and Industrial Status of American Jewry," 6; Reich, "Economic Trends," 167–69.

13. Editors of *Fortune, Jews in America*, 11; Link, *American Epoch*, 310–11.

14. Editors of *Fortune, Jews in America*, 10.

15. Daniel Toll and William Toll, "We Tried Harder: Jews in American Advertising," *AJH* 72 (September 1982): 45–46.

16. Editors of *Fortune, Jews in America*, 11; Larry May and Elaine May, "Why Jewish Movie Moguls: An Exploration in American Culture," *AJH* 72 (September 1982): 6–8.

17. Link, *American Epoch*, 311.

18. Editors of *Fortune, Jews in America*, 11. See also Charles Phillips, "New Era in the Motion Picture Industry," *AH*, 22 September 1922, 513.

19. Richard S. Tedlow and Henry L. Feingold, "Interview with Leonard Goldenson, Chairman of the Board of the American Broadcasting Company" (21 March 1981), *AJH* 72 (September 1972): 108–21.

20. Walter P. Eaton, "Jews in the American Theater," *AH*, 22 September 1922, 464.

21. May and May, "Why Jewish Movie Moguls," 17; *AH*, 22 June 1923, 114, 131; *AH*, 13 October 1922, 354.

22. John Bodnar, *The Transplanted: A History of Immigrants in Urban America* (Bloomington: University of Indiana Press, 1985), 112–15; Judd L. Teller, *Strangers and Natives: The Evolution of the American Jew from 1921 to the Present* (New York: Delacorte [Delta], 1968), 3–4; William Toll, *The Making of an Ethnic Middle Class: Portland Jewry over Four Generations* (Albany: SUNY Press, 1983); Nathan Reich, "The 'Americanization' of Jewish Unionism: A Two-Way Process," *Jewish Quarterly Review* 45 (April 1955): 540–61; Henry L. Feingold, *Zion in America*, rev. ed. (New York: Hippocrene, 1981), 158–78.

23. Will Herberg, "The Jewish Labor Movement in the U.S.," *AJYB* 53 (1952–53): 5–74; Irving Howe, *World of Our Fathers* (New York: Simon and Schuster, 1976), 332–33.

24. Melech Epstein, *The Jew and Communism: The Story of Early Communist Victories and Ultimate Defeats in the Jewish Community, USA, 1919–1941* (New York: Trade Union Sponsoring Committee, 1959), 126–50; Arthur Liebman, "The Ties That Bind: The Jewish Support for the Left in the U.S.," *AJHQ* 66 (December, 1976): 285–305; David Dubinsky and A. H. Raskin, *David Dubinsky: A Life with Labor* (New York: Simon and Schuster, 1977), 56–72; Howe, *World of Our Fathers*, 330–59; Albert Fried, *The Rise and Fall of the Jewish Gangster in America* (New York: Holt, Rinehart and Winston, 1980), 135 ff.

25. George L. Berlin, "The Jewish Labor Committee and American Immigration Policy in the 1930's," *Studies in Jewish Bibliography, History and Literature in Honor of I. Edward Kiev* (pamphlet) (New York: Ktav, 1971) 45–73.

26. Irving Howe and Israel Knox, "The Jewish Labor Movement in America: Two Views" (pamphlet) (n.p.: Jewish Labor Committee, 1958), 19; Moses Rischin, "The Jewish Labor Movement in America: A Social Interpretation," *Labor History,* Fall 1963, 227–47; Selig Perlman, "Jewish American Unionism: Its Birth Pangs and Contributions to the General American Labor Movement," *Publications of the American Jewish Historical Society* 41 (June 1952): 297–338.

27. Editors of *Fortune, Jews in America,* 15.

28. The term commercial or business elite is employed by Barry Supple to describe the "Our Crowd" phenomenon in "A Business Elite: German-Jewish Financiers in Nineteenth Century New York," *Business History Review* 31 (Summer 1957): 143–78. See also Stephen Birmingham, *Our Crowd: The Great Jewish Families of New York* (New York: Harper, 1967); Feingold, *Zion in America,* 68–81.

29. Eli Ginzberg, "Jews in the American Economy: The Dynamics of Opportunity," in *Jewish Life in America: Historical Perspectives,* ed. Gladys Rosen (New York: Ktav, 1978), 109–19; Joel Perlmann, *Ethnic Differences: Schooling and Social Structure among the Irish, Italians, Jews, and Blacks in an American City, 1880–1935* (New York: Cambridge University Press, 1988), 157–62.

30. Norman Podhoretz, *Making It* (New York: Random House, 1967), xvi–xvii.

31. Werner Sombart, *The Jews and Modern Capitalism* (London, 1913); Nathan Reich, "Capitalism and the Jews: A Critical Examination of the Sombart Thesis," *MJ* 18 (January 1930): 5–31.

32. Letchinsky, "Position of Jews," 403–4.

33. Simon Kuznets, "Economic Structure of U.S. Jewry: Recent Trends" (pamphlet) (Jerusalem: Institute of Contemporary Jewry, 1972), 10.

34. Korman, *Outsiders,* 17–24, 44–45.

35. Irving Howe, "A Memoir of the Thirties," in *Steady Work: Essays in the Politics of Democratic Radicalism, 1953–1956* (New York: Harcourt, Brace and World, 1966), 356–57.

36. Quoted from the testimony of Herbert Fordham, *AH,* 11 March 1927, 597.

37. Jerold S. Auerbach, *Unequal Justice* (New York: Oxford University Press, 1976), 101 ff., 127, 145–59; Albert I. Goldberg, "Jews in the Legal Profession: A Case of Adjustment to Discrimination," *JSS* 32 (April 1970): 148–61.

38. C. B. Sherman, "Jewish Economic Adjustment," in *American Jewry: The Tercentenary and After, 1654–1954,* ed. Eugene Kohn (New York: Reconstructionist Press, 1955), 53; Richard L. Zweigenhaft, "Recent Patterns of Jewish Representation in the Corporate and Social Elites," *Studies in Contemporary Jewry* 6 (1990): 36–46; Bayor, "Italians, Jews, and Ethnic Conflict," 379–80.

39. Stephen G. Mostov, "Dun and Bradstreet Reports as a Source of Jewish Economic History, Cincinnati, 1840–1875," *AJH* 72 (March 1983): 333–53; Bodnar, *Transplanted,* 134–36; Shelley Tennenbaum, "Immigrants and Capital: Jewish Loan Societies in the U.S., 1880–1945," *AJH* 76 (September 1986): 67–77.

40. Tennenbaum, "Immigrants and Capital," 69; see also Shelley Tennenbaum, "Culture and Context: The Emergence of Hebrew Free Loan Societies in the U.S.," *Social Science History* 13 (Fall 1989): 211–36.

41. Tennenbaum, "Immigrants and Capital," 77; editorial, *AH,* 27 January 1922, 297; *AH,* 4 May 1923, 803.

42. Bodnar, *Transplanted,* 196; Moore, *At Home in America,* 103; Selma Berrol,

"Educational and Economic Mobility: The Jewish Experience in New York City, 1880–1920," *AJHQ* 65 (March 1976): 259–70; Perlmann, *Ethnic Differences,* 139–54.

43. Perlmann, *Ethnic Differences,* 141–44; Barry R. Chiswick, "The Earnings and Human Capital of American Jews," *Journal of Human Resources* 17 (Summer 1983): 313–36; Charles K. Feinberg, "Census for Jewish Students for 1916–1917," *MJ* 3 (October 1917): 252–53. Next were Hunter, with 44 percent, and Brooklyn Polytechnical with 30 percent.

44. Editorial, *AH,* 23 September 1921, 428; Perlmann, *Ethnic Differences,* 157–62.

45. Barton J. Bledstein, *The Culture of Professionalism: The Middle Class and the Development of Higher Education in America* (New York: Norton, 1976), 111–15, 173–75; Jerold S. Auerbach, "From Rags to Robes: The Legal Profession, Social Mobility and the American Jewish Experience," *AJHQ* 66 (December 1976): 249–84.

46. Nathan Goldberg, "Economic Trends," 11–14, 17; Letchinsky, "Position of Jews," 406–10, 414, estimates that most Jewish workers had converted to white-collar employment by 1930. The comparable rate of professionalism among Italian-Americans was 1.1 percent. See Bayor, "Italians, Jews and Ethnic Conflict," 380.

47. Memoir of the Bureau of Jewish Social Research, "Professional Tendencies among Jewish Students in Colleges, Universities and Professional Schools," *AJYB* 22 (1920–21): 383–86; Teller, *Strangers and Natives,* 79–81; Goldberg, "Economic Trends," 11; Bledstein, *Culture of Professionalism,* 111–15.

48. John Erskine, "The Young Intellectuals," *AH,* 18 April 1924, 661.

49. Cyrus Adler, *Selected Letters,* ed. Ira Robinson (Philadelphia: Jewish Publication Society, 1985), 2:176–77 (Adler to Racie Adler, 29 October 1929).

50. Ibid., 2:232 (Adler to Bruno Bloch, 20 January 1932).

51. Rubinow, "Economic and Industrial Status," 8; Irwin Rosen, "The Economic Position of Jewish Youth" (1936), mimeographed report found in AJC file, U.S., Economic Conditions, 1932–53.

52. Neil M. Cowan and Ruth S. Cowan, *Our Parents' Lives: The Americanization of Eastern European Jews* (New York: Basic Books, 1989), 242–43, testimony of Rose Janofsky.

53. Irwin Rosen, "Professional Careers for Jewish Youth," *Jewish Social Service* 15 (June 1939): 345–57.

54. Melvin M. Fagen, "The Social Pathology of the Refugee Problem," *Jewish Social Service* 15 (March 1939): 283–89; Auerbach, *Unequal Justice,* 50, 126–27, 169–87, 213–19.

55. Teller, *Natives and Strangers,* 121; Murray Friedman, ed., *Jewish Life in Philadelphia, 1830–1940* (Philadelphia: Institute for the Study of Human Issues, 1983), 18–19.

56. Judah J. Shapiro, *The Friendly Society: A History of the Workmen's Circle* (New York: Media Judaica, 1970), 164–65.

57. Zallmen Yoffeh, "Crisis in Boston," *MJ* 18 (May 1930): 444–56; Milton Plesur, *Jewish Life in Twentieth Century America: Challenge and Accommodation* (Chicago: Nelson-Hall, 1982), 78; Joseph P. Schultz, ed., *Mid-America's Promise: A Profile of Kansas City's Jewry* (Kansas City, Mo.: American Jewish Historical Society, 1982), 325–27; Benjamin Glassberg, "The Philanthropy Boom Collapses," *MJ* 19 (June 1931): 434–46.

58. Henry Hurwitz, "Chaos or Creation," *MJ* 19 (October 1930): 5–14.

59. I. M. Rubinow, "What Do We Owe Peter Stuyvesant?" *MJ* 19 (March 1931):

209–22; Harry L. Lurie, *A Heritage Affirmed: The Jewish Federation Movement in America* (Philadelphia: Jewish Publication Society, 1961), 110–14; Maurice J. Karpf, "Jewish Community Organization in the U.S.," *AJYB* 39 (1937–38): 130–33; G. Berger, "American Jewish Communal Service, 1776–1976: From Traditional Self-Help to Increasing Dependence on Government Support," *JSS* 38 (Summer–Fall 1976): 225–46.

60. Isaac Metzker, *A Bintel Brief: Sixty Years of Letters from the Lower East Side to the Jewish Daily Forward* (New York: Doubleday, 1971), 160–61.

61. Ibid., 157. Ditty quoted in Abraham J. Karp, *Haven and Home: A History of the Jews in America* (New York: Schocken, 1985), 278.

62. Plesur, *Jewish Life in Twentieth Century America,* 81–82; Gabriel Davidson, *Our Jewish Farmers and the Story of the Jewish Agricultural Society* (New York: Fischer, 1943), 125–30; Morton L. Gordon, "The History of the Jewish Farmer in Eastern Connecticut" (D.H.L. diss., Bernard Revel Graduate School, 1974), 15; Manners, *Poor Cousins,* 302.

63. Kessner, "Jobs, Ghettoes and the Urban Economy," 234–36; Bayor, "Italians, Jews and Ethnic Conflict," 379–80; Barry Chiswick and June O'Neil, *Human Resources and Income Distribution: Issues and Policies* (New York: Norton, 1977), 91–93, 172–73; Ginzburg, "Jews in the American Economy," 109–19; Lucy S. Dawidowicz, *On Equal Terms: Jews in America, 1881–1891* (New York: Holt, Rinehart and Winston, 1982), 95.

64. *CJR* 3 (June 1942): 318–24 (Magazine Digest); Uriah Z. Engelman, "Medurbia: The People," *CJR* 4 (August 1943): 339–48.

65. Chiswick and O'Neill, *Human Resources and Income Distribution,* 313–34; Chiswick, "Earnings and Human Capital of American Jews," 313–36; Perlmann, *Ethnic Differences,* 122–39, 154–62.

Chapter Six. Zionism and the Restructuring of Jewish Political Life

1. Arthur Goren, *New York Jews and the Quest for Community: The Kehillah Experiment, 1908–1922* (New York: Columbia University Press, 1970), 236; *AJYB* 26, 1924–1925: 579; A. G. Duker, "Structure of the Jewish Community," in *The American Jew: A Composite Portrait,* ed. Oscar Janowsky (Philadelphia: Jewish Publication Society, 1964), 134–60. Henry L. Feingold, *Zion in America,* rev. ed. (New York: Hippocrene, 1981), 209. The term "communalism" is used by Charles Liebman, "The Religion of American Jews," in *Understanding American Judaism,* vol. 1, *The Rabbi and the Synagogue,* ed. Jacob Neusner (New York: Ktav, 1975), 46–47.

2. AJC file, Jews in U.S., Communal Organizations, speech of Uriah Z. Engelman (typscript, n.d.).

3. Harry S. Linfield, *The Communal Organization of Jews in the United States* (New York: American Jewish Committee, 1930), 18–21; Daniel J. Elazar, *Community and Polity: The Organizational Dynamics of American Jewry* (Philadelphia: Jewish Publication Society, 1976), 182–87; Michael N. Dobkowski, *Jewish American Voluntary Organizations* (Westport, Conn.: Greenwood, 1986).

4. Kenneth D. Rosenman, "Power in a Midwestern Jewish Community," in Neusner, *Understanding American Judaism,* 1:141–63.

5. Isaac E. Rontch, "The Present State of the Landsmanshaften," *Jewish Social Service Quarterly* 15 (June 1939): 360–78; Duker, "Structure of the Jewish Community," 144.

6. Irwin Yellowitz, "American Jewish Labor: Historiographical Problems and Prospects," *AJHQ* 65 (March 1976): 203–4, 209–11.

7. Linfield, *Communal Organization*, 18–21.

8. Bernard Richards, interview, Oral History Research Office, Columbia University, 1967, 130; Yonathan Shapiro, *Leadership of the American Zionist Organization, 1897–1930* (Urbana: University of Illinois Press, 1971), 94–98, 110–13; Melvin Urofsky, *A Voice That Spoke for Justice: The Life and Times of Stephen S. Wise* (Albany: SUNY Press, 1982), 159–60

9. Quoted in Bernard Richards, interview, 130; Samuel M. Blumenfeld, "Pearl Harbor and American Jewry," *New Palestine*, 4 December 1942, 11.

10. Morris Frommer, "The American Jewish Congress: A History" (Ph.D. diss., Ohio State University, 1978), 169–89, 206–12, 218.

11. Goren, *New York Jews and the Quest for Community,* 53–55; Henry L. Feingold, "A Jewish Survival Enigma: The Strange Case of the American Jewish Committee" (pamphlet) (New York: American Jewish Committee, 1981).

12. Louis L. Gerson, *The Hyphenate in Recent American Politics and Diplomacy* (Lawrence: University of Kansas Press, 1964), 105.

13. Naomi Cohen, *Not Free to Desist: The American Jewish Committee, 1906–1972* (Philadelphia: Jewish Publication Society, 1972), 147–48.

14. Editorial, *AH,* 25 March 1921, 521; *AH*, 21 April 1922, 645.

15. Samuel Halperin, *The Political World of American Zionism* (Detroit: Wayne State University Press, 1961), 198–99; Bernard Richards, "The Problem of Democratic Jewish Organization," *Jewish Forum*, April 1943, 1–4.

16. Milton Goldin, *Why They Give: American Jews and Their Philanthropies* (New York: Macmillan, 1976); Henry L. Feingold, "United Jewish Appeal in American Jewish Consciousness" (bound unpublished manuscript in United Jewish Appeal archives), 2.

17. Deborah D. Moore, *At Home in America: Second Generation New York Jews* (New York: Columbia University Press, 1981), 131.

18. Boris D. Bogen, *Born a Jew* (New York: [American Jewish Joint Distribution Committee?], 1930), 57–58, 235; Harry L. Lurie, *A Heritage Affirmed: The Jewish Federation Movement in America* (Philadelphia: Jewish Publication Society, 1961), 36.

19. Maurice B. Hexter, "Historical Reminiscences," *AJH* 68 (December 1978): 122–30.

20. Duker, "Structure of the Jewish Community," 150.

21. Lurie, *Heritage Affirmed,* 83–87, 129–31, 143–45, Graenum Berger, "American Jewish Communal Service, 1776–1976: From Traditional Self-Help to Increasing Dependence on Government Support," *JSS* 38 (Summer–Fall 1976): 238–46; Isaac Franck, "The Changing American Jewish Community," in *American Jewry: The Tercentenary and After, 1654–1954,* ed. Eugene Kohn (New York: Reconstructionist Press, 1955), 18–45; B. M. Selekman, "The Federation in the Changing American Scene," *AJYB* 36 (1934–35): 65–87.

22. Ernest Stock, *Partners and Pursestrings: A History of the United Israel Appeal* (New York: University Press of America, 1987), 49–64; Julius Haber, *Odyssey of an American Zionist: Fifty Years of Zionist History* (New York: Twayne, 1956), 216.

23. Lurie, *Heritage Affirmed,* 83–87, 119, 125; Franck, "Changing American Jewish Community," 18–27; Berger, "American Jewish Communal Service," 235–38.

24. Marc Lee Raphael, *A History of the United Jewish Appeal, 1939–1982* (Providence, R.I.: Brown University Press, 1982), 13–27; Abraham J. Karp, *To Give Life: The*

UJA in the Shaping of the American Jewish Community (New York: Schocken, 1981), 71, 77–85.

25. Jacob de Haas, "Brandeis in Zionism," *MJ* 14 (February 1928): 134–35, 136–47. Quoted by Herbert Solow, "The Vindication of Jewish Idealism," *MJ* 15 (September 1928): 259–70; Melvin I. Urofsky, *American Zionism: From Herzl to Holocaust* (New York: Doubleday, 1957), 246–83.

26. Urofsky, *American Zionism,* 247–98; Shapiro, *Leadership of the American Zionist Organization,* 135–50; Naomi W. Cohen, *American Jews and the Zionist Idea* (New York: Ktav, 1975), 25–27; Ben Halpern, *A Clash of Heroes: Brandeis, Weizmann and American Zionism* (New York: Oxford University Press, 1987); Ben Halpern, "The Americanization of Zionism," in *Solidarity and Kinship: Essays on American Zionism,* ed. Nathan Kaganoff (Waltham, Mass.: American Jewish Historical Society, 1980), 37–55; Mitchell Cohen, "Zion and State: Nation, Class and the Shaping of Modern Israel," *Jewish Frontier* 54 (March–April 1987): 11–14; George Berlin, "The Brandeis-Weizmann Dispute," *AJHQ* 60 (September 1970): 37–68.

27. Chaim Weizmann, *Trial and Error: The Autobiography of Chaim Weizmann* (New York: Harper, 1949), 267.

28. Sarah L. Schmitt, "Horace M. Kallen and the Americanization of Zionism" (Ph.D. diss., University of Maryland, 1973), 271; David Rudavsky, "Louis D. Brandeis at the London International Zionist Conference in 1920," *YIVO Annual of Jewish Social Science* 15 (1974): 145–65.

29. Cyrus Adler, *Selected Letters,* ed. Ira Robinson (Philadelphia: Jewish Publication Society, 1985), 2:41 (Adler to Louis Marshall, 2 May 1921). Bernard A. Rosenblatt, *Two Generations of Zionism: Historical Recollections of an American Zionist* (New York: Sheingold, 1967), 90.

30. *AH,* 2 September 1921, 365; Haber, *Odyssey of an American Zionist,* 178. The statement regarding Pinsk and Washington was first made at the Hebrew Girls' Trade School. See Rosenblatt, *Two Generations of Zionism,* 97.

31. Editorial, *AH,* 29 April 1921, 709.

32. Stephen Wise, *The Personal Letters of Stephen Wise,* ed. J. W. Polier and J. W. Wise (Boston: Beacon, 1956), 191 (Wise to Justine Polier, 14 April 1921).

33. Schmitt, "Horace M. Kallen," 66–73.

34. Louis Lipsky, *Memoirs in Profile* (Philadelphia: Jewish Publication Society, 1975), ix–xvii, 11–57.

35. Esther Panitz, "Louis Dembitz Brandeis and the Cleveland Conference," *AJHQ* 65 (December 1975): 140–62.

36. Lipsky, *Memoirs,* 108; Adler, *Selected Letters,* 2:34–35 (Adler to Louis Marshall, 20 April 1921).

37. Herbert Parzen, "The Lodge-Fish Resolution," *AJHQ* 60 (September 1970): 71–80; Irwin Oder, "American Zionism and the Congressional Resolution of 1922 on Palestine," *Publications of the American Jewish Historical Society* 45 (September 1955): 35–47.

38. Herbert Solow, "The Vindication of Jewish Idealism," *MJ* 15 (September 1928): 259–70; Zalman Yoffeh, "Peace in American Zionism," *MJ* 19 (October 1930): 50–62.

39. Halperin, *Political World,* 190–92.

40. Arthur A. Goren, *Dissenter in Zion* (Cambridge: Harvard University Press, 1982), 145; *New York Times,* 24 November 1929, 12; Rosenblatt, *Two Generations of*

Zionism, 145; Naomi W. Cohen, *The Year after the Riots: American Response to the Palestine Crisis of 1929–1930* (Detroit: Wayne State University Press, 1987), 72, 109–10, 160–64.

41. Louis Berg, "American Public Opinion on Palestine," *MJ* 17 (October 1919): 67–85.

42. Stuart E. Knee, *The Concept of Zionist Dissent in the American Mind, 1917–1941* (New York: Speller, 1979), 211–14.

43. Cohen, *Year after the Riots,* 176–77.

44. Halperin, *Political World,* 13.

45. Joseph Hyman, *Twenty-five Years of American Aid to Jews Overseas* (New York: Joint Distribution Committee, 1939), 30; Bogen, *Born a Jew,* 275; Allan L. Kagedan, "The Formation of Soviet Jewish Territorial Units, 1924–1937" (Ph.D. diss., Columbia University, 1985), 68.

46. Yehuda Bauer, *My Brother's Keeper: A History of the American Jewish Joint Distribution Committee, 1929–1939* (Philadelphia: Jewish Publication Society, 1974), 57–58, 61–62.

47. Editorial, *AH,* 4 September 1925, 473; Lawrence P. Bachman, "Julius Rosenwald," *AJHQ* 66 (September 1976): 88–105; Jerome M. Kutnick, "Non-Zionist Leadership: Max Warburg, 1919–1927" (Ph.D. diss., Brandeis University, 1983).

48. Goren, *Dissenter,* 259; Haber, *Odyssey of an American Zionist,* 218; Zosa Szajkowski, " 'Reconstruction' vs. 'Palliative Relief' in American Jewish Overseas Work (1919–1939)," *JSS* 32 (January 1970): 39–41; *AH,* 3 July 1925, 275, 259; Kagedan, "Formation of Soviet Jewish Territorial Units," 40–42.

49. Kagedan, "Formation of Soviet Jewish Territorial Units," 59.

50. William Zuckerman, "The Jewish Colonization Movement in Soviet Russia," *MJ* 21 (April–June 1933): 73 ff.

51. Israel S. Wechsler, "On Palestinian and Russian Colonization," *MJ* 13 (August 1927): 391–98.

52. Kagedan, "Formation of Soviet Jewish Territorial Units," 197; "From Crimea to Siberia," *New Palestine,* 23 July 1926, 60; *AJYB* 24 (1922–23): 24–48; *AJYB* 26 (1924–25): 565; Urofsky, *Voice That Spoke for Justice,* 210–11.

53. Charles Reznikoff, ed., *Louis Marshall, Champion of Liberty: Selected Papers and Addresses* (Philadelphia: Jewish Publication Society, 1957), 2:763–64; Jerome Rosenthal, "Dealing with the Devil: Louis Marshall and the Partnership between the Joint Distribution Committee and Soviet Russia," *American Jewish Archives* 39 (April 1987): 1–22 (Marshall to Julius Rosenwald, 9 February 1927); *AH,* 11 September 1925, 495.

54. Quoted in Kagedan, "Formation of Soviet Jewish Territorial Units," 195.

55. Walter Laqueur, *A History of Zionism* (New York: Holt, 1972), 462.

56. Reznikoff, *Marshall,* 2:738; Morton Rosenstock, *Louis Marshall, Defender of Jewish Rights* (Detroit: Wayne State University Press, 1966), 45; Cohen, *Not Free to Desist,* 149–50.

57. *AH,* 25 March 1927, 689.

58. Reznikoff, *Marshall,* 2:756; Urofsky, *Voice That Spoke for Justice,* 215.

59. Quoted by Herbert Solow, "The Sixteenth Zionist Congress," *MJ* 17 (October 1929): 24.

60. Reznikoff, *Marshall,* 2:786–89 (Marshall to Weizmann, 6 June 1929).

61. Adler, *Selected Letters,* 2:234–35 (Adler to Moses Leavitt, 11 February 1932);

Herbert Parzen, "The Enlargement of the Jewish Agency for Palestine, 1923–1929: A Hope Hamstrung," *JSS* 39 (1977): 129–58.

62. David H. Shpiro, "From Philanthropy to Activism: The Political Transformation of American Zionism in the Holocaust Years" (Ph.D. diss., Hebrew University of Jerusalem, Institute of Contemporary Jewry, n.d.), xviii, 24–27; Michael Meyer, *Response to Modernity: A History of the Reform Movement in Judaism* (New York: Oxford, 1988), 326–34; N. Cohen, "Reaction of Reform Judaism to Political Zionism, 1897–1922," in *The Jewish Experience in America,* ed. Abraham Karp (New York: Ktav, 1969), 154–82; Halperin, *Political World of American Zionism,* 42–43, 327; Adler, *Selected Letters,* 2:344–45 (Adler to David Werner, 14 February 1938).

63. Halperin, *Political World of American Zionism,* 196; Judd L. Teller, *Strangers and Natives: The Evolution of the American Jew from 1921 to the Present* (New York: Delacorte [Delta], 1968), 130.

Chapter Seven. American Jewish Political Behavior during the Interwar Period

1. "Annual Report of the Executive Committee," *AJYB* 26 (1924–25): 637–39; Charles Reznikoff, ed., *Louis Marshall, Champion of Liberty: Selected Papers and Addresses* (Philadelphia: Jewish Publication Society, 1957), 2:812–13 (Marshall to Felix Fuld, 31 October 1924); "Twenty-first Annual Report of the AJC," *AJYB* 30 (1928–29): 287–89; Morton Rosenstock, *Louis Marshall, Defender of Jewish Rights* (Detroit: Wayne State University Press, 1966), 55–56.

2. Louis L. Gerson, *The Hyphenate in Recent American Politics and Diplomacy* (Lawrence: University of Kansas Press, 1964), 5–6, 25–26, 30, 97 ff.

3. Ronald Bayor, "Italians and Jews in New York: The La Guardia Elections," *Proceedings of the Seventh Annual Conference of the American Italian Historical Association,* 14, 15 November 1974, 3–4; Ronald Bayor, "Italians, Jews and Ethnic Conflict," *International Migration Review* 6 (Winter 1972): 377–91.

4. "Review of the Yiddish Press," *CJR* 7 (December 1944): 658–59; "You Can Stop Hillmanism" (full-page advertisement in Stanford, Connecticut, *Advocate*), in AJC file, Election, Anti-Semitism.

5. AJC file, Election, Anti-Semitism, Constitutional Americans leaflet, 1944.

6. Arthur Mann, *La Guardia: A Fighter against His Times, 1882–1933* (New York: Lippincott, 1954), 155–57; Irving Howe, *World of Our Fathers* (New York: Simon and Schuster, 1976), 381; Robert P. Ingalls, *Herbert H. Lehman and New York's Little New Deal* (New York: New York University Press, 1975), 23.

7. *AH,* 10 October 1924, 686; Michael Dobkowski, *The Tarnished Dream* (Westport, Conn.: Greenwood, 1979), 200. There is some question about the percentage of Jewish votes cast for Debs and La Follette. These figures come from Alan Fisher, "Continuity and Erosion of Jewish Liberalism," *AJHQ* 66 (December 1976): 322–62.

8. Deborah D. Moore, *At Home in America: Second Generation New York Jews* (New York: Columbia University Press, 1981), 211.

9. Ande Manners, *Poor Cousins* (New York: Coward, 1972), 288–89; Howe, *World of Our Fathers,* 375; Sol Bloom, *The Autobiography of Sol Bloom* (New York: Putnam, 1948), 53.

10. Lawrence H. Fuchs, *The Political Behavior of American Jews* (New York: Free Press, 1956), 87; also "Introduction," *AJHQ* 66 (December 1976): 181–89; Arthur A. Goren, *Dissenter in Zion* (Cambridge: Harvard University Press, 1982); Journal of Magnes, 31 May 1921, 195–96; Arthur Liebman, "The Ties That Bind: The Jewish Support for the Left in the U.S.," *AJHQ* 66 (December 1976): 285–321; Arnold M. Eisen, *The Chosen People in America: A Study in Jewish Religious Ideology* (Bloomington: Indiana University Press, 1983), 70; Maurice Hindus, "The Jew as a Radical," *MJ* 13 (August 1927): 368.

11. Ben Halpern, "The Roots of American Jewish Liberalism," *AJHQ* 66 (December 1976): 190–214; Daniel Elazar, *Community and Polity: The Organizational Dynamics of American Jewry* (Philadelphia: Jewish Publication Society, 1976), 4, 79–80; Daniel Elazar, ed., *Kinship and Consent: The Jewish Political Tradition and Its Contemporary Uses* (New York: University Press of America, 1983), 4.

12. Werner Cohn, "Sources of American Jewish Liberalism" (Ph.D. diss., New School for Social Research, 1956).

13. Zosa Szajkowski, *Jews, Wars and Communism,* vol. 1, *The Russian Revolution, 1917* (New York: Ktav, 1972), 368, 408; Howe, *World of Our Fathers,* 396.

14. Judd L. Teller, *Strangers and Natives: The Evolution of the American Jew from 1921 to the Present* (New York: Delacorte [Delta], 1968), 32; quoted in Paul Jacobs, *Is Curly Jewish?* (New York: Atheneum, 1965), 17; Manners, *Poor Cousins,* 289; Hindus, "Jew as a Radical," 375.

15. David Burner, *The Politics of Provincialism: The Democratic Party in Transition, 1918–1932* (New York: Putnam, 1967), 240–41.

16. Quoted in Manners, *Poor Cousins,* 289.

17. Thomas Kessner, "Jobs, Ghettoes and the Urban Economy, 1880–1935," *AJH* 71 (December 1981): 232.

18. *AJYB* 21 (1919–20): 599; 33 (1931–32): 262; 39 (1937–38): 735; 40 (1938–39): 529. In addition, there were two Jewish governors—Julius L. Meier (Oregon) and Arthur Seligmann (New Mexico).

19. For background to the conflict see Rudolf Glanz, *Jews and Irish: Historic Group Relations and Immigration* (New York: Walden, 1966), and Esther Y. Feldblum, *The American Catholic Press* (New York: Atheneum, 1977); Robert E. Quigley, "American Catholic Opinions of Mexican Anticlericalism, 1910–1936" (Ph.D. diss., University of Pennsylvania, 1965).

20. Moore, *At Home in America,* 217; editorial, *AH,* 17 August 1923, 285; Howe, *World of Our Fathers,* 374; John F. Stack, *International Conflict in an American City* (Westport, Conn.: Greenwood, 1979), 33–55. For general background see David J. O'Brien, *American Catholics and Social Reform: The New Deal Years* (New York: Oxford University Press, 1968).

21. Kessner, "Jobs, Ghettoes and the Urban Economy," 236; Ronald H. Bayor, *Neighbors in Conflict: The Irish, Germans, Jews and Italians of New York City, 1929–1941* (Baltimore: Johns Hopkins University Press, 1978), 24–28; Robert A. Dahl, *Who Governs: Democracy and Power in an American City* (New Haven: Yale University Press, 1961), 42–48; Alter F. Landesman, *Brownsville: The Birth, Development and Passing of a Jewish Community in New York* (New York: Bloch, 1971), 294–307.

22. Edward J. Flynn, *You're the Boss* (New York: Viking, 1947), 28–97; Warren Moscow, *Politics in the Empire State* (New York: Knopf, 1948); Elizabeth E. Perry, *Belle*

Moskowitz: Feminine Politics and the Exercise of Power in the Age of Alfred E. Smith (New York: Oxford University Press, 1987).

23. Howe, *World of Our Fathers,* 388. For general background see also Joseph M. Proskauer, *A Segment of My Time* (New York: Farrar, Straus, 1950).

24. Samuel Lubell, *The Future of American Politics* (New York: Harper, 1956), 35–43.

25. Quoted in John L. Shover, *Politics of the Nineteen Twenties* (Waltham, Mass.: Ginn, 1970), 173; William E. Leuchtenberg, *The Perils of Prosperity, 1914–1932* (Chicago: University of Chicago Press, 1958), 238–39.

26. Marc L. Raphael, *Abba Hillel Silver: A Profile in American Judaism* (New York: Holmes and Meier, 1989), 109, 112–13.

27. Reznikoff, *Marshall,* 1:193–94 (Marshall to Major de Rothschild, 16 November 1921); *AH,* 14 October 1921, 585; 18 November 1921, 6; 13 July 1923, 177; 8 August 1924, 373.

28. American Jewish Archives, Max Kohler MS, box 4, file Q–Z (John Simons to Kohler, 2 October 1933); *AJYB,* 23 (1921–22), 329–45, 348–51; *AJYB* 25 (1923–24), 60–63; Naomi Cohen, *Not Free to Desist: The American Jewish Committee, 1906–1972* (Philadelphia: Jewish Publication Society, 1972), 144–45; Morris D. Waldman, *Nor by Power* (New York: International Universities Press, 1953), 24 ff.; Reznikoff, *Marshall,* 2:646–75 (Marshall to Nicolas Tiulesco, 5 January 1926; Marshall to George Cretziano, 31 January 1927); editorial, *AH,* 12 December 1924, 164.

29. Quoted in Szajkowski, *Jews, Wars and Communism,* 389. The speaker was Leo M. Glassman, 8 December 1929.

30. Waldman, *Nor by Power,* 67 ff.

31. The AJCOMM commissioned polls to survey reaction. AJC file, Anti-Semitism, "Report by Towhey Associates, 27 September 1941" (typed); Buel W. Patch, "Anti-Semitism in the U.S.," *Editorial Research Reports* 2 (14 November 1941); *CJR* 4 (December 1941): 637–48; Edward S. Shapiro, "The Approach of War: Isolationism and Anti-Semitism," *AJH* 74 (September 1984): 45–65.

32. Charles H. Stember, "The Recent History of Public Attitudes," in *Jews in the Mind of America,* ed. Charles H. Stember (New York: Basic Books, 1966), 142–44, 214–16.

33. Alfred O. Hero, Jr., *American Religious Groups View Foreign Policy: Trends in Rank and File Opinion 1937–1969* (Durham, N.C.: Duke University Press, 1973), 26, 145–46, 279–84. See also Cyrus Adler and Aaron Margalith, *With Firmness in the Right: American Diplomatic Action Affecting Jews, 1840–1945* (New York: Arno, 1977); J. D. Walaik, "In the Days before Ecumenicism: Anti-Semitism and the Spanish Civil War," *Journal of Church and State* 13 (Autumn 1971): 465–77.

34. The estimates of the proportion of Jews in the International Brigade and its American component are approximations, since volunteers were listed by nationality. Cecil B. Eby, *Between the Bullet and the Lie: Volunteers in the Spanish Civil War* (New York: Holt, Rinehart and Winston, 1969), makes no estimate. Chaim V. Lipschitz, *Franco, Spain, the Jews and the Holocaust,* ed. Ira Axelrod (New York: Ktav, 1984), 15, observes only that the proportion of Jewish volunteers was "disproportionately high." But Haim Avni, *Spain, the Jews and Franco* (Philadelphia: Jewish Publication Society, 1982), 50, estimates that 10 percent (approximately 3,000 to 5,000) of the 40,000 man brigade was Jewish. For varying estimates see Albert Prago, "Fifty Long Years Later:

Commemorating the Spanish Civil War," *Jewish Currents*, March 1987, 4–7; Jeffrey Hart, "For Whom the Bell Tolled," *Commentary* 82 (December 1986): 59–62.

35. Hero, *American Religious Groups*, 279–84; Leo V. Kanawanda, Jr., *Franklin D. Roosevelt's Diplomacy and American Catholics, Italians and Jews* (Ann Arbor: University of Michigan Press, 1982), 60 ff., 133 ff.; Allen Guttmann, *The Wound in the Heart: Americans and the Spanish Civil War* (New York: Free Press, 1962), 9–13.

36. Moshe Gottlieb, "The American Controversy over the Olympic Games," *AJHQ* 61 (March 1972): 181–213; Leon Jick, "The Olympic Boycott—Then," *Moment,* July–August 1980, 60–63; George N. Shuster, "General Sherrill and the Olympics," *Commonweal,* 8 November 1935.

37. Deborah E. Lipstadt, *Beyond Belief: The American Press and the Coming of the Holocaust, 1933–1945* (New York: Free Press, 1986), 104–10; Haskel Lookstein, *Were We Our Brothers' Keepers? The Public Response of American Jews to the Holocaust, 1938–1944* (New York: Hartmore House, 1985), 35–80; Henry L. Feingold, *The Politics of Rescue: The Roosevelt Administration and the Holocaust, 1938–1945* (New York: Holocaust Library, 1982), 40–44.

38. Quoted in *New York Post,* 25 March 1936, 38; American Jewish Archives, Max Kohler MS, box 3, State Department file (Wilbur Carr to Kohler, 2 June 1933; Kohler to Carr, 3 June 1933), touches on the delicate question of the department's anti-Semitism. For a varying opinion on the prevalence of anti-Semitism, see Richard Breitman and Alan Kraut, *American Refugee Policy and European Jewry, 1933–1945* (Bloomington: Indiana University Press, 1987), 4–5, 126–27, 224–25.

39. Carl H. Voss, *Rabbi and Minister: The Friendship of Stephen S. Wise and John Haynes Holmes* (New York: World, 1964), 275–76.

40. Flynn, *You're the Boss,* 183. Others claim it was first conceived by Samuel Rosenman.

41. AJC file, Voting, Jews, 1927–67, "Election 1940" (mimeographed); Lubell, *Future of American Politics,* 55; Bayor, *Neighbors in Conflict,* 5–6; Gerson, *Hyphenate,* 119–24.

42. AJC file, Election, Anti-Semitism, "You Can Stop Hillmanism" (full-page advertisement in Stamford, Connecticut, *Advocate,* n.d.).

43. AJC file, Voting, Jews, 1927–67 (mimeographed analysis of election returns in Jewish districts); David Dubinsky and A. H. Raskin, *David Dubinsky: A Life with Labor* (New York: Simon and Schuster, 1977), 262–73; Moore, *At Home in America,* 220; Howe, *World of Our Fathers,* 390 ff.

44. *New York Times,* 6 March 1933, 11; Stephen S. Wise, *Challenging Years: The Autobiography of Stephen Wise* (New York: Putnam, 1949), 231.

45. Emanuel Celler, *You Never Leave Brooklyn: The Autobiography of Emanuel Celler* (New York: Day, 1953), 12.

46. Richard T. Goldberg, *The Making of Franklin Roosevelt: Triumph over Disability* (Cambridge, Mass.: Abt Books, 1982), 1, 36.

47. Stember, *Jews in the Mind of America,* 76–86; *Nation,* 28 August 1938, 167–68; Dov Fish, "The Libel Trial of Robert Edward Edmondson: 1936–1938," *AJH* 71 (September 1981): 80.

48. Jerold S. Auerbach, *Unequal Justice: Lawyers and Social Change in Modern America* (New York: Oxford University Press, 1976), 188; Harold Ickes, *The Secret Diary of Harold L. Ickes,* vol. 2; *The Inside Struggle, 1936–1939* (New York: Simon and

Schuster, 1954), 676; Myron Scholnick, "The New Deal and Anti-Semitism in America" (Ph.D. diss., University of Maryland), 37 n.1.

49. Max Freedman, ed., *Roosevelt and Frankfurter: Their Correspondence, 1928–1945* (Boston: Little, Brown, 1967), 173, 303, 310; Michael E. Parrish, *Felix Frankfurter and His Times: The Reform Years* (New York: Free Press, 1982), 220–21.

50. Parrish, *Frankfurter and His Times,* 132; Freedman, *Roosevelt and Frankfurter,* 164 (Frankfurter to Roosevelt, 17 October 1933).

51. Parrish, *Frankfurter and His Times,* 132; Bruce A. Murphy, *The Brandeis-Frankfurter Connection: The Secret Political Activities of the Two Supreme Court Justices* (New York: Oxford University Press, 1982), 34; H. N. Hirsch, *The Enigma of Felix Frankfurter* (New York: Basic Books, 1981).

52. Nelson L. Dawson, "Louis D. Brandeis, Felix Frankfurter and Franklin D. Roosevelt: The Origins of a New Deal Relationship," *AJH* 68 (September 1978): 36–41.

53. Scholnick, "The New Deal and Anti-Semitism," 122 ff.; Frank Freidel, *Launching the New Deal* (Boston: Little, Brown, 1973), 393.

54. Quoted in Auerbach, *Unequal Justice,* 188.

55. Dean Banks, "Creating an 'American Dilemma': The Impact of Nazi Racism upon Intergroup Relations, 1933–1945" (Ph.D. diss., University of Texas at Austin, 1975).

56. Henry L. Feingold, "'Courage First and Intelligence Second': The American Jewish Secular Elite, Roosevelt and the Failure to Rescue," *AJH* 72 (June 1983): 424–60; Peter Lowenburg, *Walter Rathenau and Henry Kissinger: The Jew as a Modern Statesman in Two Political Cultures,* Leo Baeck Memorial Lecture 14 (New York: Leo Baeck Institute, 1980); Joseph Alsop and Robert Kinter, *Men around the President* (New York: Harper, 1939).

57. Roy Lubove, *Poverty and Social Welfare in the United States* (New York: Holt, 1971); Jacob Fisher, *The Response of Social Work to the Depression* (Boston: Hall, 1980); Maurice J. Karpf, "Jewish Community Organization in the U.S.," *AJYB* 39 (1937–38): 47–48.

58. AJC file, Communism and Jews, 1920–49, "Memorandum on Statistics on Jews and Communism," 4 February 1939, NB to FNT(?) (typescript). The memorandum concludes that all statistics are of questionable validity. Nathaniel Weyl, *The Jew in American Politics* (New Rochelle, N.Y.: Arlington House, 1968), 116–19.

59. Morris Frommer, "The American Jewish Congress: A History" (Ph.D. diss., Ohio State University, 1978), 408–9.

60. Arthur Liebman, "The Ties That Bind: The Jewish Support for the Left in the U.S.," *AJHQ* 66 (December 1976): 304.

61. AJC file, Communism and Jews, handbills, November 1939, 23 January 1941.

62. *CJR* 2 (September–October 1939): 43–51; *CJR* 2 (November–December 1939): 35–42; Sidney Hook, "Promise without Dogma: A Social Philosophy for Jews," *MJ* 25 (October–December 1937): 273–75.

63. Liebman, "Ties That Bind," 292; Alexander Kohansky, "Communist Propaganda for Jews: The New Line," *CJR* 3 (September–October 1940): 470–83; Earl Browder, *The Jewish People and the War* (New York: Worker's Library, May 1940), found in AJC file, Communism, Jews.

64. Kohansky, "Communist Propaganda."

65. *Yiddisher Kemfer,* 9 July 1943, in *CJR* 6 (October 1943): 504, 529 (Magazine Digest).

66. Alexander Bloom, *Prodigal Son: The New York Intellectuals and Their World* (New York: Oxford University Press, 1986), 45, 55.

67. *AH,* 28 May 1926, 69; "Nazi Red Charge Draws Denial from Jews Here," *New York Evening Journal,* 25 September 1936.

68. Quoted in Banks, "Creating an 'American Dilemma,'" 175; *Time* 23 (2 April 1934): 10–11.

Chapter Eight. The American Jewish Response to the Holocaust

1. For contrasting views see David S. Wyman, *The Abandonment of the Jews: America and the Holocaust, 1941–1945* (New York: Pantheon, 1984); Henry L. Feingold, *The Politics of Rescue: The Roosevelt Administration and the Holocaust, 1938–1945* (New York: Holocaust Library, 1980); and Richard Breitman and Alan M. Kraut, *American Refugee Policy and European Jewry, 1933–1945* (Bloomington: Indiana University Press, 1987). Haskel Lookstein, *Were We Our Brothers' Keepers? The Public Response of American Jews to the Holocaust, 1938–1945* (New York: Hartmore, 1986), and Seymour M. Finger, ed., *American Jewry during the Holocaust* (New York: Holmes and Meier, 1984), indict American Jewry for its imagined passivity.

2. The fullest description of these stages is contained in Raul Hilberg, *The Destruction of the European Jews,* 3 vols. (New York: Holmes and Meier, 1987).

3. David S. Wyman, *Paper Walls: America and the Refugee Crisis, 1938 to 1941* (New York: Pantheon, 1985), 69–78; Breitman and Kraut, *American Refugee Policy,* 28–51; Feingold, *Politics of Rescue,* 16–20; American Jewish Archives, Max Kohler MS, box 4 (Judge Irving Olehman to Max Kohler, 12 October 1933). The fullest synthesis of the refugee crisis is found in Michael R. Marrus, *The Unwanted: European Refugees in the Twentieth Century* (New York: Oxford University Press, 1985).

4. *Fortune* poll, April 1939, 102, 104, 107; 8 July 1938, 85; Charles H. Stember, ed., *Jews in the Mind of America* (New York: Basic Books, 1966), 144–54.

5. Feingold, *Politics of Rescue,* 111–13, 122–23; Haim Genizi, "New York Is Big—America Is Bigger: The Resettlement of Refugees from Nazism, 1936–1945," *JSS* 46 (Winter 1984): 61–72.

6. Cyrus Adler, *Selected Letters,* ed. Ira Robinson (Philadelphia: Jewish Publication Society, 1985), 2:292–93 (Adler to Joseph Hyman, 22 March 1935); Ginizi, "New York Is Big," 69; David Brody, "American Jewry: The Refugees and Immigration Restriction, 1932–1942," *PAJHS* 45 (June 1956): 219–84; Zosa Szajkowski, "The Attitude of American Jews to Refugees from Germany in the 1930s," *AJHQ* 61 (December 1971): 101–43.

7. Edwin Black, *The Transfer Agreement: The Untold Story of the Secret Pact between the Third Reich and Jewish Palestine* (New York: Macmillan, 1984), 371–82. For the best estimate regarding the actual date of the "final solution" decision, see Christopher R. Browning, "The Decision regarding the Final Solution," in *Unanswered Questions: Nazi Germany and the Genocide of the Jews,* ed. François Furet (New York: Schocken, 1989), 96–118.

8. Feingold, *Politics of Rescue,* 149–53; Wyman, *Paper Walls,* 75–79.

9. Barbara M. Stewart, *United States Government Policy on Refugees from Nazism, 1933–1940* (New York: Garland, 1984), 495–553; House Committee on Immigration and Naturalization, *Hearings on Joint Resolution to Authorize the Admission . . . of a Limited Number of Refugee Children* (76th Cong., 1st sess., 1939).

10. AJC file, World War, 1939–45, Atrocities, Reactions, Statements. The delegation was limited to five people: Stephen Wise (AJCONG), who headed the delegation; Maurice Wertheim (AJCOMM); Henry Monsky (B'nai B'rith); Adolph Held (Jewish Labor Committee); and Israel Rosenberg (Union of Orthodox Congregations); Minutes, Governing Council of AJCONG, 10 December 1942; Wyman, *Abandonment,* 71–72.

11. AJC file, World War, 1939–45, Atrocities, Reactions, Statements, Martha Jelenko, "Reaction of Church Leaders and Groups to Atrocities" (typescript); Deborah Lipstadt, *Beyond Belief: The American Press and the Coming of the Holocaust, 1933–1945* (New York: Free Press, 1986), 135–58.

12. Feingold, *Politics of Rescue,* 191–213.

13. Sharon R. Lowenstein, *Token Refuge: The Story of the Jewish Refugee Shelter at Oswego, 1944–1946* (Bloomington: Indiana University Press, 1986). See also her "A New Deal for Refugees: The Promise and Reality of Oswego," *AJH* 71 (March 1982): 325–41; Ruth Gruber, *Haven: The Unknown Story of One Thousand World War II Refugees* (New York: Coward-McCann, 1983); *CJR* 7 (October 1944): 556–58 (Review of Yiddish Press).

14. Quoted in Stephen Wise, *Challenging Years: The Autobiography of Stephen Wise* (New York: Putnam, 1949), 237.

15. Moshe R. Gottlieb, *American Anti-Nazi Resistance, 1933–1941* (New York: Ktav, 1982), 341–49; Black, *Transfer Agreement,* 187–92.

16. Waldman, *Nor by Power,* 49.

17. AJC file, Germans in U.S., Nazism, Anti-Semitic Propaganda, news clipping, n.d.; AJC file, German (Nazi) Boycott, AJCOMM press release, 13 March 1939.

18. Arguments summarized in Louis Mirsky, "The Policy of Aggression," *MJ* 23 (April–June 1935): 7–17; Moshe Gottlieb, "The First of April Boycott and the Reaction of the American Jewish Community," *AJHQ* 57 (June 1968): 516–56; and Gottlieb, *American Anti-Nazi Resistance,* 341–49; American Jewish Archives, Max Kohler MS, box 10, file T–V (Untermeyer to Kohler, 23 May 1934); Wise, *Challenging Years,* 248–49; "Annual Report of the Executive Committee," *AJYB* 36 (1934–35): 429.

19. Frommer, "The American Jewish Congress: A History" (Ph.D. diss., Ohio State University, 1978), 321–22.

20. Ibid., 342–74; Frederick A. Lazin, "The Response of the American Jewish Committee to the Crisis of German Jewry, 1933–1939," *AJHQ* 58 (March 1979): 283–304.

21. Adler, *Selected Letters,* 2:273–76 (Adler to Lewis Strauss, 19 October 1933).

22. Isaac Neustadt, "The Unending Task: Efforts to Unite American Jewry from the American Jewish Congress to the American Jewish Conference" (Ph.D. diss., Brandeis University, 1976), 107 ff.; Edward D. Pinsky, "Cooperation among American Jewish Organizations in Their Efforts to Rescue European Jewry during the Holocaust, 1939–1945" (Ph.D. diss., New York University, 1980), 460–507.

23. Hayim Greenberg, "Bankrupt," *Yiddishe Kemfer,* 12 February 1943, 1–3, reprinted in *Midstream* 10 (March 1964): 5–10.

24. Samuel Halperin, *The Political World of American Zionism* (Detroit: Wayne State University Press, 1961), 155.

25. Ibid., 190–92; Doreen Bierbrier, "The American Zionist Emergency Committee: An Analysis of a Pressure Group," *AJHQ* 60 (September 1970): 32–105; Emanuel

Neumann, *In the Arena: An Autobiographical Memoir* (New York: Herzl, 1976); Carl H. Voss, "The American Christian Palestine Committee: The Mid-1940s in Retrospect," *Midstream* 25 (June–July 1979): 49–53.

26. Feingold, *Politics of Rescue,* 86–87, 238–39.

27. Monty N. Penkower, "In Dramatic Dissent: The Bergson Boys," *AJH* 70 (March 1981): 281–309; Michael Brown, "The New Zionism in the New World: Vladimir Jabotinsky's Relations with the United States in the Pre-Holocaust Years," *Modern Judaism* 4 (February 1989): 71–99; Aaron Berman, *Nazism, the Jews and American Zionism, 1933–1948* (Detroit: Wayne State University Press, 1990), 119–23.

28. Ben Hecht, *Child of the Century* (New York: Simon and Schuster, 1954); Yitshaq Ben Ami, *Years of Wrath, Days of Glory: Memoirs from the Irgun* (New York: Speller, 1982), 283–91.

29. Julius Haber, *The Odyssey of an American Zionist: Fifty Years of Zionist History* (New York: Twayne, 1956), 260–61; Dina Porat, *The Blue and the Yellow Star of David: The Zionist Leadership in Palestine and the Holocaust, 1939–1945* (Cambridge: Harvard University Press, 1990), 18 ff.

30. Michael N. Dobkowski, *Jewish American Voluntary Organizations* (Westport, Conn.: Greenwood, 1986), 11–14; Michael Meyer, *Response to Modernity: A History of the Reform Movement in Judaism* (New York: Oxford University Press, 1988), 334.

31. Bernard Wasserstein, *Britain and the Jews of Europe, 1939–1945* (London: Oxford University Press, 1979), 40.

32. David Shpiro, "From Philanthropy to Activism: The Political Transformation of American Zionism in the Holocaust Years" (Ph.D. diss., Hebrew University of Jerusalem, Institute of Contemporary Jewry, n.d.), 147; Bernard A. Rosenblatt, *Two Generations of Zionism: Historical Recollections of an American Zionist* (New York: Sheingold, 1967), 198; Dan Kurtzman, *Ben Gurion, Prophet of Fire* (New York: Simon and Schuster, 1983), 235–37.

33. Aaron Berman, "American Zionism and the Rescue of European Jewry: An Ideological Perspective," *AJH* 70 (March 1983): 320–30; Feingold, *Politics of Rescue,* 237–39, 300–301.

34. Marc L. Raphael, *Abba Hillel Silver: A Profile in American Judaism* (New York: Holmes and Meier, 1989), 128–34.

35. Arthur A. Goren, *Dissenter in Zion* (Cambridge: Harvard University Press, 1982), 46–47.

36. *Congress Weekly,* 24 September 1943, 2; *CJR* (December 1943): 659–62 (Magazine Digest). The best source for organization of the American Jewish Conference is Alexander S. Kohanski, ed., *The American Jewish Conference: Its Organization and Proceedings of the First Session, August 20 to September 30, 1943* (New York: American Jewish Conference, 1944).

37. Quoted in *CJR* 6 (December 1943): 659–60 (Magazine Digest).

38. Shpiro, "From Philanthropy to Activism," 227–30.

39. House Committee on Foreign Affairs, Hearings on *Resolutions Relative to the Jewish National Home in Palestine* (H.R. 418, 419), 78th Cong., 2d sess., February 1944, 91 ff., 122.

40. Rosenblatt, *Two Generations of Zionism,* 193; Selig Adler, "Franklin Roosevelt and Zionism: The Wartime Record," *Judaism* 21 (Summer 1974): 265–76.

41. Wise, *Challenging Years,* 232.

42. H. L. Feingold, "'Courage First and Intelligence Second': The American Jewish Secular Elite, Roosevelt and the Failure to Rescue," *AJH* 72 (June 1983): 459.

43. Lipstadt, *Beyond Belief,* 250–63, 272–78; H. C. Peterson, *Propaganda for War: The Campaign against American Neutrality, 1914–1917* (Norman: University of Oklahoma Press, 1939).

44. Wasserstein, *Britain and the Jews,* quoted on book jacket.

45. Stember, *Jews in the Mind of America,* 54; Nathan Belth, *A Promise to Keep* (New York: New York Times Books, 1979), 150–51.

46. AJC file, Anti-Semitism, American 1933–, National Opinion Research Center, July 1942, March 1944 (mimeographed).

47. Editors of *Fortune, Jews in America* (New York, 1936), 3–5; William Zuckerman, "The Jewish Spirit in Crisis," *MJ* 30 (July–September 1942): 108–10.

48. Sander E. Diamond, *The Nazi Movement in the United States, 1924–1941* (Ithaca, N.Y.: Cornell University Press, 1974), 244 ff., 333, 339; Leland V. Bell, *In Hitler's Shadow: The Anatomy of American Nazism* (Port Washington, N.Y.: Kennicat, 1973), 56–58, 65–68; Belth, *Promise to Keep,* 118; Glen Jeansonne, *Gerald L. K. Smith: Minister of Hate* (New Haven: Yale University Press, 1988).

49. Alan Brinkley, *Voices of Protest: Huey Long, Father Coughlin and the Great Depression* (New York: Vintage, 1983), 268–69, 273; Belth, *Promise to Keep,* 117; Charles J. Tull, *Father Coughlin and the New Deal* (Syracuse, N.Y.: Syracuse University Press, 1965); Mary A. Christine, "The Fahey-Coughlin Connection . . . and Religious Anti-Semitism in the United States, 1938–1945" (Ph.D. diss., Graduate Theological Union, 1982).

50. Feingold, *Politics of Rescue,* 41–42; Lipstadt, *Beyond Belief,* 98–104; Sander Diamond, "The Kristallnacht and the Reaction in America," *YIVO Annual of Jewish Social Science* 14 (1969): 196–208.

51. Louis L. Gerson, *The Hyphenate in Recent American Politics and Diplomacy* (Lawrence: University of Kansas Press, 1964), 119–24; AJC file, Ethnic Groups, 1942–69 (typed report, December 1942).

52. Dean Banks, "Creating an 'American Dilemma': The Impact of Nazi Racism upon Intergroup Relations, 1933–1945" (Ph.D. diss., University of Texas at Austin, 1975), 445–46.

53. Quoted in "The War of Nerves: Hitler's Helper," *Fortune* 22 (November 1940): 85–86, 108–10, 112.

54. Ronald Bayor, "Italians, Jews and Ethnic Conflict," International Migration Review 6 (Winter 1972): 387–89.

55. David G. Singer, "The Prelude to Nazism: The German-American Press and the Jews, 1919–1933," *AJHQ* 66 (March 1977): 417–33; Diamond, *Nazi Movement in the United States,* 40–44, 85–103.

56. Haim Genizi, "The Attitude of American Catholics toward Catholic Refugees from Nazism: 1933–1945," *Proceedings of the Seventh World Congress of Jewish Studies Holocaust Research* (Jerusalem: World Union of Jewish Studies, 1980).

57. Isabel B. Price, "Black Response to Anti-Semitism: Negroes and Jews in New York to World War II" (Ph.D. diss., University of New Mexico, 1973), 247–48, 347; Naomi Cohen, *Not Free to Desist: The American Jewish Committee, 1906–1972* (Philadelphia: Jewish Publication Society, 1972), 137–83.

58. Hasia Diner, "In the Almost Promised Land: Jewish Leaders and Blacks, 1915–1935" (Ph.D. diss., University of Illinois, Chicago Circle, 1975), xii–xvii, 237.

59. *Amsterdam News,* 26 April 1933, quoted by Price, "Black Response," 184.

60. Belth, *Promise to Keep,* 120; Cohen, *Not Free to Desist,* 193–238; Benjamin Fine, "The Springfield Plan for Education against Intolerance and Prejudice," *MJ* 32 (October–December 1944): 161 ff.

61. Patricia Erens, *The Jew in American Cinema* (Bloomington: Indiana University Press, 1984), 157 ff.

62. Oswald K. Fraenkl, "For Free Speech," *MJ* 24 (April–June 1936): 100; William Shack, "Is There a Limit to Free Speech?" *MJ* 26 (October–December 1938): 276–83; Robert Gordis, "Make Free Speech Responsible," *MJ* 27 (April–June 1939): 138–46.

63. AJC file, Anti-Semitism, 1933–45, published in *Bluejacket,* 31 December 1942, base newspaper, U.S. Naval Training School, Memphis, Tennessee.

64. Eli Cohen, "Toward Economic Adjustment of Jews," *CJR* 5 (October 1942): 463.

65. See especially Isidor Kaufmann, *American Jews in World War II: The Story of 550,000 Fighters for Freedom,* 2 vols. (New York: Dial, 1947); and Mac Davis, *Jews Fight Too* (New York: Jordan, 1945).

66. *CJR* 7 (August 1944): 439 (Magazine Digest); Ruth Karpf and Judd Teller, "The Jews Fight Back," *American Mercury,* June 1944.

67. H. L. Feingold, "Finding a Conceptual Framework for the Study of American Antisemitism," *JSS* 47 (Summer–Fall 1985): 313–26.

68. Salo W. Baron, "The Effect of the War on Jewish Community Life" (pamphlet), H. L. Glicksman Memorial Lecture, 1942.

69. William Zuckerman, "Towards Regeneration in Europe: Against the Folly of 'Evacuation,'" *MJ* 31 (October–December 1943): 215–16. See also Morris R. Cohen, "Jewish Studies of Peace and Post-war Problems," *CJR* 4 (April 1941): 110–25; Banks, "Creating an 'American Dilemma,'" 450. Asked whether Jewish leaders knew the "extent to which lives were being taken," Bernard Richards replied that he did not think they did: "No, nobody knew the exact figures." Bernard Richards, interview, Columbia University Oral History Project.

70. Reinhold Niebuhr, "Jews after the War," *Nation,* 21 February 1942, 4 ff.

71. Lionel Gelber, "American Jewry, Bethink Ye! A Plea for a Realistic Policy Abroad," *MJ* 31 (January–March 1943): 1–14.

72. John Morton Blum, *Roosevelt and Morgenthau: A Revision and Condensation of "From the Morgenthau Diaries"* (Boston: Houghton Mifflin, 1970), 583.

73. AJC file, Reconstruction, World War, 1939–45, press release, 21 March 1945, "President Roosevelt Discusses Post-war Problems with AJC Head, Judge Proskauer Presents Suggestions in Connection with San Francisco Conference."

74. *CJR* 7 (October 1944): 557–58, Review of Yiddish Press; Hannah Arendt, "German Guilt," *Jewish Frontier,* December 1979, 36–41 (reprinted from January 1945 issue).

75. Frommer, "American Jewish Congress," 440; *Congress Weekly,* 6 October 1944, 3–4; Wise, *Challenging Years,* 210.

BIBLIOGRAPHICAL ESSAY

General

Although research on specific aspects of the American Jewish experience between 1920 and 1945 is extensive, there is no single work that deals with all aspects of this period. Deborah D. Moore's *At Home in America: Second Generation New York Jews* (New York: Columbia University Press, 1981) is a useful social history that takes the story to the mid-thirties. The well-written *World of Our Fathers: The Journey of the East European Jews to America and the Life They Found and Made,* by Irving Howe (New York: Simon and Schuster, 1976), presents a highly selective reading of this period. My own *Zion in America: The Jewish Experience from Colonial Times to the Present* (New York: Hippocrene, 1974) and *A Midrash on American Jewish History* (Albany: SUNY Press, 1982), as well as Lucy S. Dawidowicz, *On Equal Terms: Jews in America, 1881–1981* (New York: Holt, 1982), and Arthur Hertzberg, *The Jews in America: Four Centuries of an Uneasy Encounter: A History* (New York: Simon and Schuster, 1989), are general overviews. Hertzberg should be used with great care. That is also true of Abraham J. Karp, *Haven and Home: A History of the Jews in America* (New York: Schocken, 1985), and Stanley Feldstein, *The Land That I Show You: Three Centuries of Jewish Life in America* (New York: Anchor, 1978). Nathan Glazer's *American Judaism* (Chicago: University of Chicago Press, 1972) is now dated but remains useful for overarching concepts.

Most useful for the general immigrant and ethnic context are John Bodnar, *The Transplanted: A History of Immigrants in Urban America* (Bloomington: University of Indiana Press, 1985); Thomas Kessner, *The Golden Door: Italian and Jewish Immigrant Mobility in New York City, 1880–1915* (New York: Oxford University Press, 1977); John Higham, *Send These to Me: Jews and Other Immigrants in Urban America* (New York: Atheneum, 1975); and Ronald Bayor, *Neighbors in Conflict: The Irish, Germans, Jews and Italians of New York City* (Baltimore: Johns Hopkins University Press, 1978).

The demographic data, catalogs of communal and religious organizations, and statistics on Jewish participation in national and local politics are found in the *American Jewish Year Book (AJYB)* published by the American Jewish Committee. It is indispensable for such an undertaking. It has been supplemented in this work by the files carefully maintained by the staff of the AJCOMM library, which contain newspaper clippings, internal memoranda, and scholarly papers on all public aspects of Jewish life during the interwar period. They are referred to in the footnotes by their file classification; for example, "AJC file, World War, 1939–45," or "Jews in the United States, Cultural Life." The bulk of the journal articles that form the backbone of this work are found in the *American Jewish Historical Quarterly (AJHQ)*, which was renamed *American Jewish History (AJH)* in 1978. These articles are supplemented by those appearing in the *American Jewish Archives (AJA)*, *Jewish Social Studies (JSS)*, the *YIVO Annual of Jewish Social Science*, and occasionally in journals such as *Commentary* and its predecessor the *American Jewish Record, Midstream, Jewish Quarterly Review, Jewish Social Service*, and *Jewish Frontier*. *Menorah Journal (MJ, 1915–45)* is indispensable for contemporary analysis. Although it represented a distinct "uptown view" of events and issues, the weekly *American Hebrew (AH)* is the best Anglo-Jewish journal for serving the historian as a newspaper of record. It should be supplemented by the Yiddish dailies the *Forward, Der Tag*, and *Der Morgen Dzhurnal*.

The most recent archival research in this book is gleaned from doctoral dissertations. Most useful were Sheldon M. Neuringer, "American Jewry and U.S. Immigration Policy, 1881–1953" (University of Wisconsin, 1971); Morris Frommer, "The American Jewish Congress: A History" (Ohio State University, 1978); Sarah L. Schmitt, "Horace M. Kallen and the Americanization of Zionism" (University of Maryland, 1973); Allen L. Kadegan, "The Formation of Soviet Jewish Territorial Units, 1924–1937" (Columbia University, 1985); Jerome M. Kutnick, "Non-Zionist Leadership: Max Warburg, 1919–1927" (Brandeis University, 1983); David H. Shpiro, "From Philanthropy to Activism: The Political Transformation of American Zionism in the Holocaust Years" (Hebrew University of Jerusalem, n.d.); Werner Cohn, "Sources of American Jewish Liberalism" (New School for Social Research, 1956); Michele H. Pavin, "Sports and Leisure of the American Jewish Community, 1848–1976" (Ohio State University, 1981); Robert E. Quigley, "American Catholic Opinion of Mexican Anticlericism, 1910–1936" (University of Pennsylvania, 1965); Myron Scholnick, "The New Deal and Anti-Semitism in America" (University of Maryland, 1978); Dean Banks, "Creating an 'An American Dilemma': The Impact of Nazi Racism upon Intergroup Relations, 1933–1945" (University of Texas at Austin, 1975); Isaac Neustadt, "The Unending Task: Efforts to Unite American Jewry from the American Jewish Congress to the American Jewish

Conference" (Brandeis University, 1980); Edward D. Pinsky, "Cooperation among American Jewish Organizations in Their Efforts to Rescue European Jewry during the Holocaust, 1939–1945" (New York University, 1980); Isabel B. Price, "Black Response to Anti-Semitism: Negroes and Jews in New York to World War II" (University of New Mexico, 1973); Hasia Diner, "In the Almost Promised Land: Jewish Leaders and Blacks, 1915–1935" (University of Illinois, Chicago Circle, 1975); and Leo Kanawanda, Jr., "Franklin D. Roosevelt's Diplomacy and American Catholics, Italians and Jews" (University of Michigan, 1982).

Much information and local color can be gleaned from published memoirs, correspondence, biographies and autobiographies, oral interviews, collections, and transcriptions, and from journalistic accounts of these years. The most useful of the last mentioned is Judd Teller's *Strangers and Natives: The Evolution of the American Jew from 1921 to the Present* (New York: Dell, 1968). Isaac Metzker, *A Bintel Brief: Sixty Years of Letters from the Lower East Side to the Jewish Daily Forward* (New York: Doubleday, 1971), is good for immediacy of the individual experience. I have used the oral history collection of Columbia University and the Wiener Library of the AJCOMM. The most useful of the transcribed interviews is that of Bernard Richards at the Columbia University Oral History Library. Two published books based on oral interviews are useful primarily for color and atmosphere. They are Neil M. Cowan and Ruth S. Cowan, *Our Parents' Lives: The Americanization of the Eastern European Jews* (New York: Basic Books, 1989), and Howard Simons, *Jewish Times: Voices of the American Jewish Experience* (Boston: Houghton Mifflin, 1988). Most useful was my own interview, done with Richard Tedlow, of Leonard Goldenson in *American Jewish History* 72 (September 1982): 108–21.

Indispensable for gaining a knowledge of the period are several collections of published correspondence. Most important are Cyrus Adler, *Selected Letters,* ed. Ira Robinson (Philadelphia: Jewish Publication Society, 1985); Charles Reznikoff, ed., *Louis Marshall, Champion of Liberty: Selected Papers and Addresses,* 2 vols. (Philadelphia: Jewish Publication Society, 1957); Arthur Goren, *Dissenter in Zion: From the Writings of Judah L. Magnes* (Cambridge: Harvard University Press, 1982); Max Freedman, ed., *Roosevelt and Frankfurter: Their Correspondence, 1928–1945* (Boston: Little, Brown, 1967)

Much of the best history for the interwar period is contained in memoirs, autobiographies, and biographies. The following have been most useful. Morton Rosenstock, *Louis Marshall, Defender of Jewish Rights* (Detroit: Wayne State University Press, 1965); Carl H. Voss, *Rabbi and Minister: The Friendship of Stephen S. Wise and John Haynes Holmes* (New York: World, 1964); Melvin Urofsky, *A Voice That Spoke for Justice: The Life and Times of Stephen S. Wise* (Albany: SUNY Press, 1982); Stephen S. Wise, *Challenging Years: The Auto-*

biography of Stephen Wise (New York: Putnam, 1949); Morris R. Cohen, *A Dreamer's Journey* (Boston: Beacon, 1949); Emanuel Celler, *You Never Leave Brooklyn: The Autobiography of Emanuel Celler* (New York: Day, 1953); Ronald M. Steel, *Walter Lippmann and the American Century* (New York: Vintage, 1981); William S. Paley, *As It Happened* (New York: Doubleday, 1979); Norman Podhoretz, *Making It* (New York: Random House, 1967); Julius Haber, *The Odyssey of an American Zionist: Fifty Years of Zionist History* (New York: Twayne, 1956); Bernard Rosenblatt, *Two Generations of Zionism: Historical Recollections of an American Zionist* (New York: Sheingold, 1967); Alfred Kazin, *A Walker in the City* (New York: Harcourt, 1951); Louis Lipsky, *Memoirs in Profile* (Philadelphia: Jewish Publication Society, 1975); Joseph Hyman, *Twenty-five Years of American Aid to Jews Overseas* (New York: Joint Distribution Committee, 1939); Sol Bloom, *The Autobiography of Sol Bloom* (New York: Putnam, 1948); Elizabeth Perry, *Belle Moskowitz: Feminine Politics and the Exercise of Power in the Age of Alfred E. Smith* (New York: Oxford, 1987); Marc L. Raphael, *Abba Hillel Silver: A Profile in American Judaism* (New York: Holmes and Meier, 1989); David Dubinsky and A. H. Raskin, *David Dubinsky: A Life with Labor* (New York: Simon and Schuster, 1977); Emanuel Neumann, *In the Arena: An Autobiographical Memoir* (New York: Herzl, 1976); Ben Hecht, *Child of the Century* (New York: Simon and Schuster, 1954); Dan Kurtzman, *Ben Gurion: Prophet of Fire* (New York: Simon and Schuster, 1983); Alan Brinkley, *Voices of Protest: Huey Long, Father Coughlin and the Great Depression* (New York: Vintage, 1983); John Morton Blum, *Roosevelt and Morgenthau: A Revision and Condensation of "From the Morgenthau Diaries"* (Boston: Houghton Mifflin, 1970); Arthur Mann, *La Guardia, A Fighter against His Time* (New York: Lippincott, 1954); Paul Jacobs, *Is Curly Jewish?* (New York: Atheneum, 1965); Joseph M. Proskauer, *A Segment of My Time* (New York: Farrar, Straus, 1950); Michael E. Parrish, *Felix Frankfurter and His Times: The Reform Years* (New York: Free Press, 1982); Bruce A. Murphy, *The Frankfurter-Brandeis Connection: The Secret Political Activities of the Two Supreme Court Justices* (New York: Oxford University Press, 1982); Ronald Sanders, *Reflections in a Teapot: The Personal History of a Time* (New York: Harper, 1972).

Important information is also contained in histories of local Jewish communities. Most useful are Alter F. Landesman, *Brownsville: The Birth, Development and Passing of a Jewish Community in New York* (New York: Bloch, 1969); Louis Switchkow and Lloyd Gartner, *History of the Jews of Milwaukee* (Philadelphia: Jewish Publication Society, 1962); Max Vorspan and Lloyd P. Gartner, *History of the Jews of Los Angeles* (San Marino, Calif.: Huntington Library, 1970); Selig Adler, *From Ararat to Suburbia: The History of the Jewish Community of Buffalo* (Philadelphia: Jewish Publication Society, 1960); Jeffrey

Gurock, *When Harlem Was Jewish* (New York: Columbia University Press, 1979); and William Toll, *The Making of an Ethnic Middle Class: Portland Jewry over Four Generations* (Albany: SUNY Press, 1983). Important for demographic and sociological data on the Jews of Providence, Rhode Island, is Sidney Goldstein and Calvin Goldscheider, *Jewish Americans: Three Generations in a Jewish Community* (Englewood Cliffs, N.J.: Prentice-Hall, 1968). A collective model for writing community history is presented in Murray Friedman, ed., *Philadelphia Jewish Life, 1940–1985* (Ardmore, Pa.: Seth Press, 1986). The precedent has been followed by the Jewish community of Kansas City, Missouri.

Anti-Semitism

The impact of latent and overt anti-Semitism on Jewish perception is a major theme of this book. I have used my own "Finding a Conceptual Framework for the Study of American Antisemitism," *Jewish Social Studies* 47 (Summer–Fall 1985):313–26, as the conceptual underpinning. It can be supplemented by Gertrude Selznick and Stephen Steinberg, *The Tenacity of Prejudice: Anti-Semitism in Contemporary America* (New York: Harper, 1969). The best collection of survey research for this period is found in Charles H. Stember, ed., *Jews in the Mind of America* (New York: Basic Books, 1966). Two anthologies worth noting are Leonard Dinnerstein, *Uneasy at Home: Antisemitism and the American Jewish Experience* (New York: Columbia University Press, 1987), and David A. Gerber, ed., *Anti-Semitism in American History* (Urbana: University of Illinois Press, 1986). Morton Borden, *Jews, Turks and Infidels* (Chapel Hill: University of North Carolina Press, 1984), and Milton Plesur, *Jewish Life in Twentieth Century America: Challenge and Accommodation* (Chicago: Nelson-Hall, 1982), contain much new information. The nativist aspect is examined by John Higham, *Strangers in the Land: Patterns of American Nativism, 1860–1925* (New York: Atheneum, 1970). It should be supplemented by David H. Bennett, *The Party of Fear: From Nativist Movement to the New Right in American History* (Chapel Hill: University of North Carolina Press, 1988). Restriction in the universities is examined in Stephen Steinberg, *The Academic Melting Pot: Catholics and Jews in American Higher Education* (New York: McGraw-Hill, 1974); Harold Wechsler, *The Qualified Student: A History of Selective College Admission in America* (New York: Wiley, 1977); Marcia G. Synnott, *The Half-Opened Door: Discrimination and Admissions at Harvard, Yale, and Princeton, 1900–1970* (Westport, Conn.: Greenwood, 1979); Dan A. Oren, *Joining the Club: A History of the Jews at Yale* (New York: Yale University Press, 1987). Michael Dobkowski, *The Tarnished Dream: The Basis of American Anti-Semitism* (Westport, Conn.: Greenwood, 1979); and Saul Friedman, *The Inci-*

dent at Messina: The Blood Libel in America (New York: Stein, 1978), are good for specific incidents. Examining the linkage between Jews and political radicalism, a major theme of anti-Semites, see Melech Epstein, *The Jew and Communism: The Story of Early Communist Victories and Ultimate Defeats in the Jewish Community, USA, 1919–1941* (New York: Trade Union Sponsoring Committee, 1959); Leo P. Ribuffo, "Henry Ford and the International Jew," *American Jewish History* 69 (June 1980): 437–77; Henry L. Feingold, "Anti-Semitism and the Anti-Semitic Imagination: A Case Study, the 1920s," in *A Midrash on American Jewish History* (Albany: SUNY Press, 1983), 171–91; Nathan Belth, *A Promise to Keep* (New York: New York Times Books, 1979). Donald S. Strong, *Organized Anti-Semitism in America: The Rise of Group Prejudice during the Decade 1930–1940* (Washington, D.C.: American Council on Public Affairs, 1941), is a good summary of the topic. Foreign support of anti-Semitism during the thirties is examined by Sander E. Diamond, *The Nazi Movement in the United States, 1924–1941* (Ithaca, N.Y.: Cornell University Press, 1974); Leland Bell, *In Hitler's Shadow: The Anatomy of American Nazism* (Port Washington, N.Y.: Kennicat, 1973); and Glen Jeansonne, *Gerald L. K. Smith, Minister of Hate* (New Haven: Yale University Press, 1988).

The motivation of immigration restrictionists can be gleaned from the congressional hearings, especially the House Committee on Immigration and Naturalization, *A Bill to Provide for the Protection of the Citizens of the U.S.* (H.R. 14461), 67th Cong., 3rd sess., 5 January 1921; idem, *Restriction of Immigration* (H.R. 5, 101, 561), 68th Cong., 1st sess., 3 January 1924. Michael R. Marrus, *The Unwanted: European Refugees in the Twentieth Century* (New York: Oxford University Press, 1985), contains the best general examination of the refugee problem.

Religion

Research on the American Jewish religious scene is prolific. Indispensable for a conceptual framework are Arnold M. Eisen, *The Chosen People in America: A Study of Jewish Religious Ideology* (Bloomington: Indiana University Press, 1983); Jonathan Woocher, *Sacred Survival: The Civil Religion of American Jews* (Bloomington: Indiana University Press, 1987); Charles S. Liebman, *The Ambivalent American Jew: Politics, Religion and Family in American Jewish Life* (Philadelphia: Jewish Publication Society, 1973); and Will Herberg, *Protestant, Catholic, Jew: An Essay in Religious Sociology* (Garden City, N.Y.: Doubleday, 1955). A readable general view is Joseph L. Blau, *Judaism in America: From Curiosity to Third Faith* (Chicago: University of Chicago Press, 1976). An essential collection of essays on American Judaism is Jacob Neusner, ed., *Understanding American Judaism*, vol. 1, *The Rabbi and the Synagogue*, and vol. 2, *Sectors of American Judaism* (New York: Ktav, 1975). The best study of the Reform movement is Michael Meyer, *Response to Modernity: A History of the Reform Movement in Judaism* (New York: Oxford University Press, 1988). Marshall Sklare, *Conservative Judaism: An American Religious Movement* (New York: Schocken, 1972); Mordecai Waxman, ed., *Tradition and Change: The Development of Conservative Judaism* (New York: Burning Bush Press, 1958); Moshe Davis, *The Emergence of Conservative Judaism* (Philadelphia: Jewish Publication Society, 1963); and Abraham Karp, *A History of the United Synagogue of America, 1913–1963* (New York: United Synagogue of America, 1964), tell the story of the Conservative movement. There is no compendium of works that examine the fragmented Orthodox movement in its entirety. The best conceptualization can be found in Charles S. Liebman, "Orthodoxy in American Jewish Life," *American Jewish Yearbook* 66 (1964–65). Gilbert Klaperman, *The Story of Yeshiva University: The First Jewish University in America* (New York: Macmillan, 1969), is good for the story of that faction. William Helmreich, *The World of the Yeshiva: An Intimate Portrait of Orthodox Jewry* (New York: Free Press, 1982), presents sociological insights. The entire issue of *American Jewish History,* vol. 69 (December 1979), is devoted to Orthodoxy. Solomon Poll, *The Hasidic Community of Williamsburg* (New York: Free Press, 1962), examines that European transplant, and Jacob Agus, "The Conservative Movement: Reconstructionism," in Neusner, *Understanding American Judaism,* 2:213, and Mordecai Kaplan, *Judaism as a Civilization: Towards Reconstruction of American Jewish Life* (New York: Macmillan, 1934), examine this dissident branch of the Conservative movement. Lloyd Gartner, *Jewish Education in the U.S.: A Documentary History* (New York: Columbia Teachers College Press, 1969), presents a picture of the uneven religious education enterprise.

Culture and Acculturation

A good collection of material is available in AJC file, Jews in the U.S., Cultural Life. The conceptual framework is set in Salo Baron, "Can American Jewry Be Culturally Creative?" in *Steeled by Adversity: Essays and Addresses on American Jewish Life,* ed. Salo Baron and Jeannette Baron (Philadelphia: Jewish Publication Society, 1971). The development of Yiddish theater is described in Nahama Sandrow, *Vagabond Stars: A World History of Yiddish Theater* (New York: Harper, 1977), and David Lifson, *The Yiddish Theater in America* (New York: Yoseloff, 1965). Howe's *World of Our Fathers* (see above) is strong in the culture area. Louis Harap, *The Image of the Jew in American Literature* (Philadelphia: Jewish Publication Society, 1974), and John J. Appel, "Jews in American Caricature, 1845–1950," *American Jewish History* 71 (September 1981): 103–33, examine some cultural aspects of anti-Semitism. The place of Jews in journalism is examined by Stephen J. Whitfield, "The American Jew as Journalist," in *Studies in Contemporary Jewry,* ed. Ezra Mendelsohn (New York: Oxford University Press, 1987), 3:162 ff. The Jewish cultural and intellectual scene is probed in Whitfield's *Voices of Jacob, Hands of Esau: Jews in American Life and Thought* (Hamden, Conn.: Archon, 1984). A cursory view of Jewish impact on American culture is found in Charles A. Madison, *Jewish Publishing in America: The Impact of Jewish Writing on American Culture* (New York: Sanhedrin, 1976). Alexander Bloom, *Prodigal Son: The New York Intellectuals and Their World* (New York: Oxford University Press, 1986) gives a picture of an intellectual scene in which Jews were prominent, as does Irving Howe, "The New York Intellectuals: A Chronicle and a Critique," *Commentary* 46 (October 1968): 29–51, and Charles Kadushin, *The American Intellectual Elite* (Boston: Little, Brown, 1974). Jonathan D. Sarna, *JPS: The Americanization of Jewish Culture* (Philadelphia: Jewish Publication Society, 1989), serves as a model of the history of an agency devoted to the dissemination of Judaic culture.

Frederick L. Allen, *Only Yesterday* (New York: Harper, 1959), is a good beginning for a picture of the changing behavioral mores of the twenties. Mark Zborowski and Elizabeth Herzog, *Life Is with People: The Culture of the Shtetl* (New York: Schocken, 1952), presents a background for the residual immigrant culture but should be used with care. The changing role of Jewish women is examined in Rudolf Glanz, *The Jewish Women in America: Two Generations,* 2 vols. (New York: Ktav, 1976); Jacob R. Marcus, *The American Jewish Woman: A Documentary History* (New York: Ktav, 1981); and Charlotte Baum et al., *The Jewish Woman in America* (New York: Dial, 1976).

The delicate subject of Jewish criminality is examined in Edward Bristow, *The Jewish Fight against White Slavery* (New York: Schocken, 1983). Daniel Bell, "Crime as an American Way of Life: A Queer Ladder of Mobility," in *The End of Ideology* (New York: Collier/Harper, 1962), establishes a useful conceptual context. These works need to be supplemented with Albert Fried, *The Rise and Fall of the Jewish Gangster in America* (New York: Holt, 1980), and Jena Joselit, *Our Gang: Jewish Crime and the New York Jewish Community, 1900–1940* (Bloomington: University of Indiana Press, 1983). Harold P. Gastwirt, *Fraud, Corruption and Holiness: The Controversy over the Supervision of Jewish Dietary Practices in New York City* (New York: Kennicat, 1974), gives a good picture of crime related to the kashrut problem.

Commercial Activity

Success in the commercial sphere is at the center of the Jewish experience during the years of this study. Nathan Glazer and Daniel Moynihan, *Beyond the*

Melting Pot: The Negroes, Puerto Ricans, Jews, Italians, and Irish of New York City (Cambridge: MIT Press, 1963), is a good starting point. A conceptual framework for the Jewish approach to business is found in Abraham Korman, *The Outsiders: Jews and Corporate America* (Lexington, Mass.: Lexington Books, 1988). The general background of the economy of the twenties is related in William Leuchtenberg, *The Perils of Prosperity, 1914–1932* (Chicago: University of Chicago Press, 1960). It is supplemented by James W. Prothro, *The Dollar Decade: Business Ideas of the 1920s* (Baton Rouge: Louisiana State University Press, 1954). A revisionist view regarding how mobility was achieved is presented by Selma Berrol, "Education and Economic Mobility: The Jewish Experience in New York City, 1880–1920," *American Jewish Historical Quarterly* 65 (March 1976): 251–71. A fuller view is presented by Henry L. Feingold, "Investing in Themselves: The Harvard Case and the Origins of the Third American-Jewish Commercial Elite," *American Jewish History* 77 (June 1988): 530–53. A complete picture of comparative mobility is presented in Joel Perlmann, *Ethnic Differences: Schooling and Social Structure among the Irish, Italians, Jews and Blacks in an American City, 1880–1835* (New York: Cambridge University Press, 1988). Vincent P. Carosso, "A Financial Elite: New York's German Jewish Investment Bankers," *Amerian Jewish Historical Quarterly* 66 (September 1976): 84–87, touches on the Jewish banking story in the twenties. The role of communal credit lines is examined by Shelley Tennenbaum, "Immigrants and Capital: Jewish Loan Societies in the U.S., 1880–1945," *American Jewish History* 76 (September 1986): 67–77. The best specific data come from the study by the editors of *Fortune, Jews in America* (New York, 1936). There are dozens of books on Jewish businesses and businessmen. Representative are Leon Harris, *Merchant Princes: An Intimate History of Jewish Families Who Built Great Department Stores* (New York: Harper, 1979); E. Rosenbaum and A. J. Sherman, *M. M. Warburg and Co., 1798–1938* (London: Hurst, 1976); and Stephen Birmingham, *Our Crowd: The Great Jewish Families of New York* (New York: Harper, 1967).

The story of Jewish labor during the interwar years is told by Nathan Reich, "The 'Americanization' of Jewish Unionism: A Two-Way Process," *Jewish Quarterly Review* 45 (April 1955): 540–61, and Will Herberg, "The Jewish Labor Movement in the U.S.," *American Jewish Yearbook* 53 (1952–53): 5–74. Melech Epstein, *Jewish Labor in the U.S.A.*, 2 vols. (New York: Ktav, 1969), is complete but difficult to read. The professionalization process is examined in Barton J. Bledstein, *The Culture of Professionalism: The Middle Class and the Development of Higher Education in America* (New York: Norton, 1976). The development of professional social work, which was favored by Jews, is examined in Roy Lubove, *The Professional Altruist: The Emergence of Social Work as a Career, 1880–1930* (Cambridge: Harvard University Press, 1965).

Bibliographical Essay

Organization, Politics and Zionism

For a conceptual framework of Jewish organizational life it is best to begin with Daniel J. Elazar, *Community and Polity: The Organizational Dynamics of American Jewry* (Philadelphia: Jewish Publication Society, 1976), and Arthur A. Goren, *New York Jews and the Quest for Community: The Kehillah Experiment, 1908–1922* (New York: Columbia University Press, 1970). The far-flung organizational network is annually cataloged in the *American Jewish Yearbook* and is supplemented by Michael N. Dobkowski, ed., *Jewish-American Voluntary Organizations* (Westport, Conn.: Greenwood, 1986). The fund-raising apparatus is described in Milton Goldin, *Why They Give: American Jews and Their Philanthropies* (New York: Macmillan, 1976); Harry L. Lurie, *A Heritage Affirmed: The Jewish Federation Movement in America* (Philadelphia: Jewish Publication Society, 1961); Marc Raphael, *Understanding American Jewish Philanthropy* (New York: Ktav, 1979), and idem, *A History of the United Jewish Appeal, 1939–1982* (Providence, R.I.: Brown University Press, 1982); Yehuda Bauer, *My Brother's Keeper: A History of the American Jewish Joint Distribution Committee, 1929–1939* (Philadelphia: Jewish Publication Society, 1974); Naomi Cohen, *Not Free to Desist: The American Jewish Committee, 1906–1966* (Philadelphia: Jewish Publication Society, 1972); Deborah D. Moore, *B'nai B'rith and the Challenge of Ethnic Leadership* (Albany: SUNY Press, 1981). The far-flung landsmanshaften and their relation to communal credit lines is probed in Hannah Kliger, "Tradition of Grass Roots Organization and Leadership: The Continuity of Landsmanshaften in New York," *American Jewish History* 76 (September 1986): 25–39; I. E. Rontch, "The Present State of the Landsmanshaften," *Jewish Social Service Quarterly* 15 (June 1939): 360–78; and Daniel Soyer, "Between Two Worlds: The Jewish Landsmanshaften and Questions of Immigrant Identity," *American Jewish History* 76 (September 1986): 7–8.

The emergence of American Zionism is examined in Naomi Cohen, *American Jews and the Zionist Idea* (New York: Ktav, 1975), and idem, *The Year after the Riots: American Response to the Palestine Crisis of 1929–1930* (Detroit: Wayne State University Press, 1987); Ben Halpern, *The American Jew: A Zionist Analysis* (New York: Schocken, 1983); Melvin Urofsky, *American Zionism: From Herzl to Holocaust* (New York: Doubleday, 1975); Ben Halpern, *A Clash of Heroes: Brandeis, Weizmann and American Zionism* (New York: Oxford University Press, 1987); Yonathan Shapiro, *Leadership of the American Zionist Organization, 1897–1930* (Urbana: University of Illinois Press, 1971); Aaron Berman, *Nazism, the Jews and American Zionism, 1933–1948* (Detroit: Wayne State University Press, 1990); Stuart E. Knee, *The Concept of Zionist Dissent in the American Mind, 1917–1941* (New York: Speller, 1979); Nathan Kaganoff, ed., *Solidarity and Kinship: Essays on American Zionism* (Waltham, Mass.: American Jewish Historical Society, 1980); Samuel Halperin, *The Political World of American Zionism* (Detroit: Wayne State University Press, 1961); Walter Laqueur, *A History of Zionism* (New York: Holt, 1972).

Jewish politics and political culture are best viewed in the context of American politics, as in Warren Moscow, *Politics in the Empire State* (New York: Knopf, 1948); Edward Flynn, *You're the Boss* (New York: Viking, 1948); Samuel Lubell, *The Future of American Politics* (New York: Harper, 1965); and John L. Shover, *Politics in the Nineteen Twenties* (Waltham, Mass.: Ginn, 1970). Foreign policy issues are fully explored in Alfred O. Hero, Jr., *American Religious Groups View Foreign Policy: Trends in Rank and File Opinion, 1937–1969* (Durham, N.C.: Duke University Press, 1973); Cyrus Adler and Aaron Margalith, *With Firmness in the Right: American Diplomatic Action Affecting Jews, 1840–1945* (New York: Arno, 1977); and Louis L. Gerson, *The Hyphenate in Recent American Politics and Diplomacy* (Lawrence: University of Kansas Press, 1964); Nathaniel Weyl, *The Jew in American Politics* (New Rochelle, N.Y.: Arlington House, 1976); Daniel Elazar, ed., *Kinship and Consent: The Jewish Political Tradition and Its Contemporary Uses* (New York: University Press of America, 1983; Arthur Liebman, "The Ties That Bind: The Jewish Support of the Left in the U.S.," *American Jewish Historical Quarterly* 66 (December 1976): 285–321; Edward S. Shapiro, "The Approach of War: Isolationism and Anti-Semitism," *American Jewish Historical Quarterly* 74 (September 1984): 45–65. Lawrence Fuchs, *The Political Behavior of American Jews* (Glencoe, Ill.: Free Press, 1956), should be used with care.

American Jewry and World War II

Virtually a book a year now appears on the relation of the Roosevelt administration to the Holocaust, but there are few reliable works on Roosevelt's relationship with American Jewry. Contrasting views are presented in two books: David S. Wyman, *The Abandonment of the Jews: America and the Holocaust, 1941–1945* (New York: Pantheon, 1984), and Henry L. Feingold, *The Politics of Rescue: The Roosevelt Administration and the Holocaust, 1938–1945* (New York: Holocaust Library, 1980). Richard D. Breitman and Alan M. Kraut, *American Refugee Policy and European Jewry, 1933–1945* (Bloomington: Indiana University Press, 1987), places the refugee problem in a broader historical context. Haskel Lookstein, *Were We Our Brothers' Keepers? The Public Response of American Jews to the Holocaust, 1938–1945* (New York: Hartmore, 1986), and Seymour M. Finger, ed., *American Jewry during the Holocaust* (New York: Holmes and Meier, 1984), are polemical, as is Edwin Black, *The Transfer Agreement: The Untold Story of the Secret Pact between the*

Third Reich and Jewish Palestine (New York: Macmillan, 1984). Barbara M. Stewart, in *United States Government Policy on Refugees from Nazism, 1933–1940* (New York: Garland, 1984), has used the private papers of her father, James G. McDonald, who served as chairman of the President's Advisory Committee on Political Refugees. Shlomo Shafir, "American Diplomats in Berlin (1933–1939) and Their Attitude to the Nazi Persecution of Jews," *Yad Vashem Studies* 9 (1973): 71–104, is a good probe of a complex issue. Most helpful is "AJC file, World War, 1939–45, Atrocities, Reactions, Statements."

Henry L. Feingold, " 'Courage First and Intelligence Second': The American Jewish Secular Elite, Roosevelt and the Failure to Rescue," *American Jewish History* 72 (June 1983): 459, presents the activities of the "Jew Deal." It can be supplemented with Zosa Szajkowski, "The Attitude of American Jews to Refugees from Germany in the 1930s," *American Jewish Historical Quarterly* 61 (December 1971): 101–43. Moshe Gottlieb, *American Anti-Nazi Resistance, 1933–1941* (New York: Ktav, 1982), examines the boycott and other activities. Deborah Lipstadt, *Beyond Belief: The American Press and the Coming of the Holocaust, 1933–1945* (New York: Free Press, 1986), examines the press coverage of the Holocaust. Sharon R. Lowenstein, *Token Refuge: The Story of the Jewish Refugee Shelter at Oswego, 1944–1946* (Bloomington: Indiana University Press, 1986), and Ruth Gruber, *Haven: The Unknown Story of One Thousand World War II Refugees* (New York: Coward-McCann, 1983), present the story of the episode that marked the zenith of the American rescue effort. The Holocaust saga is concluded with Robert Abzug's *Inside The Vicious Heart: America and the Liberation of the Nazi Concentration Camps* (New York: Oxford University Press, 1987).

The story of how the immigrants fared in America and their contribution is told by Herbert A. Strauss, "The Immigration and Acculturation of the German Jew in the U.S. of A.," *Leo Baeck Yearbook* 16 (1971); Haim Genizi, "New York Is Big—America Is Bigger: The Resettlement of Refugees from Nazism, 1936–1945," *Jewish Social Studies* 46 (Winter 1984): 61–72; Anthony Heilbut, *Exiled in Paradise: German Refugee Artists and Intellectuals in America from the 1930s to the Present* (New York: Viking, 1983); and Steven M. Lowenstein, *Frankfurt on the Hudson: The German Jewish Community of Washington Heights, 1933–1983, Its Structure and Culture* (Detroit: Wayne State University Press, 1988), present various aspects of the accommodation of and to refugees.

Jewish activity during the war is explored in Isidore Kaufman, *American Jews in World War II: The Story of 550,000 Fighters for Freedom*, 2 vols. (New York: Dial, 1947), and in Clayton R. Koppes and Gregory Black, *Hollywood Goes to War: How Politics, Profits and Propaganda Shaped World War II Movies* (Glencoe, Ill.: Free Press, 1987).

Black-Jewish relations during the thirties and the war are covered in Robert Weisbord and Arthur Stein, *Bittersweet Encounter: The Afro-American and the American Jew* (Westport, Conn.: Negro University Press, 1970). Much of the information for Jewish postwar planning comes from "AJC file, Reconstruction, World War, 1939–45."

INDEX

A

Abel, Lionel, 79
Abie's Irish Rose (Nichols), 82, 87
Acculturation, 35–37, 62, 82–83, 219, 234;
    anti-Semitism and, 2, 54; and crime, 37,
    44–45, 48–54; education and, 23, 47,
    54–58, 205; and families, 37–39, 42,
    44–45, 48; and Judaism, 36, 43, 58, 97,
    98; in literature and film, 72–73, 81,
    86–87; popular culture and, 60; social
    organizations and, 58–60; sports in,
    20–21, 60, 61; transitional culture, 36,
    59, 63, 75; and women, 36, 38, 39–40,
    41, 42–48, 49; and Zionism, 172. *See
    also* Americanization; Assimilation
Adenauer, Konrad, 263
Adler, Cyrus: and American anti-Semi-
    tism, 8, 10; on immigration and
    Judaism, 32; on Jewish crime, 50; at
    Jewish Theological Seminary, 92, 112;
    and Nazi Germany, 223; on stock mar-
    ket crash, 146; and Yiddish press, 70;
    and Zionism, 166–67, 183, 185, 186, 238
Adler, Stella, 67
Adorno, Theodor, 256
Adreyev, Leonid, 65
Adultery, 40
Advertising industry, 130
African-Americans, 254–55
Agriculture: Great Depression and, 125;
    in Palestine, 168, 180, 182; poultry
    farming, 151; Russian Jewish resettle-
ment and, 178–79, 180; Stalinist
    collectivization of, 181, 207
Agudath HaRabbanim, 108, 109, 116
Agudath Israel of America, 110
Alexander, Hartley B., 76
Alfred A. Knopf, Inc., 83, 130
Algonquin Circle, 78
Alien Deportation and Exclusion League,
    229
Amalgamated Clothing Workers of Amer-
    ica (ACWA), 133, 136
American Continental Corporation, 128
American Council for Judaism (ACFJ),
    102, 103, 243, 246, 247
American Federation of Labor, 132–33
American Hebrew, 35, 70, 160; on Ameri-
    can anti-Semitism, 13, 19, 85; and
    Jewish educational performance, 19,
    20, 22, 23, 143–44; on Jewish literature,
    81; on Judaism, 93, 96; and philan-
    thropy, 59; on Yiddish language, 75, 88;
    and Zionism, 170, 183
American Israelite, 70
Americanization, 36, 38, 59; interfaith
    movement and, 123; Jewish law and,
    108–9; and politics, 200, 214; and role
    of synagogues, 31, 93; women, 47; and
    Yiddish culture, 70, 88. *See also*
    Acculturation; Assimilation
American Jewish Committee (AJC), 32,
    38; and Americanization, 31, 88, 160,
    234; and anti-Semitism, 7, 11, 160, 208,
    216, 224, 251, 255; attempt to unify

American Jewry, 159–60, 164, 185, 187, 238–39; conflict with American Jewish Congress, 159–61, 189, 261; founding of, 159; and German boycott, 235–36; membership and constituency, 157, 158, 159, 160, 234; and rise of Nazism and the Holocaust, 160, 208, 236, 238–39, 261, 262; and Zionism, 159, 161, 182, 240, 245, 246

American Jewish Conference, 239, 260, 262

American Jewish Congress: attempt to unify American Jewry, 96, 158, 159, 164, 187, 238, 239, 245; and Communism, 221; conflict with American Jewish Committee, 159–61, 189, 261; and Crimean resettlement, 179, 180; founding of, 158; and German boycott, 236, 237; membership and constituency, 100, 156, 158–59; and rise of Nazism and the Holocaust, 159, 209, 235, 238, 261, 262; and Soviet Union, 207; and women's rights, 42; and Zionism, 158, 159, 180

American Jewish Joint Distribution Committee. *See* Joint Distribution Committee

American Jewish Yearbook, 192

American Labor party, 213–14

American Mizrachi Women, 46

American Organization for Rehabilitation through Training (ORT), 165

American Relief Administration, 177

American Smelting and Refining Company, 141

American Society for Jewish Farm Settlements, 181

American Youth Congress, 221

American Zion Commonwealth, 173

American Zionist Emergency Committee (AZEC), 240–41, 243, 245, 247

Ami, Ben, 65

Amsterdam News, 255

Anarchism, 42

Anathema (Adreyev), 65

Anglo-American Declaration (1943), 246–47

Anglo-Palestine Bank, 230–31

Anti-Catholicism, 3, 25, 199, 252

Anti-Defamation League (ADL), 8, 150, 238, 255–56, 257

Antin, Mary, 81

Anti-Semitism, 82, 148; academic enrollment limits, 1, 14, 15–20, 23, 54–55, 140–41; of blacks, 254–55; blood libel, 2, 4–5, 203; Communism, association of Jews with, 6, 7–8, 199–200, 221, 223–24; in Communist movement, 195; Communist opposition to, 222, 223; employment discrimination, 2–3, 139, 140–41, 144, 150, 153, 253, 258; in Europe, 2, 8, 160, 253; Ford and *Dearborn Independent,* 2, 6, 8–11, 25, 33, 54; Holocaust and, 259–60, 262; and immigration restrictions, 1, 24, 25, 26–27, 28, 227–28; intellectuals and, 77, 79; interfaith movement and, 122, 124, 256; international Jewish conspiracy theory, 6, 7–8, 11, 189, 224, 231, 263; "Jew Deal" epithet, 191, 215–16, 217, 218, 225; Jewish criminality and, 50, 54; Jewish fears of exacerbating, 8, 228; Jewish media control stereotype, 71, 84, 131–32; Jewish reactions to, 2, 5, 8, 9–10, 19, 251; Jewish self-defense, 7, 8, 9–11, 12–13, 135, 160, 165, 223–24, 235, 251–52, 255–56, 257, 258–59; Ku Klux Klan, 3, 183, 190; Nazi, 160, 191, 207–8, 209, 224, 226, 251, 253, 256–57; political opposition to, 3, 191; in politics, 190–92, 204, 208, 210–11, 215–16, 217, 221, 223–24, 252–53; socioeconomic mobility and, 128, 138, 140–41, 253, 255; in the Soviet Union, 27, 180, 206, 223; in the U.S., 1, 204, 242–43, 250–53, 254–56, 257–58, 259–60, 263–64; in U.S. Congress, 1, 6, 208

Anti-Zionism, 149, 170, 177–78, 187, 243–44; Great Britain, 175; labor movement, 135; Palestinian Arabs, 174, 175, 185, 247; Reform Judaism, 101–2, 159, 172–73, 243

Appel, Benjamin, 81

Arabs: opposition to Zionism, 174, 175,

185, 247; of Palestine, Britain and, 228, 243; of Palestine, Zionist concern for protection of, 166–67, 174, 245, 246, 247; Palestine riots, 77, 149, 164–65, 172, 174, 185, 228; U.S. and, 248, 249
Arbeiter Ring. *See* Workmen's Circle
Arbeiter Theater Farband, 67
Arendt, Hannah, 262
Argentina, 177
Arnold, Benedict, 11
Asch, Nathan, 81
Asch, Sholem, 70
Assimilation, 56, 75, 82, 87, 90, 97. *See also* Acculturation; Americanization
Association of Hebrew Orthodox Rabbis of America, 49
Atlantic Charter (1941), 191, 247
August Belmont and Company, 128
Austrian Anschluss, 229
Austrian Jews, 165, 229
Authoritarian Personality (Adorno), 256
Automobile industry, 129
Avukah, 57

B

Babbitt (Lewis), 82
Balfour Declaration (1917), 14, 74; American Jewish organizations and, 159, 161, 166–67, 182; Reform rabbis and, 100, 102; U.S. and, 167, 190; U.S. Congress and, 1, 172, 190
Baltimore, Md., 48, 127, 148, 162, 255
Bankers, 9, 11
Bank failures, 125, 146
Banking, 128–29, 138, 141, 142, 143, 231
Bank of the United States, 146
Baron, Salo W., 260
Baron de Hirsch Fund, 179
Baruch, Bernard, 11, 216, 218, 224
Behrman, Samuel N., 67–68, 82
Beilis, Mendel, 5
Bell, Daniel, 79–80
Benderly, Samson, 56, 74, 118, 120
Ben-Gurion, David, 217, 241–42, 244, 246
Beranger, Clara, 86
Berg, Louis, 77

Bergson, Peter (Hillel Kook), 242, 243, 245
Berkman, Alexander, 6
Berkson, Isaac B., 56, 118, 120
Berle, Adolf, Jr., 194
Berlin, Irving, 60, 80
Berlin, Rabbi Meier, 123–24
Bermuda conference (1943), 233, 242, 260
Bernheimer, Charles, 36
Bernstein, Herman, 7, 13
Bernstein, John L., 27, 30–31
Bernstein, Rabbi Philip, 100
Beth Medrash Govoha, 109–10
Bialik, Hayyim Nahman, 74, 183
Bible Belt, 85
Bingham, Theodore, 48
Blacks. *See* African-Americans
Blood libel, 2, 4–5, 203
Bloom, Sol, 193–94, 247
B'nai B'rith, 94, 100, 157, 164, 236, 238–39, 240, 258
Bootlegging, 49–50
Borscht belt, 62
Boston, Mass., 26, 57, 142, 149, 162, 196, 199–200
Brandeis, Louis D.: as American Zionist leader, 156, 167–68, 172, 174, 176, 182, 218; anti-Semitic attacks on, 216, 224; and development of Palestine, 101, 168, 182, 240; and financial mismanagement in Zionist movement, 168, 169, 173–74; and German Jews, 235; split with Weizmann and WZO, 46, 169, 170, 171–72, 217; as Supreme Court justice, 17, 167, 169, 218
Brasol, Boris, 8–9
Brennglass, Rabbi Berel, 5
Breuer community, 110
Brickner, Rabbi Barnett, 100
Brinig, Myron, 81
Brisbane, Arthur, 11, 12
B'rith Abraham, 59
British Board of Deputies, 262
British Guiana, 242
Bronx County, N.Y., 3, 36, 55, 136, 194
Brooklyn, N.Y., 3, 36, 53, 55, 57, 121, 126, 192, 201

Brooklyn Tablet, 201
Broun, Heywood, 71
Browder, Earl, 222
Brundage, Avery, 209
Bublick, Gedaliah, 24
Buffalo ZOA convention (1920), 170
Bund (General Jewish Workers' Union), 32, 119
Bureau of Jewish Education, 120
Bureau of Jewish Social Research, 38, 145, 163
Burlingham, Charles, 219
Burnett, John L., 25
Business employment, 126, 127-28, 139, 140, 141-42, 152
Businessmen, 54, 82-83, 130, 152
Businesswomen, 44
Butler, Nicholas Murray, 54-55

C

Cahan, Abraham, 14, 69, 73, 197
California, 29, 49, 50
Calish, Rabbi Edward N., 205
Calles, Plutarco Elías, 199
Call It Sleep (Roth), 81
Cameron, E. B., 8-9, 12
Cantor, Eddie, 60
Capitalism, 137, 138, 147, 153
Cardozo, Benjamin N., 203
Carr, Wilbur, 25, 210-11
Celler, Emanuel, 27, 201, 209-10, 214
Central Conference of American Rabbis (CCAR), 205, 255; and Jewish army, 103, 243; and Jewish-Christian relations, 123; and "wine rabbis," 50; and Zionism, 100-101, 102, 186, 243
Chamber, William Astor, 7
Chamberlain, Joseph, 229
Chaplin, Charles, 256-57
Chapman, John Jay, 7
Chicago, Ill., 49, 57, 149, 196
Chicago UAHC convention (1924), 98
Children: acculturation, 35-36, 37, 38, 39, 58; delinquency, 44-45; dependency, 38-39; religious education, 94, 100, 118, 120; secular education, 55, 57; war

and Holocaust refugees, 228, 231-32, 241
Chipkin, Israel, 57, 118, 120
Christian Front, 252
Christianity, 17, 93, 107, 162, 226
Christians, 5, 12; fundamentalism, 4, 96; and German Jewry, 236; interfaith movement, 122-23, 124; missionaries, 94, 123; students, 19, 20; and Sunday laws, 1, 4; and Zionism, 241
Christian Science, 36
Church-state separation, 120, 193, 199
Cincinnati, Ohio, 162
Cities, 14-15, 48, 58, 153, 204, 255; Jewish neighborhoods, 3, 55, 58, 196
City College of New York (CCNY), 15, 20, 21, 22, 56-57, 143, 196
Civil religion, 97, 114, 124
Class struggle, 132, 133
Cleveland, Ohio, 108, 116, 136, 145; ZOA convention (1921), 46, 168, 170-71, 172, 174, 182, 187; ZOA convention (1930), 174
Cohen, Benjamin V., 170, 171, 172, 217-18, 219
Cohen, Elliot E., 62, 77, 79
Cohen, Felix, 218
Cohen, Morris, 21, 78, 218
Cohn, Harry, 85, 86, 130
Columbia Broadcasting System (CBS), 84, 141
Columbia Law Review, 22
Columbia (S.C.) *State,* 15
Columbia University, 15, 16, 20, 21, 22, 104
Columbus platform (1937), 101, 102, 243
Commission on Fair Labor Employment Practices, 150
Committee on Goodwill between Christians and Jews, 122
Committee for a Jewish Army, 242
Committee for Jewish Writers, 223
Communism: anti-Semitic association of Jews with, 6, 7-8, 199-200, 221, 223-24; Great Depression and, 99, 220-21; in labor movement, 50, 51, 134, 135, 175, 179; opposition to anti-Semitism, 222,

223; in politics, 193, 195, 213, 220–22; Soviet Union, 195, 207, 222, 223

Communist International, 195

Communist party, 67, 78, 196, 221–23, 254; and labor movement, 135; Soviet Union, 178, 181, 222, 223; and Zionism, 178

Conklin, Edwin G., 25

Conservative movement. *See under* Judaism

Construction industry, 136

Contraception, 39, 47–48

Coolidge, Calvin, 3, 10, 29, 30, 56, 192, 199, 203

Corcoran, Tom, 217–18

Cotillo, Salvatore, 24–25

Coughlin, Rev. Charles E., 191, 199–200, 252, 254

Council of Jewish Federations and Welfare Funds (CJF), 163–64, 165, 166, 239

Country clubs, 59

Cox, James M., 205

Credit agencies, 142–43

Crime, 37, 44–45, 48–54, 94

Crimean resettlement, 161, 166, 177–80, 207; failure of, 164–65, 180–82, 185; Zionist opposition to, 157, 176, 178, 179, 180, 182, 183, 187, 230

Cronkite, Alexander, 6

Cultural pluralism, 55–56, 57, 75, 89, 122

Culture and Democracy (Kallen), 55–56

Czechoslovakia, 206, 227

D

Dahlberg, Edward, 81

Damascus affair (1840), 5

Daniels, C. C., 8–9

Daughters of the American Revolution, 33–34

Davies, E. J., 12

Davis, John W., 198, 203

Day/Warheit, 69, 70

Dearborn Independent, 2, 6, 8, 9–11, 33

Debs, Eugene V., 68, 192, 205

Democracy, 86, 156, 190, 193; and anti-Semitism, 255, 256; and cultural plu-ralism, 56, 124; World War I and, 205; Zionism and, 176, 187

Democratic party, 3, 190, 191, 197, 207; Jewish allegiance to, 196, 198, 199, 202–4; and Zionism, 248

Denmark, 30

Department stores, 129, 235

Deportation, 6, 28, 229

De Sola Pool, David, 118

De Sola Pool, Tamar, 245

Detroit, Mich., 53, 163, 255

Dewey, John, 56, 57

Dewey, Thomas E., 191, 213

Diamond, Jack ("Legs"), 51

Dickstein, Samuel, 28, 194, 224, 257

Dillon, Reed and Company, 128

Discrimination: academic enrollment limits, 1, 14, 15–20, 23, 54–55, 140–41; employment, 2–3, 139, 140–41, 144, 150, 153, 253, 258; housing, 3; social, 3

Divorce, 38, 42–43, 106

Dominican Republic, 230, 232, 242

Dominican Republic Settlement Association (DORSA), 230, 232

Doubleday, Page and Company, 8

Dreyfus, Alfred, 5

Drob, Rabbi Max, 105

Dubinsky, David, 134, 135, 195, 213, 218

Dun, R. G., 142

Durkheim, Emile, 111–12, 113

Dushkin, Alexander, 56, 118, 120

Dynamic America and Those Who Own It (Klein), 126

E

Eastern European Jews, 205, 206; Americanization, 59; Crimean resettlement, 176–77; criminality, 48, 49; economic and social mobility, 138, 141–42, 144; and education, 14, 18, 21–22, 140, 143; German Jews and, 18; immigration restrictions, 26, 29, 30, 32, 33, 228; and Jewish culture, 32, 64, 88; and labor movement, 132; Palestinian resettlement, 32–33; philanthropies, 164; political radicalism, 214; shtetl culture, 40;

stock market crash and, 146; U.S. immigration, 30–31, 156; World War I refugees, 27, 46; and Yiddish, 64, 72, 74, 76; and Zionism, 100, 161, 169, 171, 174

Eaton, Walter, 21

Edman, Irwin, 77

Edmondson, Robert Edward, 210, 216, 252

Education: and acculturation, 23, 47, 54–58, 205; anti-Semitic discrimination, 1, 14, 15–20, 23, 54–55, 140–41; defense against anti-Semitism, 256, 257; and economic and social mobility, 23–24, 139–41, 143–45, 151, 152, 153; Hebraist movement, 55, 56–58, 120, 122; Jewish attainment levels, 14, 15, 143–44, 145, 214; Jewish esteem for, 14–15, 19, 55; public schools, 55, 56–58, 118, 120–22; religious, 93, 104, 117, 118–20; women, 47, 144

Educational Alliance, 41

Einstein, Albert, 20, 60–61, 170

Eisenstein, Ira, 115

Eliot, T. S., 72, 79

Elkus, Abraham, 202

Ellis Island, 26

Emergency Committee on Jewish Refugees, 29

Employment: anti-Semitic discrimination, 2–3, 139, 140–41, 144, 150, 153, 253, 258; garment industry, 107, 132, 133, 135–36, 137, 144, 147; Great Depression and, 146, 147–48, 150, 151; occupations, 126–30, 137–39, 144–45, 150–52; professional, 125, 126–27, 139–41, 144–45, 148; women, 2, 43–45, 127, 144

Encyclopaedia Britannica, 7

Engels, Friedrich, 47

English language, 59, 66, 76–77, 108; acculturation and, 64, 68–69, 70, 74, 75, 78, 88

Entrepreneurs, 44, 84–85, 126, 128–31, 138–39, 142

Erskine, John, 145

Ethical Culture, 36

Ethnicity, 87; cultural pluralism and, 55–56, 75; ethnic politics, 190, 192, 203, 211–12, 213; and Jewish identity, 63, 90, 96–97; and Judaism, 90, 96–97, 102; socioeconomic mobility and, 138, 145–46; Yiddish and, 56; Zionism and, 161, 234

Europe, 75–76, 138–39, 197; anti-Semitism in, 2, 8, 253; U.S. immigration from, 26, 27, 32

European Jews, 204–5; Allied war priorities and, 260–61, 263; American Jewish rescue efforts, 160, 187–88, 189, 219–20, 226, 234, 239, 248–49, 250, 264; American Zionists and, 240, 242, 244, 245, 260, 263; Holocaust refugees, 234, 244, 248–49, 262; immigration restrictions, 24; and Zionism, 186, 235. *See also* Eastern European Jews

Evian-les-Bains refugee conference (1938), 229–30, 232, 242

Ezekiel, Mordecai, 218

F

Fadiman, Clifton, 77

Fahey, Dennis, 252

Families: desertion and dependency, 38–39, 126, 147, 149–50, 162, 163; immigration, 26, 37–38; women and, 39, 42, 44–45, 47–48

Farband National Workers' Alliance, 119. *See also* Poale Zion

Farley, Jim, 213, 215

Farmers, 11, 150–51

Fascism, 222, 223, 256

Federal Bureau of Investigation (FBI), 255–56

Federal Council of Churches of Christ, 11, 122

Federal Theater Project, 66

Federation of American Zionists (FAZ), 167

Federation of Jewish Women's Organizations, 120

Feener, Harry, 54

Feffer, Itzik, 223

Feminism, 47

Index

Ferber, Edna, 80-81, 83, 95
Fiedler, Leslie, 79-80
Film industry, 3, 68, 84-87, 129-32, 139, 153, 208, 256-57
Fish, Hamilton, 173
Fisher, Louis, 179
Flexner, Bernard, 171
Ford, Henry, 180, 183; anti-Semitism, 2, 6, 8-11, 25, 33, 54; Jewish self-defense against, 8, 9-11, 12-13, 160, 178
Ford Motor Company, 9, 10, 13
Fortas, Abe, 218
Fortune, 128-29, 217, 229, 251
Foster, William Z., 191
Fox, William, 130
France, 99, 141, 209, 212, 217, 232
Frank, Henry, 190-91
Frank, Jerome, 218
Frank, Waldo, 77
Frankfurter, Felix, 193, 220; anti-Semites and, 216, 217, 224; in Roosevelt administration, 216, 217-18, 228; as Supreme Court justice, 218; in Zionist movement, 169, 170-71, 217, 219
Frankfurt school, 79
Franklin, Rabbi Leo, 8-9
Freeman, Joseph, 78
Freiheit, 66, 73, 175
Freud, Sigmund, 39
Friedlander, Israel, 118
Fuchs, Daniel, 81

G

Galicia, 27
Gallager, Michael (bishop of Detroit), 254
Gamoran, Emanuel, 118
Garment industry, 138, 141, 144, 147; crime in, 50, 51, 52, 54, 134-35; labor strikes, 51, 133, 134; unionization, 133-34, 135-36, 137; women in, 44
Gary, Ind., 121
General Jewish Council for Jewish Rights, 239
Gentiles, 19, 36, 82, 87, 93, 217
German-American Bund, 251, 253, 257
German-Americans: anti-Semitism, 251,

252, 253, 257; counterboycott of Jews, 236; and immigration restriction, 24, 28; and politics, 190, 212, 250; and World War I, 24, 250
German Jews: and anti-Semitism, 82, 160; in banking and commerce, 128, 138, 141-42; and eastern European Jews, 18; economic and social mobility, 126, 144; and education, 16, 18, 21, 143; expulsion from Germany, 185, 227-28, 230-31, 236-37; and Jewish culture, 32; and Judaism, 97, 98-99; as leaders of American Jewry, 155-56, 159, 160; in Nazi Germany, 206, 223, 226-27, 236, 238, 252; in newspapers and publishing, 70, 83; philanthropies, 162, 164; and politics, 189; refugees from Nazism, 165, 211-12, 227-28, 229-31, 234; social organizations, 59; stock market crash and, 146; U.S. immigration, 32, 33, 229, 230; women, 42, 45
Germany, 128, 141; U.S. immigration quotas, 29, 229; Weimar constitution (1919), 226
Germany, Nazi: American Jewish boycott, 235-36, 237; American Jewish efforts to counter, 135, 159, 160, 208, 226, 234, 235, 237, 260; anti-Semitism, 160, 191, 207-8, 209, 224, 226, 251, 253, 256-57; Berlin Olympic Games (1936), 209-10; Britain and, 241-42, 244, 252; Communist opposition to, 222, 223; death camps, 250, 259, 260-61; expulsion of Jews, 185, 227-28, 229, 230-31, 236-37; "final solution," 217, 231, 232-33, 239, 244, 250, 251, 260; invasion of Poland, 227; Jewish refugees from, 165, 211-12, 227-28, 229-31, 234; Kristallnacht (1938), 210, 222, 227, 230, 252; Nuremberg laws (1935), 226-27; occupation of Europe, 124, 226, 232; rise of Nazism, international alarm, 82, 165, 207, 217, 252; Soviet invasion, 222, 227, 232; Soviet Non-Aggression Pact (1939), 222, 223; Transfer Agreement, 230-31, 236-37; U.S. diplomatic and political protests,

321

191, 210; U.S. government and rescue of Jews from, 228–34, 250, 262, 263; war guilt and reparations, 233, 250, 261–63

Gershwin, George, 60, 80

Gibbon, James, Cardinal, 11

Gibson, Hugh, 160

Giglotti, Cairoli, 24–25

Ginzberg, Rabbi Louis, 50, 112

Glass, Montague, 83

Glatstein, Jacob, 73

Glazer, Nathan, 79–80

Gold, Michael, 78, 81

Goldberg, Rube, 71, 83

Goldenson, Leonard, 85, 131

Goldman, Emma, 6

Goldman, Sachs and Company, 128

Goldmann, Nahum, 243, 247

Goldwyn, Samuel, 86, 130

Gompers, Samuel, 132–33

Goode, Rabbi Alexander D., 259

Goodman, Benny, 254

Goodman, Paul, 79

Gordin, Jacob, 64

Gordis, Rabbi Robert, 257

Gordon, "Waxey," 50

Göring, Hermann, 231

Gottheil, Rabbi Gustav, 100

Grant, Madison, 7

Great Britain, 141; control of Palestine, 167, 168, 185, 222, 228, 263; Judaism in, 99; and Kristallnacht, 210, 252; U.S. immigration quotas, 29, 30; and war refugees, 228, 233, 244, 263; in World War II, 208–9, 241, 244; and Zionist movement, 175, 241–42, 243, 246–47

Great Depression: in agriculture, 125; and anti-Semitism, 34, 128, 252–53; bank failures, 125, 146; and economic mobility, 81–82, 146, 147–48, 150, 151–53; film industry in, 84, 153; and garment industry, 135, 147; German boycott and, 235–36; and German refugees, 211–12, 226, 227–28, 230, 250, 263, 264; and Jewish culture, 120; and political behavior, 198, 201, 204, 208, 211; and political radicalism, 66, 77, 78, 81,

99, 113, 204, 214, 220–21; poverty in, 146–47; public employment, 148; relief efforts, 148–50, 163, 220; and synagogue membership, 91, 98, 99; unemployment, 146, 147, 149, 150, 151; and Zionist movement, 149, 150–51, 184

Greenberg, Clement, 79

Greenberg, Hank, 61

Greenberg, Hayim, 76, 239

Greenberg, Jack, 254

Griffith, Barbara, 4–5

Group Theater, 67

Gruening, Ernest, 218

Guide to Jewish Ritual, 115

H

Ha'am, Ahad (Asher Ginsberg), 111–12

Habimah Troupe, 64

Habonim, 150

Hadassah, 45, 46, 100, 158, 164, 173, 185, 246

Hadoar, 57, 74, 75

Hakoah soccer team, 20, 60

Halakah. See Jewish law

Halkin, Simon, 74

Halper, Albert, 77, 81

Halpern, Moshe Leib, 72

Hamid, Sufi Abdul, 255

Hanukkah, 93, 96, 100

Harding, Warren G., 10, 27, 189–90, 198, 205

Hart, Moss, 67–68, 78

Harvard Alumni Bulletin, 96

Harvard Law Review, 220

Harvard University, 22; Jewish enrollment, 16, 18, 23; Jewish enrollment limitations, 1, 13–14, 16–18, 19–20, 23–24, 30, 33, 54; Menorah Society, 16, 17, 19, 77

Hasidim, 110

Hatorem, 74

Havurot movement, 114

Haynes, Patrick (archbishop of New York), 11

Hays, Will H., 85–86, 191

Hearst, William Randolph, 203, 217

Hebraism, 56–57, 73–74, 120

Hebrew, 64, 88, 119; literature and journalism, 73–74, 75; public school education, 55, 56–57, 120, 122; in synagogue services, 100, 106

Hebrew American League of New Jersey, 3

Hebrew Free Loan Society, 142

Hebrew Immigrant Aid Society (HIAS), 26–27, 157, 165

Hebrew Teachers Institute, 108

Hebrew Theological College, 91, 109

Hebrew Union College (HUC), 18, 46, 91, 98, 99–100

Hebrew University, 74

Hebron massacre (1929), 175

Hecht, Ben, 81, 242–43

Heiman, Rabbi Shlomo, 109

Heller, Rabbi Bernard, 100

Heller, Rabbi James G., 174

Hellman, Lillian, 67–68, 80, 82

Hendrick, Burton J., 8, 50

Herberg, Will, 78, 124

Herbert, Arthur ("Tootsie"), 53

Hertz, John D., 129

Herzliah Institutes, 119

High schools, 55, 143; Hebrew instruction, 56–58, 118, 120, 122

Hillel Foundation, 94

Hillman, Sidney, 191, 194, 212–13, 218

Hillquit, Morris, 195, 197, 201

Hindus, Maurice, 7

Hirsch, Rabbi Emil G., 103

Hirsch, Rabbi Samson Raphael, 110

Hirschbein, Peretz, 65

Histadrut, 135

Histadruth Ivrith, 57, 74

History of a Lie (Bernstein), 7

Hitler, Adolf, 210, 235, 255

Hitti, Philip K., 247

Holiday, Billie, 254

Holmes, Rev. John H., 211

Holocaust: American Jewish response to, 2, 71–72, 145, 156, 165, 166, 189, 212, 220, 225–26, 259–61, 264–65; death camps, 250, 259, 260–61; and decline of Yiddish, 74; "final solution," 217, 231, 232–33, 239, 244, 250, 251, 260; and Orthodox Judaism, 110; refugees, 227–28, 229–30, 231, 234, 248–49; U.S. immigration restrictions and, 33, 228–29, 231–32, 250; U.S. rescue effort, 232–34, 248, 249–50; war guilt and reparations, 233, 250, 261–63; Zionist movement and, 103, 186, 230, 235, 239–40, 242, 244–45, 249, 260

Hook, Sidney, 77, 79

Hoover, Herbert C., 30, 133–34, 175, 177, 178, 204, 228

Hopkins, Harry L., 194, 220

Horkheimer, Max, 256

Horowitz, Morris, 64

Hoskins, Harold P., 246

Hospitals, 163

Housing, 3, 136

Howe, Irving, 65, 79–80, 140

Howe, Louis, 211, 215

Hughes, Charles Evans, 25, 30

Hull, Cordell, 210, 236

Hungarian Jews, 33, 233–34, 248

Hunter College, 15

Hurley, Patrick, 246

Hurst, Fannie, 80, 83

Hurwitz, Henry, 77

I

I Can Get It for You Wholesale (Weidman), 81

Ickes, Harold L., 216, 218, 243

Illiteracy, 31–32

Immigrants, 33, 155; acculturation, 35, 38, 61, 62, 86; Americanization, 31, 117, 123; and anti-Semitism, 1, 24; criminality in, 48–49; deportation, 6, 28, 229; economic and social mobility, 125, 127–28, 137, 143; and education, 14, 15, 21–22, 23, 143; family reunification, 26; fourth generation, 59; Jewish, number of, 26, 29, 229, 232, 233; and Jewish culture, 32, 58, 62–63, 64, 75, 81, 264; literacy and health, 26, 31–32; and politics, 200, 202; relief efforts, 29, 149,

162–63; return to Russia, 6–7; social organizations, 59; third generation, 59, 68, 74, 88, 98–99, 156, 157; transitional culture, 36, 59, 63, 75; women, 43, 44, 47; and Yiddish, 56, 64, 74; and Zionism, 170. *See also* Second generation

Immigration: anti-Semitism and, 1, 24, 25, 250; Great Depression and, 228, 230, 250, 263; Holocaust refugees, restrictions and, 33, 212, 228, 231–32, 233, 248, 250, 263; nativist opposition to, 1, 24, 25, 26, 29–30, 227–29; opposition to restrictions, 28–29, 30, 190, 241; refugee children, 231–32; restrictive laws and quotas, 1, 13, 24–30, 32–33, 38, 74, 197, 229

Immigration Restriction League, 26

"In Sikh" (Introspectivists), 72, 73

Institute of Jewish Affairs, 261, 262–63

Institute on Peace and Post-war Problems, 261

Intellectuals, 73, 76, 77–80, 133, 197, 221–22

Intercollegiate Menorah Association, 96

Interfaith movement, 122–24, 256, 259

Intergovernmental Committee on Political Refugees, 230–31

Intergovernmental Union, 205

Intermarriage, 42, 87

Internal Revenue Service, 50

International Brigade, 209

International Brotherhood of Chauffeurs and Teamsters, 53

Internationalist Workers Order, 119

International Jew, The, 9, 13

International Jewish Women's Organization, 46

International Ladies' Garment Workers Union (ILGWU), 51, 66, 133, 134–36, 192

Interracial Council, 28

Irgun Z'vai Leumi, 242

Irish-Americans, 24, 86, 193, 198, 199–200, 201–2, 250, 254

Irving Place Theater, 65

Island Within (Lewisohn), 82

Israel, 74, 102, 105, 110–11

Italian-Americans, 24–25, 26, 127, 133, 141, 151, 197, 212, 252, 253

Italian immigrants, 42

Italy, 212, 253

J

Jabotinsky, Eri, 242

Jabotinsky, Vladimir, 100, 167, 242

Jacobs, Joseph, 7

James, William, 56

Jeffers, Robinson, 72

Jellinek, Rabbi Adolf, 91

Jewish Agency for Palestine, 101, 159, 161, 164–65, 166, 175, 182, 183, 184–85, 187

Jewish Agricultural Society, 151

Jewish army, 103, 242–43

Jewish Army Committee, 243

Jewish Art Theater, 65

Jewish Braille Society, 46

Jewish center movement, 91, 116–17

Jewish Colonization Association, 177

Jewish Communal Register, 155

Jewish Contributions to Civilization (Jacobs), 7

Jewish Council for Russian War Relief, 223

Jewish culture, 164, 264; Americanization and, 64, 70, 74, 75, 87–89, 122; cosmopolitanism, 63–64, 75–76; film industry, 84–87; Great Depression and, 66, 77, 78, 81; Hebrew instruction and, 56, 58; immigrants and, 32, 58, 62–63, 64, 75, 81, 264; intellectuals and, 73, 76, 77–80; journalism in, 69–72, 75; literature and poetry, 70, 72–74, 76–77, 80–82, 83–84; religion in, 63, 88, 90, 122; theater, 64–69, 80, 82–83, 85; transitional culture, 36, 59, 63, 75

Jewish Daily Bulletin, 15

Jewish Daily Forward, 68, 69, 73

Jewish Education Association, 121

Jewish Education Committee, 120

Jewish federations, 46, 156, 157, 161–64, 187; Depression relief assistance, 148–49, 163; and Zionism, 164–65, 166, 187, 240

Jewish Frontier, 239

Jewish holidays, 58, 93, 94, 97, 106, 107, 121

Jewish identity: acculturation and, 2, 76; anti-Semitism and, 2, 189; Hebrew instruction and, 55; intellectuals and, 76, 79; and politics, 189, 191–92; religion in, 90, 97; secularism and, 63, 188

Jewish Institute of Religion (JIR), 91, 98

Jewish Labor Committee (JLC), 135, 213, 237, 238, 245, 246, 261

Jewish law: Americanization and, 90, 94, 108–9; dietary, 50, 51, 106, 109; Orthodoxy and, 50, 91, 104–5, 106–7, 108–9; and philanthropy, 162; rabbis and, 92, 102, 106, 107; Reconstructionism and, 113–14, 115; Zionism and, 167

Jewish Morning Journal, 31, 69–70, 204

Jewish National Fund, 164

Jewish neighborhoods, 3, 55, 58, 196

Jewish organizations, 100, 155, 156–61, 245; and anti-Semitism, 11, 223–24, 251–52, 255–56, 258; and European Jewry under Nazism, 159, 160, 186–87, 221, 238–39, 261; German boycott, 235–36, 237; immigrant and refugee assistance, 29; women's, 43, 45–47, 158. *See also* Jewish federations

Jewish People's Committee for United Action against Fascism and Anti-Semitism, 221

Jewish People's Fraternal Order, 222

Jewish press, 5, 31, 208, 255. *See also* Yiddish press

Jewish Publication Society of America (JPS), 83

Jewish Telegraph Agency, 70

Jewish Theological Seminary (JTS), 91, 98, 99–100, 104, 105, 108, 116; Teachers Institute, 104, 112, 118

Jewish War Veterans, 189, 235, 238

Jewish welfare agencies, 148–49, 151

Jewish Welfare Board (JWB), 258, 259

Jewish Workers' University, 196

Jewish Working Girls Vacation Society, 41

Jew in Love (Hecht), 81

Jews: U.S. population, 14, 157

Jews in America (Hendrick), 8

Jews without Money (Gold), 81

Johnson, Albert, 25, 26–27, 28, 30

Joint Boycott Council, 236, 237

Joint Consultive Council, 238

Joint Distribution Committee (JDC), 29, 157, 161, 163; and Crimean resettlement, 176–77, 178–80, 181–82, 183, 185; and Dominican resettlement, 230; fund raising, 46, 164, 165, 178, 179, 186, 187; and Palestine development, 183, 186; and rescue of European Jewry, 230, 233, 239

Joint Emergency Committee on European Jewish Affairs (JEC), 239

Jolson, Al, 87

Jonas, Nathan S., 128

Jordan, David Starr, 7, 8–9

Joseph, Rabbi Jacob, 52

Judaism, 6, 18–19, 56, 264; Americanization and, 36, 88, 90, 93; as civil religion, 97, 114, 124; congregations and membership, 90–91, 97; immigration and, 32, 88; interfaith movement, 122–24, 256; marriage in, 39–40; religious education, 94, 117–22; religious holidays, 58, 93, 94, 97, 106, 107, 121; religious observance, 32, 93–94, 96, 97; secularism and, 90, 92–93, 94, 95, 96–97, 162; Soviet Union and, 207, 222; transformationists, 90, 95; and women, 42; Zionism and, 186

—Conservative, 90, 103–6, 124; congregations and membership, 91; Great Depression and, 98; and Hebraist movement, 57, 74; Jewish centers movement, 91, 117; rabbinical seminaries, 91, 92, 98, 99, 103–4; rabbis, 92, 93, 94, 104, 105, 106; Reconstructionism and, 111, 114; religious observance, 105, 106; religious schools, 119; and secularization, 93, 96, 97, 106; synagogue worship practices, 106; and Zionism, 105, 114–15

—Orthodox, 95, 123, 124, 183; congregations and membership, 90–91, 98, 99, 107–8; Conservative movement and,

99, 103–5; Great Depression and, 99; and Hebrew as vernacular, 75; Holocaust and, 110; and immigration restrictions, 33; and Jewish law, 50, 91, 104–5, 106–7, 108–9; and kosher food industry, 52, 53; rabbinical seminaries, 91, 92, 98, 108, 109–10; rabbis, 50, 52, 91, 92, 107, 109, 116; and Reconstructionism, 111, 112, 114, 116; religious observance, 4; religious schools, 119; and secularism and Americanization, 108–9, 110–11; and "wine rabbis," 50; and women's movement, 43, 48, 109
—Reconstructionist, 96, 97, 111–17, 123
—Reform, 90, 95, 107; and Americanization, 88, 93, 97, 98–99, 102–3, 234; Columbus platform (1937), 101, 102, 243; congregations and membership, 91, 100; Conservative movement and, 99, 103–5, 106; and interfaith movement, 123, 124; and Jewish army, 103, 243; Jewish centers movement, 117; Pittsburgh platform (1885), 100, 101, 102; and political liberalism, 194–95; rabbinical seminaries, 18, 91, 99–100; rabbis, 50, 91–92, 98, 100–101, 102, 103, 123, 199, 243; Reconstructionism and, 111, 114, 115; religious observance, 4, 102, 105; and rescue of European Jewry, 103; and "wine rabbis," 50; and women's movement, 42, 43; worship practices, 4, 100, 115; and Zionism, 100–102, 159, 172–73
Judaism as a Civilization (Kaplan), 112
Jung, Rabbi Leo, 109
Junior Order of American Mechanics, 30

K

Kadushin, Rabbi Max, 112
Kahn, Otto, 11
Kallen, Horace M., 21, 77, 195; cultural pluralism, 55–56, 57, 89, 122; on Judaism and rabbis, 96; in Zionist movement, 171
Kaplan, Rabbi Mordecai: founding of

Reconstructionism, 111–15; and Hebrew education, 56, 58, 74; and Jewish centers movement, 116–17; at Jewish Theological Seminary, 91, 104, 112, 116, 118; on Judaism, 95, 96, 102, 112–13; Orthodox excommunication of, 116; and Zionism, 114–15, 171
Karski, Jan, 217
Kashrut, 93, 107, 109; kosher food industry, 50, 51–53, 54, 129
Kashruth Association, 53
Kaufman, George S., 78, 80, 82
Kaufman, S. J., 71
Kazin, Alfred, 36, 79–80
Kehillah (New York), 155, 156, 160, 187; and crime, 38, 48, 49, 54; demise of, 116; and Jewish education, 118, 120
Kellogg-Briand Pact (1928), 205, 207
Kelly, Colin, 258
Kennedy, Joseph P., 132, 216, 218
Kennicott Copper Company, 141
Keren Hayesod, 168, 169, 182–84
Keren Kayemeth, 184
K'hal Adath Jeshurun, 110
Kibbutzim, 168, 180
Kiddush, 50
Kingsley, Sidney, 82
Kirstein, Louis, 171
K'lal Yisrael, 105
Klausner, Joseph, 123
Klein, Henry, 126
Knabeshue, Paul, 175
Kohler, Kaufmann, 114
Kohn, Eugene, 115
Kohut, Rebecca, 46
Kol Nidre, 115
Konvitz, Milton, 254
Kosher food industry, 50, 51–53, 54, 129
Kotler, Rabbi Aaron, 109–10
Kramer, Victor, 17
Kristallnacht (1938), 210, 222, 227, 230, 252
Kristol, Irving, 79–80
Kuhn, Fritz, 251, 252, 253
Kuhn, Loeb and Company, 128
Ku Klux Klan: anti-Semitism, 3, 183, 190; Jewish self-defense against, 193, 251–52;

membership in, 3, 34, 172; political resistance to, 3, 197, 199, 203, 204

L

Labor strikes, 51, 53, 133–34, 137
Labor unions, 157–58, 254; communism and socialism in, 50, 132–33, 134, 135, 137, 175, 179, 213; crime in, 50–51, 134–35; garment industry, 51, 133–36, 137; and Nazi Germany, 235; Protocol of Peace (1911), 50; and Sunday laws, 4; women in, 42, 43, 45, 47; and Zionism, 175. *See also* Amalgamated Clothing Workers of America; International Ladies' Garment Workers Union
Labor Zionism. *See* Poale Zion
Laemmle, Carl, 130
La Follette, Robert M., 192, 198
La Guardia, Fiorello H., 31–32, 53, 190–91, 194, 200–201, 210, 213
Landau, Jacob, 70
Landman, Rabbi Isaac, 123
Landsmanshaftn, 58–59, 157
Langer, Frances, 258
Lansky, Meyer, 53
Lasker, Albert, 11
Lasky, Jesse, 130
Lateiner, Joseph, 64
Latin America, 229
Lazaron, Rabbi Morris S., 172–73, 243
League of Nations, 32, 167, 168, 183, 190, 198, 205, 206, 238
Lecky, William, 56
Lehman, Herbert, 121, 183, 192, 203, 213
Lehman, Irving, 228
Lehman Brothers, Inc., 128
Leibowitz, Samuel, 254
Leivick, Halper, 72
Lemlich, Clara, 47
Lend-Lease Act (1941), 208–9
Lenin, Vladimir Ilich, 195, 206
Leonard, Benny, 60
Lessing, Bruno, 83
Levenberg, Rabbi Judah, 108
Levin, Meyer, 81, 258
Levinson, Salmon O., 207

Levinson-Borah plan, 205
Levy, Rabbi Felix, 101
Levy, Samuel, 109
Lewis, Sinclair, 82
Lewisohn, Ludwig, 21, 77, 82
Liberalism, 193, 194, 195
Liberal Judaism, 223
Liberal party, 213
Lilienthal, David E., 218
Lincoln Brigade, 209
Lindbergh, Charles A., 132, 208
Lippmann, Walter, 60, 71–72, 171, 204
Lipset, Seymour Martin, 79–80
Lipsky, Louis, 156, 165, 169, 171, 172, 173
Literature, 70, 72–74, 80–82, 83–84
Lodge, Henry Cabot, 24, 173, 190
Lodge-Fish resolution (1922), 1, 172–73, 190, 205
Loeb, Carl M., 128
Loew, Marcus, 86, 130
London, Meyer, 192, 197
London WZO conference (1920), 168–69
Long, Breckinridge, 233
Long, Huey P., 252
Longworth, Alice Roosevelt, 214
Lord's Day Alliance, 4, 85
Low, Seth, 200–201
Lowell, Abbott Lawrence, 1, 16–17, 19, 54–55
Lubin, Isador, 218
Ludlow amendment, 208
Luther, Hans, 210

M

McCloy, John J., 247–48
McDonald, James G., 232
McFadden, Louis, 224, 252
Mack, Julian, 46, 169, 171, 174
McKee, "Holy Joe," 191
Magnes, Rabbi Judah, 88, 194–95; criticism of Reconstructionism, 115; in Zionist movement, 100, 166–67, 174–75, 178, 245, 246
Magruder, Calvert, 217
Main Street (Lewis), 82
Malkiel, Theresa, 47

Manufacturers Trust Company, 128
Margolin, Nathan, 218
Marriage, 39–42; intermarriage, 42, 87
Marshall, George C., 247–48
Marshall, Louis, 156; and Americanization, 31, 36; as American Jewish Committee president, 3, 159, 182, 262; antilynching law effort, 254; and anti-Semitism, 3, 5, 7, 8, 9–11, 12–13, 25; and Crimean resettlement, 179, 180, 183; death of, 155, 172, 175, 181, 184–85; and European minority rights clauses, 27, 160, 206, 262; financial support of Jewish Theological Seminary, 98, 104; and immigration restrictions, 25, 27, 28–29, 31, 33, 190; and Jewish education, 118; and politics, 189–90; and rescue of European Jewry, 33; and university quotas, 18; and Yiddish, 31, 88; and Zionism, 159, 161, 172, 175, 182–83, 184
Marshalliah High School (New York), 119
Marx, Karl, 47, 138
Marxism, 78, 80, 99, 204, 222
Massachusetts, 200
Materialism, 82
Mayer, Louis B., 86, 130
Medalie, George Z., 204
Mellon, Andrew William, 30
"Melting pot" theme, 86
Memphis, Tenn., 162
Mencken, H. L., 3
Mendlowitz, Rabbi Shraga, 109
Menorah Journal, 75, 76–78, 112
Menorah Societies, 16, 17, 19, 56–57, 77, 96
Merchants, 129, 138, 141–42, 147, 152
Merlin, Samuel, 242
Mesifta Torah Vodaas, 109
Mexico, 29, 199, 201–2
Meyer, Eugene, Jr., 171, 192
Michoels, Solomon, 223
Middle class, 13, 83, 125, 137, 140; and criminality, 49, 54; education and, 14, 143, 152; film industry and, 131–32;

Great Depression and, 81–82, 146, 150; and Judaism, 98–99, 117; occupations, 126–27, 132, 145, 152, 153; and response to the Holocaust, 264; secularism, 117; women, 44, 45, 47, 48; and Yiddish, 66, 75
Middle East, 175, 204–5, 246, 247
Miller, Nathan J., 29
Miller, Sidney, 81
Minneapolis, Minn., 148
Minority Rights Congress (1927), 206
Mitchell, Purroy, 200–201
Mitnagdim, 110
Mitzvot, 113
Mizrachi, 108, 164, 182, 244
Mobility, economic and social, 125–26, 152–54; and anti-Semitism, 128, 131, 138, 141, 153, 255; education and, 23–24, 139–41, 143–45, 151, 152, 153; and ethnic identity, 145–46; Great Depression and, 81–82, 146, 147–48, 150, 151–53; occupations and, 126–30, 132, 137–38, 139, 145, 152. *See also* Middle class
Modernism, 72
Moley, Raymond, 217
Monsky, Henry, 240, 245
Montor, Henry, 247
Morgen Journal. See Jewish Morning Journal
Morgenstern, Julian, 18, 99
Morgenthau, Henry, Jr., 160, 194, 216–17, 219, 233, 261–62
Morison, Samuel E., 16
Morrow, Felix, 77
Moscow Art Theater, 64, 65
Moses, Robert, 203
Moskowitz, Belle, 194, 197, 202, 203
Moskowitz, Henry, 194, 202
Movies. *See* Film industry
Mumford, Lewis, 77
Mundelein, George, Cardinal, 254
Muni, Paul (Muni Weisenfreund), 65
Murder, Inc., 53, 54
Murphy, Charles F., 203
Murrow, Dwight, 199
Mussolini, Benito, 253

N

Nation, 55–56, 82, 122

National Advocate, 71

National Association for the Advancement of Colored People (NAACP), 254, 255

National Broadcasting Company (NBC), 84, 141

National Civic Federation, 33–34

National Committee on Jewish Aid to Great Britain, 207

National Community Relations Advisory Council, 164

National Conference of Christians and Jews, 123

National Conference of Jewish Charities, 162

National Conference on Jewish Employment, 150

National Conference of Jewish Social Service, 220

National Coordinating Committee (NCC), 229

National Council of Jewish Women (NCJW), 42, 45–46, 158, 240

National Desertion Bureau, 38–39

National Education Association, 121

National Emergency Committee for Palestine, 186

National Emergency Committee for Zionist Affairs, 240

National Federation of Temple Sisterhoods, 45, 46, 158

National Information Appeals Service, 163–64

National Liberal Immigration League, 28

National Refugee Service, 229

National Society of Hebrew Day Schools, 110

Nativism, 24, 25, 26, 33, 193, 251–52

Naye Theater (National Art Theater), 65

Nazism: in U.S., 191, 251, 252, 253, 255–56, 257. *See also* Germany, Nazi

Nazi-Soviet Non-Aggression Pact (1939), 222, 223

Neumann, Emanuel, 171, 241

Neutrality Act (1939), 208–9

New Deal, 133, 250; "Jew Deal" epithet, 191, 215–16, 217, 218, 225; Jewish influence on, 193, 194, 212, 214–16, 219–20, 225, 226; Jews in administration, 191, 212–13, 215, 216–18, 220; labor legislation, 135–36

New Jersey, 4, 151

Newman, Pauline, 47

Newspapers, 69–72, 130. *See also* Yiddish press

New York (state), 120–21, 254; Hebrew education in, 56–57; Jewish educational success in, 22, 144; kosher food law, 52; labor law, 133; libel law, 10; politics, 3, 191, 199, 203–4, 213, 221; Sunday laws, 4

New York, N.Y.: child dependency in, 38; crime in, 48, 49, 53; garment industry, 135; German-American counterboycott, 236; Great Depression in, 91, 146, 147, 148; Hebrew education in, 56–57, 118, 119, 120; high schools, 20–21, 55, 57, 118, 119, 120, 200; intellectuals, 73, 76, 77–80; Jewish education in, 118, 119, 120, 121; Jewish employment in, 126, 127, 128, 129, 148; Jewish federation, 148–49, 163; Jewish immigration to, 31–32, 38; Jewish neighborhoods, 3, 55, 196; Jewish organizations, 155; Jewish population, 37, 127; labor movement in, 135, 136; Palestinian Arab rally, 175; politics, 79, 194, 196, 198–99, 200–201, 204, 211, 212; racial tensions, 255; synagogues, 117; universities, 14–15, 20, 143, 147; Yiddish theater, 65–66, 68. *See also* Kehillah

New York Dramatic Troupe, 68

New York Telephone Company, 2

New York Times, 71, 130

New York University (NYU), 15, 22

New York *World,* 71

Nichols, Anne, 82

Niebuhr, Reinhold, 261

Niger, Shmuel, 76

Niles, David, 190, 218

Noah, Mordecai, 4, 71

"Nordic supremacy," 22, 25, 28, 29-30, 31, 145, 227, 251
Norway, 30
Numerus clausus, 14
Nuremberg laws (1935), 226

O

Occupations, 126-30, 137-39, 144-45, 150-52
Ochs, Adolph S., 71
O'Connell, William, Cardinal, 11
Odets, Clifford, 67-68, 82
Oko, Adolph, 77
Old Bunch (Levin), 81
Olympic Games (1936), 209-10, 255
Ornitz, Samuel, 81
Osborn, Henry Fairchild, 25
Oswego, N.Y., 212, 233
Ottinger, Albert, 191
Ottoman Empire, 74
Outline of Jewish Knowledge, 118
Overman, Lee, 8

P

Padover, Saul K., 218
Page, Walter Hines, 24
Pale of Settlement, 138, 177
Palestine, 161; agriculture, 168, 180, 182; American Jewish fund-raising for, 149, 164-66, 168, 169, 180, 183-84, 185; American Jewish investment in, 101, 170, 176, 179-80, 182-83; Arab population of, 166-67, 174-75, 245, 247; Arab riots, 34, 77, 149, 164-65, 172, 174, 185, 228; Crimean resettlement and, 164-65, 176-78, 179, 181, 182, 185; economic development, 168, 170, 172, 175, 184, 236-37; Hebrew and Yiddish in, 73; Holocaust refugee resettlement in, 186, 229, 230-31, 236-37, 241-42, 243-45, 250, 263; illegal immigration to, 244; immigration to, 32-33, 150-51, 174, 228, 262; Lodge-Fish resolution (1922), 1, 172-73, 190, 205; opposition to Zionist state in, 174-75, 185, 228, 244, 246-47; Reconstructionism and, 114-

15; Reform Judaism and, 100-101; U.S. government and, 167, 175-76, 224, 246-48; women's organizations for, 46; in World War II, 243; yishuv, 101, 165, 167, 172, 182, 185, 206, 242. *See also* Balfour Declaration; Zionism
Palestine Development Corporation, 171
Palestine Development Fund, 101
Palestine Economic Corporation (PEC), 179-80, 183
Palestine Foundation Fund, 164
Paley, William S., 85
Palma, Joseph, 12
Palmer raids, 6
Paris Peace Conference (1919), 158, 160
Parker, Dorothy, 78
Parsons, William, 15
Partisan Review, 79
Passover, 93, 115, 121
Peculiar Treasure (Ferber), 81
Pelley, William Dudley, 252
Pennsylvania Society of the Order of Founders and Patriots, 35
Peretz, Isaac L., 70
Perkins, Frances, 213, 219, 220
Permanent Court of International Justice, 205, 206
Petlyura, Symon, 206
Phi Beta Kappa, 20, 22
Philadelphia, Pa., 141, 148, 149, 196
Philadelphia Jewish Exponent, 18-19
Philanthropy, 59, 152, 261; for Crimean resettlement, 157, 176, 177, 180, 181, 187; Depression relief, 149; immigrant assistance, 162-63; Judaic tradition, 162; for Palestine, 149, 164-65, 166, 172, 176, 180, 240; professional fund-raising, 157, 163
Philipson, Rabbi David, 101-2, 172-73
Phillips, William, 79, 210-11
Picon, Molly, 67
Pinski, David, 70
Pipp, E. G., 9
Pittsburgh, Pa., 48
Pittsburgh platform (1885), 100, 101, 102
Poale Zion (Labor Zionists), 63, 174, 221, 223, 246

Podhoretz, Norman, 104
Poetry, 72–73
Pogroms, 71, 179
Poland, 119, 231; American Jewish
    assistance to, 176–77; anti-Semitism in,
    160; minority rights in, 25, 32, 160,
    206; Nazi invasion of, 227; Nazi-Soviet
    partition of, 222; Soviet cession, 250;
    Warsaw ghetto uprisings, 233, 258–59
Polish-Americans, 250
Polish Jews, 7, 159; American anti-Semitism
    and, 25, 26, 31; U.S. immigration, 8, 25,
    27, 29, 33
Politics, 166, 187; anti-Semitism in,
    190–92, 204, 208, 210–11, 215–16, 217,
    221, 223–24, 252–53; ethnic, 190, 192,
    203, 211–12, 213; Holocaust refugees
    and, 211–12, 215, 219–20, 222, 224,
    225–26, 255; Jewish army issue, 242–43;
    Jewish Democratic affiliation, 196, 198,
    199, 202–4; Jewish devotion to Roose-
    velt, 212–15, 234; Jewish disunity,
    189–90, 194, 224, 225–26, 234; Jewish
    officeholders, 192, 193–94, 198, 200–
    201, 214, 215, 216–18; liberalism,
    193, 194–95; machines, 190, 200, 201,
    202; New Deal, Jewish influence on,
    193, 194, 212, 214–20, 225, 226; New
    York City, 79, 194, 196, 198–99, 200–
    201, 204, 211, 212; New York State, 3,
    191, 199, 203–4, 213, 221; opposition to
    the Klan, 3, 193, 197, 199, 203; opposi-
    tion to Nazism, 210–11; radicalism, 6,
    77, 79, 196–97, 214, 220–22, 223; school
    prayer issue, 199; socialism in, 192–93,
    194, 195, 197–98, 200, 201, 207, 213,
    220–21; women's rights, 42, 43; World
    War II intervention debate, 207–9; Yid-
    dish newspapers and, 69, 191, 192, 223;
    Zionism and, 241
Pope, Genoroso, 253
Popular culture, 60, 254
Populism, 9, 204
Portrait of the Historic Jesus (Klausner),
    123
Portugal, 232
Potash and Pearlmutter, 82–83

Potofsky, Jacob, 254
Poultry farming, 151
Pound, Ezra, 72, 79
Poverty, 140, 146–47, 162, 194
Presbyterians, 94
President's Advisory Committee on Politi-
    cal Refugees (PACPR), 232
Princeton University, 22
Progressivism, 193
Prohibition, 49–50
Proletarianism, 45, 126
Proskauer, Joseph, 191, 203, 238, 246, 262
Prostitution, 27, 49
Protestantism, 96, 162; Hebraist move-
    ment and, 56; influence on Judaism, 98;
    interfaith movement, 94, 122–23, 124,
    256
Protestants: discrimination against Jews,
    15, 141; fundamentalism, 3–4, 122; and
    public schools, 121, 199; and Sunday
    laws, 3–4
Protocol of Peace (1911), 50
Protocols of the Elders of Zion, 7–8, 9,
    13
Providence, R.I., 201
Public schools, 55, 56–58, 118, 120–22, 199
Publishing industry, 83–84, 130
Pulitzer, Joseph, 71
Pulitzer Prize, 80, 82
Purim, 96, 100
Puritanism, 56, 114
Purple gang, 53

R

Rabbi Isaac Elchanan Theological Semi-
    nary (RIETS), 91, 108, 109, 110, 112
Rabbi Jacob Joseph Yeshiva, 109
Rabbinical seminaries, 91–92, 108,
    109–10
Rabbinic Assembly (RA), 105, 106, 205
Rabbinic Council of America (RCA), 109
Rabbis: Conservative, 92, 93, 94, 104,
    105, 106; and Hebraism, 74; and kosher
    food industry, 51–52; Orthodox, 50, 52,
    91, 92, 107, 109, 116; Reform, 50, 91–
    92, 98, 100–101, 102, 103, 123, 199,

243; secularization and, 58, 90, 92–93, 95, 96; and Zionism, 100–101, 102, 243
Race riots, 255
Racial discrimination, 255
Racism, 191
Radio, 68, 84, 122, 130
Radio Corporation of America, 84
Rahv, Philip, 79
Randolph, Philip, 254
Reconstructionist, 111, 222
Reconstructionist movement. *See under* Judaism
Reform. *See under* Judaism
Reisen, Abraham, 70
Reles, Abe ("Kid Twist"), 53
Religion: Americanization and, 36, 96, 113; church-state separation, 120, 193, 199; civil religion, 97, 114, 124; freedom of, 191; intellectuals and, 79; in Jewish culture, 63, 88, 96; in public schools, 120, 193, 199; religious observance, 4, 32, 58, 93–94, 97, 102, 105; students and, 94, 95. *See also* Judaism
Republican party, 3, 191, 198, 200, 204, 248
Research Institute for Jewish Post-war Problems, 261
Revel, Bernard, 108, 109
Revisionist Zionists, 167, 174, 186, 242–43, 244–45, 246
Rhoades and Company, 128
Rice, Elmer, 82
Richards, Bernard, 159, 190
Riegner, Gerhard, 239
Robins, Raymond, 6
Robinson, Jacob, 262
Rockefeller, John D., 180
Roman Catholic church, 199, 201–2, 254
Roman Catholicism, 96, 124, 140
Roman Catholics: anti-Catholicism and, 3, 25, 199, 252; and anti-Semitism, 11; and Nazi Germany, 256; in politics, 198, 200, 201, 204, 215; tensions with Jews, 198, 199–200, 201–2; universities, 23
Romania, 32, 206, 231
Romanian Jews, 159, 160, 231; U.S. immigration, 29, 33

Rommel, Erwin, 243
Roosevelt, Eleanor, 194, 220
Roosevelt, Franklin D.: anti-Semitic attacks on, 191, 208, 216; and Brandeis, 171, 218; and fair employment practices, 150, 254; and freedom of religion, 191; and German boycott, 236; gubernatorial campaign (1928), 191, 194, 203–4; and Holocaust refugees, 175, 201–2, 212, 215, 226, 228, 229, 230, 232–33, 249–50, 262, 263; Jewish appointees, 215–16, 218, 219, 225; Jewish influence on, 208, 212–13, 216–18, 219–20, 249–50, 263; Jewish support for, 194, 198, 204, 211, 212–15, 234, 247, 249; polio attack, 214; presidential campaigns, 198, 204, 212, 247; resistance to immigration liberalization, 212, 229, 232, 250; and Soviet Union, 207; and World War II intervention, 208, 209; and Zionist movement, 243, 246–47, 248, 249
Roosevelt, Theodore, 203
Root, Elihu, 6
Roots in the Sky (Miller), 81
Rosen, Joseph, 177, 178, 180, 230
Rosenberg, Harold, 79
Rosenberg, James, 178, 223
Rosenblatt, Bernard, 171
Rosenbloom, Rabbi William F., 214
Rosenbluth, Robert, 5–6
Rosenfeld, Jonah, 70
Rosenman, Samuel, 190, 217, 218, 219
Rosenthal, Henry, 77
Rosenwald, Julius, 11, 98, 99–100, 129, 177, 181, 254
Rosenwald, Lessing, 11, 247
Rosenwald, William, 165
Rosh Hashanah, 121
Rosolosky, Otto, 120
Roth, Henry, 81
Rothstein, Arnold, 51, 53
Rublee, George, 230–31, 237
Russian civil war, 27, 176–77, 180, 207
Russian Empire, 14, 197; Pale of Settlement, 138, 177; in World War I, 27
Russian Jews, 159, 206–7; college enroll-

ment limits, 14, 16, 18; in Communist movement, 7; Crimean resettlement scheme, 176–79, 180–82, 187, 207; emigrant return, 6–7; U.S. immigration, 6, 29; war refugees, 27, 176–77, 222; women, 45
Russian Revolution (1917), 6, 7, 134, 195, 206–7

S

Sabath, Adolph, 28
Sabbath, 3–4, 58, 106, 107, 108, 115
Sabbath Crusade Committee, 4
Sabbath Prayer Book, 115–16
Sacco, Nicola, 193
Saint Louis, Mo., 57, 255
Samuel, Maurice, 63, 167–68
San Francisco, Calif., 141–42
San Francisco conference (1945), 262
San Francisco *Jewish Times,* 70
San Remo protocol, 100
Sapiro, Aaron, 11–12
Sarnoff, David, 85, 95
Saturday Evening Post, 256
Saud (king of Saudi Arabia), 249
Scandinavian-Americans, 28
Schechter, Solomon, 111
Schiff, Jacob, 8, 98, 99–100, 118, 128, 155, 156, 162
Schildkraut, Rudolf, 65
Schlossberg, Joseph, 254
Schneider, Benno, 67
Schneider, Isidor, 81
Schneiderman, Rose, 43, 47
Schulberg, Budd, 81, 86
Schultz, "Dutch" (Arthur Flegenheimer), 50
Schwartz, Delmore, 79–80
Schwartz, Maurice, 65, 68
Schwartzbard, Sholem, 206
Scopes "monkey trial" (1925), 96, 193
Scrap-metal business, 129
Sears, Roebuck Company, 129, 141
Second generation: acculturation, 2, 35–38, 40, 117, 160, 214; and anti-Semitism, 2, 13; economic and social mobil-
ity, 13, 75, 127, 138, 139, 140, 150, 151; education, 18, 21–22, 55, 65, 140, 144, 205, 214; Great Depression and, 150, 151; and the Holocaust, 230, 235, 240; and Jewish culture, 64, 68, 75, 83; and Jewish identity, 2, 55, 88, 97, 191–92; and Jewish leadership, 155, 156, 157, 160, 161, 171; and Judaism, 36, 65, 75, 90, 91–92, 94, 97, 98–99, 100, 117; in literature, 81; and politics, 191–92, 193, 194, 196, 198, 200, 202–3, 205, 220; secularism, 97, 100, 161; transitional culture, 36, 59, 63, 75; women, 40, 42–43, 44, 47, 144; and Yiddish and English, 64, 65, 68–69, 74, 88. *See also* Immigrants
Secularism, 234; Hebraism and, 58; and Jewish culture, 58, 63, 90, 140, 188; and Judaism, 90, 92, 93–94, 97, 106, 110–11, 117, 122, 162; and philanthropy, 157, 162, 166; rabbis and, 92–93, 108–9; in schools, 119, 121; students, 18–19, 58
Seligman Company, 128
Sephardic Jews, 32, 137–38
Settlement house movement, 194, 202, 220
Seventh-Day Adventists, 1, 4
Sexual behavior, 39–40, 41, 47–48
Shapiro, Meyer, 79
Shaw, Irwin, 82
Shaw Commission of Inquiry (Britain), 175
Sherman Anti-Trust Act (1890), 52
Sholem Aleichem *folkshuln,* 119
Shorenstein, Hymie, 201
Siegel, "Bugsie," 53
Silver, Rabbi Abba Hillel: and politics, 194–95, 197, 204; in Zionist movement, 100, 101, 102, 166, 245, 246, 247, 248
Silverman, Jesse, 194
Simon and Schuster, Inc., 60, 83, 130
Simons, Rev. George A., 7, 8, 26
Singer, Isaac Bashevis, 70
Singer, Israel, 70
Singermann (Brinig), 81
Skulnik, Menashe, 67
Slawson, John, 256

Slesinger, Tess, 77
Slovakian Jews, 248
Smith, Alfred E., 191, 243; as governor of
New York, 3, 199; Jewish support for,
192, 194, 197, 198–99, 201, 202–4, 218;
presidential campaigns, 3, 190, 198,
202, 203, 204
Smith, "Cotton Ed," 25
Smith, Gerald L. K., 251, 252
So Big (Ferber), 80
Social discrimination, 3
Social Gospel movement, 122, 162
Socialism, 56, 63; in electoral politics,
192–93, 194, 195, 197–98, 200, 201,
207, 213, 220–21; intellectuals and, 76,
78, 79, 197; in labor movement, 137;
Orthodoxy and, 99; and religion, 79,
195, 199; and women's rights, 42, 47;
and Zionism, 167
Socialist party, 47, 192, 213, 214
Socialist realism, 81
Social Security Act (1935), 217
Social services, 126, 149, 157, 161, 194,
220, 229
Society for the Advancement of Judaism
(SAJ), 74, 112, 114, 115, 117
Solomon, Mose, 60
Soloveitchik, Rabbi Joseph B., 108
Solow, Herbert, 77
Soltes, Mordecai, 56
Sombart, Werner, 138
Sons of the American Revolution, 30
Sosua (Dominican Republic), 230, 242
Soviet Jews. *See* Russian Jews
Soviet Union, 32, 33; anti-Semitism in, 27,
180, 206, 223; collectivization of agri-
culture, 181, 207; Communist party,
Jews in, 7, 178, 181, 224; and Crimean
resettlement, 177, 178, 179, 180–81, 182,
183; economic conditions in, 176–77,
206–7; Jewish disillusionment with, 77,
79, 195, 207; Jewish emigrant return to,
6–7; Jewish support for, 207, 222, 223;
Nazi Non-Aggression Pact (1939), 222,
223; partition of Poland, 222, 250;
pogroms, 71, 179; U.S. assistance to,
176–77, 209; U.S. diplomatic recogni-
tion, 180, 207; in World War II, 209,
222, 223, 227, 232
Spain, 232, 235
Spanish civil war, 199, 208, 209
Spellman, Francis, Cardinal, 201–2, 254
Speyer and Company, 128
Spingarn, Arthur, 254
Sports, 19, 20–21, 60, 61
Springfield, Mass., 256
Stalin, Josef V., 79, 181, 195, 207
Stalingrad, battle of, 261
Starr, Harry, 17
Steel industry, 129
Steffens, Lincoln, 193
Steinberg, Rabbi Milton, 112
Steinhardt, Laurence, 171
Stern, Horace, 183
Steuben Society, 237
Stevenson, Adlai E., 216
Stimson, Henry L., 175, 247–48
Stock market crash (1929), 66, 91, 146,
163
Stoddard, Lothrop, 56
Stokes, Rose Pastor, 47
Stone, Elihu D., 171
Strasberg, Lee, 67
Strasser, Gregor, 253
Straus, Michael W., 218
Straus, Nathan, 171
Straus, Oscar, 155
Strinsky, Simeon, 71, 80
Strobing, Irving, 258
Students, 200; acculturation, 18–19,
20–21, 23, 54–55, 61; economic and
social mobility, 127–28, 140, 145, 148;
educational success, 18, 20, 21–24,
143–44, 145, 147, 148; enrollment lim-
itations, 14–20, 23–24, 54–55, 140–41;
Hebrew instruction, 55, 58; and reli-
gious education, 94, 95, 108, 118, 121;
and socialism, 78, 221–22
Studies in Prejudice, 256
Stuyvesant, Peter, 149
Suicide, 37
Sulzberger, Arthur Hays, 71
Summer camps, 41–42, 60
Sunday laws, 1, 3–4

Sweatshops, 44, 135

Sylvester, Charles, 251

Synagogues: and Americanization, 31, 58, 93, 97; building boom, 91, 117; congregations and membership, 90–91; service and worship practices, 100, 106, 109, 115

Syrkin, Marie, 246

Syrkin, Nahman, 76

T

Taft, Robert A., 248

Tageblatt, 69

Talmud, 92, 106, 139–40

Talmud Torahs, 58, 119

Tammany Hall, 193–94, 197, 198, 200, 201, 202, 203, 211

Teachers, 147–48

Telshe and Mirrer Yeshiva, 109

Terman, Lewis M., 22

Thalberg, Irving, 86

Theater, 73, 78, 82–83, 85; Yiddish, 32, 64–69, 71, 72, 75, 80

Thomas, Norman, 201, 213

Time, 224

Torah, 114, 167

Townsend, Charles, 252

Townsend Harris High School (New York), 196

Trachtenberg, Joshua, 246

Transfer Agreement (1933), 236–37

Trilling, Diana, 79

Trilling, Lionel, 77, 79

Trotsky, Leon, 7

Trujillo Molina, Rafael Leónidas, 230

Trumpeldor, Joseph, 100

Turkey, 244

U

Ukraine, 178, 181, 187

Unemployment, 146, 147, 149, 151, 194, 211, 258

Union of American Hebrew Congregations (UAHC), 94, 98, 99, 103, 107; Chicago convention (1924), 98; membership, 100; National Federation of Temple Sisterhoods, 45, 46, 158

Union of Orthodox Jewish Congregations (UOJC), 52, 107–8, 109

Union of Orthodox Rabbis, 246

Union Prayer Book, 99

United Hebrew Trades, 53, 133

United Jewish Appeal (UJA), 164–65, 166, 186, 261

United Nations, 247

United Palestine Appeal (UPA), 123–24, 164, 165, 166, 176, 183, 185, 186, 187

United States: Anglo-American Declaration (1943), 246–47; anti-Semitism in, 1, 204, 242–43, 250–53, 254–56, 257–58, 259–60, 263–64; German refugee policy, 224, 226, 228–29, 230, 232–34, 240, 248, 250; immigration restrictions, 32–33, 228–29, 233, 248; Jewish population, 14, 157; Palestine policy, 224, 247–48; Soviet diplomatic recognition, 180, 207; in World War I, 250; in World War II, 223, 226, 232, 253, 255, 258, 263; World War II intervention debate, 207–9

U.S. Congress, 208, 257; and German refugees, 232; immigration restrictions, 1, 24, 25–30, 197; Jewish members of, 192, 193–94, 198, 247; Lodge-Fish resolution (1922), 1, 172–73, 190, 205; Soviet relief, 180; and Zionism, 240–41, 247

U.S. Constitution: 18th Amendment, 42

U.S. Department of Agriculture, 11

U.S. Department of Labor, 219, 238

U.S. Department of State, 175, 210–11, 237, 249; and German refugees, 229, 230, 232, 233, 238

U.S. Department of Treasury, 210, 257

U.S. Department of War, 94

U.S. Navy, 3

U.S. Public Health Service, 32

U.S. Supreme Court, 17, 167, 169, 212, 218, 254

United Synagogue of America, 94, 104, 105, 106, 109, 121, 122

United Way of America, 149

Universities: Jewish enrollment limita-
tions, 1, 13-20, 23-24, 54-55; Jewish
success at, 20, 21-24, 143; Menorah
Societies, 16, 17, 19, 56-57, 77, 96
University of Chicago, 256
University of South Carolina, 15-16
Untermeyer, Samuel, 171, 212, 235, 236
Upstream (Lewisohn), 82
Urban League, 255

V

Vanzetti, Bartolomeo, 193
Variety, 2
Versailles, Treaty of (1919), 25, 205, 206
Viking Press, Inc., 83, 130
Vilna Troupe, 64
Vladeck, Baruch, 195
Volstead Act (1919), 30, 49, 50
Voluntarism, 43, 45-46, 156-57

W

Wagner, Robert F., 243
Wagner Act (1935), 136
Wagner-Rogers bill, 231-32
Wagner-Taft resolution (1944), 247
Wald, Lillian, 194, 195, 197, 202
Waldman, Louis, 238
Waldman, Morris, 235
Walker, James John ("Jimmy"), 53, 211
Wallace, Henry A., 248
Wallis, Frederick, 26
Warburg, Felix M., 95, 98, 181, 183, 184
Warburg, Max, 128
Warburg, Paul, 128
War crimes, 233, 250, 262
War Refugee Board (WRB), 233, 248
Warsaw ghetto uprisings, 233, 258-59
Washington Disarmament Conference
(1921), 30, 205
Washington Post, 71, 130
Wasserman, Oskar, 236
Wealth, 126
Weidman, Jerome, 81
Weimar Republic, 226
Weizmann, Chaim, 60-61, 102, 217, 245;
and development of Palestine, 172, 175,
176, 182, 183; as Jewish Agency for Pal-
estine president, 184-85; as World
Zionist Organization executive, 161,
169-70, 171, 173
Wendell, Barrett, 56
West, Nathaniel, 81
Western Union, 2
West Germany, 263
Wexler, Irvin, 50
What Makes Sammy Run? (Schulberg), 81
What's in It for Me? (Weidman), 81
White, William A., 243
Who's Who in American Jewry, 44
Willkie, Wendell L., 191, 212, 243
Wilson, Hugh, 210
Wilson, Woodrow, 24, 167, 190, 198, 205,
250, 257
"Wine rabbis," 49, 50
Winrod, Gerald, 251, 252
Wirt, William, 121
Wise, Rabbi Isaac M., 4
Wise, James, 93-94
Wise, Jonah, 165
Wise, Rabbi Stephen S., 93, 170; as
American Jewish Congress president,
171, 179, 221; and anti-Semitism, 13;
and Crimean resettlement, 179, 183;
and Hebrew instruction, 56, 120; and
immigration restrictions, 29; Jesus
speech, 123-24, 183; and Jewish army,
243; Jewish Institute of Religion founding, 91, 98, 112; and Nazi Germany,
207, 236, 237; and politics, 194-95, 197,
211, 214, 219; on secularism, 37; and
women's rights, 43; in Zionist movement, 100, 164, 167, 171, 238, 244, 245,
247, 248, 249
Wolf, Simon, 31
Wolfe, Bertram, 78
Wolfson, Harry, 77
Women, 36; education, 47, 144; employment, 2, 43-45, 127, 144; and family
life, 38, 39, 40, 41, 42, 44-45, 47-48; in
labor movement, 42, 43, 45, 47; organizations, 43, 45-47, 158; Orthodox
Judaism and, 109; prostitution, 27, 49;

women's rights movement, 42–43, 46–47; writers, 80–81
Women's Democratic Union, 197
Women's Trade Union League, 47
Workers' compensation, 126
Working class, 64–65, 125, 127, 132–33, 152
Workmen's Circle (Arbeiter Ring), 59, 66, 119, 134, 149, 157
Works Progress Administration (WPA), 148
World Conference of Protestant Christianity, 94
World Jewish Congress (WJC), 230, 238, 239, 261, 262–63
World's Work, 8
World War I, 128, 211, 241, 250; and anti-Semitism, 6, 8; effects on European Jews, 25, 27, 38, 59; and immigration restriction, 24, 25, 26, 38; and women's employment, 43; and Zionism, 74
World War II, 79–80, 136; and American anti-Semitism, 253, 255–56, 257–58, 259; American Jews in, 258–59, 260–63; German invasion of Poland, 227; German invasion of Soviet Union, 222, 227, 232; Jewish army, 242–43; Jewish refugees, 222, 227–28, 232–34, 241–42, 244, 248–50; Jews and U.S. intervention debate, 207–9; U.S. in, 223, 226, 232, 253, 255, 258, 263; Yalta conference (1945), 250; and Zionist movement, 230, 241–42, 243–45, 246–48
World Zionist Congress, 185–86
World Zionist Organization (WZO), 46, 167, 168–69, 170, 176, 182, 184
Wouk, Herman, 41
Wright-Compton resolution (1944), 247
Wyzanski, Charles, 218

Y

Yale University, 19, 20, 22
Yalta conference (1945), 250
Yellow Cab Company, 129
Yeshiva College, 23, 108, 109
Yeshivas, 109–10
Yeshiva University, 110

Yezierska, Anzia, 40, 80, 81, 86
Yiddish, 31, 47; acculturation and, 57, 59, 66, 88; Communists and, 196, 222; in education, 75, 119, 196; Hebraist movement and, 56, 57, 73, 74, 120; intellectuals and, 76, 77; in Jewish culture, 63, 66, 73, 74, 88, 157–58, 263; literature, 72–73, 74, 196; in politics, 191, 198–99, 203; socialists and, 56
Yiddish Art Theatre, 62, 67, 68
Yiddish Dramatic Players, 68
Yiddish Ensemble Theater, 68
Yiddisher Kemfer, 223
Yiddish press, 52; and anti-Semitism, 8, 71, 191; circulation, 69–70, 75; decline of, 32, 68, 70–71, 75; and European Jewry, 71–72, 158, 206, 223; and immigration restrictions, 28–29; and politics, 69, 191
Yiddish theater, 32, 64–69, 71, 72, 75, 80
Yom Kippur, 115, 121
Young Communist League (YCL), 221–22
"Yunge, Die," 70, 72

Z

Zangwill, Israel, 189
Zentralverein, 236
Zhitlovsky, Chaim, 76, 77, 195
Zimmerman, Charles S., 135
Zionism, 14, 97; American Jewish Committee and, 159, 161, 182, 238; American Jewish Congress and, 158, 159, 236, 238; and American Jewish identity, 88, 234–35; Arab riots and, 174–75, 185; British government and, 241–42, 243, 244, 246–47, 263; Conservative Judaism and, 105; Crimean resettlement controversy, 161, 166, 176, 177–82, 183, 185, 187; fund-raising, 164–65, 166, 168, 169, 172, 173, 174, 176, 180, 183–84, 185–86, 187, 240; and German boycott, 236, 237; and German Transfer Agreement, 236–37; Great Depression and, 149, 184; and Hebrew revival, 55, 56, 57, 74, 75, 119; Holocaust and, 186, 230, 239–40,

241–42, 244–45, 249, 260, 262, 263;
Jewish Agency for Palestine expansion,
161, 164–65, 166, 175, 182–85, 187;
Lodge-Fish resolution (1922), 1,
172–73, 190, 205; Nazi Germany's rise
and, 82, 165, 185, 235, 237; organizational factionalism, 161, 166–74, 186,
187, 237–38, 240, 242, 245, 246, 249,
263; Palestine immigration, 32–33,
150–51, 174, 228, 262; Palestine yishuv
investment, 165, 170, 172, 176, 179–80,
182–83; Reconstructionist Judaism and,
114–15, 117; Reform Judaism and, 100–
102, 186, 243; Revisionist Zionists, 167,
174, 186, 242–43, 244–45, 246; U.S.
government and, 175–76, 230, 240–41,
243, 246–48; women's organizations,
46, 158. *See also* Anti-Zionism; Balfour
Declaration

Zionist Organization of America (ZOA),
158; Biltmore convention (1942), 244;
Buffalo convention (1920), 161, 170;
Cleveland convention (1921), 46, 168,
170–71, 172, 182, 187; Cleveland convention (1930), 174; financial mismanagement, 173–74; and Lodge-Fish resolution, 172–73, 190; membership, 172,
185; Palestine funding, 170, 176; resignation of Brandeis faction, 171–72, 217;
split with World Zionist Organization,
169–70, 187
Zukor, Adolph, 84, 131–32
Zurich Minority Rights Congress (1927),
206
Zurich WZO conference (1929), 184
Zwillman, "Longy," 50

ABOUT THE AMERICAN
JEWISH HISTORICAL SOCIETY

THE TWENTIETH CENTURY has been a period of change for the American Jewish community, bringing growth in numbers and in status and, most important, a new perception of itself as part of the history of the United States. The American Jewish Historical Society has also grown over the century, emerging as a professional historical association with a depth of scholarship that enables it to redefine what is *American* and what is *Jewish* in the American saga. To record and examine this saga and to honor its own centennial, the society has published this five-volume series, *The Jewish People in America.*

The society was founded on 7 June 1892 in New York City, where it was housed in two crowded rooms in the Jewish Theological Seminary. At the first meeting, its president Cyrus Adler declared that it was the patriotic duty of every ethnic group in America to record its contributions to the country. Another founding father emphasized the need to popularize such studies "in order to stem the growing anti-Semitism in this country." As late as the 1950s, the society was encouraging young doctoral students in history to research and publish material of Jewish interest, even though such research, according to Rabbi Isidore Meyer, then the society's librarian, would impede the writers' advancement in academia. In this climate, the early writings in the society's journal, *Publications of the American Jewish Historical Society,* were primarily the work of amateurs; they were narrowly focused, often simply a recounting of the deeds of the writers' ancestors. However, these studies did bring to light original data of great importance to subsequent historians and constitute an invaluable corpus of American Jewish historiography.

The situation has changed materially. One hundred years later, the society has its own building on the campus of Brandeis University; the building houses the society's office space, exhibit area, and library. The Academic Council of the society includes sixty-three professors of American history whose primary interest is American Jewish history. Articles in the society's publication, now called *American Jewish History,* meet the highest professional standards and are often presented at the annual meeting of the American Historical Association. The society has also published an extensive series of monographs, which culminates in the publication of these volumes. The purpose of *The Jewish People in America* series is to provide a comprehensive historical study of the American Jewish experience from the age of discovery to the present time that both satisfies the standards of the historical profession and holds the interest of the intelligent lay reader.

Dr. Abraham Kanof
Past President
American Jewish Historical Society
and Chairman
The Jewish People in America Project